Communication
IN OUR LIVES

EIGHTH EDITION

Julia T Wood

Lineberger Distinguished Professor of Humanities Emerita
Caroline H. and Thomas S. Royster Distinguished Professor of Graduate Education Emerita
The University of North Carolina at Chapel Hill

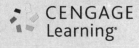

CENGAGE
Learning·

Australia • Brazil • Mexico • Singapore • United Kingdom • United States

Communication in Our Lives, Eighth Edition
Julia T. Wood

Product Director: Monica Eckman

Product Manager: Kelli Strieby

Content Developer: Kate Scheinman

Associate Content Developer: Karolina Kiwak

Product Assistant: Madeleine Ohman

Marketing Manager: Sarah Seymour

Manufacturing Planner: Doug Bertke

IP Analyst: Ann Hoffman

IP Project Manager: Kathryn B. Kucharek

Production Management, and Composition:
    Lumina Datamatics, Inc.

Text Designer: Bill Reuter

Cover Designer: Marissa Falco

Cover Image: Tara Thelen/Canopy/Corbis

© 2018, 2015, 2012 Cengage Learning

WCN: 01-100-101

For product information and technology assistance, contact us at
Cengage Learning Customer & Sales Support, 1-800-354-9706

For permission to use material from this text or product,
submit all requests online at **www.cengage.com/permissions.**
Further permissions questions can be emailed to
permissionrequest@cengage.com.

Library of Congress Control Number: 2016943761

Student Edition:
ISBN: 978-1-305-94954-6

Loose-leaf Edition:
ISBN: 978-1-305-94964-5

Cengage Learning
20 Channel Center Street
Boston, MA 02210
USA

Cengage Learning is a leading provider of customized learning solutions with employees residing in nearly 40 different countries and sales in more than 125 countries around the world. Find your local representative at **www.cengage.com.**

Cengage Learning products are represented in Canada by Nelson Education, Ltd.

To learn more about Cengage Learning Solutions, visit **www.cengage.com.**

Purchase any of our products at your local college store or at our preferred online store **www.cengagebrain.com.**

Printed in the United States of America
Print Number: 01   Print Year: 2016

For Carolyn
For so many reasons

Brief Contents

Contents

List of Boxes

Communication & Careers

Preface

When I was an undergraduate student, I discovered the field of communication. In my first communication course, I realized that communication was more central to my life than anything else I could study. That feeling grew stronger with each communication course I took during my undergraduate and graduate studies.

I wrote *Communication in Our Lives* to share with students my passion for communication and my belief that it is critically important in our everyday lives as professionals, citizens, and people in personal and social relationships. Because I want this book to engage students, I've tried to make it as interesting and substantive as communication itself. I use a conversational style of writing, and all chapters include examples, reflections from students, and applications that invite students to engage material personally. To help students develop their practical competence as communicators, I emphasize concrete skills and hands-on exercises.

Distinguishing Features of *Communication in Our Lives*

Communication in Our Lives has two distinct conceptual emphases. In addition, it includes a number of pedagogical features designed to highlight the relevance of communication to students' everyday lives and experiences. Some of these features have been retained from the seventh edition, and some are new to this eighth edition.

Conceptual Emphases

Two conceptual goals guided my writing of this book: (a) to emphasize theories and research developed by scholars of communication and (b) to integrate coverage of social diversity as it relates to communication.

Emphasis on Communication Theory, Research, and Skills *Communication in Our Lives* highlights theories, research, and skills developed by scholars of communication. For example, Chapter 7 provides coverage of relational dialectics, a theory primarily developed by Leslie Baxter, a professor of communication at the University of Iowa. Chapter 11 relies on research by scholars of social media to sharpen understanding of how various digital technologies are making our lives ever more connected. Chapters 12 through 16 draw on communication scholars' knowledge of effective public communication. For instance, James McCroskey and Jason Teven (1999) have shown that speakers who demonstrate goodwill toward listeners tend to have higher credibility than those who don't. I emphasize the work of communication scholars both because their research is valuable and because I want students to appreciate the intellectual richness of the communication field.

Although I highlight the work of communication scholars, I also include relevant research conducted by scholars in fields such as sociology, psychology, business, and anthropology.

Communication scholars have long recognized the profoundly ethical dimensions of human communication. I incorporate this tradition in communication scholarship by calling attention to ethical issues and choices in communication. In addition to identifying ethical aspects of communication in each chapter, I include two questions related to ethics at the end of each chapter, signaled with an icon, that focus on ethics.

Integrated Attention to Social Diversity　　I have woven discussion of social diversity into the basic framework of this book. I do not do this to be "politically correct." Instead, I provide integrated attention to social diversity because it is one of the most significant features of contemporary life in the United States. Our culture includes people of different ethnicities, ages, genders, physical and mental abilities, sexual orientations, gender identities, economic classes, and religious and spiritual commitments.

Communication in Our Lives encourages students to appreciate social diversity as a fact of cultural life that has important implications for our communication with others. Because social diversity affects interaction in all contexts, I incorporate discussion of diverse cultures and communication practices into all chapters of this book. For example, in discussing personal identity in Chapter 3, I point out how social views of race, economic class, gender, and sexual orientation affect self-concept. In Chapters 12–16, I note that effective speaking requires adapting to diverse audiences with varied experiences, backgrounds, and values.

In addition to weaving social diversity into all chapters, Chapter 10 is devoted exclusively to communication and culture. This chapter provides a sustained and focused exploration of the reciprocal relationship between culture and communication.

Changes in This Edition

Like communication, books are dynamic—they evolve over time. This edition of *Communication in Our Lives* attempts to retain the strengths of previous editions while also making changes in response to feedback. Before beginning work on this edition, I read feedback from hundreds of faculty members and students who used previous editions. Their suggestions and comments led me to make a number of changes in this new edition.

One significant change in this edition is **greater coverage of digital media** as they affect all forms and contexts of communication. Chapter 11 focuses on media—both mass media and digital media. In addition, in preparing this edition, I wrote a new section on digital media for every chapter other than Chapter 11, which is devoted entirely to media. This section calls students' attention to the ways in which topics covered in the chapter reflect and are affected by the pervasiveness of digital media.

A second noteworthy change is highlighting of **relationships between communication (theories, concepts, and skills) and careers**. Every chapter includes one or more Communication & Careers features that call attention to the importance of communication in a range of professions.

Third, I have **reorganized the book**. In this edition, Part II, Contexts of Interaction, includes chapters that focus on how the foundations discussed in Part I apply to communication in interpersonal relationships, group and team work, cultures and social groups, and mass and digital media.

Finally, this edition of *Communication in Our Lives* also reflects changes in scholarship. Those familiar with the sixth edition of this book will notice that the current edition includes **more than 150 new references**.

In making the above changes, I've been mindful of length. Rather than just adding new material to the former edition, I have weeded out dated material to make room for newer research and discussion of currently timely topics. As a result, this edition is the same length as its predecessor.

Pedagogical Features

In addition to the conceptually distinctive aspects of this book, several features are designed to make it interesting and valuable to students.

First, I adopt a *conversational style of writing* rather than the more distant and formal style often used by textbook authors. I share with students some of my experiences in communicating with others, and I invite them to think with me about important issues and difficult challenges surrounding communication in our everyday lives. The accessible, informal writing style encourages students to personally engage the ideas I present.

A second pedagogical feature is *student commentaries*. Every chapter is enriched by reflections written by students in my classes and other classes around the country who adopted previous editions of this book. The questions, thoughts, and concerns expressed by diverse students invite readers to reflect on their own experiences as communicators. I welcome ideas from students around the country, so students in your class may wish to send their insights to me for inclusion in future editions of this book.

Third, I encourage *students to interact directly with the text* through MindTap. Each chapter opens with a *polling question*, which is designed to prompt students to think about how the chapter's content applies to them individually. By answering these questions online, students immediately engage the chapter's focus. In addition, some of the photos in chapters are captioned with questions that students are prompted to answer online. When they answer, they can read my responses to the questions in MindTap.

Communication in Our Lives also includes pedagogical features that promote learning and skill development. Each chapter open with *learning objectives* so that students have a clear sense of how to focus their reading and studying. Within chapters, I've added a *marginal glossary* and *marginal Review It! boxes* that summarize key content. At the end of each chapter, I provide *Sharpen Your Skill* exercises to encourage students to apply concepts and develop skills discussed in the text. Many of these exercises end with a prompt to the book's online resources, which offer additional opportunities for skill application. Each chapter also includes *Communication Highlights*, which call attention to interesting communication research and examples of communication issues in everyday life, and *Communication & Careers*, which focus on connections between communication and professional life.

The chapters conclude with the following features:

A narrative *Chapter Summary* highlights the main themes throughout the chapter. This feature enables students to see whether what they retained from reading the chapter is consistent with the key content.

Video Case studies (called *Experiencing Communication in Our Lives*) are another feature that encourages students to engage ideas actively. These brief scenarios and speeches appear at the end of each chapter to bring to life the ideas and principles presented. Rather than using generic case studies, I wrote the ones used in this book so that they would directly reflect chapter content and provide students with representative examples of communication theories and skills. In addition to their presentation in the book, the case studies are featured in the MindTap for *Communication in Our Lives* as short interactive video activities that include questions for discussion and analysis. (See the section on student resources for details about MindTap.) With the multimedia enactments of the scenarios, instructors and students can analyze not only verbal messages but also nonverbal communication.

Each chapter continues with a list of *Key Concepts*, the *Sharpen Your Skill* exercises, and then a series of *For Further Reflection and Discussion* questions that encourage students to reflect on and discuss the chapter's material. Each set of these questions includes at least one question that focuses on ethics.

The final feature, *Beyond the Classroom*, appears at the end of chapters in Parts I and II. This feature offers suggestions for taking the material in the chapter beyond the classroom in three ways: considering the chapter's relevance in the workplace, probing ethical issues raised in the chapter, and connecting chapter material to civic and social engagement with the broader world.

Appendix A provides a collection of *annotated speeches* for student analysis. Appendix B covers interviewing, with emphasis on job interviews.

Resources for Instructors

Katrina Bodey and I have written an *Instructor's Resource Manual* that describes approaches to teaching the basic course, provides a wealth of class-tested exercises, including new teaching resources for the public speaking segment of your course, and provides suggested journal topics and sample test items.

The password-protected instructor companion website includes Computerized Testing via Cognero®, ready-to-use PowerPoint® presentations (with text, images, that can be customized to suit your course needs), and an electronic version of the Instructor's Manual.

MindTap from Cengage Learning represents a new approach to a highly personalized, online learning platform. A fully online learning solution, MindTap combines all of a student's learning tools—readings, multimedia, activities, and assessments—into a singular Learning Path that guides the student through the curriculum. Educators personalize the experience by customizing the presentation of these learning tools to their students; even seamlessly introducing their own content into the Learning Path via "apps" that integrate into the MindTap platform. MindTap can also be deeply integrated into an institution's Learning Management System (LMS) through a service called MindLinks.

Cengage Learning's extensive video library includes the *Student Speeches for Critique and Analysis* and *Communication Scenarios for Critique and Analysis*, which include sample student speeches and the interpersonal and group communication scenarios featured as case studies in this text. These videos provide realistic examples of communication that allow students and teachers to identify specific communication principles, skills, and practices, and to analyze how they work in actual interaction. All these videos can be found in the Speech Video Library located in MindTap.

The speech video library provides instructors an easy way to keyword search, review, evaluate, and assign exemplar student speeches into their classroom & online learning environment. There are over 150 videos, including both famous historical speeches and realistic student classroom speeches as well as communication scenarios. Student speech types include informative, persuasive, invitational, impromptu, and group presentations. All speeches are accompanied by activities to help student refine and develop their speech preparation and critical thinking skills.

With Cengage's **Flex-Text Customization Program**, you can create a text as unique as your course: quickly, simply, and affordably. As part of our flex-text program, you can add your personal touch to *Communication in Our Lives* with a course-specific cover and up to 32 pages of your own content, at no additional cost.

I encourage you to contact your local Cengage Learning representative or http://www.cengage.com/highered/ for more information, user names and passwords, examination copies, or a demonstration of these ancillary products. Available to qualified adopters.

Resources for Students

If you want your students to have access to the online resources for *Communication in Our Lives*, please be sure to order them for your course. These resources can be bundled with every new copy of the text or ordered separately. If you do not order them, your students will not have access to these online resources. *Contact your local Cengage Learning sales representative for more details.*

The *Communication in Our Lives* interactive video activities feature videos of the sample speeches and interpersonal and group communication scenarios featured in the book's case studies. This multimedia tool allows students to evaluate the speeches and scenarios, and compare their evaluation with mine.

MindTap from Cengage Learning represents a new approach to a highly personalized, online learning platform and brings course concepts to life with online interactive learning, study, and exam preparation tools like the interactive eBook, flashcards, quizzes, tested activities, Communication Highlight Activities and Sharpen Your Skills Activities that support the printed textbook. The Speech Communication MindTap for *Communication in Our Lives* goes beyond the book to deliver what you need!

Many Cengage Learning texts are available through **CengageBrain**, our textbook rental program or also available as an eBook where you can buy by the chapter. Keep CengageBrain in mind for your next Cengage Learning purchase. Visit http://cengagebrain.com for details.

A *Guide to the Basic Course for ESL Students* by Esther Yook of Mary Washington College is an aid for nonnative speakers. This guide includes strategies for accent management and overcoming speech apprehension, in addition to helpful website addresses and answers to frequently asked questions.

Finally, *The Art and Strategy of Service Learning Presentations* by Rick Isaacson and Jeff Saperstein is an invaluable resource for students in the basic course that integrates or will soon integrate a service learning component. This handbook provides guidelines for connecting service learning work with classroom concepts and advice for working effectively with agencies and organizations. It also provides model forms and reports and a directory of online resources.

Acknowledgments

All books reflect the efforts of many people, and *Communication in Our Lives* is no exception. A number of people have helped this book evolve from an early vision to the final form you hold in your hands. I am grateful to my editor, Kelli Strieby, for her support and for her management of the team that worked on this book. I am also especially indebted to my content development editor, the invincible Kate Scheinman. From start to finish, she has been an active partner in the project. This book reflects her many insights.

I am also grateful to the people who reviewed the previous editions of this book, who have been most generous in offering suggestions for improving the book.

Reviewers who worked with me in developing this edition, and to whom I am especially grateful, are:

Julie Benson-Rosston, Carrol College

Jennifer Boyenga, Indian Hills Community College

Jennifer Fairchild, Eastern Kentucky University

Clark Friesen, Lone Star College-Tomball

Amie Kincaid, University of Illinois Springfield

Jennifer Marks, Northeast Lakeview College

Felicia Stewart, Morehouse College

I could not have written this book without undergraduate students. They have helped me refine ideas and activities that appear in this book. Invariably, my students teach me at least as much as I teach them, and for that I am deeply grateful.

I also thank my friends who are sources of personal support, insight, challenges, and experience—all of which find their way into what I write. Finally, and always, I acknowledge my partner Robbie (Robert) Cox. Like everything else I do, this book has benefited from his presence in my life. Being married to him has enriched my appreciation of the possibilities for love, growth, kindness, understanding, and magic between people. In addition to being the great love of my life, Robbie is my most demanding critic and my greatest fan. Both his criticism and support have shaped the final form of this book.

Julia T. Wood
May 2016
Chapel Hill, NC

About the Author

Julia T. Wood is Lineberger Distinguished Professor of Humanities Emerita and the Caroline H. and Thomas S. Royster Distinguished Professor of Graduate Education Emerita at the University of North Carolina at Chapel Hill. After completing her Ph.D. (Pennsylvania State University) at age 24, she taught classes, conducted research, and wrote extensively about communication in personal relationships and about gender, communication, and culture. She has published more than 100 articles and chapters, she has authored or coauthored 17 books, and edited or coedited 9 others. The recipient of 12 awards for outstanding teaching and 15 awards for distinguished scholarship, Professor Wood continues to conduct research, write, and mentor students. In addition to her academic pursuits, Professor Wood enjoys volunteering at the Carolina Tiger Rescue where she works with rescued tigers, lions, cougars, servals, caracals, and ocelots. She also cherishes time and conversation with students, friends, and family.

Professor Wood lives with her partner, Robert (Robbie) Cox, who is Professor Emeritus at the University of North Carolina and who works with the national Sierra Club. Four-footed members of their family are their dog, Cassidy, and two cats, Always Rowdy and Rigby.

Introduction

- A friend comes to you with a problem, and you want to show that you support him.

- A group you belong to is working on recycling programs for the campus, and you're frustrated by the group's inefficiency. You want to make meetings more productive.

- At the end of the term, the person you've been seeing will graduate and take a job in a city 1,000 miles away, and you wonder how to stay connected across the distance.

- You met an interesting person online. At first, you enjoyed interacting with her, but lately she's been texting you incessantly, and you feel she's intrusive.

- The major project in one of your courses is an oral research report, so your grade depends on your ability to present a good speech.

Situations like these illustrate the importance of communication in our lives. Unlike some of the subjects you study, communication is relevant to every aspect of your life. We communicate with ourselves when we work through ideas, psych ourselves up to meet challenges, and rehearse ways to approach someone about a difficult issue. We communicate with others to build and sustain personal relationships, to perform our jobs and advance our careers, to connect with friends and meet new people online, and to participate in social and civic activities. Every facet of life involves communication.

Although we communicate all the time, we don't always communicate effectively. People who have inadequate communication knowledge and skills are hampered in their efforts to achieve personal, professional, and social goals. On the other hand, people who communicate well have a keen advantage in accomplishing their objectives. This suggests that learning about communication and learning how to communicate are keys to effective living.

Communication in Our Lives is designed to help you understand how communication works in your personal, professional, and social life. To open the book, I'll introduce myself and describe the basic approach and special features of *Communication in Our Lives*.

Introduction to the Author

As an undergraduate, I enrolled in a course much like the one you're taking now. In that course, I discovered the field of communication, and my interest in it has endured and grown in the years since I took that class. Communication is the basis of cultural life, and it is a primary tool for personal, social, civic, and professional satisfaction and growth. It is a field that is both theoretically rich and exceptionally practical. I know of no discipline that offers more valuable insights, skills, and knowledge.

Because you will be reading this book, you should know something about the person who wrote it. I am a middle-class, Caucasian heterosexual woman. As is true for all of us, who I am affects what I know and how I think, act, interact, and write. My race, gender, social–economic class, and sexual orientation have given me certain kinds of insight and obscured others. As a woman, I understand discrimination based on sex because I've experienced it personally. I do not have personal knowledge of racial discrimination because Western culture confers privilege on European Americans. Being middle class has shielded me from personal experience with hunger, poverty, and class bias; and my heterosexuality has spared me from being a direct target of homophobic prejudice. Who you are also influences your experiences, knowledge, and ways of communicating.

Although identity limits our personal knowledge and experiences, it doesn't completely prevent insight into people and situations different from our own. From conversations with others and from reading, we can gain some understanding of people and circumstances different from our own. What we learn by studying and interacting with a range of people expands our appreciation of the richness and complexity of humanity. In addition, learning about people different from us enlarges our personal repertoire of communication skills and our appreciation of the range of ways to communicate.

Introduction to the Book

The aim of *Communication in Our Lives* is to introduce you to many forms and functions of communication in modern life. The title reflects my belief that communication is an important part of our everyday lives. Each chapter focuses on a specific kind of communication or a particular context in which we communicate.

Coverage

Because communication is a continuous part of life, we need to understand how it works—or doesn't—in a range of situations. Therefore, this book covers a broad spectrum of communication encounters, including communication with yourself, interaction with friends and romantic partners, work in groups and teams, interaction in organizations, mass and social media, interaction between people with diverse cultural backgrounds, and public speaking. The breadth of communication issues and skills presented in this book can be adapted to the interests and preferences of individual classes and instructors.

Students

Communication in Our Lives is written for anyone interested in human communication. If you are a communication major, this book and the course it accompanies will provide you with a firm foundation for more advanced study. If you are majoring in another discipline, this book and the course you are taking will give you a sound basic understanding of communication and opportunities to strengthen your skills as a communicator.

Learning should be a joy, not a chore. I've written this book in an informal, personal style; for instance, I refer to myself as *I* rather than *the author*, and I use contractions (*can't* and *you're* instead of the more formal *cannot* and *you are*), as we do in normal conversation. I also punctuate chapters with concrete examples and insights from students at campuses around the country.

Theory and Practice

Years ago, renowned scholar Kurt Lewin said, "There is nothing so practical as a good theory." His words remain true today. In this book, I've blended theory and practice so that each draws on and enriches the other. Effective practice is theoretically informed: It is based on knowledge of how and why the communication process works and what is likely to result from different kinds of communication. At the same time, effective theories have pragmatic value: They help us understand experiences and events in our everyday lives. Each chapter in this book is informed by the theories and research generated by scholars of communication.

Features

Accenting this edition, are the following key features:

Integrated Attention to Cultural Diversity

Diversity is woven into the fabric of this book. Awareness of diversity is integral to how we communicate and think about communication; it is not an afterthought. I integrate cultural diversity into the text in several ways. First, each chapter includes research on diverse people and highlights our commonalities and differences. Second, the photos I chose for this book include people of different races, ages, religions, and so forth. Likewise, each chapter includes examples from a range of people, walks of life, and orientations.

In addition to incorporating diversity into the book as a whole, in Chapter 10, I focus exclusively on communication and culture. There you will learn about cultures and social communities (distinct groups within a single society) and the ways cultural values and norms shape how we view and practice communication. Just as important, Chapter 10 will heighten your awareness of the power of communication to shape and change cultures. In addition, it will enhance your ability to participate effectively in a culturally diverse world.

To talk about social groups is to risk stereotyping. For instance, a substantial amount of research shows that women, in general, are more emotionally expressive than men, in general. A good deal of research also reports that blacks, in general, speak with greater animation and force than whites, in general. Yet, not all women are emotionally expressive, not all men are emotionally inexpressive, not all blacks communicate forcefully, and not all whites communicate blandly. Throughout this book, I try to provide you with reliable information on social groups while avoiding stereotyping. I rely on research by members of groups being discussed whenever that is available. I also use qualifying terms, such as *most* and *in general*, to remind us that there are exceptions to generalizations.

Student Commentaries

In my classes, students teach me and each other by sharing their insights, experiences, and questions. Because I've witnessed how much students learn from one another, I've included reflections written by students at my university and other campuses. As you read the student commentaries, you'll probably identify with some, disagree with others, and be puzzled by still others. Whether you agree, disagree, or are perplexed, I think you'll find that the student commentaries valuably expand the text by adding to the voices and views it represents. In the students' words, you will find much insight and much to spark thought and discussion in your classes and elsewhere. You may have insights about material covered in this book. If so, I invite you to send me your commentaries so that I might include them in the next edition of this book.

Learning Aids

I've created three features to assist you in identifying and retaining key concepts and ideas as you read. First, each chapter opens with Learning Objectives, which you may use to guide how you read and study the chapter. Second, key terms are highlighted and defined in margins of chapters. Third, you will find Review It! boxes in the margins of the book. These summarize material you've read. By reviewing them, you increase your retention of content.

Communication and Careers

Each chapter includes one or more "Communication and Careers" features. These highlight the connections between communication principles and practices and professional paths you may pursue. This feature will enlarge your understanding of the role of communication in shaping organizations, the importance of good communication in building and maintaining effective relationships with coworkers, clients, patients, and customers.

Communication Highlights

Each chapter also includes several "Communication Highlights," which call your attention to especially interesting findings from communication research and news reports involving communication in everyday life. The "Communication Highlights" offer springboards for class discussions.

Experiencing Communication in Our Lives

Following each chapter is a case study, "Experiencing Communication in Our Lives." With each one, I invite you to think about how principles and skills we discuss in that chapter show up in everyday life. I ask a few questions about the case study that allow you to apply what you have learned in a chapter to analyzing real-life communication and developing strategies for improving interaction. A video of the case study is also available online with your MindTap Speech for *Communication in Our Lives*.

Beyond the Classroom

Following chapters in Parts I and II is a "Beyond the Classroom" feature. It asks you to take the material in the chapter and extend it in three ways: asking how it applies to the workplace, how it involves ethical issues and choices, and how it applies to civic and social life. By thinking through these three issues for each chapter, you will actively engage the material and understand it more deeply.

Sharpen Your Skill

At the end of each chapter, you will find two "Sharpen Your Skill" exercises. These bring to life the concepts we discuss by showing you how material in the text pertains to your daily life. They invite you to apply communication principles and skills as you interact with others. Some of the "Sharpen Your Skill" features suggest ways to practice particular communication skills. Others encourage you to notice how a specific communication principle or theory shows up in your interactions. If you do the "Sharpen Your Skill" exercises, you will increase your insight into communication in general and your own communication in particular.

Research in Our Lives

A final feature, "Research in Our Lives," is available from your instructor for distribution. This feature answers a question that students often raise: What does academic research have to do with the "real world"? To show you that research conducted by communication scholars has important impact on real life, I offer short summaries of six research studies that are relevant to issues in today's world and your own life.

I hope you enjoy reading this book as much as I've enjoyed writing it. I also hope that this book and the class it accompanies will help you develop the skills needed for communication in your life. If so, then both of us will have spent our time well.

1

The way we communicate with others and with ourselves ultimately determines the quality of our lives.

Anthony Robbins

The World of Communication

LEARNING OBJECTIVES

After studying the topics in this chapter, you should be able to:

1. Identify the key features that define communication.

2. Distinguish between content-level meaning and relationship-level meaning.

3. Identify the value of studying communication to four aspects of your life: personal, relationship, professional, and cultural.

4. Apply the transactional model of communication to a specific interaction.

5. List the four themes that unify the field of communication.

6. Explain how the definition of communication applies to social media and online communication.

How does communication affect your life the most?

MindTap®

Review the chapter's learning objectives and **start** with a quick warm-up activity.

Mike pockets his iPhone and shakes his head; staying in touch with Chris is awkward now that they live 800 miles apart. They were buddies in high school but drifted apart after they went to different universities. They text frequently, but it's not the same as hanging out together. Shrugging, he turns on the TV while he finishes dressing for dinner with Coreen. The top news story is about another school shooting. He grimaces, thinking that the world has become pretty violent. Turning his thoughts back to Coreen, Mike hopes she won't want to talk about their relationship again tonight. He can't see the point of analyzing and discussing their relationship unless something is wrong, but she likes to talk about it when everything is fine.

As he dresses, Mike thinks about his oral presentation for Thursday's sociology class. He has some good ideas, but he doesn't know how to turn them into an effective speech. He vaguely remembers that the professor talked about how to organize a speech, but he wasn't listening. Mike also wishes he knew how to deal with a group that can't get on track. He and six other students have worked for three months to organize a student book co-op, but the group can't get its act together. By now everyone is really frustrated, and nobody listens to anyone else. His phone alerts him to a new text message and he reads a message from a member of the group who is angry that nobody seems to be really committed to the co-op project. Mike saves the message for a later reply, turns off the TV, and leaves to meet Coreen.

L
ike Mike, most of us communicate continually in our daily lives. Effective communication is vital to friendships, romantic relationships, public speaking, participation in civic life, interviewing, classroom learning, and productive group work. Communication opportunities and demands fill our everyday lives.

Long after the college years, Mike—and the rest of us—will rely on communication. You may need to talk with clients or patients, make progress reports, work on teams, and present proposals. You may represent your company at a press conference or team up with colleagues to develop company policies. You will have conflicts with coworkers, supervisors, and subordinates. Beyond your career, you'll communicate with family members, friends, neighbors, and civic and community groups.

Why Study Communication?

Communication is one of the most popular fields of undergraduate study. One reason for this popularity is that effective communication is important in all aspects of life. In 2015, the Pew Research Center reported that adults rank communication skills as number 1 for getting ahead in life—more important than writing, reading, math, science, and other skills (GooLeave, 2015).

Communication skills can be learned. Some people have a natural aptitude for playing basketball. They become even more effective, however, if they study theories of offensive and defensive play and if they practice skills. Likewise, even if you communicate well now, learning about communication and practicing communication skills can make you more effective (Hargie, 2006).

Another reason to study communication is that theories and principles help us make sense of what happens in our lives, and they help us have personal impact. For instance, if Mike learned about different gender communities, he might understand why Coreen, like many women, enjoys talking about relationships even when there is no problem. If Mike had better insight into the communication that sustains long-distance relationships, he might be able to enrich his friendship with Chris despite the miles between them. If he knew how to develop an agenda, he might be able to get his group on track. Studying public speaking could help Mike design a good presentation for his class report. Learning to listen better would help Mike retain information like his professor's tips on organizing oral reports. Communication theory and skills would help Mike maximize his effectiveness in all spheres of his life.

Communication in Our Lives will help you become a more confident and competent communicator. Part One clarifies how communication works (or doesn't work) and explains how perception, personal identity, language, nonverbal communication, and listening affect the overall communication process. In Part Two, we'll look at communication in five contexts: personal relationships, small groups, organizations, cultures, and mediated environments. Part Three focuses on public speaking.

This chapter lays a foundation for your study of communication. We'll first define communication. Next we'll discuss the values of communication in many spheres of your life. Then we'll examine some models of communication to clarify how the process works. In the third section of the chapter, we'll describe the breadth of the communication field and careers for communication specialists.

Defining Communication

Communication* is a systemic process in which people interact with and through symbols to create and interpret meanings. Let's elaborate the key parts of this definition.

Communication is a **process**, which means it is ongoing and always in motion, moving ever forward and changing continually. It's hard to tell when communication starts and stops because what happened long before we talk with someone may influence interaction, and what occurs in a particular encounter may have repercussions in the future. We cannot freeze communication at any one moment.

Communication is also systemic because it occurs within a **system** of interrelated parts that affect one another. In family communication, for instance, each member of the family is part of the system (Galvin, Dickson, & Marrow, 2006). In addition, the physical environment and the time of day are elements of the system that affect interaction. People interact differently in a formal living room and on a beach, and we may be more alert at certain times of day than at others. If a family has a history of listening sensitively and working out problems constructively, and then when one family member says, "There's something we need to talk about," the comment is unlikely to cause defensiveness. On the other hand, if the family has a record of nasty conflicts, then the same comment might arouse strong defensiveness. A lingering kiss might be an appropriate way to show affection in a private setting, but the same action would raise eyebrows in an office. To interpret communication, we have to consider the system in which it takes place.

communication A systemic process in which people interact with and through symbols to create and interpret meanings.

process Something that is ongoing and continuously in motion, the beginnings and endings of which are difficult to identify. Communication is a process.

system A group of interrelated elements that affect one another. Communication is systemic.

---

*Boldfaced terms are defined in the margins and also in the glossary at the end of the book.

Our definition of communication also emphasizes **symbols**, which include all languages and many nonverbal behaviors, as well as art and music. Anything that abstractly signifies something else can be a symbol. We might symbolize love by giving a ring and saying "I love you" or by embracing. Later in this chapter, we'll have more to say about symbols. For now, just remember that human communication involves interaction with and through symbols.

Finally, our definition focuses on meanings, which are the heart of communication. Meanings are the significance we bestow on phenomena—what they signify to us. Meanings are not in phenomena. Instead, meaning grows out of our interaction with symbols.

There are two levels of meaning in communication. The **content level of meaning** is the literal message. For example, if someone says to you, "Get lost!" the content level of meaning is that you should go away. The **relationship level of meaning** expresses the relationship between communicators. In our example, if the person who says, "Get lost!" is a friend and is smiling, then you would probably interpret the relationship level of meaning as indicating that the person likes you and is kidding around. On the other hand, if the person who says, "Get lost!" is your supervisor, and he or she is responding to your request for a raise, then you might interpret the relationship level of meaning as indicating that your supervisor regards you as inferior and dislikes your work.

Values of Communication

From birth to death, communication shapes our personal, professional, civic, and social lives as well as the culture in which we live (Galvin, Braithwaite, & Bylund, 2015; Holt-Lunstad, Smith, & Layton, 2010; Salas & Frush, 2012). In order to advance a career, you'll need to know how to present your ideas effectively, build good relationships with colleagues, monitor your perceptions, manage conflicts constructively, and listen carefully. To have healthy, enduring relationships, you'll need to know how to listen well, communicate support, deal with conflicts, and understand communication styles that are different from your own. To be an engaged citizen, you'll need to express your points of view articulately, and you'll need to listen critically to others' ideas.

Personal Identity and Health

George Herbert Mead (1934)* said that humans are "talked into" humanity. He meant that we gain personal identity as we communicate with others. In the earliest years of our lives, family members tell us who we are: "You're smart." "You're strong." "You're a clown." Later, we interact with teachers, friends, romantic partners, and coworkers who communicate how they perceive us. Thus, how we see ourselves reflects the views of us that others communicate.

The profound connection between identity and communication is dramatically evident in children who have been deprived of human contact. Case studies of children who were isolated from others for long periods of time reveal that they lack a healthy self-concept, and their mental and psychological development is severely hindered by lack of language (Shattuck, 1980).

symbol An arbitrary, ambiguous, and abstract representation of a phenomenon. Symbols are the basis of language, much nonverbal behavior, and human thought.

content level of meaning One of the two levels of meaning in communication. The content level of meaning is the literal, or denotative, information in a message.

relationship level of meaning One of the two levels of meaning in communication; expresses the relationship between communicators.

---

*I am using the American Psychological Association's (APA) method of citation. For example, if you see "Mead (1934)," I am referencing a work by Mead that was written in 1934. If you see "Mead (1934, p.10)" or "(Mead, 1934, p. 10)," I am referencing page 10 specifically of Mead's 1934 work. The full bibliographic citations for all works appear in the References section at the end of the book.

A large body of research shows that communicating with others promotes health, whereas social isolation is linked to stress, disease, and early death (Fackelmann, 2006; Holt-Lunstad et al., 2010). Families that practice good communication are more cohesive and stable (Galvin & Braithwaite, 2015). College students who are in committed relationships have fewer mental health problems and are less likely to be obese (Braithwaite, Delevi, & Fincham, 2010). Life-threatening medical problems are also affected by healthy interaction with others. Heart disease is more common among people who lack strong interpersonal relationships (Holt-Lunstad et al., 2010). Clearly, healthy interaction with others is important to our physical and mental well-being.

Communication skills are also essential to effective health care. Doctors, nurses, dentists, and others involved in health care need to be able to listen to patients and to communicate in ways patients understand. Equally important, patients need to be able to communicate clearly with health care professionals to explain their concerns and symptoms.

Relationship Values

Daniel Goleman, author of *Social Intelligence* (2007), says humans are "wired to connect" (p. 4). And communication is the primary way that we connect with others. Marriage counselors have long emphasized the importance of communication for healthy, enduring relationships (Gottman, 1994a, 1994b; Gottman & Carrère, 1994). They point out that the failure of some marriages is not caused primarily by troubles and problems or even by conflict because all marriages encounter challenges and conflict. A major distinction between relationships that endure and those that collapse is effective communication. In fact, results of a national poll showed that a majority of Americans perceive communication problems as the number 1 reason that marriages fail—far surpassing other reasons such as sexual difficulties, money problems, and interference from family members (http://files .umwblogs.org/blogs.dir/1160/files/2008/05/roper-poll-on-communication.pdf).

Communication is important for more than solving problems or making disclosures. For most of us, everyday talks and nonverbal interactions are the very essence of relationships (Duck & McMahon, 2012; Goleman, 2011; Wood & Duck, 2006). Unremarkable, everyday interaction sustains intimacy more than the big moments, such as declarations of love. By sharing news about mutual acquaintances and discussing ordinary topics, partners keep up the steady pulse of their relationship (Duck, 2006; Schmidt & Uecker, 2007; Wood, 2006a). For this reason, one of the biggest challenges of long-distance relationships is not being able to share small talks.

> **MYCA** *Last year, I did study abroad, and it was really hard to stay connected with my friends and family. I was in the Philippines so it was night here when it was day there—forget texting back and forth or even IMs. Plus, the Internet was spotty so sometimes I couldn't get on to share something cool that was happening in the moment. That was the hardest part—not being able to share the little things when they happened.*

Professional Values

One reason that communication is among the most popular majors is that communication skills are closely linked to professional success. The importance of

Communication & Careers

Poor Communication = Preventable Death

As many as 98,000 preventable deaths each year have been traced to poor communication among doctors, nurses, and other members of health care teams (Harris, 2011). This disturbing fact has made effective team work a priority in training health care providers (Salas & Frush, 2012).

As a result, a number of medical schools, including those at Stanford, Los Angeles, and Cincinnati, now base admissions to medical school not only on academic record but also on the ability to collaborate with others. In addition, they require students to take courses in teamwork.

communication is obvious in professions such as patient care, teaching, business, law, sales, and counseling, in which talking and listening are prominent.

In other fields, the importance of communication is less obvious but nonetheless present. Most employers list communication skills as one of the top qualities in job candidates (Hart Research, 2013; Rhodes, 2010; Selingo, 2012). Leaders at organizations such as the *New York Times*, FedEx, and GlaxoSmithKline list communication as vital to their organizations' success (O'Hair & Eadie, 2009). Doctors who do not listen well are less effective in treating patients, and they're more likely to be sued than doctors who listen well (Levine, 2004; Milia, 2003). The pivotal role of communication in health care makes it unsurprising that an increasing number of medical schools base admissions, in part, on applicants' communication skills, especially their ability to communicate empathy to patients (Rosenbaum, 2011).

In the workplace, poor communication means that errors and misunderstandings occur, messages must be repeated, productivity suffers, and—sometimes—people lose jobs. No matter what your career goals are, developing strong communication skills will enhance your professional success.

Cultural Values

Communication skills are important to the health of our society. To be effective, citizens in a democracy must be able to express ideas and evaluate the ideas of others. One event typical of presidential election years is a debate between or among candidates. To make informed judgments, viewers need to listen critically to candidates' arguments and their responses to criticism and questions. We also need listening skills to grasp and evaluate opposing points of view on issues such as abortion, environmental policies, and health care reform. To be a good community member, you need skills in expressing your point of view and responding to those of others.

Living in our era means living with people who have diverse cultural and ethnic backgrounds. In 2000, 64% of Americans were Caucasian, but the prediction is that there will be no single majority race by 2043 (Milbank, 2014). Nearly half of first-year students at colleges and universities think that learning about other cultures is essential or very important (Hoover, 2010). In addition, there is great value in interacting with people from different cultures. The number of international students who enroll in U.S. colleges and universities is at an all-time high: 723,277 (McMurtrie, 2011). U.S.-born students appreciate the presence of peers

Communication Highlight

U.S. Demographics in the Twenty-First Century

Demographics in the United States are changing rapidly. Currently, one in three U.S. residents is a minority, but that number is growing quickly. The latest Census reports that for the first time ever, there are more births of minorities in the United States (Yen, 2012). The following table shows demographic shifts from 2010 to projections for 2050 ("Demographics," 2009; Milbank, 2014; Yen, 2012):

	2010 (Percentage)	2050 (Percentage)
African Americans	13	13
Asians	4	8
White, not Hispanic	64	46
Hispanics or Latino/a	16	30
Other	3	5

All figures are rounded off.

More and more people are convinced that a key function of higher education is to prepare people to function effectively and comfortably in a diverse society. Two-thirds of Americans polled by the Ford Foundation (1998) say it is very important for colleges and universities to prepare students to live and work in a society marked by diversity. Fully 94% of Americans polled say that it is more important now than ever before for all of us to understand people who are different from us, and the majority of respondents believe that every college student should be required to study different cultures and social groups to graduate.

Go to the book's online resources for this chapter to learn more about diverse groups and their impact on the United States.

from around the globe. In fact, exposure to students from a range of backgrounds is one of the best predictors of whether first-year college students return for a second year (Berrett, 2011).

AVA *There are so many people from different cultures on this campus that you can't get by without knowing how to communicate in a whole lot of ways. In my classes and my dorm, there are lots of Asian students and some Hispanic ones, and they communicate differently than people raised in the United States. If I don't learn about their communication styles, I can't get to know them or learn about what they think.*

Ava is right. When she was a student in one of my courses, she and I talked several times about the concern she expresses in her commentary. Ava realized she needed to learn to interact with people who differ from her if she is to participate fully in today's world. She has learned a lot about communicating with diverse people, and no doubt she will learn more in the years ahead. Like Ava, you can improve your ability to communicate effectively with the variety of people who make up our society.

Communication, then, is important for personal, relationship, professional, and cultural reasons. Because communication is a cornerstone of human life, your choice to study it will serve you well. To understand what's involved in communication, let's now define the process.

Models of Communication

Over the years, scholars in communication have developed a number of models, which reflect increasingly sophisticated understandings of the communication process.

Linear Models

One of the first models (Laswell, 1948) described communication as a linear, or one-way, process in which one person acted on another person. This model consisted of five questions that described early views of how communication worked:

Who?
Says what?
In what channel?
To whom?
With what effect?

A year later, Shannon and Weaver (1949) advanced a model that included **noise**, which is anything that can interfere with the intended message. Figure 1.1 shows two versions of the Shannon and Weaver's model. Although linear models were useful starting points, they were too simple to capture the complexity of most kinds of human communication.

Interactive Models

The major shortcoming of linear models was that they portrayed communication as flowing in only one direction, from a sender to a receiver. This suggests that speakers only speak and never listen and that listeners only listen and never send messages.

noise Anything that interferes with intended communication.

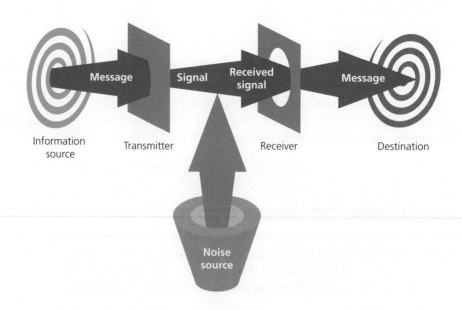

FIGURE 1.1
A Linear Model of Communication
Source: Adapted from Shannon, C., & Weaver, W. (1949). *The Mathematical Theory of Communication.* Urbana: University of Illinois Press.

Verbal and nonverbal communication reflect cultural backgrounds and understandings.

Realizing that receivers respond to senders and senders attend to receivers led communication theorists (Schramm, 1955) to adapt models to include feedback. Feedback may be verbal, nonverbal, or both, and it may be intentional or unintentional. Research has confirmed Schramm's insight that feedback is important. Supervisors report that communication accuracy and on-the-job productivity rise when they encourage their subordinates to give feedback: ask questions, comment on supervisors' messages, and respond to supervisory communication (Deal & Kennedy, 1999).

The interactive model also shows that communicators create and interpret communication within their personal fields of experience. This recognizes communication as an interactive process in which both senders and receivers participate actively (Figure 1.2).

feedback Response to a message; may be verbal, nonverbal, or both. In communication theory, the concept of feedback appeared first in interactive models of communication.

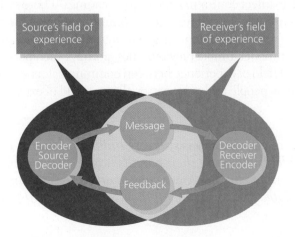

FIGURE 1.2
An Interactive Model of Communication
Source: Adapted from Schramm, W. (1955). *The Process and Effects of Mass Communication.* Urbana: University of Illinois Press.

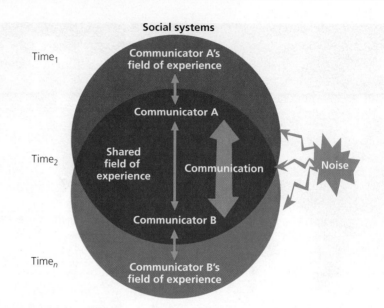

FIGURE 1.3
A Transactional Model
of Communication
Source: Adapted
from Wood, J. T.
(2010). *Interpersonal
Communication: Everyday
Encounters* (6th ed.).
Belmont, CA: Wadsworth.

Transactional Models

A serious limitation of interactive models is that they don't acknowledge that everyone involved in communication both sends and receives messages, often simultaneously. While giving a press release, a speaker watches reporters to see whether they seem interested; both the speaker and the reporters are "listening," and both are "speaking."

Interactive models also fail to capture the dynamism of communication. To do this, a model would need to show that communication changes over time as a result of what happens between people. For example, Mike and Coreen communicated in more reserved and formal ways on their first date than after months of seeing each other. What they talk about and how they talk have changed as a result of interacting. An accurate model would include the feature of time and would depict features of communication as dynamically varying rather than constant. Figure 1.3 is a transactional model of communication that highlights these features and others we have discussed.

The transactional model includes noise, which is anything that has the potential to interfere with the intended communication. This includes sounds like a lawn mower or people nearby talking on smartphones, as well as "noise" within communicators, such as fatigue and preoccupation. In addition, our model shows that communication is a continuous, constantly changing process.

The outer lines on our model emphasize that communication occurs within systems that themselves affect communication and meanings. Those systems include contexts that both communicators share (e.g., a common campus, town, and culture) as well as each person's personal systems (e.g., family, religious associations, and friends). Also notice that our model, unlike previous ones, portrays each person's field of experience and the shared field of experience between communicators as changing over time. As we encounter new people and grow personally, our field of experience expands.

NISHA   *I lived in India until I was 14, and my family is still very Indian culturally. I am always surprised by how much U.S. college students disregard their parents' wishes. My parents insist that I marry an Indian so they do not want me to date Americans or other non-Indians. My friends say it is not my parents business who I date. They don't care if their parents don't approve of their boyfriends and girlfriends.*

Finally, our model doesn't label one person a "sender" and the other a "receiver." Instead, both people are defined as communicators who participate actively in the communication process. This means that, at a given moment in communication, you may be sending a message, receiving a message, or doing both at the same time (interpreting what someone says while nodding to show you are interested).

The Breadth of the Communication Field

The discipline of communication dates back more than 2,000 years. Originally, the field focused almost exclusively on public communication. Aristotle, a famous Greek philosopher, believed that effective public speaking was essential to citizens' participation in civic life (Borchers, 2006). He taught his students how to develop and present persuasive speeches to influence public affairs.

Although public speaking remains a vital skill, it is no longer the only focus of the communication field. The modern discipline includes seven major areas of research and teaching: interpersonal communication, group communication, organizational communication, public communication, health communication, mass communication and social media, and intercultural communication.

Interpersonal Communication

A second major emphasis in the field of communication is **interpersonal communication**, which deals with communication between people. In one sense, everything except intrapersonal communication is interpersonal. But such a broad definition doesn't create useful boundaries for the area of study.

Interpersonal communication exists on a continuum from impersonal to highly personal. The most impersonal kind of communication occurs when we ignore another person or treat another as an object. In the middle of the continuum is interaction with others within social roles. The most personal communication occurs in what philosopher Martin Buber (1970) called "I–Thou" relationships, in which each person treats the other as a unique and sacred person. Figure 1.4 illustrates the communication continuum. The more we know and interact with another person as a distinct individual, the more personal the communication is. Using this criterion, we would say that a deep conversation with a friend is more personal than a casual exchange with a sales clerk.

Interpersonal communication scholars study how communication creates and sustains relationships and how partners communicate to deal with the normal and extraordinary challenges of maintaining intimacy over time (Duck & McMahon, 2012; Wood & Duck, 2006).

Research indicates that communication is the lifeblood of close friendships and romantic relationships. Communication is the primary way people develop intimacy and continuously refashion relationships to meet their changing needs and identities. Intimates who learn how to listen sensitively and talk with each other have the greatest chance of enduring over time.

Review It!

Models of Communication:
- Linear
- Interactive
- Transactional

interpersonal communication Communication between people, usually in close relationships such as friendship and romance.

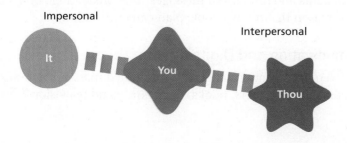

FIGURE 1.4
The Communication Continuum

Group Communication

A third important branch of communication study is small-group communication, including therapeutic groups, social groups, decision-making committees, and work teams. Small-group communication scholars study leadership, member participation, agendas for decision making, and disruptive and constructive conflict. Chapters 10 and 11 will help us understand how communication affects each of these aspects of group life and how we can participate effectively in groups.

Group communication scholars also study teams, which are special types of groups that pull together people with diverse skills and experiences and which develop especially strong cohesion. Learning to communicate effectively in teams has become a criterion for success and advancement in careers.

Organizational Communication

Communication in organizations is another growing area of interest. Communication scholars have identified communication skills that enhance professional success, and they have traced the impact of various kinds of communication on morale, productivity, and commitment to organizations.

Many organizational communication scholars study **organizational culture**, which is the understandings about identity and codes of thought and action shared by the members of an organization (Nicotera, Clinkscales, & Walker, 2002). From this understanding emerge rules for interaction and perspectives on work.

MADISON   *I've had a number of part-time jobs, and I've noticed one interesting gender difference in my bosses. Men who are in charge tend to tell staff what to do—not like in a mean way, but it's very firm, like "Get that done right away." Women bosses tend to ask, like, saying "Would you do this?" or "Could you get this to me?" The bottom line is the same: We know to do whatever the boss says. But it feels more inclusive when a boss asks you instead of telling you.*

Health Communication

Health communication is one of the fastest-growing areas in the contemporary field of communication. Health communication is a very broad area that includes patient–clinician interaction, communication on health care teams, organizational dynamics in health care settings, marketing and advocacy of healthy practices for individuals and communities, and policy making (Kreps, 2010; Schiavo, 2007).

Effective communication is essential to successful public health practice in contexts that range from homes to doctor's offices and workplaces. Health communication includes not only face-to-face interaction but also interaction on health websites such as WebMD, online support groups, web portals, and mobile devices that monitor patients and send them messages. The broad range of health communication is one reason that many people plan careers in this area.

organizational culture
Ways of thinking, acting, and understanding work that are shared by members of an organization and that reflect an organization's distinct identity.

Mass Communication and Digital Media

For some time, communication scholars have studied mass communication media such as film, radio, newspapers, books, magazines, and television. Their research has given us insight into how mass media work and how they represent and influence cultural values. For instance, the cultural value place on youth is reflected in and perpetuated by featuring young, attractive models in ads and as news reporters and anchors.

A more recent focus of media scholars is digital media. How do iPods, tablets, smartphones, and other digital media influence our thinking, working, and relating? Do they increase productivity? Are we becoming less attentive because we're so often multitasking? Are we becoming more efficient because we multitask? Are we more and more connected to others?

Clearly, the verdict on the effects of social media will not be in for some time. Meanwhile, technologies of communication pervade many aspects of our lives. Skyping allows people who are separated by many miles to talk with and see each other. Many public presentations now include PowerPoint slides and clips from the Internet.

Public Communication

Even though not everyone will enter careers that call for extensive formal speaking, most of us will have opportunities to speak publically. When we join new groups, we may be asked to "say a few words about yourself," and others' first impressions of us will be based on our self-introductions.

In addition, we all will be in situations where speaking up is a responsibility. My editor speaks to her sales representatives to explain what her books are about and how to point out important features to faculty. I recently coached my doctor in public speaking so she could address her colleagues on a development in the treatment of kidney disease. My plumber presents workshops to his staff to update them on new plumbing products and to teach them how to communicate effectively with

JOEL SARTORE/National Geographic Creative

MindTap® How satisfying do you find digital interaction systems such as Skype and FaceTime?

customers. My editor, doctor, and plumber don't consider themselves public speakers, but public speaking is a part of their lives, and doing it effectively is important to their success.

Scholars of public communication focus on critical evaluation of speeches and on principles for speaking effectively. Scholars of public communication also study principles of effective public speaking so we know a lot about what makes speakers seem credible to listeners and how credibility affects persuasion. Research has also enlightened us about the kinds of argument, methods of organizing ideas, and forms of proof that listeners find effective. Had Mike studied this research, he could have gleaned useful guidelines for his oral report in class.

Intercultural Communication

Intercultural communication is an increasingly important focus of research, teaching, and training. The United States has always been made up of many people with diverse cultural backgrounds and styles of communicating.

Scholars of intercultural communication increase awareness of different cultures' communication practices. For example, a Taiwanese woman in one of my classes seldom spoke up and wouldn't enter the heated debates that characterize graduate classes. One day after class, I encouraged Mei-Ling to argue for her ideas when others challenged them. She replied that that would be impolite. Her culture considers it disrespectful to argue or assert oneself and even more disrespectful to contradict others. Understood in terms of the communication values of her culture, Mei-Ling's deference did not mean she lacked confidence.

MEIKKO   *What I find most odd about Americans is their focus on themselves. Here, everyone wants to be an individual who is so strong and stands out from everyone else. In Japan, it is not like that. We see ourselves as parts of families and communities, not as individuals. Here* I *and* my *are the most common words, but they are not often said in Japan.*

Review It!

Breadth of Field:
- Interpersonal
- Group
- Organizational
- Health
- Media
- Public
- Intercultural

A particularly important recent trend in the study of intercultural communication is the research on different social communities within a single society. Cultural differences are obvious in communication between a Saudi Arabian and a Canadian. Less obvious are cultural differences in communication between people who speak the "same" language. Within the United States, there are distinct social communities based on race, gender, sexual orientation, and other factors. Intercultural communication scholars (Samovar, Porter, & McDaniel, 2011) have identified distinctive styles of communication used by women, men, blacks, whites, certain American Indian tribes, people with disabilities, and other groups. For example, women, more than men, tend to disclose personal information and to engage in emotionally expressive talk in their friendships (Wood, 1994a, 1994d, 2013). Many blacks are socialized in a culture that encourages dynamic talk, verbal duels, and other communication routines that have no equivalents in white speech communities (Houston & Wood, 1996). Participating effectively in a pluralistic society requires us to recognize and respect the communication practices of distinct social communities.

Unifying Themes in the Field

After reading about the major branches of the modern field of communication, you might think that the field is a collection of separate, unrelated areas of interest. Actually, the field of communication is unified by a pervasive interest in symbols, meaning, critical thinking, and ethics.

Review It!

Unifying Themes:
- Symbols
- Meaning
- Critical Thinking
- Ethics

Symbols

Symbols are the basis of language, thinking, and much nonverbal behavior. A wedding band is a symbol of marriage in Western culture; your name is a symbol for you; and a smile is a symbol of friendliness. Because symbols are abstract, they allow us to lift experiences and ourselves out of the present concrete world in order to reflect on past experiences and imagine future ones. Because symbols let us represent ideas and feelings, we can share experiences with others, even if they have not had those experiences themselves.

Whether we are interested in social media or intrapersonal, interpersonal, group, public, or intercultural communication, symbols are central to what happens. Thus, symbols and the mental activities they enable are a unifying focus of study and teaching about all forms of communication.

Meaning

Closely related to interest in symbols is the communication field's pervasive concern with meaning. The human world is one of meaning. We don't simply exist, eat, drink, sleep, and go through motions. Instead, we imbue every aspect of our lives with significance or meaning. When I feed my dog, Cassie, she eats her food and then returns to her canine adventures. For her, eating is a necessary and enjoyable activity. Unlike Cassie, we humans layer food and eating with significance. For example, kosher products reflect commitment to Jewish heritage, turkey is commonly associated with commemorating the first Thanksgiving in the United States (although vegetarians symbolize their commitment by *not* eating turkey), eggnog is a Christmas tradition, candles are part of Kwanzaa, and birthday cakes celebrate an individual.

To study communication, then, is to study how we use symbols to create meaning in our lives. Communication scholars see romantic bonds, friendships, families, teams, organizations, and cultures as growing out of human communication.

> **BENITA**   *It's funny how important a word can be. Nick and I had been going out for a long time, and we really liked each other, but I didn't know if this was going to be long term. Then we said we loved each other, and that changed how we saw each other and the relationship. Just using the word love transformed who we are.*

Critical Thinking

A third enduring concern in the communication field is **critical thinking**. To be competent communicators, we must examine ideas carefully to decide what to believe, think, and do in particular situations. Someone who thinks critically weighs ideas thoughtfully, considers evidence carefully, asks about alternative

critical thinking Examining ideas reflectively and carefully to decide what you should believe, think, or do.

Table 1.1	Critical Thinking Skills for Effective Communication

- Identify assumptions behind statements, claims, and arguments.
- Distinguish between logical and illogical reasoning.
- Separate facts from inferences.
- Evaluate evidence to determine its reliability, relevance, and value.
- Connect new information and ideas to familiar knowledge; apply concepts learned in one context to other contexts; recognize when and where specific principles are and are not appropriate.
- Distinguish between personal experiences, attitudes, behaviors, and generalizations about human beings.
- Identify and consider alternative views on issues, solutions to problems, and courses of action.
- Define problems and questions clearly and precisely.
- Draw reasonable conclusions about the implications of information and argument for thought and action.
- Determine how to find answers to important questions by considering what needs to be known and what sources might provide relevant knowledge.

conclusions and courses of action, and connects principles and concepts across multiple contexts. Table 1.1 identifies key skills of critical thinking that affect communication competence.

Critical thinking is important in all aspects of our lives. The skills of critical thinking can enhance communication in friendships, romantic relationships, and family relationships. Critical thinking is also important to your success as a student. In class discussions and exams, you are asked to compare and contrast different policies or historical eras and to apply theories to particular situations—doing so requires critical thinking. Likewise, critical thinking is important in professional life. People who score low on measures of critical thinking are more likely to be unemployed than people who score highly (9.6% vs. 3.1%) (Berrett, 2012).

Ethics and Communication

A final theme that unifies research and teaching is ethical communication and interpretation of others' communication. Because all forms of communication involve ethical issues, this theme infuses all areas of the discipline. For instance, ethical dimensions of intrapersonal communication include the influence of stereotypes on our judgments of others. Ethical issues in the realm of interpersonal communication include honesty, compassion, and fairness in relationships. Pressures to conform that sometimes operate in groups are an ethical concern in group communication. Ethical issues also surface in public communication. For example, speakers who misrepresent facts or deliberately lie are violating an ethical principle.

Another ethical issue relevant to a range of communication contexts concerns attitudes and actions that encourage or hinder freedom of speech: Are all members of organizations equally empowered to speak? What does it mean when audiences shout down a speaker with unpopular views? How does the balance of power between relationship partners affect each person's freedom to express himself or herself? Because ethical issues infuse all forms of communication, we will discuss ethical themes in each chapter of this book. In the questions at the end of each chapter, the ethics icon will call your attention to a question focused on ethics of communication.

Thinking Critically About Language and Social Groups

MindTap®

It's especially important to think critically when using, listening to, or reading generalizations about social groups. The value of generalizations is that they allow us to recognize general patterns that can be useful starting points in understanding others. We can't learn about Koreans, blacks, whites, or Buddhists if we cannot use group labels such as *Korean* and *black*. At the same time, generalizations do not necessarily apply to particular individuals. For instance, it is true that Koreans in general are more communal than native-born Americans, particularly whites, in general, but a particular Korean may be very individualistic, and a particular native-born American may be very communal.

In this book, you will read many generalizations about various social groups. These generalizations are based on research, usually including research conducted by members of the social group being discussed. That doesn't mean that a generalization about men or whites is true about all men or all whites. You may well be a living exception to some of the generalizations about groups to which you belong.

To prevent ourselves from mistaking generalizations for absolute truths, it's important to use qualifying words such as *usually, in general, typically,* and *in most cases.* These remind us that there are exceptions to generalizations. As you read this book, notice how I qualify generalizations so we don't mistake them for universal truths. Notice also whether generalizations are appropriately qualified on television, in newspaper stories, in magazine articles, and in everyday conversations.

What Can I Do with a Degree in Communication?

MindTap®

A strong background in communication prepares people for success in an amazing array of careers. Consider William Ellwood. Once a professor, Ellwood is now the OppNet Facilitator for the Office of Behavioral and Social Sciences Research at the National Institutes of Health. Or consider Marsha Vanderford who is the director of the Emergency Communication Center for the National Center for Health Marketing, which is part of the Centers for Disease Control. Or James Stiff, who owns and is a consultant at Trial Analysts (Kellerman, 2011). Go to the book's online resources for this chapter to learn more about careers of communication professionals.

Careers in Communication

As we've seen, communication skills are essential to success in most fields. In addition, people who major in communication are particularly sought after in a number of occupations.

Research

Communication research is a vital and growing field of work. A great deal of study is conducted by academics who combine teaching and research in faculty careers.

In addition to academic research, communication specialists do media research on everything from message production to marketing. Companies want to know how people respond to different kinds of advertisements, logos, and labels for products. Before a new cereal or beer is named, various names are test marketed to test how customers will respond to different names. In addition, hospitals and other health care organizations need communication specialists to develop media campaigns for new products and services.

Education

Teachers are needed for communication curricula in secondary schools, junior colleges, colleges, universities, technical schools, and community colleges. The level at which a person is qualified to teach depends on how extensively he or she has studied communication. Generally, a bachelor's degree in communication education and certification by the board of education are required of teachers in elementary and secondary schools. A master's degree in communication qualifies a person to teach at community colleges, technical schools, and some junior colleges and colleges. The doctoral degree (Ph.D.) in communication is usually required for a career in university education, although some universities offer short-term positions to people with master's degrees.

Although generalists are preferred for many teaching jobs, university faculty often teach in specialized areas of communication. For instance, my research and teaching focus on interpersonal communication and gender and communication. Another faculty member specializes in environmental advocacy. Other college faculty concentrate on oral traditions, intercultural communication, family communication, organizational dynamics, and mass media on cultural values.

Communication educators are not limited to communication departments. People with advanced degrees in communication hold positions in other areas. Because communication is essential for doctors and businesspeople, increasing numbers of medical and business schools are creating permanent positions for communication specialists.

Media Production, Analysis, and Criticism

Increasingly, students are attracted to careers in mass communication and technologies of communication. There are many careers paths in media production, all of which demand good communication skills (Gregory, Healy, & Mazierkska, 2007). News reporters need skill not only in presenting information clearly but also in conducting interviews and fostering trust so that people will open up to them. To be effective, broadcasters must speak clearly and engagingly, and they must communicate credibly. Script writing and directing also require solid understanding of human communication.

Because our society is media saturated, we rely on media critics to help us understand what media are doing: Are they representing information fairly? Are they biased? Are they offering messages that are healthy for us?

Training and Consulting

Consulting is another field that welcomes people with backgrounds in communication. Organizations have programs to train employees in effective group communication skills, interview techniques, and group and team work. Some large hospitals and major corporations, such as IBM, have entire departments devoted to training and development. People with communication backgrounds often join these departments and work with the corporation to design and teach courses or workshops that enhance employees' communication skills.

Communication specialists may also join or form consulting firms that provide particular kinds of communication training to government and organizations. One of my colleagues consults with organizations to help them develop work teams that interact effectively. Another advises a hospital on communication training program for members of health care teams. Other communication specialists work with politicians to improve their presentation styles and sometimes to write their speeches. I consult with attorneys on cases involving charges of sexual harassment and sex discrimination: I help them understand how particular communication patterns create hostile, harassing environments, and I collaborate with them to develop trial strategy. Other communication consultants work with attorneys on jury selection and advise attorneys on courtroom communication strategies.

Human Relations and Management

Because communication is the foundation of human relations, it's no surprise that many communication specialists build careers in public relations, human resources, grievance management, negotiations, customer relations, and development and fund-raising. In each of these areas, communication skills are essential.

Communication degrees also open the door to career in management. The most important qualifications for management are not technical skills but the ability to interact with others and communicate effectively. Good managers are skilled in listening, expressing their ideas, building consensus, creating supportive work environments, and balancing task and interpersonal concerns in dealing with others.

SHARPEN YOUR SKILL

At the end of this chapter, refer to the Sharpen Your Skill feature, Giving a Speech of Self-Introduction, to apply concepts from Chapter 1.

Pressmaster/Shutterstock.com

People with strong communication skills have a range of career options.

Digital Media and Communication

How are digital media relevant to the ideas presented in this chapter? First, consider how the values of communication that we identified are achieved using social media. For instance, we rely on social media to maintain personal relationships and sometimes to form relationships. We post updates and photos on social networking sites to let friends know what's happening in our lives and to learn what is happening in others' lives. We also use social media in careers. Many companies now request online submission of job applications. Once we have a job, we use digital media to establish and maintain professional ties. LinkedIn, for example, allows people to network professionally. Digital media also enlarge our ability to engage in civic life—online we can sign petitions for causes, blog about issues that matter to us, and read the blogs of others whose opinions we respect.

You might also consider what the definition of communication implies for interacting via social media. When we talk with people face-to-face, we are aware of their immediate physical context, which is not always the case with digital interaction. We may not know who else is present and what else is happening around a person we text. When the systems within which communication occurs are unknown to us, it's more difficult to interpret others. For instance, does a delayed response mean the person you texted is angry, is thinking over what you said, is talking with people he or she is with, or is participating in a work meeting? Feedback is sometimes delayed when we interact via digital media. Also, because nonverbal communication in digital media is restricted, we may miss out on meaning, particularly on the relationship level.

Our definition also emphasizes process—changes in communication that happen over time. Think about how online and digital communication have evolved in just your lifetime. When email first became available to the general public, most people treated it much like letter writing: An email started with "Dear" or "Hello" and ended with a closing such as "Thank you" or "Sincerely." As email became more popular and as all of us were flooded with email messages, the opening and closing courtesies largely disappeared. As email traffic continued to increase, abbreviations started being used: BRB (be right back), LOL (laughing out loud), and so forth. Texting and tweeting brought more innovation in use of symbols. Vowels are often dropped, single letters serve for some words (u for you, r for are), phrases, rather than complete sentences, are acceptable, and emoticons and emojis are used to convey feelings. The rules of grammar, syntax, and spelling have also been loosened by digital natives who assume the autocorrect function edits correctly.

You might also reflect on the ways that digital media are integrated into the careers we discussed for people with strong backgrounds in communication. For instance, much research today is conducted online; human relations and management rely on digital communication to announce policies, update employees on issues, and even conduct meetings. There are few professions today that do not involve digital media.

SHARPEN YOUR SKILL

At the end of this chapter, refer to the Sharpen Your Skill feature, Your Mediated World, to apply concepts from Chapter 1.

Chapter Summary

In this chapter, we took a first look at human communication. First, we defined communication, and then we discussed its value in our lives. Next, we considered a series of models, the most accurate of which is transactional. The transactional model emphasizes that communication is a systemic process in which people interact to create and share meanings.

Like most fields of study, communication has developed over the years. Today, communication scholars and teachers are interested in a range of communication activities. This broad range of areas is held together by abiding interests in symbolic activities, meanings, critical thinking, and ethics, which together form the foundation of personal, interpersonal, civic, and social life.

The central role of communication in our lives explains why it provides foundations for a range of careers. The final section of the chapter noted ways in which definitions and models of communication apply to digital media.

Experiencing Communication in Our Lives

MindTap

CASE STUDY: A Model Speech of Self-Introduction

Apply what you've learned in this chapter by analyzing the following case study, using the accompanying questions as a guide. These questions and a video of the case study are also available online with your MindTap Speech for *Communication in Our Lives*.

Hi. My name is Adam Currier, and I'm going to be introducing myself to you today. When I was first told that I had to introduce myself using a collage, I was afraid because I think collage, and I immediately think art, which is a subject that I have never been any good at.

So I was stuck on what I wanted to do for my collage to introduce myself. So when I'm stuck and when I need any kind of inspiration, I usually turn to my wall. And that's where I went—I turned to my wall. And when I look at my bedroom wall, I see quotes like "Be mindful of yourself and the world around you" and "Time is not a thing you have lost; it is not a thing you ever had." And I wondered why I had some of those quotes on my wall and other quotes like "We're not here to find a way to heaven. The way is heaven." And I started thinking about why I had these themes on my wall. And I realized that it was because of two major events that have happened in my life.

The first one was the theme that really got me thinking about pursuing the goals I wanted to pursue, even when other people told me that it wasn't possible. And that was my sophomore year of high school. I had decided that I wanted to take eight classes instead of the normal six. So instead of being at school from 8 a.m. to 3 p.m., I'd be there from 7 in the morning to 7 at night.

And the minute people heard that I was going to do this, everyone said it couldn't be done. My mom, my dad, the people who have been most supportive of me in my life, told me that I couldn't do it. And that I would wreck my grade point average, and I would end up not being able to get into a college that I wanted to go to. My friends, who have also supported me right by my parents, told me that I couldn't do it.

And I did it anyways. And I made it through without wrecking my GPA. I finished up with A's and B's just like I had all the years that I'd been in school. Realizing that even when no one was supporting me, I set my mind to a goal and

achieved that goal; I realize that it's important to never let people tell you what you are capable of. If someone says you can't do that and it's something you really want to do, do it anyways.

The second theme on my wall was to enjoy every minute of life. And I was thinking about the main thing that made me think about that, and I realized that it was my grandfather. Every year since I ever remember, we've gone back to Iowa and spent a week of that summer just being with my dad's parents, my grandparents. And each year as I grew, I grew closer and closer to my grandfather. And it got to the point where I no longer just knew him as a relative, but I knew him as a human being.

Sitting outside on his porch one day, right before he died, he told me about his life and we were talking about what he had done—being in World War II, being a dentist, being a community leader—all the things that he had ever achieved in his life, and it all sounded so perfect. I said, "Grandfather, what do you regret most in your life?" And he said, "Adam, I regret not seeing more sunsets." A couple months later he passed on, and I realized that I didn't enjoy every single minute with him as much as I could have and I didn't have the time with him that I thought that I'd have.

So I look at my wall now and I see the quotes on it and I see the stories on it and the pictures on it, and I realize that everyone I've ever come into contact with, everyone I've ever met, everything I've ever done has all contributed to shaping the person I am, and my wall reflects the person that I am. So if I can pass on anything to you, I would hope that it would be to enjoy every minute of your life, and in that enjoyment never let people tell you what is possible, because only you know your potential. Thank you.

QUESTIONS FOR ANALYSIS AND DISCUSSION

1. In his short speech, does Adam convey who he is?

2. Based on Adam's speech, what characteristics do you think describe him?

3. Does the closing of the speech reflect back to the opening?

MindTap

Use flashcards to learn key concepts and take a quiz to test your knowledge.

Key Concepts

communication
content level of
    meaning
critical thinking
feedback

interpersonal
    communication
noise
organizational
    culture

process
relationship level of
    meaning
symbol
system

Sharpen Your Skill

1. Giving a Speech of Self-Introduction

This exercise serves two purposes: It gives you a first experience in public speaking and it allows you to introduce yourself to your classmates. You may choose to develop your speech on your own, or you may use criteria specified by your instructor. If you want a basic blueprint for your speech, try this:

Reflect on yourself and your life. Identify one interesting or unusual aspect of your identity of your life, and use that as the focus of your speech. Possible foci for your speech are experience of living in another country, the origin of an unusual name, a unique event in your life, or an interesting hobby or skill. Use the following basic structure for your speech:

I.   My name is _____
     I want to tell you this about myself: _____
II. Describe the interesting or unusual aspects of yourself or your life. _____
     _____

III. Conclude by restating your main idea. _____
     _____

You may want to review the sample speech of introduction at the end of this chapter and via MindTap.

2. Your Mediated World

How do social media affect your interactions? How are posts, tweets, and texts different from face-to-face interactions? Have you made any acquaintances or friends through social media? Did those relationships develop differently from ones formed through face-to-face contact? Do you feel differently about people you have never seen and those you see?

For Further Reflection and Discussion

1. Using each of the models discussed in this chapter, describe communication in your family. What does each model highlight and obscure? Which model best describes and explains communication in your family?

2. Interview a professional in the field you plan to enter to discover what kinds of communication skills he or she thinks are the most important for success. Which of those skills do you already have? Which skills do you need to develop or improve? How can you use this book and the course it accompanies to develop the skills you will need to be effective in your career?

3. Think critically about the impact of digital technologies of communication. In what ways do you think these technologies improve professional, personal, and social communication? In what ways may they be counterproductive?

4. Go to the book's online resources for this chapter to check out the NCA's online magazine, *Communication Currents*, which was launched in November 2006.

Beyond the Classroom

Each chapter in this book concludes with suggestions for taking the material in the chapter beyond the classroom. We'll focus on three extensions: considering the chapter's relevance in the workplace, probing ethical issues raised in the chapter, and connecting chapter material to civic and social engagement with the broader world. For his first chapter, you'll learn what the National Communication

Association (NCA) and the International Communication Association (ICA) have to offer relevant to all three of those foci. Go to the book's online resources for this chapter to find NCA's home page and ICA's welcome page. I suggest more specific links that will allow you to become familiar with the impressive scope of the organization and the discipline it represents.

1. **Workplace.** Go to the book's online resources for this chapter to access NCA's page on communication in the workplace. Follow links there to learn about multiple ways that communication intersects the workplace.

2. **Ethics.** Go to the book's online resources for this chapter to access ICA's statement on ethics. Carefully consider what the documents advocate and condemn. Do you agree with the ethical principles identified in the documents?

3. **Engagement.** Go to the book's online resources for this chapter to learn about NCA's "Communicating Common Ground" program that was launched in 1999 to encourage faculty, students, and practitioners in the field of communication to work actively in their communities to reduce prejudice and hateful acts based on racial, ethnic, religious, and other human differences.

2

Gail Mooney/Masterfile Corporation

> We see the world
> as "we" are, not
> as "it" is; because
> it is the "I" behind
> the "eye" that
> does the seeing.
>
> **Anaïs Nin**

Perception and Communication

LEARNING OBJECTIVES

After studying the topics in this chapter, you should be able to:

1. Recognize that perception is made up of a series of steps in which we select, organize, and interpret information to create meaning.

2. List reasons that we notice certain information and ignore other.

3. Explain how our background and previous experiences shape the way we organize information.

4. Describe how attributions affect the way we interpret information.

5. Provide examples of the reciprocal relationship between your perceptions and your use of social media.

6. Apply this chapter's guidelines to improve the accuracy of your perceptions.

When the perceptions of you and a friend differ, how do you determine who is correct?

MindTap®

Review the chapter's learning objectives and **start** with a quick warm-up activity.

One of my research projects involved interviewing inmates in a medium-security men's prison. On the first day of interviewing, I arrived at the security station through which all visitors must pass. The guard looked at me and asked me to remove my necklace, a simple gold chain. "The inmates could use that to choke you," he explained. He then checked my purse, a standard procedure for visitors. He found my key ring, which is a two-inch piece of metal shaped like a cat's head with pointed ears. Pointing to the ears of the cat, he said, "This could be a weapon—they could put out your eyes." For the same reason, the guard confiscated my nail clipper and nail file. The guard also suggested that on future visits I should not wear a belt.

The guard's experience with prisoners led him to perceive dangers that I didn't perceive. The necklace that I saw as a fashion accent he saw as a means of choking me. What I perceived as a key ring and manicure tools he saw as potential weapons. Our perceptions differed because we had different experiences and roles, which affected how we perceived necklaces, key chains, and nail files, clippers, and belts.

This chapter focuses on **perception**, which is the heart of communication. As we will see, perception is intricately intertwined with communication. Perception shapes how we communicate and how we interpret others' communication. In addition, communication influences our perceptions of people and situations. In the first part of this chapter, we elaborate the three-part process of perception. Next, we'll consider factors that affect our perceptions. Third, we will discuss perception in relation to digital media. Finally, we will explore ways to improve our abilities to perceive and communicate effectively.

Human Perception

Perception is the active process of selecting, organizing, and interpreting people, objects, events, situations, and activities. The first thing to notice about this definition is that perception is an active process. Phenomena do not have intrinsic meaning that we passively receive. Instead, we actively work to make sense of ourselves, others, situations, and other phenomena. To do so, we focus on only certain things, and then we organize and interpret what we have selectively noticed. What something means to us depends on which aspects of it we attend to and how we organize and interpret what we notice.

Perception consists of three processes: selecting, organizing, and interpreting. These processes are overlapping, so they blend into and influence one another. They are also interactive, so each affects the other two.

Selection

Stop for a moment and notice what is going on around you right now. Is there music in the background? Is the room warm or cold, messy or clean, large or small, light or dark? Is there laundry in the corner waiting to be washed? Can you smell anything—food cooking, traces of cologne? Is anyone else in the room? Do you hear other conversations or music? Can you hear muted sounds of activities outside? What about this book—what do you notice about it? On what kind of paper

perception The active process of selecting, organizing, and interpreting people, objects, events, situations, and activities.

is the book printed? Is the type large, small, or easy to read? Do you like the size of the book, the colors used, and the design of the text? Now think about what's happening inside you: Are you alert, sleepy, hungry, or comfortable? Do you have a headache or an itch anywhere?

You probably weren't conscious of most of these phenomena when you began reading the chapter. Instead, you focused on reading and understanding the material in the book. You narrowed your attention to what you defined as important at that moment, and you were unaware of many other things going on around you. This is typical of how we live our lives. We can't attend to everything in our environment because there is simply far too much there, and most of it isn't relevant to us at any particular time.

Selective perception explains why it is dangerous to use social media while driving. Recent research (Lowy, 2013) shows that when drivers text or use a speech-to-text system, their attention focuses on the messages and commands they are generating. As a result, they stop scanning the road ahead, fail to check side and rear-view mirrors, and may not notice stop signs or pedestrians. When texting or giving voice commands, brain waves, eye movements, and reaction times demonstrate inattention to driving.

Which stimuli we notice depends on a number of factors. First, some qualities of external phenomena draw attention. For instance, we notice things that **STAND OUT** because they are immediate, relevant, or intense. We're more likely to hear a loud voice than a soft one and to notice a bright shirt than a drab one. Second, our perceptions are influenced by the acuity of our senses. For instance, if you have a good sense of smell, you're likely to be enticed by the smell of freshly baked bread. People whose vision or hearing is limited or nonexistent often develop greater sensitivity in their other senses.

Third, change or variation compels attention, which is why we may take for granted all the pleasant interactions with a friend and notice only the tense moments. Effective public speakers apply the principle that change compels notice

We notice things that stand out or differ from their surroundings.

to keep listeners focused on their speaking. For instance, they may raise or lower their voices or move to a different place to maintain listeners' attention.

Sometimes we deliberately call phenomena to our attention. Self-indication occurs when we point out certain things to ourselves. Right now you're learning to indicate to yourself that you perceive selectively, so in the future you will be more aware of the selectivity of your perceptions. People who want to eat healthy diets deliberately notice nutritional content of food items. Health care professionals notice aspects of appearance that are clues to a person's health.

What we select to notice is also influenced by who we are and what is going on inside us. Our motives and needs affect what we see and don't see. If you've just broken up with someone, you're more likely to notice attractive people, than if you are in an established romantic relationship. People tend to perceive things they desire as more accessible than they really are. In one study, the researchers (Balcetis & Dunning, 2010) had people sit across the table from a full bottle of water and then had them either eat pretzels or drink water from a glass. The participants were then asked to estimate how close they were to the bottle of water. Consistently, the participants who were thirsty from eating pretzels perceived the water bottle as being closer than the other participants.

We are also more likely to perceive what we expect to perceive. This explains the phenomenon of the **self-fulfilling prophecy,** in which one acts in ways consistent with how one has learned to perceive oneself. Children who are told they are unlovable may perceive themselves that way and notice rejecting but not affirming communication from others. Recent research shows that lonely people tend to perceive others more negatively than nonlonely people (Tsai & Reis, 2009). The negative judgments may lead those judging to make less effort to engage others. In turn, this leads to unsatisfying interactions and perhaps alienates others so loneliness continues or increases. Go to the book's online resources for this chapter to learn more about self-fulfilling prophecies.

LEE TENG-HUI   *Before I came to school here, I was told that Americans are very pushy, loud, and selfish. For my first few months here, I saw that was true of Americans just as I had been told it would be. It took me longer to see also that Americans are friendly and helpful because I had not been taught to expect these qualities.*

self-fulfilling prophecy An expectation or judgment of ourselves brought about by our own actions.

constructivism Theory that claims we organize and interpret experience by applying cognitive structures called schemata.

schemata (singular: schema) Cognitive structures we use to organize and interpret experiences. I our types of schemata are prototypes, personal constructs, stereotypes, and scripts.

prototype A knowledge structure that defines the clearest or most representative example of some category.

Organization

We don't simply string together randomly what we've noticed. Instead, we organize what we've selectively noticed to make it meaningful to us. The most useful theory for explaining how we organize what we've attended to is **constructivism,** the theory that we organize and interpret experience by applying cognitive structures called **schemata** (singular: *schema*). Originally developed by George Kelly in 1955, constructivism has been elaborated by scholars in communication and psychology. We use four kinds of cognitive schemata to make sense of phenomena: prototypes, personal constructs, stereotypes, and scripts (Burleson & Rack, 2008; Fehr, 1993; Hewes, 1995).

Prototypes   A prototype is a knowledge structure that defines the best or most representative example of some category (Fehr, 1993). For example, you probably have prototypes of best teachers, friends, public speakers, and romantic partners. Each of these categories is exemplified by a person who is the ideal case; that's the prototype.

We use prototypes to define categories: Jane is the ideal friend; Luke is the ideal romantic partner; Robin is the ideal work associate. We may then consider how close a particular phenomenon is to our prototype for that category. As Alicia's commentary points out, our prototypes can be faulty, leading us to fail to perceive someone as belonging in the appropriate category because he or she does not match our prototype for the category.

> **AMELIA**   *I was working with a male nurse. Every time he met a new patient, the patient would say, "Hi, doctor." Even when he told them he was a nurse, they treated him as a doctor. No one ever confused me with a doctor. Patients just assume that men in white are doctors and women in white are nurses.*

Personal Constructs   Personal constructs are bipolar mental yardsticks that allow us to position people and situations along dimensions of judgment. Examples of personal constructs are intelligent–not intelligent, responsible–not responsible, kind–not kind, and attractive–not attractive. To size up a person, we measure him or her by personal constructs that we use to think about people. How intelligent, responsible, kind, and attractive is this person? Whereas prototypes help us decide into which broad category a person or situation fits, personal constructs let us make more detailed assessments of particular qualities of phenomena we have selectively perceived. Our personal constructs shape our perceptions because we define something only in terms of how it compares to the constructs we use. Thus, we may not notice qualities of people that are outside the constructs we use to perceive them.

Stereotypes   Stereotypes are predictive generalizations about people and situations. Based on the category in which we place a phenomenon and how the phenomenon measures up to the personal constructs we apply, we predict what it will do. For instance, if you classify Meredith into the prototype of liberal, and you perceive her as compassionate, generous, and kind (personal constructs), you might predict that she is likely to support government-funded programs to help disadvantaged citizens.

Stereotypes may be accurate or inaccurate. They are generalizations, which are sometimes based on facts that are generally true of a group and sometimes on prejudice or assumptions. Even if we have accurate understandings of a group, generalizations may not apply to particular individuals in it. Although college students as a group are more liberal than the population as a whole, some college students are very conservative. A particular individual may not conform to what is typical of his or her group as a whole. Ethical communicators keep in mind that stereotypes are generalizations that can be both useful and misleading.

personal construct A bipolar mental yardstick that allows us to measure people and situations along specific dimensions of judgment.

stereotype A predictive generalization about people and situations.

> **SCOTT**   *The stereotype that really ticks me off is "dumb jock." I'm a fullback on the team, and I'm big just like any good fullback. But I'm also a good student. I study, and I put a lot into papers and homework for classes. But a lot of the professors here and the students, too, assume I'm dumb just because I'm an athlete. Sometimes I say something in class, and you can just see surprise all over everyone's faces because I had a good idea. When you think about it, athletes have to be smart to do all of their schoolwork plus practice and work out about 30 hours a week.*

Gary Crabbe/Enlightened Images/Alamy Stock Photo

MindTap®   What stereotypes do you have of the men in this photograph?

Scripts   To organize what we notice, we also use **scripts,** which are guides to action. A script consists of a sequence of activities that define what we and others are expected to do in specific situations.

Many of our daily activities are governed by scripts, although we're often unaware of them. You have a script for greeting casual acquaintances: "Hey, how ya doing?" "Fine. See ya around." You have scripts for checking in with friends online: "hi. where r u? gotta go. brb." You also have scripts for managing conflict, talking with professors, interacting with superiors on the job, dealing with clerks, and relaxing with friends. Christine Bachen and Eva Illouz (1996) studied 184 people to learn about their views of romance. They found that most people agree on the scripts for appropriate sequences of events for first dates and romantic dinners. Similarly, Sandra Metts (2006b) has identified consistent scripts for heterosexual flirting.

script One of four cognitive schemata. A script defines an expected or appropriate sequence of action in a particular setting.

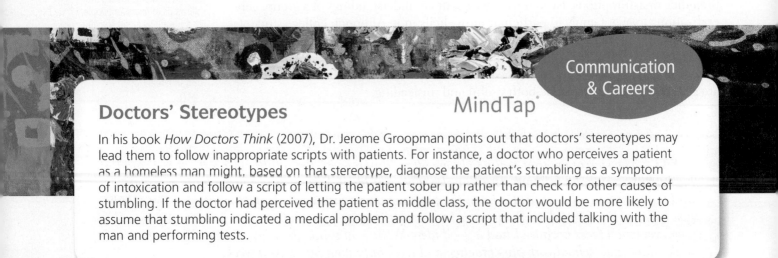

Communication & Careers

Doctors' Stereotypes

MindTap®

In his book *How Doctors Think* (2007), Dr. Jerome Groopman points out that doctors' stereotypes may lead them to follow inappropriate scripts with patients. For instance, a doctor who perceives a patient as a homeless man might, based on that stereotype, diagnose the patient's stumbling as a symptom of intoxication and follow a script of letting the patient sober up rather than check for other causes of stumbling. If the doctor had perceived the patient as middle class, the doctor would be more likely to assume that stumbling indicated a medical problem and follow a script that included talking with the man and performing tests.

Communication Highlight

Expectations and Perceptions

How we perceive others is influenced by past experiences and expectations. This has been demonstrated repeatedly in experiments (Bargh, 1997). In one study, two groups of research participants were asked to complete what was described as a language test. One group of participants worked with a list of words related to character, such as *honesty*. The other group of participants worked with a list of randomly selected words. Then both groups were asked to complete what they were told was a second, independent study, in which they read a short description of a person and then gave their impressions of the person. Participants who worked with the words related to character described the person they read about in the second study as more honest than did the participants who worked with words unrelated to honesty (Bargh, 1999).

Prototypes, personal constructs, stereotypes, and scripts are cognitive schemata that we use to organize the phenomena to which we selectively attend. They help us make sense of what we notice and help us anticipate how we and others will act in particular situations. Our cognitive schemata are not entirely individualistic. Rather, they reflect our membership in a culture and in specific social groups. As we interact with others, we internalize their ways of classifying, measuring, and predicting interaction in various situations. Each of us has an ethical responsibility to assess social perspectives critically before relying on them to organize our perceptions and direct our activities.

> **Review It!**
>
> Cognitive Schemata:
> - Prototypes
> - Personal Constructs
> - Stereotypes
> - Scripts

Interpretation

To assign meaning, we must interpret what we have noticed and organized. **Interpretation** is the subjective process of explaining perceptions to assign meaning to them.

Attributions **Attributions** are explanations of why things happen and why people act as they do (Fehr, 1993; Fehr & Russell, 1991; Heider, 1958; Kelley, 1967). It's good to remind ourselves that the attributions we make aren't necessarily correct— they are our subjective ways of assigning meaning.

Attributions have four dimensions (Table 2.1). The first is *locus*, which attributes what a person does to either internal factors ("He's sick.") or external factors ("The traffic jam frustrated him."). The second dimension is *stability*, which explains actions as resulting either from stable factors that won't change ("She's a Type A person.") or from temporary, unstable factors ("She's irritable because she's just had a fight with the boss."). *Scope* (sometimes called *specificity*) is the third dimension, and it defines behavior as part of a global pattern ("He's a mean person.") or a specific instance ("He gets angry when he's tired."). Finally, the dimension of *responsibility* attributes behaviors either to factors people can control ("She doesn't try to control her outbursts.") or to ones they cannot ("She has a chemical imbalance that makes her moody.").

A student who was reading this book for a class at another university emailed me with a question about attributions. He asked whether scope and stability are really distinct dimensions. This is a good question. Most global attributions are also stable. However, there are exceptions. For example, you might say that someone is

> **SHARPEN YOUR SKILL**
>
>
>
> At the end of this chapter, refer to the Sharpen Your Skill feature, Perceiving Others, to apply concepts from Chapter 2.

> **interpretation** The subjective process of evaluating and explaining perceptions.
>
> **attribution** A causal account that explains why a thing happened or why someone acted a certain way.

Table 2.1	Dimensions of Interpersonal Attributions	
Locus	Internal	External
Stability	Stable	Unstable
Scope	Global	Specific
Responsibility	Within personal control	Beyond personal control

always efficient at work but inefficient during leisure time. In this case, the attribution is stable and specific. If the person were efficient in all spheres of life, the attribution would be stable and global.

Investigations have shown that happy and unhappy couples have distinct attributional styles (Manusov & Harvey, 2001; Segrin, Hanzal, & Domschke, 2009; Tavris & Aronson, 2007). Happy couples make relationship-enhancing attributions. They attribute nice things a partner does to internal, stable, and global reasons that the partner controls: "She got the film because she is a good person who always does sweet things." They attribute unpleasant things a partner does to external, unstable, and specific factors and sometimes to influences beyond personal control: "He yelled at me because all the stress of the past few days made him irritable."

In contrast, unhappy couples make relationship-diminishing attributions. They explain nice actions as results of external, unstable, and specific factors: "She got the tape because she had some time to kill today." Negative actions are attributed to internal, stable, and global factors: "He yelled at me because he is a nasty person who never shows any consideration for anybody else." Thus, we should be mindful of our attributions because they influence how we experience our relationships.

The Self-Serving Bias   Research indicates that we tend to construct attributions that serve our personal interests (Hamachek, 1992; Hinton, 2016; Manusov & Spitzberg, 2008; Sypher, 1984). Thus, we are inclined to make internal, stable, and global attributions for our positive actions and successes. We're also likely to claim that good results come about because of our efforts. On the other hand, people tend to attribute negative actions and failures to external, unstable, and specific factors that are beyond personal control. In other words, we tend to attribute our misconduct and mistakes to outside forces that we can't help but attribute all the good we do to our personal qualities and effort. This **self-serving bias** can distort our perceptions, leading us to take excessive credit for what we do well and to abdicate responsibility for what we do poorly. Like many human tendencies, the self-serving bias is influenced by culture. Mexicans (Tropp & Wright, 2003), Native Americans (Fryberg & Markus, 2003), Chileans (Heine & Raineri, 2009), and some East Asians (Heine & Hamamura, 2007) are less likely than Western Caucasians to engage in the self-serving bias.

Review It!

Dimensions of Attributions:

- Locus
- Stability
- Scope
- Responsibility

self-serving bias The tendency to attribute our positive actions and successes to stable, global, internal influences that we control and to attribute negative actions and failures to unstable, specific, external influences beyond our control.

MEG   *Last summer, I worked at a day-care center for 4- to 6-year-olds. Whenever a fight started and I broke it up, each child would say the other one made them fight or the other one started it or they couldn't help hitting. They were classic cases of self-serving bias.*

We've seen that perception involves three interrelated processes. The first of these, selection, allows us to notice certain things and ignore others. The second process is organization, in which we use prototypes, personal constructs, stereotypes, and scripts to order what we have selectively noticed. Finally, we engage in interpretation by using attributions to explain what we have noticed and organized. Although we discussed these processes separately, in reality they interact continually.

Influences on Perception

In opening this chapter, I mentioned an incident in which a prison guard's perceptions differed from mine. His experience and priorities as a guard who dealt with dangerous men led him to perceive that objects that I saw as harmless as potential weapons. Similarly, able-bodied people may not notice the lack of elevators or ramps in a building, but someone with a physical disability quickly perceives the building as inaccessible.

White students at predominantly white schools often don't notice that few people of color are in their classes, but the ethnic ratio is very obvious to students who are not white. Let's consider some reasons why people differ in how they perceive situations and other people.

Physiology

The most obvious reason perceptions vary is that people differ in sensory abilities and physiologies. Music that one person finds deafening is barely audible to

> ### Review It!
> Perception Processes:
> - Selection
> - Organization
> - Interpretation

Communication Highlight

I'm Right; You're Wrong

When you are in conflict with a close friend or romantic partner, how do you see your role and the other person's? Do you often think you were being reasonable and the other person was being unreasonable? Do you tend to see yourself as having good intentions and the other person as having bad ones? If so, you're not alone. In 1999, Astrid Schütz separately asked husbands and wives to describe conflicts between them. Typically, each spouse described the problem as the other's fault. Each spouse saw his or her own behavior as justified and reasonable but described the partner's behavior as unfair, inconsiderate, inappropriate, or wrong. Participants also described their own intentions positively and their partners' intentions negatively—as unfair, irrational, mean-spirited, and so forth.

Schütz concluded that the self-serving bias is likely to affect how partners perceive themselves, each other, and conflicts between them. Resolution and positive feelings about each other are undermined when each partner perceives himself or herself as behaving well and the other as behaving wrongly.

In another experiment (Jaffe, 2004), peace proposals created by Israelis were labeled proposals created by Palestinians and proposals actually created by Palestinians were labeled proposals created by Israelis. Then Israeli citizens were asked to evaluate the proposals. The Israelis liked the proposal that was attributed to Israelis but actually authored by Palestinians better than they liked the proposal actually drafted by Israelis that was attributed to Palestinians. This displays how profoundly perceptions can be shaped by biases.

another. On a given day on my campus, students wear everything from shorts and sandals to jackets, indicating that they have different sensitivities to cold. Some people have better vision than others, and still others are color blind.

Our physiological states also influence perception. If you are tired, stressed, or sick, you might perceive a comment from a coworker as critical of you, but the same comment wouldn't bother you if you felt good. If you interact with someone who is sick, you might attribute his or her irritability to temporary factors rather than to enduring personality.

Age also influences our perceptions. The older we get, the more complex is our perspective on life and people. Many people 18–22 years old consider it normal to pay over $3 for a gallon of gas, but to a 60-year-old person who recalls when gas cost 20 cents a gallon, current prices seem high. The extent of discrimination still experienced by women and minorities understandably leads some young people to see inequities as unalterable. When I attended college, women weren't admitted on an equal basis with men, and almost all students of color attended minority colleges. The substantial progress made during my lifetime leads me to perceive remaining inequities as changeable.

Culture

A **culture** consists of beliefs, values, understandings, practices, and ways of interpreting experience that are shared by a number of people. It is a set of taken-for-granted assumptions that form the pattern of our lives and guide how we perceive as well as how we think, feel, and act.

Consider a few aspects of modern Western culture that influence our perceptions. One characteristic of our culture is an emphasis on technology and its offspring, speed. We expect things to happen fast—almost instantly. We fax or email PDFs of letters, jet across the country, engage in instant messaging and texting, and microwave our meals.

North America is also a fiercely individualistic culture in which personal achievement and independence are rewarded. When children become adults, they often move away from their parents. Some other cultures are more communal, and identity is linked to family rather than being perceived as an individual quality. In communal cultures, children are looked after by the whole community instead of just their parents, and elders are given great respect and care.

The culture in which we live can even affect how we interpret visual stimuli. Look at Figure 2.1. Does line a or b seem longer to you? The lines are actually identical in length, but most Westerners perceive line b as longer. San Foragers of

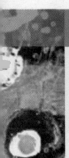

SHARPEN YOUR SKILL

At the end of this chapter, refer to the Sharpen Your Skill feature, Noticing Individualism, to apply concepts from Chapter 2.

culture Beliefs, understandings, practices, and ways of interpreting experience that are shared by a number of people.

Communication in Everyday Life

DIVERSITY

Which Line Is Longer?

Is line *a* or line *b* in the figure longer? The lines are known as the **Müller-Lyer illusion**. The lines are actually identical in length, but they don't appear so to some people. If you are a Westerner, it's likely that you perceive line b as longer. However, if you are a San Forager of the Kalahari, you are likely to perceive the lines as equal in length? Why the difference?

Researchers (Henrich & Norenzayan, 2010; Watters, 2013) have found that cultures shape not just our behaviors and values, but also our perceptions. Westerners live in a world with lots of carpentered corners—squared corners in rooms and buildings—so they learn to perceive lines in three dimensions. People who live in less industrialized cultures see fewer carpentered corners, and their perceptions are not trained to see lines as three dimensional. Of more than a dozan cultures studied, Americans emerge as the most likely to perceive line *b* as longer.

FIGURE 2.1
The Müller-Lyer Illusion

the Kalahari, however, perceive the two lines as equal in length. The reason for this difference in perception is that Westerners live in a world with carpentered corners, so we learn to see flat lines in three dimensions. People in less developed cultures are unaccustomed to carpentered corners so they tend not to perceive flat lines in three dimensions (Henrich & Norenzayan, 2010; Watters, 2013).

In recent years, scholars have realized that we are affected not only by the culture as a whole but also by our particular location within the culture (Haraway, 1988; Harding, 1991; Wood, 2005). **Standpoint theory** claims that a culture includes a number of social communities that have different degrees of social status and privilege. Each social community distinctively shapes the perceptions, identities, and opportunities of its members. If a member of a social group gains political insight into the group's social location, then he or she can develop a standpoint. For example, a Muslim has the social location of Muslims. If that person learns about ways in which Western society discriminates against Muslims, the person may develop a Muslim standpoint. Without political awareness, however, a person cannot achieve a standpoint.

standpoint theory The theory that a culture includes a number of social groups that differently shape the knowledge, identities, and opportunities of members of those groups.

ASHER *I'll admit that when Krista and I had a child, I expected Krista to stay home and take care of her. Actually, we both did, and that worked fine for 3 months. Then Krista got cancer, and she was in the hospital for weeks and then in and out for nearly a year for treatments. Even when she was home, she didn't have the energy to take care of little Jennie. I had to take over a lot of the child care. Doing that really changed me in basic ways. I had to learn to tolerate being interrupted when I was working. I had to tune into what Jennie needed and learn to read her. Before that experience, I thought women had a maternal instinct. What I learned is, anyone can develop a parental sensitivity.*

Gendered locations explain the difference between the amount of effort women and men, in general, invest in communication that maintains relationships. Socialized into the role of "relationship expert," women are often expected by others and themselves to take care of relationships (Wood, 1994d, 2007a, 2013).

Social and Professional Roles

Our perceptions are also shaped by social roles that others communicate to us. Messages that tell us that we are expected to fulfill particular roles, as well as the actual demands of those roles, affect how we perceive and communicate.

Speakers are more likely than audience members to notice the acoustics of presentation rooms. Teachers often perceive classes in terms of whether the students are interested, whether they have read material, and whether they engage in class discussion. On the other hand, many students perceive classes in terms of the number and difficulty of tests, whether papers are required, and whether the professor is interesting.

The careers people choose influence what they notice and how they think and act. Doctors are trained to be highly observant of physical symptoms, and they may detect a physical problem before a person knows that he or she has it. For example, some years ago at a social gathering, a friend of mine who is a doctor asked me how long I had had a herniated disk. Surprised, I told him I didn't have one. "You do," he insisted, and sure enough, a few weeks later a magnetic resonance imaging examination confirmed a ruptured disk in my back. His medical training enabled him to perceive subtle changes in my posture and walk that I hadn't noticed.

Cognitive Abilities

In addition to physiological, cultural, and social influences, perception is shaped by our cognitive abilities. How elaborately we think about situations and people, and the extent of our personal knowledge of others, affects how we select, organize, and interpret experiences.

Cognitive Complexity   People differ in the number and types of knowledge schemata they use to organize and interpret people and situations. **Cognitive complexity** refers to the number of constructs used, how abstract they are, and how elaborately they interact to shape perceptions. Most children have fairly simple cognitive systems. They rely on few schemata, focus more on concrete categories (tall–not tall) than on abstract ones (introspective–not introspective), and often don't perceive relationships between different perceptions. For instance, infants may call every man Daddy because they haven't learned more complex ways to distinguish among men.

Adults also differ in cognitive complexity. If you perceive people only as nice or mean, you have a limited range for perceiving others. Similarly, people who focus exclusively on concrete data tend to have less sophisticated understandings than people who also perceive psychological data. For example, you might notice that a coworker is assertive, tells jokes, and contributes on task teams. These are concrete perceptions. At a more abstract, psychological level, you might infer that these concrete behaviors reflect a secure, self-confident personality. This is a more sophisticated cognition because it integrates three perceptions to develop an explanation of why the person acts as he or she does.

What if you later find out that the person is reserved in one-to-one conversations? Someone with low cognitive complexity would have difficulty integrating the new information into prior observations. Either the new information would be dismissed because it doesn't fit or the most recent information would alter

cognitive complexity The number of constructs used, how abstract they are, and how elaborately they interact to create perceptions.

the former perception, and the person would be redefined as shy. A more cognitively complex person would integrate all the information into a coherent account. Perhaps a cognitively complex thinker would conclude that the person is confident in social situations but less secure in more personal ones.

Cognitively complex people tend to be flexible in interpreting complicated phenomena and integrating new information into their thinking about people and situations. Less cognitively complex people are likely to ignore information that doesn't fit neatly with their impressions or to use it to replace the impressions they had formed (Delia, Clark, & Switzer, 1974). Either way, they fail to recognize some of the nuances and inconsistencies that are part of human life. The complexity of our cognitive systems affects the fullness and intricacy of our perceptions of people and interpersonal situations. Cognitively complex people also tend to communicate in more flexible and appropriate ways with a range of others. This probably results from their ability to recognize differences in people and to adapt their own communication accordingly.

Person-Centered Perception   **Person-centered perception** reflects cognitive complexity because it entails abstract thinking and a broad range of schemata. Person-centered perception is the ability to perceive another as a unique and distinct individual. Our ability to perceive others as unique depends both on the general ability to make cognitive distinctions and on our knowledge of particular others. As we get to know individuals, we gain insight into how they differ from others in their groups ("Rob's not like most campus politicos"; "Janet's more flexible than most managers."). The more we interact with one another and the greater variety of experiences we have together, the more insight we gain into other people. In long-term relationships, we fine-tune our perceptions throughout the life of relationships.

person-centered perception The ability to perceive another as a unique and distinct individual apart from social roles and generalizations.

Camille Tokerud/Stone/Getty Images

MindTap°   Was there an older person who took your perspective when you were a child?

Person-centered perception is not the same as empathy. **Empathy** is the ability to feel with another person—to feel what he or she feels. Feeling with another is an emotional response. Because feelings are guided by our own experiences and emotions, it may be impossible to feel exactly and completely what another person feels. A more realistic goal is to try to recognize another's perspective and adapt your communication to how he or she perceives situations and people (Muehlhoff, 2006). With commitment and effort, we can learn a lot about how others see the world, even if that differs from how we see it.

When we take others' perspectives, we try to grasp what something means to them and how they perceive things. We can't really understand someone else's perspective when we're judging whether it is right or wrong, sensible or crazy. Instead, we have to let go of our own perspective and perceptions long enough to enter the thoughts and feelings of another person. Doing this allows us to understand issues from the other person's point of view so we can communicate more effectively (Servaty-Seib & Burleson, 2007). You might learn why your boss thinks something is important that you've been disregarding. You might find out how a friend interprets your behavior in ways inconsistent with what you intend to communicate.

At a later point in interaction, we may choose to express our own perspective or to disagree with another's views. This is appropriate and important in honest communication, but voicing our own views is not a substitute for the equally important skill of recognizing another's perspective. In sum, differences based on physiology, culture, membership in social groups, social roles, and cognitive abilities affect what we perceive and how we interpret others and experiences.

Digital Media and Perception

We now want to consider how the ideas that we've discussed in the foregoing pages apply to social media and online communication. We'll focus on two connections between social media and perception.

First, our choices of social media shape our perceptions of events, issues, and people. If you follow Rush Limbaugh's tweets, you will get a conservative perspective on national and international issues and on the people involved in them. If you follow Rachel Maddow's tweets, you will get a much more liberal perspective on the same issues and people. Limbaugh frequently disparages feminists, by labeling them "feminazis"; Maddow identifies as a feminist and speaks favorably about feminist issues. Limbaugh sympathizes with corporate interests and tends to support lowering corporate taxes and boosting capitalism; Maddow is inclined to be distrustful of corporate interests, to think corporations should pay more taxes, and to favor reigning in some capitalist tendencies. Who's right? There is no objective answer to that question, but your views on such issues are shaped by the bloggers and digital media sources you choose to follow.

Second, consider how membership in social communities affects what we say and post on social media. Try this experiment: Look at the social network profiles of people you know who belong to different ethnic groups. How often do their postings include boasting about individual accomplishments, which reflects Western but not Eastern values? Do people from communal and collectivist cultures post more photos of families and themselves with families than do people from individualist cultures? Now look at the profiles of women and men you know. To what extent does each sex tweet and post about relationships, sports, fashion, and politics? Are the trends that you note consistent with research we've discussed about Western and non-Western cultural values and feminine and masculine social communities?

Review It!

Influences on
Perception:

- Physiology
- Culture
- Roles
- Cognitive Abilities

empathy The ability to feel with another person or to feel what that person feels in a given situation.

Guidelines for Effective Perception

To be a competent communicator, you need to realize how perception and communication affect each other. We'll elaborate on the connection between perception and communication and then discuss guidelines for enhancing communication competence.

Perceptions, Communication, and Abstraction

Words crystallize perceptions. When we name feelings and thoughts, we create precise ways to describe and think about them. But just as words crystallize experiences, they can also freeze thought. Once we label our perceptions, we may respond to our own labels rather than to actual phenomena.

Consider this situation. You and five others form a study group, and a student named Andrea monopolizes the whole meeting with her questions and concerns. Leaving the meeting, one person says, "Gee, Andrea is so selfish and immature! I'll never work with her again." Another person responds, "She's not really selfish. She's insecure about her grades in this course, so she was hyper in the meeting." Chances are these two people will perceive and treat Andrea differently depending on whether they label her selfish or insecure. The point is that the two people respond not to Andrea herself but to how they selectively perceive and label her.

Communication is based on a process of abstracting from complex stimuli. Our perceptions are not equivalent to the complex reality on which they are based because we can never fully describe or even apprehend total reality. This means that what we perceive is a step removed from stimuli because perceptions are always partial and subjective. We move a second step from stimuli when we label a perception. We move even further from stimuli when we respond not to behaviors or our perceptions of them but to the judgments we associate with the label we have imposed. This process can be illustrated as a ladder of abstraction, as shown in Figure 2.2 (Korzybski, 1948). Go to the book's online resources for this chapter to learn more about the abstraction process.

Thinking of communication as a process of abstracting suggests ways to enhance competence in interaction. Five guidelines help us avoid the problems abstraction may invite.

Communication Highlight

Eye Witness Testimony: Fact or Fiction? MindTap

Many a defendant has been convicted because of eyewitness testimony. And many an *innocent* defendant has been convicted by eyewitness testimony. In recent years, a number of convicted felons have been given new trials because DNA evidence could now be introduced. Nearly 75% of cases in which DNA exonerated a person serving time involved eye-witness testimony that the imprisoned person was the person who committed the crime (Beil, 2011).

The eyewitnesses weren't lying, at least not intentionally. They simply misremembered. Researchers studying memory point out that most people perceive only a few details when an event happens. Later police questioning and line ups, coupled with repeating a false memory to themselves, make eyewitness very confident when they testify erroneously.

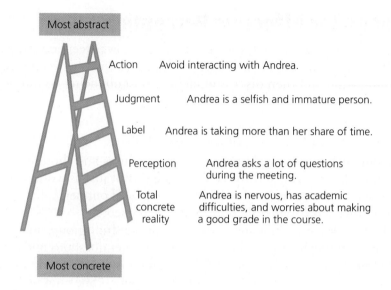

Most abstract

Action   Avoid interacting with Andrea.

Judgment   Andrea is a selfish and immature person.

Label   Andrea is taking more than her share of time.

Perception   Andrea asks a lot of questions
during the meeting.

Total   Andrea is nervous, has academic
concrete   difficulties, and worries about making
reality   a good grade in the course.

Most concrete

FIGURE 2.2
Perception,
Communication, and
Abstraction

Recognize That All Perceptions Are Subjective   Our perceptions are partial and subjective because each of us perceives from a unique perspective. A class you find exciting may put another student to sleep. Writing is a creative, enjoyable activity for some people and a tedious grind for others. There is no truth or falsity to perceptions; they represent what things mean to individuals based on their individual social roles, cultural backgrounds, cognitive abilities, standpoints, and physiology. Effective communicators realize that perceptions are subjective and don't assume that their own perceptions are the only valid ones.

Avoid Mind Reading   One of the most common problems in communication is **mind reading**—assuming we understand what another person thinks or perceives. When we mind read, we act as if we know what's on another's mind, and this can get us into trouble. Marriage counselors identify mind reading as one of the behaviors that contributes to interpersonal tension (Gottman, 1993). According to communication scholar Fran Dickson (1995), one exception may be mind reading between spouses in long-lasting marriages. After living together for a long time, partners may have sufficient person perception to mind read with great accuracy.

For the most part, however, mind reading is more likely to harm than help communication. Doctors sometimes assume they know what patients think or feel and don't ask patients to express their perspectives (Chen, 2012). Mind reading invites problems when we say or think, "I know why you're upset" or "You don't care about me." We also mind read when we tell ourselves we know how somebody else will feel or react or what they'll do. The truth is we don't really know—we're only guessing. When we mind read, we impose our perceptions on others, which can lead to resentment and misunderstandings.

mind reading Assuming that we understand what another person thinks or how another person perceives something.

SAWYER   *I learned my lesson about mind reading. A friend I'd known since childhood recently lost her mother to cancer. When I visited the friend, I said I was sorry for her sadness. She told me she wasn't sad at all; she said she was relieved. She had been sad to see her mother suffering so much. To her, death was a blessing.*

Check Perceptions with Others   Because perceptions are subjective and mind reading is ineffective, we need to check our perceptions with others. Perception checking is an important communication skill because it helps people understand each other and their relationships. To check perceptions, you should first state what you have noticed. For example, a person might say, "Lately you've seemed less attentive to me." Second, the person should check to see whether the other perceives the same thing: "Do you feel you've been less attentive?" Third, it's appropriate to offer alternative explanations of your perceptions: "It might be that you're annoyed with me or that you're stressed out at work or that you're focused on other things." Finally, you may ask the other person to clarify how he or she perceives the behavior and the reasons for it: "What do you think is going on?" If the other person doesn't share your perceptions, ask him or her to explain the behaviors on which your perception is based: "Why have you wanted to be together less often lately?"

Speak tentatively when checking perceptions to minimize defensiveness and encourage open dialogue. Just let the other person know you've noticed something and would like him or her to clarify his or her perceptions of what is happening and what it means. It's also a good idea to check perceptions directly with the other person. It is more difficult to reach a shared understanding with another person when we ask someone else to act as a go-between or when we ask others whether they agree with our perceptions of a third person.

Distinguish Between Facts and Inferences   Competent communicators know the difference between facts and inferences. A fact is a statement based on observation or other data. An inference involves an interpretation that goes beyond the facts. For example, it is a fact that my partner, Robbie, forgets a lot of things. Based on that fact, I might infer that he is thoughtless. Defining Robbie as thoughtless is an inference that goes beyond the "fact" of his forgetfulness, which is equally well explained by preoccupation or general absentmindedness.

The self-serving bias can distort fans' perceptions of their team.

It's easy to confuse facts and inferences because we sometimes treat the latter as the former. When we say, "He is irresponsible," we make a statement that sounds factual, and we may then regard it that way ourselves. To avoid this tendency, substitute more tentative words for *is*. For instance, "Parker's behaviors seem thoughtless" is more tentative than "Parker is thoughtless." Tentative language helps us resist the tendency to treat inferences as facts.

Monitor the Self-Serving Bias   The self-serving bias exemplifies humans' broad tendency to protect self-image (Tavris & Aronson, 2007). We want to be competent, good, smart, and right. If we make dumb decisions, we're inclined to deny or justify them. A primary means of doing this is to engage in the self-serving bias, which distorts our perceptions. Monitoring the self-serving bias also has implications for how we perceive others. Just as we tend to judge ourselves generously, we may also be inclined to judge others too harshly. Monitor your perceptions to see whether you attribute others' successes and admirable actions to external factors beyond their control and their shortcomings and blunders to internal factors they can (should) control. If you do this, substitute more generous explanations for others' behaviors, and notice how that affects your perceptions of them.

Perceiving accurately is a communication skill that can be developed. Following the five guidelines we have discussed will allow you to perceive more carefully and accurately.

Chapter Summary

In this chapter, we've explored human perception, which involves selecting, organizing, and interpreting experiences. These three processes are not separate in practice; they interact such that each one affects the others. What we selectively notice affects what we interpret and evaluate. In addition, our interpretations act as lenses that influence what we notice in the world around us. Selection, interpretation, and evaluation interact continuously in the process of perception.

Perception is shaped by many factors. Our physiological abilities and conditions affect what we notice and how astutely we recognize stimuli around us. In addition, our cultural backgrounds and social locations shape how we see and interact with the world. Social roles are another influence on perception. Thus, professional training and roles in families affect what we notice and how we organize and interpret it. Finally, perception is influenced by cognitive abilities, including cognitive complexity, person-centered perception, and perspective taking.

The factors that shape our perceptions affect our use of digital media. Our moods and cultural backgrounds, for example, influence the sites and blogs we visit and what we post in our own digital communication.

Thinking about communication as a process of abstracting helps us understand how perception works. We discussed five guidelines for avoiding the problems abstraction sometimes causes. First, realize that all perceptions are subjective, so there is no absolutely correct or best understanding of a situation or a person. Second, because people perceive differently, we should avoid mind reading or assuming we know what others perceive, think, and feel. Third, it's a good idea to check perceptions, which involves stating how you perceive something and asking how another person perceives it. A fourth guideline is to distinguish facts from inferences. Finally, avoiding the self-serving bias is important because it can lead us to perceive ourselves too charitably and others too harshly.

MindTap®

Experiencing Communication in Our Lives

CASE STUDY: College Success

Apply what you've learned in this chapter by analyzing the following case study, using the accompanying questions as a guide. These questions and a video of the case study are also available online with your MindTap Speech for *Communication in Our Lives.*

Your friend Jim tells you about a problem he's having with his parents. According to Jim, his parents have unrealistic expectations of him. He tends to be an average student, usually making Cs, a few Bs, and an occasional D in his courses. His parents are angry that his grades aren't better. Jim tells you that when he went home last month, his father said this: "I'm not paying for you to go to school so you can party with your friends. I paid my own way and still made Phi Beta Kappa. You have a free ride, and you're still just pulling Cs. You just have to study harder."

Now Jim says to you, "I mean, I like to hang out with my friends, but that's got nothing to do with my grades. My dad's this brilliant guy, I mean, he just cruised through college, he thinks it's easy. I don't know how it was back then, but all my classes are hard. I mean, no matter how much studying I do, I'm not gonna get all As. What should I do? I mean, how do I convince them that I'm doing everything I can?"

Jason Harris/© 2001 Wadsworth

QUESTIONS FOR ANALYSIS AND DISCUSSION

1. Both Jim and his parents make attributions to explain his grades. Describe the dimensions of Jim's attributions and those of his parents.

2. How might you assess the accuracy of Jim's attributions? What questions could you ask him to help you decide whether his perceptions are well founded or biased?

3. What constructs, prototypes, and scripts seem to operate in Jim's and his parents' thinking about college life?

4. What could you say to Jim to help him and his parents reach a shared perspective on his academic work?

MindTap

Use flashcards to learn key concepts and take a quiz to test your knowledge.

Key Concepts

attribution	mind reading	schemata
cognitive complexity	perception	script
constructivism	personal construct	self-fulfilling prophecy
culture	person-centered	self-serving bias
empathy	perception	standpoint theory
interpretation	prototype	stereotype

Sharpen Your Skill

1. Perceiving Others

Pay attention to the cognitive schemata you use the next time you meet a new person. First, notice how you classify the person. Do you categorize him or her as a potential friend, date, coworker, or neighbor? Next, identify the personal constructs you use to assess the person. Do you focus on physical characteristics (attractive–not attractive), mental qualities (intelligent–not intelligent), psychological features (secure–not secure), or interpersonal qualities (available–not available)? Would different personal constructs be prominent if you used a different prototype to classify the person? Now note how you stereotype the person. What do you expect him or her to do, according to the prototype and personal constructs you've applied? Finally, identify your script: How do you expect interaction to unfold between the two of you?

2. Noticing Individualism

How do the individualistic values of our culture influence our perceptions and activities? Check it out by observing the following:

How is seating arranged in restaurants? Are there large, communal eating areas or private tables and booths for individuals, couples, and small groups?

_____

How are living spaces arranged? How many people live in the average house?

_____

Do families share homes? How many common spaces and individual spaces are there in homes? _____

How many people share a car in your family? How many cars are there in the United States? _____

How does the Western emphasis on individualism affect your day-to-day perceptions and activities? _____

For Further Reflection and Discussion

1. Identify an occasion when you engaged in the self-serving bias. Explain what you did, using the language of attributions.

2. Identify ethical issues involved in perceiving. What ethical choices do we make—perhaps unconsciously—as we selectively perceive, organize, and interpret others, particularly people whom we think are different from us in important ways?

3. Use the ladder of abstraction to analyze your perceptions and actions in a specific communication encounter. First, identify the concrete reality, what you perceived from the totality, the labels you assigned, and the resulting inferences and judgments. Second, return to the first level of perception and substitute different perceptions—other aspects of the total situation you might have perceived selectively. What labels, inferences, and judgments do the substitute perceptions invite? With others in the class, discuss the extent to which our perceptions and labels influence "reality."

Beyond the Classroom

Let's take the material in this chapter beyond the classroom by thinking about how what you've learned about perception might apply to the workplace, ethical choices, and engagement with the broader world.

1. **Workplace.** This chapter discusses ways that culture and cultural values influence our perceptions. Think about how cultural values such as efficiency and individualism affect communication in your workplace or a former workplace. Continue this line of thinking by identifying other strong aspects of U.S. culture and tracing their impact on the workplace.

2. **Ethics.** This chapter presents five guidelines for enhancing competence in perceiving. Each guideline has ethical implications and assumptions. For example, the first guideline is to recognize that all perceptions are subjective. This assumes that there are multiple ways of perceiving any phenomena; in turn, this implies that there is no automatic validity to any particular perception. If you accept those assumptions, the implication is that we can't assume others are wrong if their perceptions differ from our own. Thus, the guideline implies that ethical communication requires awareness of and respect for others' perceptions. Now you analyze the ethical assumptions and implications of the other four guidelines for increasing competence in perceiving.

3. **Engagement.** Volunteer to work in a context that allows you to interact with a people you have not spent time with—for example, volunteer at a homeless shelter. Make a list of schemata (i.e., prototypes, personal constructs, stereotypes, and scripts) you have about these people before you interact with them. After spending time with them, review your list of schemata and evaluate how accurate they were.

3

Go confidently in the direction of your dreams.

Henry David Thoreau

Comstock/Stockbyte/Getty Images

Communication and Personal Identity

How do social media affect your self-esteem?

MindTap®

Review the chapter's learning objectives and **start** with a quick warm-up activity.

LEARNING OBJECTIVES

After studying the topics in this chapter, you should be able to:

1. Provide examples of a direct definition, a reflected appraisal, and a social comparison that have shaped your self-concept.

2. Recall a time when a fulfilling prophecy guided your behavior.

3. Provide two examples of how your identity has been influenced by particular others.

4. Identify messages of identity formation you received in response to a posting you made on a social networking site.

5. Reflect on how the predominant identity categories of Western society have influenced your self-concept.

6. Apply the guidelines in this chapter to set a goal for personal improvement.

"**W**ho are you?" asks Greta as an elderly man sits in a chair beside her.

"I am Sam, your husband," he replies taking her hand.

"Who am I?" she asks.

"You are Greta Williams," he says softly. "You taught school for many years, you loved to hike, and loved practical jokes. We have two daughters."

"Who liked jokes?" Greta asks.

Greta was also a star ballerina at age 5, a college student, and an amateur artist, but she isn't aware of any of these parts of her identity. On good days, she remembers fragments of her life. On bad days, like today, she has no memory of who she was for 70 years before she developed dementia.

Can you imagine not knowing who you are, what you loved doing, or who your partner is? Greta has lost a key anchor that most of us take for granted: her personal identity.

MindTap°

Read, highlight, and take notes online.

L   ike Greta, you've defined yourself in different ways over the years, and you'll redefine yourself further in the future. This reminds us that the self is not fixed firmly at one time and constant thereafter. Instead, the self is a process that evolves and changes throughout our lives. In this chapter, we explore how communication with others allows us to develop and refine personal identities. We begin by defining the self. Next, we consider how social media affects our identities. We conclude with guidelines for enhancing your identity.

What Is the Self?

The **self** is a process of internalizing and acting from social perspectives that we learn in the process of communication. At first, this may seem like a complicated way to define the self. As we will see, however, this definition directs our attention to some important insights into what is complicated: the human self.

The Self Arises in Communication with Others

The most basic insight into the self is that it isn't something we are born with. Instead, the self develops only as we communicate with others and participate in the social world. From the moment we are born, we interact with others. We learn how they see us, and we internalize many of their views of who we are and should be.

Communication with Family Members   For most of us, family members are the first important influence on how we see ourselves (Bergen & Braithwaite, 2009). Parents and other family members communicate who we are and what we are worth. They rely primarily on three kinds of communication: *direct definition*, *identity scripts*, and *attachment styles*.

Direct definition, as the term implies, is communication that explicitly tells us who we are by labeling us and our behaviors. For instance, parents might say, "You're my little girl" or "You're a big boy" and thus communicate to the child what sex he or she is. Having been labeled *boy* or *girl*, the child then pays attention to how others talk about boys and girls to figure out what it means to be a certain sex. Parents' own gender stereotypes typically are communicated to children, so daughters

self A multidimensional process in which the individual forms and acts from social perspectives that arise and evolve in communication with himself or herself.

direct definition Communication that explicitly tells us who we are by specifically labeling us and reacting to our behaviors. Direct definition usually occurs first in families and then in interaction with peers and others.

may also be told, "Be nice to your friends" and "Don't mess up your clothes." Sons, on the other hand, are more likely to be told, "Stick up for yourself" and "Don't cry." As we hear these messages, we pick up our parents' and society's gender expectations. Direct definition also takes place as family members respond to children's behaviors. If a child is praised for dusting furniture, being helpful is reinforced as part of the child's self-concept. Positive labels enhance our self-esteem: "You are smart," "You're great at baseball." Negative labels can damage children's self-esteem: "You're a troublemaker" and "You're stupid" are messages that can demolish a child's sense of self-worth.

Identity scripts are another way family members communicate who we are and should be. Psychologists define identity scripts as rules for how we are supposed to live and who we are supposed to be (Berne, 1964; Harris, 1969). Like the scripts for plays, identity scripts define our roles, how we are to play them, and basic elements in the plot we are supposed to have for our lives. Think back to your childhood to identify some of the principal scripts that operated in your family. Did you learn, "Always be prepared for emergencies," "We give back to our community," or "Live by God's word"? These are examples of identity scripts families teach us.

Children seldom author, or even edit, initial identity scripts. In fact, children are generally not even conscious of learning identity scripts. As adults, however, we are no longer passive recipients of others' definitions. We have the capacity to review the identity scripts that were given to us and to challenge and change those that do not fit who we now choose to be.

Finally, parents communicate who we are through **attachment styles,** which are patterns of parenting that teach us who we and others are and how to relate to others. From extensive studies of interaction between parents and children, John Bowlby (1973, 1988) developed the theory that most of us learn attachment styles in our relationship with our first caregivers—usually with parents. They communicate how they see us, others, and relationships. In turn, we are likely to internalize their views as our own. The first relationship is especially important because it shapes expectations for later relationships (Rhodewalt, 2007). Four distinct attachment styles have been identified (Figure 3.1).

A child is most likely to develop a *secure attachment style* when the primary caregiver interacts in a consistently attentive and loving way with the child. In response, the child develops a positive sense of self-worth ("I am lovable") and a positive view of others ("People are loving and can be trusted"). People with secure attachment styles tend to be outgoing, affectionate, and able to handle the normal challenges and disappointments of close relationships without losing self-esteem.

SHARPEN YOUR SKILL

At the end of this chapter, refer to the Sharpen Your Skill feature, Reflecting on Your Identity Scripts, to apply concepts from Chapter 3.

identity script A guide to action based on rules for living and identity. Initially communicated in families, identity scripts define our roles, how we are to play them, and basic elements in the plot of our lives.

attachment style Any of several patterns of attachment that result from particular parenting styles that teach children who they are, who others are, and how to approach relationships.

FIGURE 3.1
Styles of Attachment

Parents' communication is a major influence on identity.

Securely attached individuals tend to have more secure relationships (Rowe & Carnelley, 2005) than less securely attached individuals.

A child may develop a *fearful attachment style* if the primary caregiver communicates in negative, rejecting, or abusive ways to the child. Children who are treated negatively often conclude that they are unlovable and others are rejecting. Although they may want close bonds with others, they fear that others will not love them and that they themselves are not lovable.

A caregiver who is disinterested, rejecting, or abusive may also lead a child to develop a *dismissive attachment style*, which often leads children to scorn others. People with dismissive attachment styles have a positive view of themselves and a low regard for others and relationships. This may lead them to regard relationships as unnecessary and undesirable.

Review It!

Attachment Styles:
- Secure
- Fearful
- Dismissive
- Anxious/ambivalent

OLIVIA *When I was in high school, I babysat to make money. One little girl I watched was very standoffish. No matter how hard I tried to play with Liza and be friends, she kept her distance. But sometimes I would see her looking at me almost longingly like she wanted to play with me. When her parents were around, they were focused on work or each other. If Liza needed something or spoke up, they acted as if she was interrupting them.*

Last is the *anxious/ambivalent attachment style*, which is the most complex of the four. Each of the other three styles results from a consistent pattern of treatment by a caregiver. However, the anxious/ambivalent style is fostered by *inconsistent* treatment from the caregiver. Sometimes the adult is loving and attentive, at other times indifferent or rejecting. The caregiver's communication is not only inconsistent but also unpredictable. He or she may respond positively to something a child does on Monday and react negatively to the same behavior on Tuesday. Naturally, this unpredictability creates anxiety in a child. Because children tend to assume that adults are right, they often believe they themselves are the source of any problem—that they are unlovable or deserve others' abuse. People who have high anxiety about attachments are likely to avoid or minimize attachments (Brenning, Soenens, Braet, & Bosmans, 2011).

In adult life, people who have anxious/ambivalent attachment styles know that others can be loving and affirming, but they also know that others can hurt them and be unloving. Reflecting the pattern displayed by the caregiver, people with anxious/ambivalent attachment styles often are inconsistent themselves. One day they invite affection; the next day they deny needing closeness. An interesting study by Tim Cole and Laura Leets (1999) found that people with anxious/ambivalent attachment styles often form relationships with television characters. It may feel safer to be in relationships with television characters than with real people.

Unless we consciously work to change the attachment styles we learned in our first close relationships, they tend to affect how we communicate in our adult relationships (Bornstein & Languirand, 2003; Bowlby, 1988; Guerrero, 1996). However, we can modify our attachment styles by challenging unconstructive views of us communicated in our early years and by forming relationships that foster secure connections today (Banse, 2004). To learn more about attachment theory, go to the book's online resources for this chapter.

Edwin Verin/Shutterstock.com

We measure our abilities against those of peers.

Communication with Peers   A second major influence on our self-concepts is communication with peers. From childhood playmates to work associates, friends, and romantic partners, we interact with peers throughout our lives. As we do, we gain further direct definitions that tell us how others see us. In turn, this affects how we see ourselves. As we interact with peers, we engage in **social comparison**, which involves comparing ourselves with others to gauge our talents, attractiveness, abilities, skills, and so forth (Stapel & Blanton, 2006). We measure ourselves in relation to others in two ways. First, we compare ourselves with others to decide whether we are like them or different from them. Are we the same age, color, or religion? Do we have similar backgrounds and social and political beliefs?

Peers are particularly strong in commenting directly on conformity to expectations of gender. Some college-age men think drinking and sexual activity embody masculinity. Men who are not interested in drinking and hooking up may be ridiculed and excluded for not being "real men" (Cross, 2008; Kimmel, 2008). Women who don't wear popular brands of clothing or who weigh more than what is considered ideal may be belittled and excluded for being unfeminine (Adler, 2007; Barash, 2006).

Assessing similarity and difference allows us to decide with whom we fit. Research has shown that people generally are most comfortable with others who are like them, so we tend to gravitate toward those we regard as similar (Amodio & Showers, 2006; Chen, Luo, Yue, Xu, & Zhaoyang, 2009; Lutz-Zois, Bradley, Mihalik, & Moorman-Eavers, 2006). However, interacting only with people like us can impoverish our understandings of ourselves and the world.

Social Comparison in the Workplace   MindTap

Communication & Careers

Performance reviews give professionals feedback on job performance. It's only natural to want to know not only how you are evaluated, but also how you compare to your peers. But what happens when you find out that your performance is regarded less well than that of coworkers? Recent research offers answers (Edelman & Larkin, 2014). It turns out that employees of higher status and track records of success are more likely to engage in deception in response to negative social comparisons than are employees of lesser status and success. In an effort to maintain their standing, higher-status employees employ deceptive practices to make themselves look better. For example, higher-ranking professors downloaded their own publications to elevate the ranking of the publications.

We also use social comparison to measure ourselves in relation to others. Am I as good a goalie as Jenny? Am I as smart as Sam? We continuously refine our self-image by comparing ourselves to others on various criteria of judgment. This is normal and necessary if we are to develop realistic self-concepts. However, we should be wary of what psychologists call upward comparison, which is the tendency to compare ourselves to people who exceed us in what they have or can do (Tugend, 2011). While stretching to be better is desirable, it isn't constructive to judge our attractiveness in relation to that of movie stars and models or our athletic ability in relation to that of professional athletes.

WYATT *I learned more about myself and about being white when I was assigned to room with a black guy my freshman year. I'd never interacted much with blacks, and I'd never had a black friend, but I got really close with my roommate. Carl helped me see a lot of things I take for granted that he can't because of his skin. For example, people assume I'm here because I earned a good record in high school, but a lot of people think Carl got in just because he's black and the college had to meet its minority quota. His SAT was higher than mine and so are his grades, but people believe I'm smart and he's a quota admission.*

Communication with Society   A third influence on our identity is interaction with society in general. As we observe and interact with others and media and as we participate in institutions, we learn how society regards each sex, race, sexual orientation, and socioeconomic class. We also learn broad cultural values.

Media are primary in teaching social perspectives. When we read popular magazines, watch films, and visit sites on the Web, we are inundated with messages about which careers carry status, which clothes and hairstyles are cool, how women and men are supposed to look and act, and so forth. Media shape teens' views of sex and sexuality—what is appropriate and "cool" (Bodey & Wood, 2009; Wood, 2010; Wood & Fixmer-Oraiz, 2017).

Self-Help: A Healthier Self?

Do you love too much, too little, or the wrong people? Are you guilty of negative thinking? If so, there's a self-help book—or a dozen—for you. Don't want a book? No problem, buy self-help video and audio products, attend seminars, or hire a personal coach. You can join a support group with 12 steps or 7 principles. It's all part of the multibillion dollar self-help industry. And don't forget television programs such as *The Swan* (aired 2004), *Extreme Makeover* (aired 2002–2006), and *The Biggest Loser* (is being aired 2004–present), which also tell us to take charge of fixing ourselves with self-discipline perhaps along with multiple surgeries.

Although the self-help industry is wildly popular today, it's not exactly new. The first self-help book was published in 1859 by Samuel Smiles. Titled *Self-Help* and appropriately self-published, Smiles' book opened by telling readers "Heaven helps those who help themselves." Within a year of publication, the book sold 20,000 copies, extraordinary for that era. Another early self-help author was Dale Carnegie. After a short stint as a salesman, Carnegie failed as an actor and wound up broke, unemployed and living at the YMCA in New York. That's where he started teaching a public speaking course that formed the basis of *How to Win Friends and Influence People* (1936), which was a self-help manual for millions of readers.

Despite the popularity of self-help, caution may be wise. Steve Salerno, former editor of *Men's Health* magazine's books program, doesn't think much of self-help books. In *SHAM (2005),* a critique of the self-help industry, he writes that "self-help is an enterprise wherein people holding the thinnest of credentials diagnose in basically normal people symptoms of inflated or invented maladies, so that they may then implement remedies that have never been shown to work" (p. 1).

The institutions that organize our society further communicate social perspectives by the values they uphold. For example, our judicial system reminds us that as a society we value laws and punish those who break them. The number of schools and the levels of education in America inform us that our society values learning. At the same time, institutions reflect prevailing social prejudices. For instance, we may be a lawful society, but wealthy defendants often can buy better "justice" than poor ones. Similarly, although we claim to offer equal educational opportunities to all, students whose families have money and influence often can get into better schools than students whose families have fewer resources. These and other values are so thoroughly woven into the fabric of our culture that we learn them with little effort or awareness.

The Self-Fulfilling Prophecy   One particularly powerful way in which communication shapes the self is the self-fulfilling prophecy, which we discussed in Chapter 2. Self-fulfilling prophecies operate when we act in ways that bring about expectations or judgments of ourselves. If you have done poorly in classes in which teachers didn't seem to respect you and have done well with teachers who thought you were smart, then you know what a self-fulfilling prophecy is. The prophecies that we act to fulfill usually are first communicated to us by others' direct definitions, identity scripts, and attachment styles. Because we often internalize others' perspectives, we may act to fulfill the labels.

> **MILO** *I can really identify with the self-fulfilling prophecy idea. In the second grade, my family moved from our farm to a city where my dad could find work. The first week of class in my new school, we had show and tell. When it was my turn, as soon as I started talking the other kids started laughing at me. I had been raised on a farm in the rural South, and the other kids were from the city. They thought I talked funny, and they made fun of my accent—called me "hillbilly" and "redneck." From then on, I avoided public speaking like the plague. I thought I couldn't speak to others. Last year, I finally took a course in public speaking, and I made a B. It took me a long time to challenge the label that I was a bad public speaker.*

Many of us believe things about ourselves that are inaccurate. Sometimes labels that were once true aren't any longer, but we continue to believe them and act to fulfill them. In other cases, the labels were never valid, but we may believe them anyway. Unfortunately, children often are labeled "slow" or "stupid" when the real problem may be that they have impaired vision or hearing or are too hungry to concentrate in school. Even when the true source of difficulty is discovered, the children may have already internalized a destructive self-fulfilling prophecy.

The Self Is Multidimensional

Although we use the word *self* as if it referred to a single entity, in reality the self has many dimensions. You have a physical self that includes your size, shape, skin, hair and eye colors, and so forth. In addition, you have a cognitive self that includes your intelligence, aptitudes, and education. You have an emotional self concept. Are you interpersonally sensitive? Do you have a hot temper? Are you generally optimistic or pessimistic? You have a social self. Some people are extraverted, whereas others are more reserved. Our social selves also include our roles: daughter or son, student, worker, parent, volunteer, partner in a committed relationship. Each of us also has a moral self that is composed of ethical and spiritual principles we believe in and try to follow. As Carlyle points out, the different dimensions of ourselves sometimes seem at odds with one another.

> **EZRA** *On my own, like with friends or family, I'm pretty quiet—even shy, you could say. But my job requires me to be real outgoing and sociable. I tend bar, and people expect me to kid around and talk with them and stuff. Believe me, if I were as quiet with my customers as I am with my friends, my tips would drop to nothing. It's like when I'm in my work role, I'm Mr. Hail-fellow-well-met, but away from work I'm pretty reserved.*

The Self Is a Process

The self develops over time; it is a process. A baby perceives no boundaries between its body and a nipple, a hand that tickles, or a breeze. As an infant has experiences and as others respond to him or her, the child gradually begins to develop **ego boundaries,** which define where the self stops and the rest of the world begins. This is the beginning of a self-concept: the realization that one is a separate entity.

ego boundaries A person's internal sense of where he or she stops and the rest of the world begins.

Ego boundaries develop as an infant distinguishes the self from the rest of the world.

As infants begin to differentiate themselves from the rest of the world, the self starts to develop. Infants and young children listen to and observe others to define themselves and to become competent in the identities others assign to them (Kohlberg, 1958; Piaget, 1932/1965). For instance, children work to figure out what it takes to be nice, tough, and responsible, and they strive to become competent at embodying those qualities. The ways we define ourselves vary as we mature. Struggling to be a good mud-cake maker at age 4 gives way to striving for popularity in high school and to succeeding in professional and family roles later in life.

Of course, we all enter the world with certain abilities and limits, which constrain the possibilities of who we can be. Someone without the genes to be tall and coordinated, for instance, probably is not going to be a star forward in basketball. Beyond genetic limits, however, we have considerable freedom to create who we will be.

We Internalize and Act from Social Perspectives

We've already noted that in developing a self, we internalize many of the perspectives of others. Let's now look more closely at how we internalize both the perspectives of specific individuals who are significant in our lives and the general perspective of our society.

particular others One source of social perspectives that people use to define themselves and guide how they think, act, and feel. The perspectives of particular others are the viewpoints of people who are significant to the self.

Particular Others   We first encounter the perspectives of **particular others**. As the term implies, these are the viewpoints of specific people who are significant to us. Mothers, fathers, siblings, and often day-care providers are particular others who are significant to most infants. In addition, we may be very close to aunts, uncles, grandparents, godparents, and others. Children who grow up in large, extended families often have a great many particular others who affect how they come to see themselves.

> **SHENNOA**   *My grandmother was the biggest influence on me. I lived with her while my mama worked, and she taught me to take myself seriously. She's the one who told me I should go to college and plan a career so that I wouldn't have to depend on somebody else. She's the one who told me to stand up for myself and not let others tell me what to do or believe in. But she did more than just tell me to be a strong person. That's how she was, and I learned just by watching her. A lot of who I am is modeled on my grandmother.*

The process of seeing ourselves through others' eyes is called **reflected appraisal.** It means that we see ourselves in terms of the appraisals reflected in others' eyes. The process has also been called the "looking-glass self" because others are mirrors who reflect how they perceive us (Cooley, 1912). Reflected appraisals are not confined to childhood but continue throughout our lives. When a teacher communicates that a student is smart, the student may come to see himself or herself that way. In professional life, coworkers and supervisors reflect their appraisals of us when they communicate that we're on the fast track, average, or unsuited to our position. The appraisals that others communicate shape how we see ourselves. In turn, how we see ourselves affects how we communicate. Thus, if you see yourself as an interesting conversationalist, you're likely to communicate that confidence when you talk with others.

SHARPEN YOUR SKILL

At the end of this chapter, refer to the Sharpen Your Skill feature, Your Looking-Glass Self, to apply concepts from Chapter 3.

reflected appraisal Our perceptions of others' views of us.

Leigh M. Wilco

MindTap   Who are the looking glasses through which you see yourself?

The Generalized Other   The second social perspective that influences how we see ourselves is called the **perspective of the generalized other**. The generalized other is the rules, roles, values, and attitudes endorsed by the specific culture in which we live (Mead, 1934). Modern Western culture emphasizes gender, race, sexual orientation, and economic class as central to personal identity (Andersen & Collins, 2013; Wood, 2005).

North American culture views race as a primary aspect of personal identity (González, Houston, & Chen, 2012). The white race historically has been privileged in the United States. In the early years of this country, it was considered normal and right for white men to own black women, men, and children and to require them to work for no wages and in poor conditions. Later, it was considered natural that white men could vote but black men could not. Clearly, racial prejudice has diminished substantially. Even so, the upper levels of government, education, and business are dominated by white men, whereas people of color continue to fight overt and covert discrimination in many spheres of society.

> **WEN-SHU**   *My family moved here when I was 9 years old. Because I look Asian, people make assumptions about me. They assume I am quiet (true), I am good at math (not true), and I defer to men and elders (true with regard to elders but not men). People also see all Asians as the same, but Taiwanese are as different from mainland Chinese as French Caucasians are from U.S. Caucasians. The first thing people notice about me is my race, and they make too many assumptions about what it means.*

Sex and gender are also key aspects of identity in Western culture. Western cultures recognize only two sexes and genders, but an increasing number of countries including New Zealand, Australia, and Nepal recognize multiple sexes (Bendavid, 2013), and some societies regard sex as changeable so a man can become a woman and vice versa (Baird, 2014; Bilefsky, 2008).

In the United States, historically, men—specifically, white men—have been seen as more valuable than women and more entitled to privileges. In the 1800s, women weren't allowed to own property, attend college, or vote. Although there has been great progress in achieving equality between the sexes, in some respects women and men still are not considered equal or treated as such (Kaufman & Kimmel, 2011; Wood & Fixmer-Oraiz, 2017).

Western cultures have strong gender prescriptions. Girls and women are expected to be caring and cooperative, whereas boys and men are supposed to be

perspective of the generalized other The collection of rules, roles, and attitudes endorsed by the whole social community in which we live.

independent and competitive. Consequently, women who are competitive and men who are gentle may receive social disapproval for violating gender prescriptions (Kimmel & Messner, 2012). Gender prescriptions also specify ideal body images— tall and muscular for men; slender or thin and not too tall for women.

A third aspect of identity that cultural communication establishes as salient is sexual orientation. Western culture's view that heterosexuality is normal and right is communicated not only directly but also through privileges given to heterosexuals but denied to gay men, lesbians, bisexuals, trans and gender nonconforming people. Only in 2015 did the Supreme Court rule that all states must recognize same-sex marriage. Yet in many ways the society still communicates that gender conformity is the norm. For example, most of us can find clothes that fit, but women's blouses are too tight in the shoulders for trans women and men's pants are too tight in the hips for masculine-presenting women (Italie, 2014).

Many colleges and universities now include gender identity and expression in their nondiscrimination policies, have designated some bathrooms as available to everyone and enacted gender-neutral housing policies so that transgender students are not forced to live with people with whom they don't identify (Lazo, 2014; Tilsley, 2010).

Although biases against sexual orientation and gender identity are decreasing, they still very much affect how we are viewed and treated.

SANDI   *I've known I was lesbian since I was in high school, but only in the last year have I come out to others. As soon as I tell someone I'm lesbian, they see me differently. Even people who have known me a long time act like I've developed spots or something. Some of my girlfriends don't want to hug or touch me anymore, like they think I'm suddenly going to come on to them. Guys act as if I'm from another planet. It's really strange that sexual orientation makes so much difference in how others see you. I mean, relative to other things like character, personality, and intelligence, who you sleep with is pretty unimportant.*

A fourth dimension of identity, socioeconomic class, is also central to the generalized other's perspective in Western culture (Acker, 2013, Kendall, 2011; Scott & Leonhardt, 2013). Socioeconomic class isn't just the amount of money a person has. It's a basic part of how we understand our place in the world and how we think, feel, and act (Lawless, 2012). Socioeconomic class affects everything from the careers we pursue to the schools and lifestyles we see as possibilities for ourselves. Members of the middle and upper classes assume that they will attend college and enter good professions, whereas people from the working class may be directed toward vocational training regardless of their academic achievements. In such patterns, we see how the perspective of the generalized other shapes our identities and our concrete lives.

ROCHELLE   *I got so mad in high school. I had a solid A average, and ever since I was 12 I had planned to go to college. But when the guidance counselor talked with me at the start of my senior year, she encouraged me to apply to a technical school that is near my home. When I said I thought my grades should get me into a good college, she did this double-take, like, "Your kind doesn't go to college." My parents both work in a mill and so do all my relatives, but does that mean that I can't have a different future? What really burned me was that a lot of girls who had average grades but came from "the right families" were told to apply to colleges.*

It's important to realize that social perspectives on race, sex, sexual orientation, and socioeconomic class interact. Race intersects gender, so women of color often experience double oppression and devaluation in our culture. Class and sexual orientation also interact: Homophobia tends to be pronounced among people in the working class, so a lesbian or gay person in a poor community may be socially ostracized. Socioeconomic class and gender are also interlinked; women are far more likely than men to live at the poverty level (Andersen & Collins, 2013; Kaufman & Kimmel, 2011). Intersections of race and class mean that minority members of the working class often are not treated as well as working-class whites (Rothenberg, 2006).

As we internalize the generalized other's perspective, we come to share many of the views and values of our society. Shared understandings are essential for collective life. If we all made up our own rules, there would be no common standards and collective life would be chaotic. Yet, shared understandings are not carved in stone: People sometimes work to change how their society operates. The changes we have seen in how Western culture defines and values people of different races, genders, and sexual orientations testify to the possibility of evolution in social perceptions. Each of us has an ethical responsibility to think critically about which social views to accept and use as guides for our own behaviors, attitudes, and values. This suggests a fourth proposition about the self.

Social Perspectives on the Self Are Changeable

The generalized other's perspectives are not fixed. Because they are constructed by members of a society, they can also be changed if enough members of a society challenge them.

Social perspectives are created in particular cultures at specific times. Unsurprisingly, they tend to reflect the views and values of those who are in power at that time. Yet power relations evolve over time and, when they do, social perspectives may also change.

In the 1600s, Europeans first colonized what is now the United States. At the top of the settlers' social hierarchy were white heterosexual men, especially those of means. Later, Africans were taken from their homeland and brought to America to be slaves, and they were assigned low positions in the social hierarchy. The laws and norms that developed in the early chapters of United States history privileged the interests of straight white men of means and did little to support, much less advance, the interests of women, people of color, or people who were not heterosexual.

Centuries later, the United States still has a social hierarchy, but the society has gradually become less rigidly stratified. As that has happened, laws and norms have become increasingly respectful of a range of sexes, races, sexual orientations, and gender identities. Women and people of color can vote; gay and trans people can marry; it is illegal to discriminate on the basis of sex, race, or sexual orientation; and nobody can own another human being. These fundamental changes in how identities are understood offer clear evidence that social perspectives can and do change. As they continue to evolve, each of us will probably modify views of others' identities and our own.

Social perspectives on same-sex relationships have changed over time.

Lifesize/Getty Images

Review It!

Western Culture's Identity Categories:

- Race
- Sex and Gender
- Sexual Orientation
- Socioeconomic Class

Social perspectives change in response to individual and collective efforts to weave new meanings into the fabric of common life. Feminist, Civil Rights, and Gay Rights movements have profoundly challenged and changed how identities are understood in the United States. Changes in how we view sex, race, class, (dis)ability, and sexual orientation arc ncgotiatcd in communication contexts ranging from one-to-one conversations to mass and social media. Each of us has an ethical responsibility to speak out against social perspectives that we perceive as wrong or harmful. By doing so, we participate in the ongoing process of refining social perspectives.

> **JESSICA** *My husband and I have really worked to share equally in our marriage. When we got married 8 years ago, we both believed women and men were equal and should have equal responsibilities for the home and family and equal power in making decisions that affect the family. But it's a lot harder to actually live that ideal than to believe in it. Both of us have struggled against our socialization that says I should cook and clean and take care of the kids and he should make big decisions about our lives. I think we've done a pretty good job of creating and living an egalitarian marriage. A lot of our friends see us as models.*

Digital Media and Personal Identity

We'll discuss three of many ways that social media are relevant to personal identity. First, consider the importance of social media in providing us with direct definitions and reflected appraisals. A 2013 survey reports that nearly 30% of Americans aged 12 or older have a profile on at least one social networking site, and 60% of Americans aged 12 or older are heavy users of social networks (Quenqua, 2014). That implies we get and give a lot of appraisals through online and digital communication. When you post a photo on Instagram or Facebook, others respond by saying, "You look great!" and "Very cool outfit." Knowing that others think you look attractive probably elevates your own sense of your attractiveness. But what if others' comments are less positive? "Have you gained weight?" "What did you do to your hair?" Those reflected appraisals are likely to make you feel less good about yourself.

Girls and women are more likely than boys or men to use social media as a venue for self-development. Teen girls use their blogs and pages on social networking sites to talk about issues such as pressures to be skinny, to drink (or not), have sex (or not), and to dress in particular ways (Bodey, 2009; Bodey & Wood, 2009). As girls work out what they think and want to do in their online communities, they count on comments from others to clarify their own thinking and gain confidence in their ability to reject gender norms they find troubling.

Social networks can be—and too often are—used for cyberbullying, which includes text messages, comments, rumors, embarrassing pictures, videos and fake profiles that are meant to hurt another person and are sent by email or posted on social networking sites. Direct definitions such as "You are ugly," or "You look like a wimp" are very hurtful, regardless of whether they are true. Fully 43% of teenagers are subject to some form of cyberbullying. For LGBTQ teenagers the percentage is even higher: 53% (Burney, 2012). When asked why people were so cruel online, one young boy explained, "You can be as mean as you want on Facebook" (Hoffman, 2010, p. A12). Cyberbullying has no necessary stopping point.

Communication Highlight

Am I Pretty?

Most of us care how others see us. For many young girls, one of the key issues is whether others see them as attractive. Whereas girls once asked friends "am I pretty?," they are now likely to post the question in a YouTube video of themselves. And the responses can be extremely cruel. One-on-one evaluations between girls who are friends usually include some diplomacy, even tenderness, but comments posted as replied to YouTube videos observe no boundaries. When 13-year-old Sammie posted an Am I Pretty? video, one male responded comments, "Yes, you are really ugly. Now go cry to someone that actually cares" (Quenqua, 2014).

Am I Pretty? videos are not rare. More than 23,000, most from 13- to 15-year olds, have been posted, and they keep pouring in (Quenqua, 2014). Some psychiatrists consider these videos an alarming new form of self-mutilation, no unlike cutting. Other observers regard the ubiquity of the videos further evidence that popular culture is obsessed with superficial qualities rather than substantive ones.

The school yard bully pretty much stays on the school yard. Thus, a victim can escape by going home or visiting a friend. Online bullying can follow the victim anywhere and anytime. It is unremitting.

Social media are also key sources for social comparison. We read others' updates and compare our accomplishments to theirs, our activities to theirs, our number of friends to theirs, and so on. On social networking sites, many, perhaps most, people emphasize what is positive in their lives and downplay or omit mention of what is not so positive (Krasnova, Wenninger, Widaja, & Buxmann, 2013; Tierney, 2013). This suggests that we might be wise to be cautious in comparing ourselves to the selves others present online.

Guidelines for Enhancing the Self

So far, we've explained how the self develops in the process of communicating with others. Building on that knowledge, we'll now explore guidelines for encouraging personal growth.

Make a Strong Commitment to Improve Yourself

The first principle for enhancing who you are is to make a firm commitment to personal growth. This isn't as easy as it might sound. A firm commitment involves more than saying, "I want to listen better" or "I want to be less judgmental." Saying these sentences is simple, but actually investing the effort to change is difficult. Changing ourselves takes ongoing effort. In addition, we must realize at the outset that there will be setbacks, and we can't let them derail us.

Gain Knowledge as a Basis for Personal Change

Commitment alone is insufficient to spur changes in who you are. In addition, you need several types of knowledge. First, you need to understand how the self is formed. In this chapter, we've discussed the influence of particular others and the generalized other. You may not want to accept all the views and values you were taught.

Communication Highlight   Failure on the Way to Success

Who was Babe Ruth? If you know baseball history, you probably think of him as having hit 714 home runs. He did, but he also struck out 1,330 times. R. H. Macy, who founded Macy's department store, failed in his first seven efforts to start a business. Superstar Michael Jordan was cut from his high school basketball team because he wasn't good enough. Early in his career, Walt Disney was fired from a newspaper job because his editor thought he had no good or creative ideas. The Beatles penned 59 songs before they had their first hit.

Most people who succeed fail along the way; sometimes they fail many times. If Babe Ruth had let his strikeouts defeat him, he would never have been a champion batter. The same is true of most of us. Failures and defeats are inevitable. Letting them define who we are is not inevitable.

Another important source of knowledge is other people. Perhaps you recall a time when you began a new job. If you were fortunate, you found a mentor who explained the ropes to you and gave you helpful feedback. In much the same way, others can also provide feedback on your progress in the process of change. In addition, others can serve as models. If you know someone you think is particularly skillful in supporting others, observe him or her carefully to identify concrete skills that you can tailor to suit your personal style.

Set Realistic Goals

Changing ourselves is most likely when we set goals that are specific and realistic. Vague goals for self-improvement usually lead nowhere because they don't indicate concrete steps toward change. For instance, "I want to be better at intimate communication" is a very vague objective. You can't do anything to meet such an unclear goal until you know something about the talk that enhances and impedes intimacy. Books such as *Communication in Our Lives* will help you pinpoint concrete skills that facilitate healthy intimate communication. For instance, Chapter 4 will help you develop listening skills, and Chapter 7 will explain how communication affects personal and social relationships.

Goals should also be realistic. If you are shy and want to be more extraverted, it is reasonable to try to speak up more often. On the other hand, it may not be reasonable to try to be the life of every party. Realistic goals are based on realistic standards. In a culture that emphasizes perfection, it's easy to be trapped into expecting more than is possible. A better method is to establish a series of small, incremental goals. You might focus first on improving one communication skill. When you're satisfied with your ability at that skill, you can work on another one.

> **MIKE** *For a long time, I put myself down for not doing as well academically as a lot of my friends. They put mega-hours into studying and writing papers. I can't do that because I work 30 hours a week. Now I see that it's unfair to compare myself to them. When I compare myself to students who work as much as I do, my record is pretty good.*

Self-Disclose When Appropriate

Self-disclosure is the revelation of information about ourselves that others are unlikely to discover on their own. We self-disclose when we share private information about ourselves—our hopes, fears, feelings, thoughts, and experiences. Although we don't reveal our private selves to everyone and don't do it often even with intimates, self-disclosure is an important kind of communication.

Self-disclosure has notable values. First, sharing personal feelings, thoughts, and experiences often enhances closeness between people (Hendrick & Hendrick, 1996, 2006; Samp & Palevitz, 2009; Stafford, 2009). By extension, when others understand our private selves, they may respond to us more sensitively, as unique individuals. Self-disclosing also tends to invite others to self-disclose, so we may learn more about them. Finally, self-disclosure can affect what we know about ourselves and how we feel about who we are. For example, if we reveal a weakness or an incident of which we're ashamed, and another person accepts the disclosure without judging us negatively, we may find it easier to accept ourselves. Self-disclosure necessarily involves risk—the risk that others will not accept private information or that they might use it against us. Appropriate self-disclosure minimizes these risks by proceeding slowly and establishing trust. Begin by revealing information that is personal but not highly intimate or able to damage you if exploited. Before disclosing further, observe how the other person responds to your communication and what he or she does with it. You might also pay attention to whether the other person reciprocates by disclosing personal information to you.

Accept That You Are in Process

Accepting yourself as you are now is a starting point for any change. The self that you are results from all the interactions and experiences in your life. You don't have to like or admire everything about yourself, but it is important to accept who you are today as a basis for moving forward.

Accepting yourself as being in process also implies that you realize you can change. Don't let yourself be hindered by defeating self-fulfilling prophecies or the fallacy of thinking that you can't change. You can change if you set realistic goals, make a genuine commitment, and then work for the changes you want.

self-disclosure Revelation of information about ourselves that others are unlikely to discover on their own.

Create a Supportive Context for Change

Just as it is easier to swim with the tide than against it, it is easier to change our views of ourselves when we have some support for our efforts. You can do a lot to create an environment that promotes your growth by choosing contexts and people who help you realize your goals. First, think about settings. If you want to lose weight, it's better to go to restaurants that serve healthful foods and offer light choices than to go to cholesterol castles. If you want to become more extraverted, go to parties, not libraries. But libraries are a better context than parties if your goal is to improve academic performance.

ISLA   *I never cared a lot about clothes until I joined a sorority where the labels on your clothes are a measure of your worth. The girls compete with each other to dress the best and have the newest styles. When one of the sisters wears something out of style, she gets a lot of teasing, but really it's pressure on her to measure up to the sorority image. At first, I adopted my sisters' values, and I spent more money than I could afford on clothes. For a while I even quit making contributions at church so that I could have more money for clothes. When I finally realized I was becoming somebody I didn't like, I tried to change, but my sisters made me feel bad anytime I wasn't dressed well. Finally, I moved out rather than face that pressure all the time. It just wasn't a good place for me to be myself.*

Because how others view us affects how we see ourselves, you can create a supportive context by consciously choosing to be around people who believe in you and encourage your personal growth. Steer clear of people who put you down or say you can't change. In other words, people who reflect positive appraisals of us enhance our ability to improve who we are.

Others aren't the only ones whose communication affects our self-concepts. We also communicate with ourselves, and our own messages influence how we see ourselves. One of the most crippling kinds of self-talk we can engage in is **self-sabotage**—telling ourselves we are no good, we'll never learn something, there's no point in trying to change. We may be repeating others' judgments of us, or we may be inventing negative self-fulfilling prophecies. Either way, self-sabotage undermines belief in ourselves.

Distinguished therapist Albert Ellis (1988) suggests you should challenge negative statements you make to yourself and replace them with constructive intrapersonal communication. Following Ellis' advice, the next time you hear yourself saying, "I can't do...," challenge the self-defeating message, say out loud to yourself, "I can do it." Of course, you won't grow and improve if you listen only to praise, particularly if it is less than honest. Real friends can help us identify areas for growth without making us feel bad about ourselves.

In sum, to improve your self-concept, you should create contexts that support growth and change, and seek experiences and settings that foster belief in yourself and the changes you desire. Also, recognize uppers, downers, and vultures in yourself and others, and learn which people and which kinds of communication assist you in achieving your own goals for self-improvement.

self-sabotage Self-talk that communicates that we're no good, we can't do something, we can't change, and so forth. Undermines belief in ourselves and motivation to change and grow.

Chapter Summary

In this chapter, we explored the self as a process that evolves as we communicate with others over the course of our lives. As we interact with others, we learn and internalize social perspectives, both those of particular others and those of the generalized other, or society as a whole. Reflected appraisals, direct definitions, and social comparisons are key communication processes that shape how we see ourselves and how we change over time. The perspective of the generalized other includes social views of key aspects of identity, including gender, race, and sexual orientation. However, these are arbitrary social constructions that we may challenge and resist once we are adults. When we resist social views and values that we consider unethical, we promote change in both society and ourselves.

The second section of this chapter identified ways that social media affect personal identity. We noted that social media expand the opportunities for direct definition, reflected appraisal and social comparisons, which can be beneficial and also destructive.

In the final section of the chapter, we focused on ways to enhance communication competence by improving self-concept. Guidelines include making a firm commitment to personal growth, gaining knowledge about desired changes and the skills they involve, setting realistic goals, accepting yourself as in process, and creating contexts that support the changes you seek. We can make amazing changes in who we are and how we feel about ourselves when we commit to doing so.

MindTap®

Experiencing Communication in Our Lives

CASE STUDY: Parental Teachings

Apply what you've learned in this chapter by analyzing the following case study, using the accompanying questions as a guide. These questions and a video of the case study are also available online with your MindTap Speech for *Communication in Our Lives.*

Kate McDonald is in the neighborhood park with her two children, 7-year-old Emma and 5-year-old Jeremy. The three of them walk into the park and approach the swing set.

KATE: Jeremy, why don't you push Emma so she can swing? Emma, you hang on tight.

Jeremy begins pushing his sister, who squeals with delight. Jeremy gives an extra-hard push that lands him in the dirt in front of the swing set. Laughing, Emma jumps off, falling in the dirt beside her brother.

KATE: Come here, sweetie. You've got dirt all over your knees and your pretty new dress.

Kate brushes the dirt off Emma, who then runs over to the jungle gym set that Jeremy is now climbing. Kate smiles as she watches Jeremy climb fearlessly on the bars.

KATE: You're a brave little man, aren't you? How high can you go?

Encouraged by his mother, Jeremy climbs to the top bars and holds up a fist, screaming, "Look at me, Mom! I'm king of the hill! I climbed to the very top!"

Kate laughs and claps her hands to applaud him. Jealous of the attention Jeremy is getting, Emma runs over to the jungle gym and starts climbing. Kate calls out, "Careful, honey. Don't go any higher. You could fall and hurt yourself." When Emma ignores her mother and reaches for a higher bar, Kate walks over and pulls her off, saying, "Emma, I told you that is dangerous. Time to get down. Why don't you play on the swings some more?"

Once Kate puts Emma on the ground, the girl walks over to the swings and begins swaying.

QUESTIONS FOR ANALYSIS AND DISCUSSION

1. Identify examples of direct definition in this scenario. How does Kate define Emma and Jeremy?

2. Identify examples of reflected appraisal in this scenario. What appraisals of her son and daughter does Kate reflect to them?

3. What do Emma's and Jeremy's responses to Kate suggest about their acceptance of her views of them?

4. To what extent does Kate's communication with her children reflect conventional gender expectations in Western culture?

Key Concepts

attachment style
direct definition
ego boundaries
identity script

particular others
perspective of the gener-
    alized other
reflected appraisal

self
self-disclosure
self-sabotage
social comparison

MindTap

Use flashcards to learn key concepts and take a quiz to test your knowledge.

Sharpen Your Skill

1. Reflecting on Your Identity Scripts

Recall identity scripts your parents communicated about who you were or were supposed to become. Can you hear them saying, "Our people do . . ." or "Our family doesn't . . ."? Can you recall messages that told you what and who they expected you to be? As a youngster, did you hear, "You'll go to college" or "You're going to be a doctor"?

Now review key identity scripts. Which ones make sense to you today? Are you still following any that are irrelevant to your present life or that are at odds with your personal values and goals? If so, then commit to changing scripts that aren't productive for you or that conflict with values you hold. You can rewrite identity scripts now that you're an adult.

2. Your Looking-Glass Self

Identify three people who have been or are particularly important to you. For each person, identify one self-perception you have that reflects the appraisal of you communicated by that person.

Now imagine that you'd never known each of the three people. Describe how you would be different. How would your self-image change? For instance, Shennoa (see commentary, p. 58) might think she would be less independent had her grandmother not influenced how she sees herself.

Trace the way you see yourself to the appraisals that particular others have reflected.

Prepare a 2-minute presentation in which you describe one of the people you've identified as a looking glass for yourself. Explain how this person has influenced the way you see yourself. You may want to look ahead to Part III of this book for guidelines on preparing a speech.

For Further Reflection and Discussion

1. Set one specific goal for personal growth as a communicator. Be sure to specify your goal in terms of clear behavioral changes and make it realistic. As you study different topics during the semester, apply what you learn to your personal goal.

2. What ethical issues do you perceive in the process of developing and continuously refining self-concepts, both your own and those of people around you? Is it as important to be ethical in communicating with yourself (self-talk, or intrapersonal communication) as in communicating with others?

3. How do people you meet and get to know through social media affect your sense of who you are? Are they significant for you? Do they represent the generalized other to you? Is it useful to distinguish between the impact of face-to-face and online communication?

4. Historically, India classified people according to caste, one of the most rigid systems of social class. To learn about how a person's caste affected his or her opportunities in life, go to the book's online resources for this chapter.

Beyond the Classroom

Let's take the material in this chapter beyond the classroom by thinking about how what you've learned about personal identity might apply to the workplace, ethical choices, and engagement with the broader world.

1. **Workplace.** Recall examples of supervisors and coworkers' direct definitions of you or other employees. For example, were you defined as "a good worker" or "a quick learner"? Consider identity scripts that you were given in a particular workplace. What did others tell you about the company or workplace's identity and about how employees in this particular job were supposed to think and act?

2. **Ethics.** How does what you learned in this chapter affect ethical choices about parenting? Reflect on the ethical implications of knowing that parents affect children's self-concepts by their choices of direct definitions, identity scripts, and attachment styles. What ethical responsibilities, if any, do parents have regarding their impact on children's self-concepts and self-esteem?

3. **Engagement.** Not all children have the fortune of having parents who are able to nurture them lovingly and help them develop positive self-concepts. In 1964, the United States launched the Head Start Program to help children and their families who have limited resources. Go to the book's online resources for this chapter to access the National Head Start Program's website. Spend some time reading this page and following links it provides. Can you identify ways that the program aims to enhance the self-concepts of underprivileged children and their families?

Jose Galvez/PhotoEdit

4

The best way
to understand
people is to listen
to them.

Ralph Nichols

Listening Effectively

LEARNING OBJECTIVES

After studying the topics in this chapter, you should be able to:

1. Identify the key features that define communication.

2. Distinguish between content-level meaning and relationship-level meaning.

3. Identify the value of studying communication to four aspects of your life: personal, relationship, professional, and cultural.

4. Apply the transactional model of communication to a specific interaction.

5. List the four themes that unify the field of communication.

6. Explain how the definition of communication applies to social media and online communication.

In an average day, what percentage of your time are you listening?

MindTap

Review the chapter's learning objectives and **start** with a quick warm-up activity.

"**D**o you have a minute to talk?" Joanne asks her friend Elly as she enters her dorm room.

"Sure," Elly agrees without looking up from the text on her iPhone.

"I'm worried about what's happening between Drew and me," Joanne begins. "He takes me for granted all the time. He never asks what I want to do or where I'd like to go. He just assumes I'll go along with whatever he wants."

"Yeah, I know that routine. Steve does it to me, too," Elly says with exasperation as she looks up. "Last weekend, he insisted we go to this stupid war movie that I wouldn't have chosen in a million years. But what I wanted didn't make a lot of difference to him."

"That's exactly what I'm talking about," Joanne agrees. "I don't like it when Drew treats me that way."

"What I told Steve last weekend was that I'd had it, and from now on we decide together what we're doing, or we don't do it together," Elly says forcefully. "We've had this talk before, but this time I think I really got through to him that I was serious."

"So are you saying that's what I should do with Drew?"

"Sure," Elly says while composing a text. "Take it from me, subtlety won't work. Remember last year when I was dating Larry? I tried to be subtle and hint that I'd like to be consulted about things. What I said to him went in one ear and out the other."

"But Drew's not like Larry or Steve. I think he just doesn't understand how I feel when he makes all the decisions," Joanne says.

"Well, I really don't think Steve's 'like that' either. He's just as good a guy as Drew," Elly snaps.

"That's not what I meant," Joanne says. "I just meant that I don't think I need to hit Drew over the head with a two-by-four."

"And I suppose you think Steve does need that?"

"I don't know. I'm just thinking that maybe our relationships are different," Joanne says.

Poor listening is evident in the conversation between Elly and Joanne. The first obstacle to effective listening is Elly's preoccupation with her iPhone. A second problem is Elly's tendency to monopolize the conversation by focusing on her own problems and boyfriends instead of on Joanne's concerns about the relationship with Drew. Third, Elly listens defensively, taking offense when Joanne suggests that their relationships may differ.

Usually, when we think about communication, we focus on talking. Yet talking is not the only part—or even the greatest part—of communication. Effective communication also involves listening. As obvious as this is, few of us devote as much energy to listening as we do to talking (Brady, 2015).

This chapter focuses on listening. First, we'll consider what's involved in listening, which is more than most of us realize. Next, we'll discuss obstacles to effective listening and how to minimize them. Third, we'll consider common forms of nonlistening. The fourth section of the chapter explores listening in the realm of digital communication. Finally, we discuss guidelines for improving listening effectiveness.

Who Listens?

Dan Rather interviewed Mother Teresa shortly before her death (Bailey, 1998). She had this to say about listening.

Rather: "What do you say to God when you pray?"

Mother Teresa: "I listen."

Rather: "Well, what does God say?"

Mother Teresa: "He listens."

You spend more time listening—or trying to—than talking. Studies of people from college students to professionals indicate that the average person spends 45–75% of waking time listening to others (ILA, 2011; Nichols, 2009; Wolvin, 2009). If we don't listen effectively, we're communicating poorly most of the time.

When people don't listen well on the job, they may miss information that can affect their professional effectiveness and advancement (Darling & Dannels, 2003; Landrum & Harrold, 2003). Skill in listening is also linked to resolving workplace conflicts. Doctors who don't listen fully to patients may misdiagnose or mistreat medical problems (Joshi, 2015; Scholz, 2005; Wen & Kosowsky, 2013). Ineffective listening in the classroom diminishes learning and performance on tests. In personal relationships, poor listening can hinder understanding of others, and listening ineffectively to public communication leaves us uninformed about civic issues.

The Listening Process

Although we often use the words *listening* and *hearing* as if they were synonyms, actually they're not. **Hearing** is a physiological activity that occurs when sound waves hit our eardrums. Hearing is passive; we don't have to invest any energy to hear. Listening, on the other hand, is an active process that requires energy (International Listening Association, 2011). Listening involves more than just hearing or receiving messages through sight, as when we notice nonverbal behaviors or when people with hearing impairments read lips or receive messages in American Sign Language (ASL).

Listening is an active, complex process that includes being mindful, physically receiving messages, selecting and organizing information, interpreting communication, responding, and remembering. The complexity of listening is represented in the Chinese character for listening, which includes symbols for eyes, ears, and heart (Figure 4.1). As the character suggests, to listen effectively, we use not only our ears, but also our eyes and hearts.

Being Mindful

The first step in listening is deciding to be mindful. **Mindfulness** is being fully engaged in the moment. You focus on what is happening here and now. When you are mindful, you don't let your thoughts wander from what is happening in

hearing The physiological activity that occurs when sound waves hit our eardrums. Unlike listening, hearing is a passive process.

listening A complex process that consists of being mindful, physically receiving messages, selecting and organizing information, interpreting, responding, and remembering.

mindfulness Being fully present in the moment; the first step of listening and the foundation of all other steps.

Eyes

Ears

Heart

FIGURE 4.1
The Chinese Character
for Listening

Listening

the present conversation. You don't think about what you did yesterday or about a friend you want to text, and you don't think about your own feelings and issues. Instead, when you listen mindfully, you tune in fully to another person and try to understand that person without imposing your own ideas, judgments, or feelings on the message. You may later express your thoughts and feelings, but when you listen mindfully, you attend to another fully.

Mindfulness enhances communication in two ways. First, attending mindfully to others increases our understanding of how they feel and think about what they are saying. Second, when we listen mindfully, others tend to express themselves in greater depth.

Being mindful is a personal commitment to attend fully and without diversion to another person. No amount of skill will make you a good listener if you do not choose to attend mindfully to others. Thus, your own choice to be mindful or not is the foundation of how well you listen—or fail to.

Physically Receiving Messages

In addition to mindfulness, listening involves physically receiving messages. For many people, this happens through hearing. People who are hard of hearing, however, receive messages by reading sign language or physically sensing sound waves. Our ability to receive messages may decline when we are tired or ill. Physical reception of messages may also be impeded by background noises, such as blaring music, others talking nearby, or buzzes alerting us to incoming texts.

ELLE *Hard-of-hearing people are capable of physically feeling sound waves, and we may in fact be more in tune to the physicality of sound waves than hearing people, because we've learned to rely on noticing these vibrations as an alternative to our ears. Sometimes I can feel loud trucks coming down the street when my hearing peers either can't or don't notice because they can hear them with their ears, for instance.*

Communication Highlight

Chewing Causes Murder

MindTap®

How could chewing cause murder? Actually, it didn't, but a woman admitted that she felt like strangling her boyfriend whenever he chewed. The sound of his chewing enraged her. This woman is not a psychopath. Her problem is misophonia, which means "hatred of sound." Named in 2002, this is a condition in which particular sounds enrage or disgust a person. The most common sounds that trigger these responses are chewing, swallowing, lip smacking, breathing, typing, and pen clicking. Research suggests that misophonia is caused by hyperconnectivity between the auditory system and the part of the brain that controls emotion (Lerner, 2015).

Selecting and Organizing Material

The third part of listening is selecting and organizing material. As we noted in Chapter 2, we don't perceive everything around us. Instead, we selectively attend to some messages and elements of our environments and disregard others. What we select to attend to depends on many factors, including our physiology, interests, cognitive structures, and expectations.

We can compensate for our tendencies to attend selectively by remembering that we are more likely to notice stimuli that are intense, loud, or unusual. Thus, we may overlook communicators who speak softly. If we're aware of this tendency, we can guard against it and choose to listen mindfully to communicators who are not especially dynamic.

Once we've selected what to notice, we organize what we've received. As you'll recall from Chapter 2, we use cognitive schemata to organize perceptions. When others are talking, we make decisions—usually not consciously—about how to organize what they say: Does the communication fit the prototype of venting or problem solving or something else? We apply personal constructs to classify the message as rational or not rational, emotional or not emotional, and so forth. Based on how you construct what you are selectively attending to, you apply stereotypes to predict what the other person will do and expects you to do. Finally, based on the meanings you have constructed, you choose a script to follow in interaction.

When a friend is upset, you can reasonably predict that he or she may not want advice until he or she has first had a chance to express his feelings. On the other hand, when a coworker comes to you with a problem that must be solved quickly, you assume he or she might welcome practical advice. Your script for responding to the distraught friend might be to say, "Tell me more about what you're feeling." With a colleague who is facing a deadline, you might adopt a more directive script and say, "Let's put our heads together and come up with a solution."

Interpreting Communication

The fourth part of listening is interpreting others' communication. When we interpret, we put together all that we have selected and organized to make sense of the overall situation. The most important principle in this process is to be person centered, which means trying to take the other person's perspective. Certainly, you won't always agree with other people. However, if you want to listen well, you have an ethical responsibility to make an earnest effort to understand others' perspectives. To interpret someone with respect for their perspective is one of the greatest gifts we can give.

MAGGIE   *Don and I didn't understand each other's perspective, and we didn't even understand that we didn't understand. Once I told him I was really upset about a friend of mine who needed money for an emergency. Don told me she had no right to expect me to bail her out, but that had nothing to do with what I was feeling. He saw the situation in terms of what rights my friend had, but to me it was about feeling concerned for someone I like. Only after we got counseling did we learn to really listen to each other instead of listening through ourselves.*

Responding

Effective listening includes responding, which is communicating attention and interest as well as voicing our own views when that is appropriate. Skillful listeners give outward signs that they are interested and involved not only when others finish speaking but throughout interaction. Indicators of engagement include attentive posture, head nods, eye contact, and vocal responses such as "um hmm," "okay," and "go on." When we respond with interest, we communicate that we care about the other person and what he or she is saying. This is what makes listening such an active process.

Remembering

The final part of effective listening is remembering, or retaining what you have heard. We remember less than half of a message immediately after we hear it. As time goes by, retention decreases further; we recall only about 35% of most messages 8 hours after we hear them (Adler & Proctor, 2013). Because we forget about two-thirds of what we hear, it's important to make sure we hang onto the most important third. Later in this chapter, we'll discuss strategies for increasing retention.

Obstacles to Effective Listening

There are two broad types of obstacles to good listening: those external to us and those inside us.

External Obstacles

Although we can't always control external obstacles, knowing what situational factors hinder listening can help us guard against them or compensate for the interference they create.

Message Overload   The sheer amount of communication in our lives makes it impossible to listen fully to all of it. When we're not talking face-to-face with someone, we're likely to be texting, watching TV, listening to podcasts, or watching YouTube videos. We simply aren't able to listen mindfully all of the time.

Message overload often occurs in academic settings. If you're taking four or five classes, you confront mountains of information. Message overload may also occur when communication takes place simultaneously in two channels. For instance, you might experience information overload if a professor presents information verbally while also clicking through PowerPoint slides with complex statistical data.

Message Complexity   The more detailed and complicated ideas are, the harder it is to follow and retain them. Many jobs today are highly specialized so communication among coworkers is complex (Cooper, 1997; Hacker, Goss, & Townley, 1998). We need to guard against the tendency to tune out people who use technical terms, provide lots of detail, and use complex sentences.

Environmental Distractions   Distractions in the environment can interfere with listening (Keizer, 2010). Perhaps you've been part of a crowd at a rally or a game. If so, you probably had trouble hearing the person next to you. Although most sounds aren't as overwhelming as the roar of crowds, there is always some noise in communication situations. Music, television in the background, side conversations in a class, or rings of smart phones can hinder communication.

> **NICK**   *It's impossible to listen well in my apartment. Four of us live there, and at least two different stereos are on all the time. Also, a TV is usually on, and there may be conversations or phone calls, too. It's crazy when we try to talk to each other in the middle of all the racket. We're always asking each other to repeat something or skipping over whatever we don't hear. If we go out to a bar or something, the noise there is just as bad. Sometimes I think we don't really want to talk with each other and all the distractions protect us from having to.*

Good listeners try to reduce environmental distractions. It's considerate to turn off televisions, phones, and laptops if someone wants to talk with you. In the example that opened this chapter, Elly should have put her phone aside if she wanted to listen mindfully to Joanne.

Communication & Careers

New Epidemic: Distracted Doctors

Would you want your neurosurgeon making personal calls during an operation on your spine? Would you want a surgical nurse checking competitive air fares while attending an operation? Would you want the technician texting while operating a bypass machine? Would you be comfortable knowing doctors and nurses were shopping online while you were on the operating table? Welcome to what some call "distracted doctoring" (Richtel, 2011). All of these examples are based on observations of real doctors, nurses, and technicians in surgery.

Dr. Peter Papadakos is an anesthesiologist who directs critical care at the University of Rochester Medical Center. He says, "My gut feeling is lives are in danger" (Richtel, 2011, p. A4). Dr. Papadakos's concern is illustrated by a patient who was partially paralyzed during an operation in which his neurosurgeon made personal and business calls—at least 10 of them!

Cognitive psychologists have found that email alerts, IMs, and notifications of text messages undermine the ability to listen mindfully (Begley, 2009). Interruptions fragment concentration so we have trouble resituating ourselves in whatever we were doing before the interruption. Attending to social media may have even more substantial costs: Between 2004 and 2012, there was a 200% increase in the number of pedestrians killed or injured while wearing headphones that prevented them from hearing traffic (Newsbeast, 2012).

Internal Obstacles

In addition to external interferences, listening may be hindered by four psychological obstacles.

Preoccupation   When we are preoccupied with our own thoughts and concerns, we can't focus on what someone else is saying.

ANDY   *I've been really stressed about finding a job. I've had lots of first interviews, but no callbacks and no offers. Even when I'm not interviewing—like when I'm with friends or in class— getting a job is in the back of my mind. It just stays there so that it's hard for me to really focus on anything else happening around me.*

Prejudgments   Another obstacle to effective listening is prejudgment of others or their ideas. Sometimes we decide in advance that others have nothing to offer us, so we tune them out. If a coworker's ideas have not impressed you in the past, you might assume he or she will contribute nothing of value to a present conversation. The risk is that you might miss a good idea simply because you prejudged

Attention to social media can interfere with mindful listening.

Rich Legg/E+/Getty Images

the other person. Research shows that, on average, doctors interrupt patients 23 seconds after patients have started explaining their medical situation or need (Levine, 2004). When doctors stop listening, they risk not getting information that could help them diagnose and treat patients. It's also important to keep an open mind when listening to communication regarding issues about which you already have opinions. You might miss important new information and perspectives if you don't put your prejudgments aside long enough to listen mindfully.

Another kind of prejudgment occurs when we assume we know what another feels, thinks, and is going to say, and we then assimilate his or her message into our preconceptions. This is a form of mind reading, which we discussed in Chapter 2.

> **NOAH**   *My parents need a course in listening! They are so quick to tell me what I think and feel, or should think and feel, that they never hear what I do feel or think. Last year I approached them with the idea of taking a year off from school. Before I could even explain why I wanted to do this, Dad was all over me about being responsible and getting ahead in a career. Mom jumped on me about looking for an easy out and not having the gumption to stick with my studies. The whole point was that I wanted to work as an intern to get some hands-on experience in media production, which is my major. It had nothing to do with wanting an easy out or not trying to get ahead, but they couldn't even hear me through their own ideas about what I felt.*

Lack of Effort   Because active listening takes so much effort, we're not always able or willing to do it well. If you can't summon the effort to listen well, you might suggest postponing interaction until a time when you will be able to invest effort in listening. If you explain to the other that you want to defer communication because you really are interested and want to be able to listen well, he or she is likely to appreciate your honesty and commitment to listening.

Failure to Adjust to Diverse Communication Styles   A final internal obstacle to effective listening is not recognizing and adjusting to different listening styles that reflect diverse communities and cultures (Samovar et al., 2015). The more we understand about different people's rules for listening, the more effectively we can signal our attention in ways they appreciate. For example, in the United States it is considered polite to make frequent but not continuous eye contact in conversation. Yet in some cultures, continuous eye contact is normative, and in others almost any eye contact is considered intrusive.

Even within the United States, there are differences in listening rules based on membership in racial, gender, and other social communities. For example, men generally provide fewer verbal and nonverbal clues than women to indicate they are interested in what another person is saying. They may also respond primarily to the content level of meaning and less to the relationship level of meaning. If you understand these gender differences, you can adapt your listening style appropriately.

> **LAVONDA**   *My boyfriend is the worst listener ever. Whenever I try to tell him about some problem I have, he becomes Mr. Answer Man. He tells me what to do or how to handle a situation. That doesn't do anything to help me with my feelings or even to let me know he hears what I'm feeling.*

We have seen that there are many obstacles to effective listening. Obstacles inherent in messages and situations include message overload, message complexity, and environmental distractions. In addition, there are four potential interferences inside us: preoccupation, prejudgment, lack of effort, and failure to recognize and adapt to diverse expectations of listening.

Forms of Nonlistening

Now that we've discussed obstacles to effective listening, let's consider some forms of nonlistening. As you read about these six types of nonlistening, they may seem familiar because you and others probably engage in them at times.

Pseudolistening

Pseudolistening is pretending to listen. When we pseudolisten, we appear to be attentive, but really our minds are elsewhere. Superficial talk in social situations and boring lectures are two communication situations in which we may consciously choose to pseudolisten so that we seem polite even though we really aren't involved.

> **SOURYANA**   *I do a lot of pseudolistening in classes where the teachers are boring. I pretend I'm taking notes on my laptop, but really I'm checking email or visiting my favorite blogs. Every now and then, I look up and nod at the teacher so I look like I'm listening.*

pseudolistening Pretending to listen.

monopolizing Continually focusing communication on oneself instead of on the person who is talking.

Monopolizing

Monopolizing is hogging the stage by continually focusing communication on ourselves instead of the person talking. There are two primary forms of monopolizing. One is *conversational rerouting,* in which a person shifts the topic of talk to himself or herself. For example, if Harper tells Marla about a roommate problem,

MindTap®   Do you ever pseudolisten in classes while also using digital media?

Marla might reroute the conversation by saying, "I know what you mean. My roommate is a real jerk." Then Marla goes off on an extended description of her own roommate problems.

Another form of monopolizing is *diversionary interrupting*, which is interrupting in ways that disrupt the person speaking. Often, this occurs in combination with rerouting, so that a person interrupts and then directs the conversation to a new topic. In other cases, monopolizers fire questions that break up a speaker's concentration and impel the speaker to answer the questions before continuing. Both rerouting and diversionary interrupting are techniques for monopolizing a conversation. They are the antithesis of good listening.

It's important to realize that not all interruptions are monopolizing tactics. We also interrupt to show interest, voice support, and ask for elaboration. This type of interrupting usually takes the form of minimal communication such as "umm," "go on," and "really?" that shows interest in the person who is speaking.

Selective Listening

Selective listening is focusing on only particular parts of messages. One form of selective listening is focusing only on aspects of communication that interest us or correspond with our values. Students often become highly attentive when teachers say, "This is important for the test." In the workplace, we may become more attentive when communication addresses topics such as raises, layoffs, and other matters that may affect us directly.

A second form of selective listening occurs when we reject communication that bores us or makes us uncomfortable. For instance, we may not listen when others praise accomplishments of public officials we don't like. Being mindful allows you to curb the tendency to tune out messages you find boring or uncomfortable.

Defensive Listening

Defensive listening involves perceiving personal attacks, criticisms, or hostility in communication when no offense is intended. When we listen defensively, we read unkind motives into whatever others say. Thus, an innocent remark such as "Have you finished your report yet?" may be perceived as suspicion that you aren't doing your work. Although defensive listening is often limited to particular moments, some people perceive insults and criticism in most communication (a global, stable attribution).

Ambushing

Ambushing is listening carefully for the purpose of attacking. Unlike the other kinds of nonlistening we've discussed, ambushing involves very careful listening, but it isn't motivated by interest in another. Instead, ambushers listen intently to gather ammunition, which they then use to attack a speaker. Political candidates routinely do this as do trial attorneys. Each person listens carefully to the other for the sole purpose of undercutting the adversary. Ambushing is not advisable when openness and connection are wanted.

selective listening Focusing on only selected parts of communication. We listen selectively when we screen out parts of a message that don't interest us or with which we disagree and also when we rivet attention on parts of communication that do interest us or with which we agree.

defensive listening Perceiving personal attacks, criticisms, or hostility in communication when no offense is intended.

ambushing Listening carefully to attack a speaker.

ERIC *One of the brothers at my house is a real ambusher. He's a pre-law major, and he loves to debate and win arguments. No matter what somebody talks about, this guy just listens long enough to mount a counterattack. He doesn't care about understanding others, just about beating them. I've quit talking when he's around.*

Literal Listening

The final form of nonlistening is **literal listening**, which is listening only to the content level of meaning and ignoring the relationship level of meaning. Literal listeners get the information in a message, but they miss the feelings and relationship dimension.

In summary, nonlistening comes in many forms, including pseudolistening, ambushing speakers, monopolizing the stage, responding defensively, attending selectively, and listening literally. Being aware of forms of nonlistening enables you to exercise control over how you listen and thus how fully and mindfully you participate in communication with others.

Digital Media and Listening

We will discuss three ways that the ideas in this chapter are relevant to digital media. First, some online communication requires mindful listening. When you skype or have face time with a friend or family member, you need the same mindfulness and listening skills that you do to listen to someone face-to-face.

Second, attention to digital media can interfere with face-to-face listening. Leslie Perlow, who is on the faculty of Harvard's Business School, is the author of *Sleeping with Your Smartphone* (2013) in which she asserts that our devices threaten to overtake our lives. She recommends that professionals need blocks of time when they are entirely disconnected so that they can concentrate on listening and working together. Randi Zuckerberg (2013) also urges people to disconnect from devices and engage in real life. People need to get back to talking face to face, really looking at each other and getting energy from each other. Highly creative work environments depend on listening—truly listening (Brady, 2013; Korkki, 2013). M.I.T. Professor Sherry Turkle (2015), who is widely known and respected expert on technology, asserts that digital communication is often more shallow and fragmented than face-to-face communication. She urges people to spend less time communicating digitally and more having in person conversations. And Steve Jobs did not allow iPhones or tablets at the dinner table (Franzen, 2015).

Third, we need to exercise critical listening when communicating digitally. Anyone can post anything online, so accuracy is not guaranteed. When you read blogs and tweets, you should ask questions such as: What qualifies this person to have an informed stance on this issue? Does this person have any vested interest or any ties to others who have stakes in the issue? What is this person's track record of accuracy? Another way to keep your critical thinking sharp is to check other sources of information on the same issue to see if there is a consistent opinion. Consistency doesn't necessarily equal right, but it gives you one way to check what you read online.

It's also wise to be thoughtful about what you communicate on social media. As Randi Zuckerberg (2013) notes, the fact that you can post pictures and comments about every moment of your life doesn't mean you should.

Guidelines for Effective Listening

Effective listening is an active process that is tailored to specific purposes. Informational listening, critical listening, and relational listening entail different listening styles and behaviors. We'll discuss guidelines to improve effectiveness of each type of listening.

Informational and Critical Listening

Much of the time, we listen to gain information. We listen for information in classes, in professional meetings, when important news stories are reported, and when we need guidance on everything from medical treatment to driving directions. In all of these cases, the goal of **informational listening** is to gain and understand information.

Closely related to informational listening is **critical listening**, in which we listen to form opinions and to evaluate people and ideas. Critical listening requires us to analyze and evaluate information and the people who express it. We decide whether a speaker is credible and ethical by judging the thoroughness of a presentation, the accuracy of evidence, and the carefulness of reasoning. In Chapter 13, we discuss ways to evaluate evidence.

Be Mindful Both informational and critical listening begin with the decision to be mindful. Focus on gaining as much information as you can. Later, you may want to ask questions if material wasn't clear even though you listened mindfully.

Control Obstacles Minimize distractions when listening for information or critically listening. You might shut a window to block out traffic noises and empty your mind of preoccupations and prejudgments that can interfere with attending fully.

Ask Questions Asking speakers to clarify or elaborate on their messages allows you to understand information you didn't grasp at first and enhances insight into content that you did comprehend. Questions also compliment speakers because they indicate that you are interested and want to know more.

When listening critically, it's appropriate to ask probing questions of speakers: "What is the source of your statistics on the rate of unemployment?" "Have you talked with anyone who holds a point of view contrary to yours?" It's especially

informational listening
Listening to gain and understand information; tends to focus on the content level of meaning.

critical listening Attending to communication to analyze and evaluate the content of communication or the person speaking.

Listening to discriminate is vital when doctors communicate with patients.

Between a Rock and a Hard Place

Most of us have had the experience of being frustrated by a speaker who used specialized language that we couldn't understand. That experience is common for people in the United States for whom English is a second language.

According to communication scholar Wen-Shu Lee (1994, 2000), phrases that often defy understanding for non-native speakers include *miss the boat* (Where is the boat? I don't see a boat.), *kick the bucket* (Who's kicking what bucket?), *chew the fat* (Why would you want to chew fat?), *between a rock and a hard place* (Why is someone in such a position?), and *hit the road* (Why would anybody hit a road?).

Go to the online resources for this chapter to learn more about English slang and people for whom English is a second language.

important and appropriate for non-native speakers to ask questions if they don't understand language, particularly colloquial terms (Lee, 1994, 2000). Sensitive communicators avoid or explain idioms when non-native speakers are present. If speakers don't offer explanations, listeners should request them.

Use Aids to Recall   To understand and remember important information, we can apply the principles of perception we discussed in Chapter 2. For instance, we tend to notice and recall stimuli that are repeated. To use this principle to increase recall, repeat important ideas to yourself immediately after hearing them.

Another way to increase retention is to use mnemonic (pronounced "nemonic," rhymes with *demonic*) devices, which are memory aids that create patterns for what you've heard. You probably already do this in studying. For instance, KIM is a mnemonic to remember that Kim (K) from Iowa (I) is going into medicine (M).

Organize Information   Organizing information increases retention. For example, suppose a friend tells you he is confused about long-range goals, doesn't know what he can do with a math major, wants to locate in the Midwest, wonders whether graduate school is necessary, likes small towns, needs some internships to try out different options, and wants a family eventually. You could regroup this stream of concerns into two categories: academic information (careers for math majors, graduate school, internship opportunities) and lifestyle preferences (Midwest, small town, family). Remembering those two categories allows you to retain the essence of your friend's concerns, even if you forget many of the specifics.

Relational Listening

In some listening situations, we're as concerned or even more concerned with the relational level of meaning than the content level. We engage in **relational listening** when we listen to a friend's worries, counsel a coworker, or talk with a parent about health concerns. Whenever supporting a person and maintaining a relationship are key goals, we should engage in relational listening, which requires active involvement with the other person.

SHARPEN YOUR SKILL

At the end of this chapter, refer to the Sharpen Your Skill feature, Improving Recall, to apply concepts from Chapter 4.

relational listening Listening to support another person or to understand another person's feelings and perceptions; focuses on the relational level of meaning as much as on the content level of meaning.

Be Mindful   The first requirement for effective relational listening is to be mindful. You'll recall that this was also the first step in informational and critical listening. When we're interested in relational meanings, however, a different kind of mindfulness is needed. Instead of focusing our minds on information, we need to concentrate on understanding feelings. Thus, mindful relational listening calls on us to pay attention to subtle clues to feelings and perceptions.

Suspend Judgment   When listening to provide support, it's important to avoid highly judgmental responses. When we judge what another says, we move away from that person and his or her feelings. To curb evaluative tendencies, ask whether you really need to pass judgment in the present moment.

Only if someone asks for our judgment should we offer it when we are listening to support. Even if our opinion is sought, we should express it in a way that doesn't devalue others. Sometimes people excuse strongly judgmental comments by saying, "You asked me to be honest" or "I mean this as constructive criticism." Too often, however, the judgments are not constructive and are harsher than candor requires.

> JOSÉ   *My best friend makes it so easy for me to tell whatever is on my mind. She never puts me down or makes me feel stupid or weird. Sometimes I ask her what she thinks, and she has this way of telling me without making me feel wrong if I think differently. What it boils down to is respect. She respects me and herself, so she doesn't have to prove anything by acting better than me.*

Understand the Other Person's Perspective   One of the most important principles for effective relational listening is to grasp the other person's perspective. This means we have to step outside of our own point of view, at least long enough to understand how another person sees things. Active listening conveys effort to understand, which, in turn increases the other person's satisfaction with interaction (Weger, Minei, & Robinson, 2014).

Paraphrasing is an active listening technique to clarify another's meaning or needs by reflecting our interpretations of his or her communication back to him or her. For example, a friend might confide, "I'm really scared my kid brother is messing around with drugs." We could paraphrase this way: "It sounds as if you think your brother may be experimenting with drugs." This paraphrase allows us to clarify whether the friend has any evidence of the brother's drug involvement. **Minimal encouragers** are responses that express interest in hearing more and invite another person to elaborate. They indicate that we are listening, following, and interested. Examples of minimal encouragers are "Tell me more," "Really?" "Go on," and "Then what happened?" We can also use nonverbal minimal encouragers, such as a raised eyebrow to show we're involved, a nod to indicate we understand, or widened eyes to indicate we're fascinated. Keep in mind that these are *minimal* encouragers intended to prompt, rather than interfere with, the flow of another's talk.

To enhance understanding of what another feels or wants from us we can ask questions. For instance, we might ask, "How do you feel about that?" or "Do you want to talk about how to handle the situation, or do you just want to air the issues?" Asking directly signals that we really want to help and allows others to tell us how we can best do that.

paraphrasing A method of clarifying others' meaning by restating their communication.

minimal encouragers Communication that, by expressing interest in hearing more, gently invites another person to elaborate.

An Addition to Legal Training   MindTap®

What does it take to be an effective attorney? According to Neil Hamilton (2011–2012), listening is critical. Hamilton reports that attorneys who listen actively to clients are more effective for several reasons. First, the attorneys get more information. Second, active listening encourages clients to give fuller accounts of events and to provide more details. Third, actively listening enhances attorney–client relationships by building trust and respect. Hamilton encourages law schools to include listening in their curricula. Specifically, he advocates reflecting and paraphrasing as key skills.

Express Support   Central to relational listening is communicating support. This doesn't necessarily require you to agree with another's perspective or ideas, but you should communicate support for the person. The following conversation between a father and son illustrates how we can support a person even if we don't agree another.

> SON: Dad, I'm changing my major from business to drama.
> FATHER: Oh.
> SON: Yeah, I've wanted to do it for some time, but I kept holding back because acting isn't as safe as accounting.
> FATHER: That's true.
> SON: But I've decided to do it anyway.
> FATHER: Frankly, that worries me. Starving actors are a dime a dozen. You wouldn't have any economic security.
> SON: I know acting isn't as secure as business, but it's what I really want to do.
> FATHER: Why does acting matter so much to you.
> SON: It's the most creative, totally fulfilling thing I've ever done. Business doesn't do that for me. I feel like I have to give this a try, or I'll always wonder if I could have made it.
> FATHER: Couldn't you finish your business degree and get a job and act on the side?
> SON: No. I've got to give acting a full shot—give it everything I have, to see if I can make it.
> FATHER: Well, I still have reservations, but I guess I can understand having to try something that matters this much to you. I'm just concerned that you'll lose years of your life to something that doesn't work out.
> SON: Well, I'm kinda concerned about that too, but I'm more worried about wasting years of my life in a career that doesn't turn me on.
> FATHER: I wouldn't make the choice you're making, but I respect your decision and your guts for taking a big gamble.

This dialogue illustrates several principles of effective relational listening. First, notice that the father's first two comments are minimal encouragers that invite his son to elaborate thoughts and feelings. The father also encourages his son to explain how he feels. Later, the father suggests a compromise solution.

Daniel Bosler/Stone/Getty Images

Mindful listening is one of the greatest gifts we can give to another.

When his son rejects that, the father respects the son's position. Importantly, the father makes his own position clear, but he separates his personal stance from his respect for his son's right to make his own choices. Sometimes it's difficult to listen openly and nonjudgmentally, particularly if we don't agree with the person speaking, as in the example. However, if your goal is to support another person, then sensitive, responsive involvement without evaluation is critical.

Other Purposes of Listening

Listening for information to evaluate critically and listening to support others are two major listening purposes. In addition, we will briefly discuss other listening goals.

Listening for Pleasure   Sometimes we listen for pleasure, as when we attend concerts or enjoy conversation with witty, funny people. When we listen for pleasure, we don't need to concentrate on organizing and remembering as much as when we listen for information, although retention is important if you want to be able to tell a joke to someone else later. Yet listening for pleasure does require mindfulness, hearing, and interpretation.

Listening to Discriminate   In some situations, we listen to make fine discriminations in sounds to draw valid conclusions and act appropriately in response. For example, doctors and nurses listen to discriminate when they use stethoscopes to diagnose heart functioning or lung congestion. Parents listen to discriminate among a baby's cries for attention, food, or a diaper change. Skilled mechanics can distinguish between engine sounds that most people cannot detect.

Chapter Summary

According to Zeno of Citium, an ancient philosopher, "We have been given two ears but a single mouth, in order that we may listen more and talk less." Thousands of years later, we can still learn from his comment. Listening is a major and vital part of communication, yet too often we don't consider it as important as talking. In this chapter, we've explored the complex and demanding process of listening.

We began by distinguishing between hearing—physically receiving messages—and listening. The former is a straightforward physiological process that doesn't take effort on our part. Listening, in contrast, is a complicated and active process involving being mindful, hearing, selecting and organizing, interpreting, responding, and remembering. Listening well takes commitment and skill.

To understand what interferes with effective listening, we discussed obstacles in situations and messages and obstacles in us. Listening is hindered by message overload, complexity of material, and external noise in communication contexts. In addition, listening can be hampered by our preoccupations and prejudgments, lack of effort, and failure to recognize differences in listening styles. These obstacles to listening give rise to various types of nonlistening, including pseudolistening, monopolizing, selective listening, defensive listening, ambushing, and literal listening. Each of these forms of nonlistening signals that we aren't fully present in interaction.

We identified ways that principles of effectively listening pertain to digital communication. To conclude the chapter, we identified guidelines for different listening goals. Informational listening and critical listening require us to adopt a mindful attitude and to think critically, organize and evaluate information, clarify understanding by asking questions, and develop aids to retention of complex material. Relational listening also requires mindfulness, but it calls for other, distinct listening skills. Suspending judgment, paraphrasing, giving minimal encouragers, and expressing support enhance the effectiveness of relational listening.

MindTap

Experiencing Communication in Our Lives

CASE STUDY: Family Hour

Apply what you've learned in this chapter by analyzing the following case study, using the accompanying questions as a guide. These questions and a video of the case study are also available online with your MindTap Speech for *Communication in Our Lives*.

Over spring break, 20-year-old Josh visits his father. He wants to convince his family to support him in joining a fraternity that has given him a bid. On his second day home, after dinner Josh decides to broach the topic. His dad is watching the evening news on television when Josh walks into the living room. Josh sits down and opens the conversation.

JOSH: Well, something pretty interesting has happened at school this semester.

DAD: I'll bet you found a girlfriend, right? I was about your age when your mother and I started dating, and that was the best part of college. I still remember how she looked on our first date. She was young, and then she was very slender and pretty. I saw her and thought she was the loveliest thing I'd ever seen. Before long, we were a regular item. Yep, it was about when I was 20, like you are now.

JOSH: Well, I haven't found a girlfriend, but I did get a bid from Sigma Chi.

DAD: Sigma Chi. What is that—a fraternity?

JOSH: Yeah, it's probably the coolest fraternity on campus. I attended some rush parties this semester—mainly out of curiosity, just to see what they were like.

DAD: Why'd you do that? Before you ever went to college, I told you to steer clear of fraternities. They cost a lot of money, and they distract you from your studies.

JOSH: Well, I know you told me to steer clear of fraternities, but I did check a few out. I'd be willing to take a job to help pay the membership fee and monthly dues. Besides, it's not that much more expensive when you figure I'd be eating at the house, and . . .

DAD: Do you realize how much it costs just for you to go to that school? I'm paying $14,000 a year! When I went to school, I had to go to state college because my parents couldn't afford to send me to the school of my choice. You have no idea how lucky you are to be going to the school you wanted to go to and have me footing all the bills.

JOSH: But we could work it out so that a fraternity wouldn't cost you anything. Like I said, I . . .

DAD: If you want to take a job, fine. I could use some help paying your tuition and fees. But you're not taking a job just so you can belong to a party house.

JOSH: I thought they were just party houses too, until I attended rush. Now, I went to several houses that were that way, but Sigma Chi isn't. I really liked the brothers at Sigma Chi. They're interesting and friendly and fun, so I was thrilled when . . .

DAD: I don't want to hear about it. You're not joining a fraternity. I told you what happened when I was in college. I joined one, and pretty soon my Dean's List grades dropped to Cs and Ds. When you live in a fraternity house, you can't study like you can in your dorm room or the library. I should know. I tried it and found out the hard way. There's no need for you to repeat my mistake.

JOSH: But, Dad, I'm not you. Joining a fraternity wouldn't necessarily mean that my grades . . .

DAD: What do you mean, you're not me? You think I wasn't a good student before I joined the fraternity? You think you're so smart you can party all the time and still make good grades? Let me tell you something, I thought that too, and, boy, was I ever wrong! As soon as I joined the house, it was party time all the time. There was always music blaring and girls in the house and poker games—anything but studying. I wasn't stupid. It's just not an atmosphere that encourages academic work.

JOSH: I'd like to give it a try. I really like these guys, and I think I can handle being in Sigma Chi and still . . .

DAD: Well, you think wrong!

QUESTIONS FOR ANALYSIS AND DISCUSSION

1. What forms of ineffective listening are evident in this dialogue?

2. If you could advise Josh's father on listening effectively, what would you tell him to do differently?

3. Would you offer any advice to Josh on how he could listen to his father more effectively?

MindTap

Use flashcards to learn key concepts and take a quiz to test your knowledge.

Key Concepts

ambushing	listening	paraphrasing
critical listening	literal listening	pseudolistening
defensive listening	mindfulness	relational listening
hearing	minimal encouragers	selective listening
informational listening	monopolizing	

Sharpen Your Skill

1. Learn from the Pros

One way to improve your listening skills is to observe people who are experts at effective listening. Watch a television program that features interviews—Sunday morning news shows, for example. Select one interview to observe, and answer the following questions about it:

- How does the interviewer phrase questions to encourage the interviewee to talk? Are questions open or closed, biased or unbiased?
- How is the interviewer seated in relation to the interviewee—how close, at what angle?
- Does the interviewer paraphrase the interviewee's responses?
- Does the interviewer make minimal responses?
- How, if at all, does the interviewer show that he or she understands and respects the interviewee's perspective?
- How, if at all, does the interviewer demonstrate attentiveness?

2. Improving Recall

Apply the principles we've discussed to enhance memory.

- The next time you meet someone, repeat his or her name to yourself three times after you are introduced. After your next class, take 15 minutes to review your notes in a quiet place. Read them aloud so that you hear as well as see the main ideas.
- Invent mnemonics to create patterns that help you remember basic information in a message.

- Organize ideas into categories. To remember the main ideas of this chapter, you might use major subheadings to form categories: listening process, obstacles to listening, and listening goals. The mnemonic LOG (i.e., listening, obstacles, goals) could help you remember those topics.

For Further Reflection and Discussion

1. Select one type of nonlistening in which you engage, and work to minimize its occurrence for the next three days.

2. How do you know whether someone is really listening to you when you are texting or talking on a cell? What signals mindful listening in these settings?

3. What different ethical responsibilities accompany listening for information and listening relationally?

4. Who is your prototype of an excellent listener? Describe what the person does that makes him or her effective. Do the person's listening behaviors fit with the guidelines offered in this chapter?

5. Dave Isay set out to make an oral history of the United States by listening to the stories of everyday people—not politicians, celebrities, or CEOs, but regular people. By January of 2009, StoryCorps had recorded more than 40,000 stories of ordinary Americans—what they value and how they understand life. Isay gathered a number of these stories into a book, which he titled *Listening as an Act of Love* (2008).

6. If you want to work on your listening skills, you might be interested in Madelyn Burley-Allen's book *Listening: The Forgotten Skill* (1995). She provides a self-teaching guide for improving listening effectiveness.

7. Go to the book's online resources for this chapter for a website that offers guidelines for listening better.

Beyond the Classroom

Let's take the material in this chapter beyond the classroom by thinking about how what you've learned about listening might apply to the workplace, ethical choices, and engagement with the broader world.

1. **Workplace.** The chapter identified six forms of nonlistening. To what extent are any of these types of nonlistening evident in your current workplace or to what extent were they present in a former workplace? Reflect on particular instances of nonlistening in the workplace: Can you identify any causes or conditions that were common to them? Do you recognize any costs of the nonlistening in terms of productivity, relations among workers, and so forth? (You could apply this same analysis to a classroom or other campus location.)

2. **Ethics.** At the end of Chapter 1, I invited you to read NCA's Credo for Ethical Communication by going to the online resources for that chapter. Reread that now by going to the online resources for this chapter. Using that credo as a guideline, develop a Credo for Ethical Listening that identifies both what listeners must do and what they cannot do if they wish to listen ethically.

3. **Engagement.** American Public Media developed a radio program called "The Story," which presents interviews with people who have interesting stories to tell about their lives. Most of the people interviewed are not celebrities; they aren't famous; and they aren't particularly heroic. In other words, many of them are regular people, but the interviewer uses excellent listening skills to bring the interviewees out and make their stories sing. Go to the online resources for this chapter to find the home page for "The Story." Listen to one podcast of a story. As you listen, pay particular attention to the interviewer: How does he demonstrate engagement with the interviewee? How does he encourage the interviewee to expand on points and to move along with the story?

Syda Productions/Shutterstock.com

5

> A different
> language is a
> different vision
> of life.
>
> **Federico Fellini**

The Verbal Dimension of Communication

LEARNING OBJECTIVES

After studying the topics in this chapter, you should be able to:

1. Explain why ambiguous or abstract words can lead to misunderstandings.

2. Identify some of the communication rules you follow when interacting with friends versus strangers.

3. Provide an example of how words can define a phenomenon.

4. Provide an example of how words can evaluate a phenomenon.

5. Become aware of specialized language used in social media.

6. Apply chapter guidelines to improve your verbal communication.

To what extent do you think language influences your perceptions of reality?

MindTap®

Review the chapter's learning objectives and **start** with a quick warm-up activity.

MindTap®

Read, highlight, and
take notes online.

Perhaps you are familiar with the story of Helen Keller. As an infant, she contracted an illness that left her deaf and blind. Trapped in her dark, silent world, Helen reacted to whatever stimuli were in her immediate environment but did not show any ability to self-reflect, grasp meanings, or communicate with others. Later in life, she achieved remarkable things: She graduated with honors from Radcliffe, authored nearly a dozen books, met 12 U.S. presidents, learned to read and write four languages other than English, and lectured throughout the United States, Europe, and Asia.

What allowed Helen to move from reacting only to immediate stimuli to being an engaging, reflective person who connected with a wide range of people? Language. Learning to use language gave Helen access to the human world of meaning. When Helen was 7, Annie Sullivan became her teacher. Helen was smart, so Annie was able to teach her the manual alphabet quickly. In just a few weeks with Annie, Helen was able to use her hands to spell words, but she didn't understand what they meant. She didn't grasp that the actions of her or Annie's fingers were communicating meaning.

That changed in one electric moment. While one of Helen's hands was under the spout of a water pump, Annie spelled W-A-T-E-R into her other hand. Suddenly Helen got it; she connected the actions of Annie's fingers to the cool liquid running over her hand. Annie and Helen had shared meaning. Once Helen understood how to communicate, she was unstoppable and went on to accomplish amazing things in her life.

Library of Congress Prints and Photographs Division [LC-USZ62-69879]

Learning to use language opened the human world of meaning for Helen Keller.

In this chapter, we take a close look at language. We begin by defining symbols, which are the basis of language. Second, we explore principles of verbal communication. Next, we consider what language allows us to do. Fourth, we examine connections between language and digital media. The final section of the chapter focuses on guidelines for effective use of language.

Features of Symbols

Language consists of symbols. A **symbol** is a representation of a person, event, or other phenomenon. For instance, the word *house* is a symbol that stands for a type of building. *Tweet* and *blog* are words we have coined to represent ways we use social media to communicate. The key to understanding symbols is to realize that they are arbitrary, ambiguous, and abstract ways of representing things.

Symbols Are Arbitrary

Symbols are **arbitrary**, which means they are not intrinsically connected to what they represent. For instance, the word *book* has no necessary or natural connection to what you are reading now. We could substitute a different word, as long as we agreed it would stand for what we now call a book. Certain words seem right because as a society we agree to use them in particular ways, but they have no natural correspondence to their referents.

Because language is arbitrary, we can create private communication codes. For example, most professions rely on buzzwords that are

Customer-Savvy Language for Fast Food Executives

MindTap

People who are being trained to lead fast-food companies have a new focus of study: The language of young people who make up their primary customer base. Once a week, Taco Bell employees in their twenties email the "Millennial Word of the Week," which is featured at the company's headquarters (Choi, 2015). The email explains what the word or phrase means and gives examples of how to use it when interacting with young customers. Examples:

Lit:	an adjective used to describe a situation, person or place as awesome
Throwing shade:	publicly disrespecting a person
On fleek:	relevant; on point
Dat. . . doe:	that . . . though; something that is really awesome.

not understood by outsiders. Two primary tasks of military intelligence are to invent secret codes and to break the secret codes of others. Go to the book's online resources for this chapter to learn about code talkers in the military during World War II.

Because language is arbitrary, we can create new words and terms. Today, many people work out of *virtual offices*, a term nobody had heard 20 years ago. The word *friend* was a noun until people on social network websites such as Facebook began using it as a verb—one person *friends* another on the website.

Symbols Are Ambiguous

Symbols are also **ambiguous,** which means their meanings aren't fixed in an absolute way. The meanings of words vary based on the values and experiences of those who use them. *Government regulation* may mean positive assistance to citizens who are suffering from pollutants emitted by a chemical company. To owners of the chemical company, however, *government regulation* may mean being forced to adopt costly measures to reduce pollution. Although the words are the same, their meanings vary according to individuals' interests and experiences.

Although words don't mean exactly the same thing to everyone, many symbols have an agreed-on range of meanings within a culture. Thus, we all understand that *dog* means a four-footed creature, but each of us also has personal meanings for the word based on dogs we have known and our experiences with them. We've all experienced dynamic speakers, yet we may differ in our notions of what concrete behaviors would lead us to label a speaker *dynamic* (remember the abstraction ladder we discussed in Chapter 2).

The ambiguity of symbols explains why misunderstandings occur. Your supervisor tells you it's important to be "a team player," which you assume means you should cooperate with coworkers. However, your supervisor may mean that you are expected to initiate and participate in teams on the job. To minimize the likelihood of misunderstanding, we can offer clear, concrete translations of ambiguous words.

Symbols Are Abstract

Finally, symbols are **abstract,** which means not concrete or tangible. They stand for ideas, people, events, objects, feelings, and so forth, but they are not the things

symbol An arbitrary, ambiguous, and abstract representation of a phenomenon. Symbols are the basis of language, much nonverbal behavior, and human thought.

arbitrary Random; not determined by necessity. Symbols are arbitrary because there is no particular reason for any one symbol to stand for a certain referent.

ambiguous Subject to more than one interpretation. Symbols are ambiguous because their meanings vary from person to person and context to context.

abstract Removed from concrete reality. Symbols are abstract because they are inferences and generalizations derived from a total reality.

Lost in Translation

Language doesn't always translate well across cultures. Consider these examples of English terms that turned out to mean something very different in other cultures (Leaper, 1999).

Don't say, "I'm a Pepper" in the United Kingdom. The manufacturer of the soft drink Dr. Pepper discovered that this didn't work because *pepper* is British slang for "prostitute" (Leaper, 1999).

When General Motors exported its Chevrolet Nova to South America, there were problems. In Spanish, *no va* means "does not go"—not a great advertisement for a car! (Leaper, 1999).

To avoid such cross-cultural blunders, many U.S. companies now hire consultants to develop names that will work for their products in other countries. In China, BMW is *Precious Horse*; Reebok shoes are *Quick Steps*; Coca-Cola is *Tasty Fun*; Marriott is *Wealthy Elites*; and Heineken is *Happiness Power* (Wines, 2011).

they represent. In Chapter 2, we discussed the abstraction ladder, whereby we move farther and farther away from concrete reality. The symbols we use vary in abstractness. *Managerial potential* is an abstract term. *Presentational skills* is less abstract. Even more concrete expressions are *experience in speaking to large groups and hosting webinars.*

ADIVA   *My resident assistant told us we must observe "quiet hours" from 7 to 10 each night so that people can study. But everyone on my hall plays music and talks during quiet hours. My adviser told me I needed to take courses in social diversity, so I took a class in oral traditions of Asian cultures. Then my adviser told me that is a non-Western civilization course, not one in social diversity.*

Review It!

Features of Symbols:

- Arbitrary
- Ambiguous
- Abstract

Because symbols are arbitrary, ambiguous, and abstract, they allow us to share complex ideas and feelings with others. At the same time, symbols have the potential to create misunderstandings. When we understand that symbols are ambiguous, arbitrary, and abstract, we can guard against their potential to hinder communication.

Principles of Verbal Communication

Three principles clarify how we use verbal communication and how it affects us.

Interpretation Creates Meaning

Because symbols are arbitrary, ambiguous, and abstract, their meanings aren't self-evident or absolute. Instead, we have to interpret the meaning of symbols.

If a work associate says, "Let's go to dinner after work," the comment could be an invitation to explore transforming the work relationship into a friendship or it might indicate that the person issuing the invitation is interested in a romantic relationship. Effective communicators are alert to possible misunderstandings, and they check perceptions with others to see whether meanings match.

Communication Is Rule Guided

Verbal communication is patterned by unspoken but broadly understood rules (Argyle & Henderson, 1984; Shimanoff, 1980). **Communication rules** are shared understandings of what communication means and what kinds of communication are and are not appropriate in various situations. For the most part, rules aren't explicitly taught. In the course of interacting with our families and others, we unconsciously absorb rules that guide how we communicate and how we interpret others' communication.

Two kinds of rules guide communication (Cronen, Pearce, & Snavely, 1979; Pearce, Cronen, & Conklin, 1979). **Regulative rules** specify when, how, where, and with whom to talk about certain things. For instance, we follow regulative rules for turn taking in conversation. In formal contexts, we usually know not to interrupt when someone else is speaking, but in more informal settings, interruptions may be appropriate. Talking during formal speeches is appropriate in some contexts, as in traditional black churches and public meetings. Regulative rules also define when, where, and with whom it's appropriate or inappropriate to communicate in particular ways. It is generally not appropriate to tell somber stories at celebratory events and, conversely, it is generally inappropriate to laugh and tell jokes at funerals (but it may be okay at wakes). Some couples have the rule that it's okay to kiss in private but not in public. On the job, there are often unwritten regulative rules that executives may interrupt subordinates but that subordinates may not interrupt executives.

JUDE   *I can talk to Sam about politics all night long. Usually, we agree, but we also disagree on some issues and we enjoy arguing. I can't talk with Travis about politics. He totally disagrees with most of what I believe and he shuts down because he hates conflict. On the other hand, I can get into really deep discussions with Travis about religious stuff, and Sam has no interest in that.*

Constitutive rules tell us how to count certain kinds of communication. We learn that paying attention counts as showing respect, hugging counts as affection, and raising the middle finger counts as an insult. Social interactions tend to follow rules that are widely shared in a specific society.

Interaction between intimates also follows rules, but these may not be shared by the culture as a whole. Intimate partners negotiate private rules to guide how they communicate and what certain things mean. Couples craft personal rules that specify how to argue, express love, make decisions, and show support.

We may not realize that rules exist until one is broken and we realize that we had an expectation. Becoming aware of communication rules empowers you to consciously create ones that promote healthy interaction and relationships.

communication rules Shared understandings of what communication means and what behaviors are appropriate in various situations.

regulative rules Communication rules that regulate interaction by specifying when, how, where, and with whom to talk about certain things.

constitutive rules Communication rules that define what communication means by specifying how certain communicative acts are to be counted.

Monkey Business Images/Shutterstock.com

MindTap® What regulative and constitutive rules govern mealtime conversation in your family?

Punctuation Affects Meaning

In writing, we use periods to define where ideas stop and start. Similarly, in communication, **punctuation** is the mental mark of the beginnings and endings of particular interactions (Watzlawick, Beavin, & Jackson, 1967). For example, when a teacher steps to the front of a classroom, we perceive that class is beginning. When the CEO sits down at a conference table, we perceive the beginning of a meeting. When a speaker says, "Thank you for your attention" and folds notes, we regard that as the end of the formal speech.

When we don't agree on punctuation, problems may arise. A common instance of conflicting punctuation is the demand–withdraw pattern illustrated in Figure 5.1 (Bergner & Bergner, 1990; Caughlin & Vangelisti, 2000; Wegner, 2005).

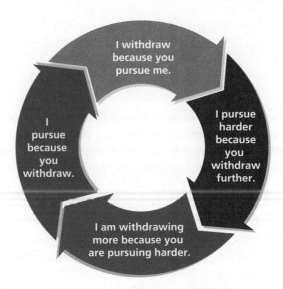

I withdraw because you pursue me.

I pursue harder because you withdraw further.

I am withdrawing more because you are pursuing harder.

I pursue because you withdraw.

FIGURE 5.1
The Demand–Withdraw Pattern

This occurs when one person tries to express closeness and the other strives to maintain autonomy by avoiding interaction. The more one partner pushes for closeness, the more the other partner withdraws. Each partner punctuates the beginning of the interaction with the other's behavior. Thus, the demander thinks, "I pursue because you withdraw," and the withdrawer thinks, "I withdraw because you pursue."

Effective communicators realize that people don't always punctuate the same way. When they punctuate differently, they ascribe different meanings interaction. To break out of destructive cycles such as demand–withdraw, partners need to discuss how each of them is punctuating the experience. This reminds us of the importance of perspective taking. Steven's comment illustrates the demand–withdraw pattern and a lack of perspective taking between him and his parents.

> **STEVEN**   *My parents say I am irresponsible if I don't tell them about something I do. So then they probe me and call more often to check up on me. I hate that kind of intrusion, so I don't return their calls and I sidestep questions. That makes them call more and ask more questions. That makes me clam up more. And we just keep going in circles.*

Symbolic Abilities

Because we use symbols, we live in a world of ideas and meanings. Instead of just reacting to others and our environments, we think about them and sometimes transform them. In much the same way, we don't simply accept ourselves as we are but continuously work to change and grow. Philosophers of language have identified five ways symbolic capacities affect our lives (Cassirer, 1944; Langer, 1953, 1979). As we discuss each, we'll consider how to realize the constructive power of symbols and minimize the problems they can generate.

Symbols Define

We use symbols to define experiences, people, relationships, feelings, and thoughts. As we saw in Chapter 2, the definitions we give to phenomena shape what they mean to us. When we label people, we focus attention on particular aspects of them, and we necessarily obscure other aspects of who they are. We might define a person as an environmentalist, a teacher, a gourmet cook, and a Republican. Each way of classifying the person directs our attention to certain, and not other, aspects of identity. We might discuss wilderness legislation with the environmentalist, talk about testing with the teacher, swap recipes with the cook, and discuss politics or not, depending on our own political stance, with the Republican. We tend to interact with people according to how we define and classify them.

Totalizing is using a single label to represent the totality of a person. We fixate on one symbol to define someone and fail to recognize many other aspects of who he or she is. Totalizing also occurs when we dismiss people by saying, "He's a liberal," "She's old," "She's preppy," or "He's a jock." When we totalize others, we negate most of who they are by spotlighting a single aspect of their identity.

totalizing Responding to people as if one aspect of them were the sum total of who they are.

NANYA   *I'm Indian, and that's all a lot of people here see in me. They see that my skin is dark and I wear a sari, and they put me in the category "foreigner" or, if they are observant, "Indian." They mark me off as different, foreign, not like them, and they can't see anything else about me. How would they feel if I categorized them as "Americans" and didn't see their individual qualities?*

Symbols influence how we think and feel about experiences and people. In one study, I and my colleagues asked romantic couples how they defined differences between them (Wood, Dendy, Dordek, Germany, & Varallo, 1994). We found that some people define differences as positive forces that energize a relationship. Others define differences as problems or barriers to closeness. There was a direct connection between how partners defined differences and how they dealt with them. Partners who labeled differences as constructive, approached disagreements with curiosity and a belief that they would grow by discussing differences. On the other hand, partners who labeled differences as problems tended to deny differences or avoid talking about them.

How we think about relationships directly affects what happens in them. People who dwell on negative thoughts about relationships heighten awareness of relationship flaws and diminish perceptions of strengths. Conversely, partners who focus on good facets of their relationships are more conscious of positive qualities of partners and relationships and less aware of imperfections (Seligman, 2002).

Wedding bands symbolize commitment.

Stewart Cohen/Blend Images/Getty Images

ABBY *About 3 years ago, my husband and I were seriously considering divorce. We decided to try marital counseling first, and that saved our marriage. The counselor helped us see that we noticed problems, aggravations, and faults in each other and didn't see all of the good qualities in each other and our relationship. Now we have a "warts-and-all" philosophy, which means we accept each other, warts and all. Changing how we think about our marriage really has changed what it is for us.*

As Abby's commentary indicates, our definitions of relationships can create self-fulfilling prophecies. Once we select a label for relationships or other phenomena, we tend to see what our label names and to overlook what it doesn't. This suggests an ethical principle for using and interpreting language: We should consider what the language that we and others use includes and excludes.

Symbols Evaluate

Symbols are not neutral. They are laden with values. We tend to describe people we like with language that accents their good qualities and downplays their flaws. The reverse is generally true of descriptions of people we don't like. My friend is *casual*; someone I don't like is *sloppy*. Restaurants use language that is designed to heighten the attractiveness of menu items. "Tender lobster accented with drawn butter" sounds more appetizing than "crustacean murdered by being boiled alive and then drenched in saturated fat."

In recent years, we have become more sensitive to different ways of naming ethnic groups. The term *African American* emphasizes cultural heritage, whereas *black* focuses on skin color. The word *Hispanic* emphasizes the Spanish language spoken in the home countries, whereas *Latino* and *Latina* highlight the geographic origin of Latin American men and women, respectively. People with roots in Spanish-speaking Caribbean countries tend to refer to themselves as *Latinos* and *Latinas* or to use more specific labels such as *Cubano*, *Peruvian*, and *Mexican* (Rodriguez, 2003). An ethical guideline for using language is to try to learn and respect others' preferences for describing their identities.

Loaded language consists of words that strongly slant perceptions and thus meanings. For example, conservative television and radio commentators sometimes disparage people with liberal social and political values as *knee-jerk liberals*. At the same time, liberal commentators sometimes describe people with conservative social and political values as *country club fat cats*. Loaded language also fosters negative views of older citizens. Terms such as *geezer* and *old fogey* incline us to regard older people with contempt or pity. Alternatives such as *senior citizen* and *elderly person* are more respectful. In 2014, the U.S. Patent and Trademark Office canceled the Washington Redskins' trademark on the name *redskins* because the term is perceived as disrespecting Native Americans (A Victory for Tolerance, 2014).

Symbols Organize Perceptions

We use symbols to organize our perceptions. As we saw in Chapter 2, we rely on cognitive schemata to classify and evaluate experiences. How we organize experiences affects what they mean to us. For example, your prototype of a good friend affects how you judge particular friends. When we place someone in the category of friend,

loaded language An extreme form of evaluative language that relies on words that strongly slant perceptions and hence meanings.

Communication Highlight

Language Shapes Our Realities

MindTap°

Language shapes our perceptions in ways that reflect a culture's values and experiences (Whorf, 1956). In one part of Australia, people speak Guugu Timithirr, a language that does not include the terms *right* and *left*. In Guugu Timithirr, special locations are described in relation to a compass. Thus, a person speaking this language might ask to have the pepper passed north (Monastersky, 2002). People recall colors more clearly if their language provides distinct terms, so English speakers do not remember shades of blue (light blue, dark blue) as precisely as Russian speakers who have different words for light blue (*goluboy*) and dark blue (*sinly*) (Gentner & Boroditsky, 2009).

SHARPEN YOUR SKILL

At the end of this chapter, refer to the Sharpen Your Skill feature, Assessing Your Stereotypes, to apply concepts from Chapter 5.

---

the category influences how we interpret that person's communication. An insult is likely to be viewed as teasing if made by someone we define as a friend but a call to battle if made by someone we classify as an enemy. The words don't change, but their meaning varies, depending on how we classify the person uttering them.

Because symbols organize thought, they allow us to think about abstract concepts such as professionalism, democracy, morality, and community. Thinking abstractly relieves us of having to consider every specific object and experience individually.

Our capacity to abstract can also distort thinking. A primary way this occurs is in stereotyping—thinking in broad generalizations about a whole class of people or experiences. Examples of stereotypes are "Sorority women are yuppies," "Ph.D.s are smart," and "Democrats tax and spend." Notice that stereotypes can be positive or negative.

REGGIE   *People say racism no longer exists, but I know it does. If I'm out walking at night, white girls cross the street because they think I'll mug them. They don't cross the street if they see a white guy. One of the guys on my hall asked me whether I thought the Bridge Program was helpful. I didn't go through it because I had a good high school record. Does he think every black needs special help?*

Stereotypes can discourage us from recognizing important differences among the phenomena we lump together. Thus, we have an ethical responsibility to stay alert to differences among the things and people that we place in a single category.

Symbols Allow Hypothetical Thought

Who was your best friend when you were 5 years old? What would you do if you won the lottery? To answer these questions, you must think hypothetically, which means thinking about experiences and ideas that are not part of your concrete, present situation. Because we can think hypothetically, we can plan, dream, remember, fantasize, set goals, and weigh alternative courses of action.

Hypothetical thought is possible because we use symbols. When we symbolize, we name ideas so that we can hold them in our minds and reflect on them.

---

hypothetical thought
Cognitive awareness of experiences and ideas that are not part of the concrete, present situation.

Communication Highlight

Fat Talk

"I'm so fat." "I hate my hips." "Why can't I get my stomach flat?" Sound familiar? Most women, including ones who are of normal weight or underweight, engage in negative talk about their bodies (Engeln, 2015). But is fat talk harmless venting or is it harmful?

Research suggests it isn't entirely benign. Women who engage in fat talk are more likely to feel ashamed of their bodies or parts of them and to develop eating disorders. The researchers also noted that engaging in fat talk doesn't lead to making healthier choices related to diet and exercise (Arroyo & Harwood, 2012; Engeln, 2015). Maybe it's time to change the conversation.

We can contemplate things that currently have no real existence. For example, you've invested many hours in studying because you imagine having a college degree. The degree is not real now, nor is the self that you will become once you have the degree. Yet the idea is sufficiently real to motivate you to work hard for many years.

Close relationships rely on ideas of history and future. One of the strongest glues for intimacy is a history of shared experiences (Bruess & Hoefs, 2006; Cockburn-Wootten & Zorn, 2006; Wood, 2006a). Just knowing that they have weathered rough times in the past helps partners get through current trials. Belief in a future also sustains intimacy. We interact with people we don't expect to see again differently than people who are continuing parts of our lives. Talking about the future also enhances intimacy because it suggests that more lies ahead.

StockLite/Shutterstock.com

Self-reflection allows us to manage the image we project to others.

Symbols Allow Self-Reflection

Just as we use symbols to reflect on what goes on outside of us, we also use them to reflect on ourselves. In an argument, you may want to hurl a biting insult at a coworker who has criticized you, but you censor that impulse. You remind yourself that it's impolite to put others down and that doing so might create future problems with that coworker.

The ability to self-reflect allows us to think about who we want to be and set goals for becoming the self we desire. We can feel shame, pride, and regret for our actions—emotions that are possible because we self-reflect. We can control what we do in the present by imagining how we might later feel about our actions.

Self-reflection also allows us to manage our image, or the identity we present to others. Because we reflect on ourselves from social perspectives, we are able to consider how we appear in others' eyes. Our ability to manage how we appear sometimes is called *facework* because it involves controlling the face we present to others. When talking with teachers, you may consciously present yourself as a respectful, engaged student. When communicating with someone you'd like to date, you may choose to be more attentive and social than you are in other circumstances. In work situations, you may do facework to create an image of yourself as responsible, ambitious, and dependable. Continuously, we adjust how we present ourselves so that we sculpt our image to fit particular situations and people.

Summing up, we use symbols to define, evaluate, and organize experiences, think hypothetically, and self-reflect. Each of these abilities helps us create meaning in our lives.

Digital Media and Verbal Communication

How does what we have learned about verbal communication apply to online and digital interaction? One of the most obvious ways is our coining new words to describe experiences and modes of communication that are unique to social media. Some of the words we invented are variations on words and phrases that already existed: *buddy list, instant message, netiquette, cyberbullying, tweet*. Other words are wholly new, invented to describe what happens in cyberspace. For instance, *blog, virtual reality,* and *avatar* are words we have created to name experiences in computer-mediated communication. What additional terms can you think of that have been created to refer to interaction on social media?

The features of symbols that we discussed are as applicable to digital media as to face-to-face communication. Consider, for instance, the ambiguity of language. The meaning of words in tweets, texts, or emails may be more ambiguous than the meaning of words in face-to-face conversations. Digital media do not allow us the full range of nonverbal communication, which often helps us understand what speakers mean—winks, scowls, and so forth give us cues to meaning. Emoticons and Emoji are great, but not as richly expressive as nonverbal communication.

The rules that we discussed apply to digital communication just as they do to face-to-face communication. What regulative rules have evolved to govern when, where, and with whom it is appropriate to communicate online and digitally? Are there people you do not text, but instead call or email? Are there people you do not email but always text? Do you follow different rules for sharing personal information online and in face-to-face conversations?

Now think about constitutive rules you follow when using social media. What counts as a timely reply to a post? A tweet? A text? What counts as rudeness in texting? What counts as supportive in commenting on postings on social networking websites?

Guidelines for Effective Verbal Communication

We've explored what symbols are and how they may be used differently in distinct social communities. Building on these understandings, we can now consider ways to improve the effectiveness of our verbal communication.

Engage in Dual Perspective

The single most important guideline for effective verbal communication is to engage in **dual perspective**. Dual perspective involves taking another person's point of view into account as you communicate. For instance, effective public speakers take listeners' values into consideration when planning and presenting speeches. The same is true of friends who communicate well: They take each other's perspective into account.

We don't need to abandon our own perspectives to recognize those of others. In fact, it would be just as unethical to stifle your own views as to dismiss those of

dual perspective The ability to understand another person's perspective, beliefs, thoughts, or feelings.

others. *Dual perspective*, as the term implies, consists of two perspectives. It entails understanding both our own and another's point of view and acknowledging each when we communicate. For example, you and your supervisor may disagree about a performance review. It's important that you understand why your supervisor assigns the ratings he or she does, even if you don't share his or her perceptions. By understanding the supervisor's perceptions and ratings, you enhance your ability to have a good working relationship and to perform effectively on the job.

Own Your Feelings and Thoughts

We sometimes use language that obscures our responsibility for how we feel and what we think. For instance, people say, "You made me feel inadequate about my job performance," or "You hurt me," as if what they feel is caused by someone else. On a more subtle level, we sometimes blame others for our responses to what they say. "You're too demanding" really means that you don't like what someone else wants or expects. The sense of feeling pressured by another's expectations is in you

Our feelings and thoughts result from how we interpret others' communication, not from their communication itself. Others sometimes exert a great deal of influence on how we feel and how we see ourselves. Yet they do not directly cause our feelings. Although how we interpret what others say may lead us to feel certain ways, we can't hold them directly responsible for our feelings. In relationships with manipulative or hurtful people, you may find it useful either to communicate in ways that don't enable the other and that do preserve your integrity or to leave the relationship before it jeopardizes your own well-being.

Effective communicators take responsibility for themselves by using language that owns their thoughts and feelings. They own their feelings and do not blame others for what happens in themselves. To take responsibility for your own feelings, rely on *I*-language instead of *you*-language. Table 5.1 gives examples of the difference.

In my work with inmates who have violent histories, one of the key skills we teach is using *I*-language. At the outset, the inmates say things such as, "She made me hit her by acting so nasty." Through instruction, exercises, and practice, they

Table 5.1	*You*-Language and *I*-Language
***YOU*-LANGUAGE**	***I*-LANGUAGE**
You hurt me.	I feel hurt when you ignore what I say.
You make me feel small.	I feel small when you tell me that I'm selfish.
My boss intimidates me.	When my boss criticizes my work, I feel intimidated.
You're really domineering.	When you shout at me, I feel dominated.
The speaker made me feel dumb.	I felt uninformed when the speaker discussed such complex information.
You humiliated me.	I felt humiliated when you mentioned my problems in front of our friends.

learn to change their *you*-language to *I*-language, saying, "I hit her because I didn't like how she was acting." The inmates tell me that learning *I*-language is empowering because it helps them see that they have more control over their actions than they had realized.

There are two differences between *I*-language and *you*-language. First, *I*-statements own responsibility, whereas *you*-statements project it onto another person. *You*-language is likely to arouse defensiveness, which doesn't facilitate healthy communication. Second, *I*-statements offer more description than *you*-statements. *You*-statements tend to be abstract accusations, which is one reason they're ineffective in promoting change. *I*-statements, on the other hand, provide concrete descriptions of behaviors and feelings without directly blaming another person for how we feel.

Some people feel awkward when they first start using *I*-language. This is natural because most of us are accustomed to using *you*-language. With commitment and practice, however, you can learn to communicate using *I*-language. Once you feel comfortable using it, you will find that *I*-language has many advantages. It is less likely than *you*-language to make others defensive, so *I*-language opens the doors for dialogue.

I-language is also more honest. We deceive ourselves when we say, "You made me feel . . . " because others don't control how we feel. Finally, *I*-language is more empowering than *you*-language. When we say, "You hurt me," or "You made me feel bad," we give control of our emotions to others. This reduces our personal sense of agency and, by extension, our motivation to change what is happening. Using *I*-language allows us to own our feelings while also explaining to others how we interpret their behaviors.

ROTH   *I never realized how often I use* you*-language. I'm always saying my girlfriend makes me feel happy or my father makes me feel like a failure. What I'm beginning to see is that they really don't control my feelings. I do.*

Respect What Others Say About Their Feelings and Ideas

Has anyone ever said to you, "You shouldn't feel that way"? If so, you know how infuriating it can be to be told that your feelings aren't valid, appropriate, or acceptable. It's equally destructive to be told our thoughts are wrong. When someone says, "How can you think something so stupid?" we feel devalued. Even if you don't feel or think what someone else does, you can still respect another person's perspective.

We also disrespect others when we speak for them instead of letting them speak for themselves. In Chapter 2, we learned about mind reading, and it is relevant to speaking for others. As we have seen, our distinct experiences and ways of interpreting life make each of us unique. We seldom, if ever, completely grasp what another person feels or thinks. Although it is supportive to engage in dual perspective, it isn't supportive to presume that we fully understand someone else's feelings or thoughts, especially when he or she differs from us in important ways. It's particularly important not to assume we understand people from other cultures or social communities.

Corporatespeak

It's not new that any profession has some language unique to it, but the jargon in the business world sometimes baffles new hires. What would you think if your supervisor asked to schedule a *bilateral* with you? What if you were asked if you have enough *bandwidth* to take on a project and to prepare some *decks* for it? Welcome to Corporatespeak 2015 (Katzman, 2015).

A *bilateral* is a one-on-one meeting. *Bandwidth* is time. Decks are PowerPoint slides.

Respecting how others express their thoughts and feelings is a cornerstone of effective communication. We also grow when we open ourselves to perspectives, feelings, and thoughts that differ from our own.

Strive for Accuracy and Clarity

Because symbols are arbitrary, abstract, and ambiguous, the potential for misunderstanding always exists. Although we cannot entirely eliminate misunderstandings, we can minimize them.

Be Aware of Levels of Abstraction   Misunderstandings are most likely when language is very abstract. For instance, suppose a professor says, "Your papers should demonstrate a sophisticated conceptual grasp of the material and its pragmatic implications." Would you know how to write a paper to satisfy the professor? You might not, because the language is very abstract and unclear. Here's a more concrete description: "Your papers should include definitions of the concepts and specific examples that show how they apply in real life." With this less abstract statement, you would have a better idea of what the professor expected.

Abstract language is particularly likely to lead to misunderstandings when people talk about how they want one another to change. Concrete language and specific examples help people share understandings of which behaviors are unwelcome and which ones are wanted. For example, "I want you to be more responsible about your job" does not explain what would count as being more responsible. Is it arriving on time, taking on extra assignments, or something else? It isn't clear what the speaker wants unless more concrete descriptions are supplied. Likewise, "I want to be closer" could mean the speaker wants to spend more time together, talk about the relationship, do things together, or anything else. Vague abstractions lend themselves to misunderstanding.

Qualify Language   Another way to increase the clarity of communication is to qualify language. Two types of language should be qualified. First, we should qualify generalizations so

"Well, then, if 'commandments' seems too harsh to me, and 'guidelines' seems too wishy-washy to you, how about 'the 10 Policy Statements'?"

we don't mislead ourselves or others. "Politicians are crooked" is a false statement because it overgeneralizes. A more accurate statement would be, "A number of politicians have been shown to have engaged in illegal activities."

We should also qualify language when describing and evaluating people. **Static evaluation** consists of assessments that suggest that something is unchanging or frozen in time. These are particularly troublesome when applied to people: "Ann is selfish," "Don is irresponsible," or "Bob is generous." Whenever we use the word *is*, we suggest that something is inherent and fixed. In reality, we aren't static but continuously changing. A person who is selfish at one time may not be at another. A person who is irresponsible on one occasion may be responsible in other situations.

Indexing is a technique developed by early communication scholars that allows us to note that our statements reflect only specific times and circumstances (Korzybski, 1948). To index, we would say "Ann$_{\text{June 6, 1997}}$ acted selfishly," "Don$_{\text{on the task committee}}$ was irresponsible," Bob$_{\text{in college}}$ was generous." See how indexing ties description to a specific time and circumstance? Mental indexing reminds us that we and others are able to change in remarkable ways.

ROY   *I had a couple of accidents right after I got my driver's license. Most teenagers do, right? But to hear my father, you'd think I am a bad driver today. Those accidents were 5 years ago, and I haven't even had a ticket since then. But he still talks about "reckless Roy."*

---

static evaluation Assessments that suggest something is unchanging or static. "Bob is impatient" is a static evaluation.

indexing A technique of noting that statements reflect specific times and circumstances and may not apply to other times or circumstances.

We've considered four guidelines for effective verbal communication. Engaging in dual perspective is the first principle and a foundation for all others. A second guideline is to take responsibility for our own feelings and thoughts by using I-language. Third, we should respect others as the experts on what they feel and think and not speak for them or presume we know what they think and feel. The fourth principle is to strive for clarity by choosing appropriate degrees of abstraction, qualifying generalizations, and indexing evaluations, particularly ones applied to people.

Chapter Summary

In this chapter, we've discussed the world of words and meaning, which make up the uniquely human universe of symbol users. Because symbols are arbitrary, ambiguous, and abstract, they have no inherent meanings. Instead, we actively construct meaning by interpreting symbols based on perspectives gleaned through interaction with others and our personal experiences. We also punctuate to create meaning in communication.

We use symbols to define, evaluate, and organize our experiences. In addition, we use symbols to think hypothetically so we can consider alternatives and inhabit all three dimensions of time. Finally, symbols allow us to self-reflect so we can monitor our own behaviors.

Digital media rely on symbols just as face-to-face communication does. We noted that there is often greater ambiguity in language used in social media than communication between people who are physically together. In other respects, symbols perform similarly in the two contexts. In both environments, regulative and constitutive rules guide communication, and in both new words are continually being created.

Because symbols are abstract, arbitrary, and ambiguous, misunderstandings can occur between communicators. We can reduce the likelihood of misunderstandings by being sensitive to levels of abstraction. In addition, we should engage in dual perspective, own our thoughts and feelings, respect what others say about how they think and feel, and monitor abstractness, generalizations, and static evaluations. In Chapter 6, we will continue our discussion of the world of human communication by exploring the fascinating realm of nonverbal behavior.

Experiencing Communication in Our Lives

MindTap°

CASE STUDY: The Roommates

Apply what you've learned in this chapter by analyzing the following case study, using the accompanying questions as a guide. These questions and a video of the case study are also available online with your MindTap Speech for *Communication in Our Lives.*

Bernadette and Celia were assigned to be roommates a month ago when the school year began. Initially, both were pleased with the match because they discovered commonalities in their interests and backgrounds. They are both sophomores from small towns, they have similar tastes in music and television programs, and they both like to stay up late and sleep in.

Lately, however, Bernadette has been irritated by Celia's housekeeping or lack of it. Celia leaves her clothes lying all over the room. If they cook in, Celia often leaves the pans and dishes for hours, and then it's usually Bernadette who cleans them. Bernadette feels she has to talk to Celia about this problem, but she hasn't figured out how or when to talk. When Celia gets in from classes, Bernadette is sitting and reading a textbook on her bed.

CELIA: Hey Bernie, how's it going?

Celia drops her book bag in the middle of the floor, flops on the bed, and kicks her shoes off on the floor. As Bernadette watches, she feels her frustration peaking and decides now is the time to talk to Celia about the problem.

BERNADETTE: You shouldn't do that. You make me nuts the way you just throw your stuff all over the room.

CELIA: I don't "throw my stuff all over the room." I just took off my shoes and put my books down, like I do every day.

BERNADETTE: No, you didn't. You dropped your bag right in the middle of the room, and you kicked your shoes where they happen to fall without ever noticing how messy they look. And you're right—that is what you do every day.

CELIA: There's nothing wrong with wanting to be comfortable in my own room. Are we suddenly going for the Good Housekeeping Seal of Approval?

BERNADETTE: Comfortable is one thing. But you're so messy. Your mess makes me really miserable.

CELIA: Since when? This is the first I've heard about it.

BERNADETTE: Since we started rooming together, but I didn't want to say anything about how angry you make me. I just can't stand it any more. You shouldn't be so messy.

CELIA: Sounds to me like you've got a problem—you, not me.

BERNADETTE: Well it's you and your mess that are my problem. Do you have to be such a slob?

QUESTIONS FOR ANALYSIS AND DISCUSSION

1. Identify examples of *you*-language in this conversation. How would you change it to *I*-language?

2. Identify examples of loaded language and ambiguous language.

3. Do you agree with Celia that the problem is Bernadette's, not hers?

4. Do Celia and Bernadette seem to engage in dual perspective to understand each other?

Key Concepts

abstract	dual perspective	regulative rules
ambiguous	hypothetical thought	static evaluation
arbitrary	indexing	symbol
communication rules	loaded language	totalizing
constitutive rules	punctuation	

Sharpen Your Skill

1. Communication Rules

Identify constitutive and regulative rules you follow when you are interacting on the job and when you are with your family.

Constitutive Rules
What counts as being attentive in a team meeting at work?
What counts as being attentive to a romantic partner?
What counts as being respectful of parents?
What counts as being responsible on the job?
What counts as showing affection to parents and stepparents?

Regulative Rules
When is it appropriate to interrupt parents, friends, or coworkers?
What topics are appropriate during family dinner conversation?
With which family members do you talk about personal issues?
With which family members do you talk about money problems?

2. Assessing Your Stereotypes

Identify a stereotype you use, and consider 10 people to whom you might apply it. Identify differences between the people. At first, this may be difficult because stereotypes gloss over differences. What do you discover as you look for individual variations in the people you lumped together under a single symbol?

For Further Reflection and Discussion

1. Pay attention to *I-* and *you*-language in your own communication and that of others. What happens when you switch a *you*-statement to an *I*-statement? Does it change how you feel or what happens in interaction?

2. What is a good term for describing someone with whom you have a serious romance? *Boyfriend* and *girlfriend* no longer work for many people. Do you prefer *significant other, romantic partner, special friend,* or another term? Why?

3. What ethical responsibilities should accompany the right to free speech? Do you think individuals have an unqualified right to say whatever they want or are there limits to what people should be allowed to say?

Ethics

4. Identify communication rules for online conversations. What counts as joking (how do you indicate you're joking)? What counts as flaming? How is interaction regulated with rules for turn taking and length of comment?

Beyond the Classroom

Let's take the material in this chapter beyond the classroom by thinking about how what you've learned about verbal communication might apply to the workplace, ethical choices, and engagement with the broader world.

1. **Workplace.** In this chapter, we discovered verbal interaction is guided by constitutive and regulative rules. Think about a place where you work or where you worked in the past. Identify two key rules of each type and analyze how they shaped communication in that work site.

2. **Ethics.** Articulate the ethical basis for the third guideline presented in this chapter: Respect what others say about their thoughts and feelings. Why might it be ethical to do so and unethical not to do so?

3. **Engagement.** Subordinate groups are often defined by others who have the power to name them. Yet subordinate groups may eventually challenge the names others confer on them. In the 1960s, blacks in the United States rejected names that had been applied to members of their race and advanced new names they chose for themselves: African American and Afro American. In the 1990s, people who are not heterosexual began resisting names that had been applied to them and using self-definitions. Thinking about these two examples, consider definitions others impose on groups that are currently subordinate in the United States. How do the labels define members of the group? If you want to extend this exercise, talk with members of these groups and ask how they would define themselves or what words they would like others to use when referring to them.

> What you do speaks so loud that I cannot hear what you say.
>
> **Ralph Waldo Emerson**

The Nonverbal Dimension of Communication

LEARNING OBJECTIVES

After studying the topics in this chapter, you should be able to:

1. Explain why ambiguous or abstract words can lead to misunderstandings.

2. Identify some of the communication rules you follow when interacting with friends versus strangers.

3. Provide an example of how words can define a phenomenon.

4. Provide an example of how words can evaluate a phenomenon.

5. Become aware of specialized language used in social media.

6. Apply chapter guidelines to improve your verbal communication.

How well can you recognize others' feelings based on their nonverbal communication?

MindTap

Review the chapter's learning objectives and **start** with a quick warm-up activity.

While a student at Yale, Kenta Koga interned with a Japanese company, hoping that would lead to a permanent position. It didn't. Kenta was criticized by his supervisors for speaking up and for crossing his arms in front of senior colleagues. A student from Brown University, also interning in a Japanese company, was told she could not be hired because she laughed too much (Tabuchi, 2012).

Maria notices a nice-looking guy who is studying two tables away from her in the library. When he looks up at her, she lowers her eyes. After a moment, she looks back at him just for a second. A few minutes later he comes over, sits down beside her, and introduces himself.

These examples illustrate the power of nonverbal communication. In the first case, the students interning in Japanese companies were perceived as being rude because they violated nonverbal norms of the host country. In the library scene, we see a gendered pattern of nonverbal communication. Maria follows feminine communication norms by indirectly signaling her interest and waiting for the man to initiate contact. In turn, he enacts the rules of masculine communication culture by gazing directly at her and moving to her table.

Ethnicity, gender, sexual orientation, and socioeconomic class are identities that we create and sustain by performing them day in and day out (Butler, 2004; West & Zimmerman, 1987). In this sense, nonverbal communication, like language, is a primary way in which we announce who we are. The intricate system of nonverbal communication helps us establish identity, negotiate relationships, and create environments.

Nonverbal behaviors account for 65–93% of the total meaning of communication (Birdwhistell, 1970; Hickson, Stacks, & Moore, 2003; Mehrabian, 1981). One reason for the impact of nonverbal communication is its breadth: It includes everything from dress and eye contact to body posture and vocal inflection.

In this chapter, we explore the fascinating realm of nonverbal interaction. We will identify principles of nonverbal communication and types of nonverbal behavior, consider relationships between nonverbal communication and digital media, and discuss guidelines to improve the effectiveness of our nonverbal communication.

Principles of Nonverbal Communication

Nonverbal communication is all aspects of communication other than words themselves. It includes how we utter words (i.e., inflection, volume), features of environments that affect communication (i.e., temperature, lighting), and objects that influence personal images and interaction patterns (i.e., dress, jewelry). Five key points highlight the nature and power of nonverbal communication.

Similar to and Different from Verbal Communication

Nonverbal communication and verbal communication are similar in some ways and different in others.

nonverbal communication All forms of communication other than words themselves; includes inflection and other vocal qualities as well as several other behaviors.

Similarities   Like verbal communication, nonverbal behavior is symbolic, which means it is arbitrary, ambiguous, and abstract. Thus, we can't be sure what a smile or a gesture means, and we can't guarantee that others understand the meanings we intend to express with our own nonverbal behaviors. Second, like verbal communication, our nonverbal behavior and our interpretations of others' nonverbal behaviors are guided by constitutive and regulative rules.

A third similarity between the two communication systems is that both are culture bound. Our nonverbal communication reflects and reproduces values and norms of the particular culture and social communities to which we belong (Knapp, Hall, & Hogan, 2013; Orbe & Harris, 2015; Samovar, Porter, McDaniel, & Roy, 2015). For instance, dress considered appropriate for women varies across cultures: Some women in the United States wear miniskirts; women in some other countries wear headscarves. Dress also reflects organizational identities: Many professionals wear business suits or dresses; carpenters usually wear jeans; medical professionals typically wear white lab coats; and military personnel wear uniforms.

Last, both verbal and nonverbal communication may be either intentional or unintentional. For instance, in a job interview we are highly conscious of our dress and posture as well as the words we use. At other times, our verbal and nonverbal communication may be unintentional. If an interviewer asks you a difficult question, your facial expression may reveal that you are caught off guard, or you may accidentally speak ungrammatically.

Differences   There are also differences between the two systems of communication. First, nonverbal communication is perceived as more honest. If verbal and nonverbal behaviors are inconsistent, most people trust the nonverbal behavior. There is little evidence that nonverbal behavior actually is more trustworthy than verbal communication; after all, we often control it quite deliberately. Nonetheless, it tends to be *perceived* as more trustworthy (Epley, 2014).

Second, unlike verbal communication, nonverbal communication is multichanneled. Verbal communication usually occurs within a single channel; oral verbal communication is received through hearing, and written verbal communication and sign language are received through sight. In contrast, nonverbal communication may be seen, felt, heard, smelled, and tasted. We often receive nonverbal communication simultaneously through two or more channels, as when we feel a hug while hearing a whispered "I love you."

Finally, nonverbal communication is more continuous than verbal communication. We begin speaking at one moment and stop speaking at another moment. In contrast, nonverbal communication tends to flow continually. Before we speak, our facial expressions and posture express our feelings; as we speak, our body movements and appearance communicate; and after we speak, our posture changes, perhaps relaxing.

> **Review It!**
>
> Similarities to Verbal:
> - Symbolic
> - Rule-Guided
> - Culture Bound
> - Intentional or Unintentional

Frans Lemmens/The Image Bank/Getty Images

Different cultures prescribe different styles of dress.

Review It!

Differences from Verbal:
- Perceived as More Honest
- Multichanneled
- Continuous

Supplements or Replaces Verbal Communication

Nonverbal behaviors interact with verbal communication in five ways. First, nonverbal behaviors repeat verbal messages. For example, you might say "yes" while nodding your head.

Second, nonverbal behaviors may highlight verbal communication, as when you use inflection to emphasize certain words ("This is the *most* serious consequence of the policy that I oppose"). Third, nonverbal behaviors may complement or add to words. Public speakers often emphasize verbal statements with forceful gestures and increases in volume and inflection. Fourth, nonverbal behaviors may contradict verbal messages, as when a group member says, "Nothing's wrong" in a hostile tone of voice. Finally, we sometimes substitute nonverbal behaviors for verbal ones. For instance, you might roll your eyes to indicate that you are exasperated by something.

Regulates Interaction

You generally know when a professor welcomes discussion from students and when someone expects you to speak. But how do you know? There are no explicit, verbal cues to tell us when to speak and when to keep silent. Instead, conversations usually are regulated nonverbally (Guerrero & Floyd, 2006). We use our eyes and body posture to indicate that we want to enter conversations. We invite people to speak by looking directly at them, often after asking a question (Knapp & Hall, 2006).

Communication Highlight

Cross-Cultural Nonverbal Clashes

Cross-cultural misunderstandings aren't limited to verbal communication, according to Siu Wa Tang, chair of the Department of Psychiatry at the University of California at Irvine (Emmons, 1998). When Tang and a colleague visited pharmaceutical plants in Changchun, China, Tang was well accepted, but his colleague was not. The Chinese took an immediate and strong dislike to the colleague. Tang says the problem was facial expressions. His U.S. colleague used facial expressions that Americans would interpret as showing honesty and directness but which the Chinese people interpreted as aggressive and rude.

Based on this experience, Tang conducted experiments to test the universality of facial expressions. He found that a few basic feelings and expressions were understood across cultures. Happiness and sadness, for example, were nonverbally expressed in similar ways. However, other facial expressions did not translate so well. Nine out of 10 Americans interpreted a photograph of a face as showing fear, yet 6 of 10 Japanese identified the same photograph as expressing surprise or sadness. A photo identified by 9 of 10 Americans as showing anger was interpreted by 75% of Japanese as expressing disgust or contempt. Another source of cross-cultural nonverbal misunderstandings is eye contact. Americans generally consider it polite to look another person in the eye when conversing, but Japanese look at each other's cheeks; to look another in the eyes is perceived as very aggressive.

Cross-cultural communication clashes may also occur over gift giving (Axtell, 2007). An American might offend a Chinese with the gift of a clock because in China clocks symbolize death. Giving a gift to an Arab on first meeting would be interpreted as a bribe. Bringing flowers to a dinner hosted by a person from Kenya would puzzle the host because in Kenya flowers are given only to express sympathy for a loss. And the Swiss consider even numbers of flowers bad luck, so giving a dozen is inappropriate, and the recipient would probably interpret the gift as reflecting ill will.

> **DARCY**   *I know one guy who dominates every conversation. I'd never noticed this until we studied how nonverbal behaviors regulate turn taking. This guy won't look at others when he's talking. He looks out into space, or sometimes he gives you a hard stare, but he never looks at anyone like he's saying, "Okay, your turn now."*

Establishes Relationship-Level Meanings

In Chapter 1, we noted that there are two levels of meaning in communication. To review: The content level of meaning concerns actual information or literal meaning; the relationship level of meaning defines communicators' identities and the relationship between them. Nonverbal communication is often more powerful than verbal language in conveying relationship-level meanings (Manusov & Patterson, 2006).

Nonverbal communication is used to convey three dimensions of relationship-level meanings: *responsiveness, liking,* and *power* (Mehrabian, 1981). Yet how we convey relationship meanings and what specific nonverbal behaviors mean depends on the communication rules we've learned in our particular cultures and social communities.

Responsiveness   We use eye contact, facial expressions, and body posture to indicate interest in others, as Maria did in one of the examples that opened this chapter. We signal friendliness by laughing. But as in the example with the interns in Japanese companies, laughter doesn't mean the same thing in all cultures.

> **MARYAM**   *Americans do more than one thing at a time. In Nepal, when we talk with someone, we are with that person. We do not also write on paper or have the television on. We talk with the person. It is hard for me to accept the custom of giving only some attention to each other in conversation.*

As Maryam's observation indicates, different cultures teach members distinct rules for showing responsiveness.

Liking   A second dimension of relationship-level meaning is liking. In Western societies, smiles and friendly touching usually indicate positive feelings, whereas frowns and belligerent postures express antagonism. Have you ever noticed how often political candidates shake hands, slap backs, and otherwise touch people whose votes they want? Similarly, in work settings, people who like one another often sit together, exchange eye contact, and smile at one another.

Power   The third aspect of relationship-level meanings is power, or control. We use nonverbal behaviors to assert dominance, express deference, and negotiate status and influence. Powerful people, such as bosses, touch those with less power, such as secretaries, more than those with less power touch those with more power (Hall, Coats, & Smith-LeBeau, 2004). In general, men assume more space and use greater volume and more forceful gestures than women (Major, Schmidlin, & Williams, 1990).

> **RAMONA**   *In my home, my father sits at the head of the table, and he has his chair in the family room and his workroom. My mother does not have her chair anywhere in the house, and she has no room of her own either.*

Review It!

Dimensions of
Relationship-Level
Meaning:
- Responsiveness
- Liking
- Power

The connection between power and space is evident in the fact that CEOs usually have spacious offices, entry-level and mid-level professionals have smaller offices, and secretaries often have minuscule workstations, even though secretaries often store and manage more material than those higher in the organizational chain of command. Regulative communication rules also tacitly specify that people with status or power have the right to enter the space of people with less power, but the converse is not true. Space also reflects power differences in families. Adults usually have more space than children; like Ramona's father, men more often than women have their own rooms and sit at the head of the table. Men are also more likely than women to move into others' space, as the man in the library moved to Maria's table in the example at the beginning of this chapter.

Reflects Cultural Values

As noted above, nonverbal communication reflects rules of specific cultures and social communities (Manusov & Patterson, 2006). This implies that most nonverbal behavior isn't instinctual but learned in the process of socialization.

Have you ever seen the bumper sticker that says, "If you can read this, you're too close"? That slogan proclaims North Americans' fierce territoriality. We value our private spaces, and we resent—and sometimes fight—anyone who trespasses on what we consider our turf. We want private homes with rooms for each person

MindTap®   What nonverbal cues to power relations do you perceive in this photo?

Jonatan Fernström/Jupiter images

and large lots. On the job, a reserved parking space and a private office with a door mark status; employees with lower status often park in satellite lots and share offices or have workstations without doors. In cultures where individuality is less valued, people are less territorial. For instance, Brazilians routinely stand close together in shops, buses, and elevators, and when they bump into each other, they don't apologize or draw back. Similarly, in countries such as Hong Kong, people are used to living and working in very close quarters, so territoriality is uncommon (Chan, 1999). In some cultures—Italy, for example—dramatic nonverbal displays of emotion are typical, but other cultures consider more reserved displays of emotion appropriate (Matsumoto, Franklin, Choi, Rogers, & Tatani, 2002).

> **SUCHENG** *In the United States, each person has so much room. Every individual has a separate room in which to sleep and sometimes another separate room in which to work. Also, I see that each family here lives in a separate house. People have much less space in China. Families live together, with sons bringing their families into their parents' home and all sharing the same space. At first when I came here it felt strange to have so much space, but now I sometimes feel very crowded when I go home.*

Patterns of eye contact also reflect cultural values. In the United States, frankness and assertion are valued, so meeting another's eyes is considered appropriate and a demonstration of personal honesty. Yet, as we've noted, in many Asian and northern European countries, direct eye contact is considered abrasive and disrespectful (Axtell, 2007; Samovar et al., 2015). On the other hand, in Brazil, eye contact often is so intense that people from the United States consider it rude staring.

Greeting behaviors also vary across cultures. In the United States and many other Western countries, the handshake is the most common way to greet. Arab men are more likely to kiss each other on both cheeks as a form of greeting. Embraces are typical greetings in Mexico. Bowing is the standard form of greeting in some Asian cultures (Samovar et al., 2015).

In sum, we've noted five features of the nonverbal communication system. First, there are similarities and differences between nonverbal and verbal communication. Second, nonverbal behavior can supplement or replace verbal communication. Third, nonverbal behaviors regulate interaction. Fourth, nonverbal communication is often especially powerful in establishing and expressing relational meanings. Fifth, nonverbal behaviors reflect cultural values and are learned, not instinctive. We're now ready to explore the many types of behavior in the intricate nonverbal communication system.

Types of Nonverbal Communication

In this section, we will consider nine forms of nonverbal behavior, noticing how we use each to communicate.

Kinesics

Kinesics is body position and body motions, including those of the face. Our bodies express a great deal about how we see ourselves. A speaker who stands erect and is relaxed announces self-confidence, whereas someone who slouches and shuffles may seem unsure of himself or herself.

kinesics Body position and body motions, including those of the face.

Communication
& Careers

Police Trained in Cultural Sensitivity   MindTap®
to Nonverbal Communication

Part of training to become police officers in New York is studying a manual titled "Policing in a Multicultural Society." The manual was developed because officers who are unaware of cultural differences in nonverbal behaviors were misinterpreting behaviors of some people who had immigrated to the United States (Goldstein, 2013). The manual includes the following:

1. Immigrants from rural Mexico are socialized to avoid direct eye contact. This should not be interpreted as deceitfulness.
2. Immigrants from Puerto Rico often engage in eye-checking with others. This should not be interpreted as sending signals not to speak honestly.
3. African immigrants often shake hands with a light touch of palms instead of a firm grip. This is not an indicator of shiftiness.
4. Arab immigrants may get out of their cars when stopped by police. This is a sign of courtesy. Do not interpret this as aggression.
5. Arab immigrants tend to speak loudly. This should not be interpreted as shouting or belligerence.

SHARPEN YOUR SKILL

At the end of this chapter, refer to the Sharpen Your Skill feature, Communicating Closeness, to apply concepts from Chapter 6.

haptics Nonverbal communication that involves physical touch.

How we position ourselves relative to others may express our feelings toward them. On work teams, friends and allies often sit together, and competitors typically maintain distance. Americans often cross their legs, but this is perceived as offensive in Ghana and Turkey (Samovar et al., 2017).

Our faces are intricate messengers. Our eyes can shoot daggers of anger, issue challenges, express skepticism, or radiate love. With our faces, we can indicate disapproval (scowls), doubt (raised eyebrows), love (eye gazes), and challenge (stares). The face is particularly powerful in conveying responsiveness and liking (Gueguen & De Gail, 2003).

Our eyes communicate some of the most important and complex messages about how we feel. If you watch infants, you'll notice that they focus on others' eyes. As adults, we often look at eyes to judge emotions, honesty, interest, and self-confidence. Among Westerners, eye contact tends to increase feelings of closeness.

Haptics

Haptics is physical touch. Touch is the first of our senses to develop, and touching and being touched are essential to a healthy life (Whitman, White, O'Mara, & Goeke-Morey, 1999).

Touching also communicates power and status. Cultural views of women as more touchable than men are reflected in gendered patterns. Women tend to touch others to show liking and intimacy, whereas men more typically rely on touch to assert power and control (Jhally & Katz, 2001).

YVETTE   *When I was pregnant, total strangers would walk up to me and touch my belly. It was amazing—and disturbing. They seemed to think they had a right to touch me or that the baby wasn't me, so they could touch him. Amazing!*

Touch conveys emotions.

Physical Appearance

Western culture places an extremely high value on **physical appearance**. For this reason, most of us notice how others look, and we form initial evaluations based on their appearance. Although our initial judgments may be inaccurate, they can affect our decisions about friendships, dating, and hiring. In fact, economist Daniel Hamermesh (2011) reports that people who are above average in attractiveness are likely to make 3–4% more than people who are below average in attractiveness. That could add up to well over $200,000 over the course of a career.

Cultures stipulate ideals for physical form. Currently, cultural ideals in the West emphasize thinness in women and muscularity in men (Davies-Popelka, 2015; Kimmel, 2013; Spar, 2013). In an effort to meet these ideals, some men engage in extreme body building or use steroids, and some women diet excessively and develop eating disorders. Go to the book's online resources for this chapter to visit the National Eating Disorders Association's website to learn about eating disorders and ways to help people who have them.

In an effort to meet cultural standards for appearance, many people elect to have cosmetic surgery. Women most often have breast augmentation, tummy tuck, liposuction, eyelid surgery, and breast lift (American Society of Plastic Surgeons, 2014). The most popular surgeries for men are liposuction, eyelid surgery, rhinoplasty, and face lifts (American Society of Plastic Surgeons, 2014). Both sexes also increasingly rely on less invasive treatments such as soft tissue filler, chemical peels, and laser hair removal—13.4 million of these procedures were performed in the United States in 2013 (American Society of Plastic Surgeons, 2014).

Standards for attractiveness vary with ethnicity. African Americans generally admire fuller figures than European Americans, and this is especially true among African Americans who identify strongly with African American culture (Berry, 2014; Walker, 2007).

physical appearance
Physical features of people and the values attached to those features; a type of nonverbal communication.

CASS *I found out how much appearance matters when I was in an auto accident. It messed up my face so that I had scars all over one side and on my forehead. All of a sudden, nobody was asking me out. All these guys who had been so crazy about me before the accident lost interest. Some of my girlfriends seemed uneasy about being seen with me. When I first had the wreck, I was so glad to be alive that I didn't even think about plastic surgery. After a couple of months of seeing how others treated me, however, I had the surgery.*

Artifacts

Artifacts are personal objects with which we announce our identities and personalize our environments. We craft our image by how we dress, the jewelry we wear, and the objects we carry and use. George W. Bush insisted on formal dress—coat and tie—at all times in the Oval Office (Stolberg, 2009). Barack Obama sometimes takes off his jacket while working in the Oval Office, and he often skips the tie on weekends. Go to the book's online resources for this chapter to learn more about norms for professional dressing.

We also use artifacts to define settings and personal territories. At annual meetings of companies, the CEO usually speaks from a podium that bears the company logo. In much the same manner, we claim our private spaces by filling them with photos of family members and other objects that matter to us and reflect our experiences and values. Lovers of art adorn their homes with paintings and sculptures. Religious families display pictures of holy scenes and the *Bible*, the *Qur'an*, the *Vedas*, the *Koran*, or another sacred text.

NAOMI *I've moved a lot since coming to college—dorm, apartment, another apartment, and another apartment. I never feel a place is home until I put the photograph of my grandmother holding me on my dresser. Then it's home.*

artifacts Personal objects we use to announce our identities and personalize our environments.

Artifacts can express personal identity. Approximately one-third of Americans in the 25- to 29-year age range have at least one tattoo (Opfer, 2011). But many people who get tattoos later want to get rid of them. Enter people like Dr. Tattoff who has performed more than 110,000 tattoo removals (Opfer, 2011).

PERHAPS A REVIEW OF OUR CASUAL DAY POLICY IS IN ORDER...

We also use artifacts to express ethnic identity. Kwanzaa is an African American holiday tradition that celebrates the centrality of home, family, and community. The kinara is a branched candleholder that holds seven candles, one of which is lit during each day of Kwanzaa (Bellamy, 1996; George, 1995). The Jewish holiday, Hanukkah, features the menorah that holds candles while Seder features an elaborate meal in which each item represents a part of Jewish history. The Christian tradition includes Christmas trees and Nativity scenes.

Proxemics

Proxemics is space and how we use it. Every culture has norms for using space and for how close people should be to one another (Samovar et al., 2015). In a classic study, Edward Hall (1966) found that in the United States, we interact with social acquaintances from a distance of 4 to 12 feet but are comfortable with 18 inches or less between us and close friends or romantic partners. In some cultures greater or lesser distances are considered comfortable.

Space also signals status; greater space is assumed by those of higher status. The prerogative of entering someone else's personal space is also linked to power; those with greater power are most likely to trespass into others' territory.

How space is arranged also tells us something about the expected form of interaction in the space. Formal businesses may have private offices with doors and little common space. In contrast, more casual businesses are likely to have fewer doors and more common space to encourage interaction between employees. Families that enjoy interaction tend to arrange furniture to invite conversation and eye contact.

proxemics A type of nonverbal communication that includes space and how we use it.

Brad Perks Lightscapes/Alamy Stock Photo

MindTap® What does this executive's space convey about his power and openness to others?

Environmental Factors

Environmental factors are elements of settings that affect how we feel and act. For instance, we respond to architecture, colors, room design, temperature, sounds, smells, and lighting. Rooms with comfortable chairs invite relaxation, whereas rooms with stiff chairs prompt formality. Dimly lit rooms can enhance romantic feelings, although dark rooms can be depressing.

Restaurants use environmental features to control how long people linger over meals. For example, low lights, comfortable chairs or booths, and soft music often are part of the environment in upscale restaurants where patrons tend to linger. On the other hand, fast-food eateries have hard plastic booths and bright lights, which encourage diners to eat and move on. To make a profit, inexpensive restaurants have to get people in and out as quickly as possible.

A New Jersey hospital recently redesigned rooms to increase natural light and otherwise create more attractive environments. Patients in the redesigned rooms asked for 30% less medication and rated food better than patients in the unremodeled rooms even though the food was the same (Kimmelman, 2014). Ron Baker is an expert on classroom environments. He says that even when constructing new classroom buildings, planners are often "making the same kinds of stupid mistakes" (Bartlett, 2003, p. A36). What are those "stupid mistakes"? Lights that cause glare on laptop screens; chairs that are too small for some students; desks that won't accommodate a notebook, a laptop, and a textbook; and inadequate air-conditioning or heating. Go to the book's online resources for this chapter to learn more about Ron Baker's ideas on ideal classrooms.

Chronemics

Chronemics is how we perceive and use time to define identities and interaction. Important people with high status can keep others waiting. Conversely, people with low status are expected to be punctual in Western society (Richmond & McCroskey, 1995b). It is standard practice to have to wait, sometimes a long while, to see a doctor, even if you have an appointment. This carries the message that the doctor's time is more valuable than ours. Professors can be late to class, and students are expected to wait, but students sometimes are reprimanded if they arrive after a class begins. Subordinates are expected to report punctually to meetings, but bosses are allowed to be tardy.

SHARPEN YOUR SKILL

At the end of this chapter, refer to the Sharpen Your Skill feature, Environmental Awareness, to apply concepts from Chapter 6.

environmental factors Elements of settings that affect how we feel and act. Environmental factors are a type of nonverbal communication.

chronemics A type of nonverbal communication concerned with how we perceive and use time to define identities and interaction.

Communication Highlight

Environmental Racism

According to Robert Cox, former president of the Sierra Club, the term *environmental racism* arose to describe a pattern whereby toxic waste dumps and hazardous industrial plants are located in low-income neighborhoods and communities of color (Cox, 2016). The pattern is clear: The space of minorities and poor people can be invaded and contaminated, but the territory of more affluent citizens cannot be.

Go to the book's online resources for this chapter to learn more about environmental racism (also called *environmental justice*). This site provides information on the Environmental Protection Agency's strategies for preventing environmental racism.

Chronemics express cultural attitudes toward time. In Western societies, time is valuable, so speed is highly valued (Calero, 2005; Honoré, 2005). Thus, we replace our computers and cell phones as soon as faster models hit the market. We often try to do several things at once to get more done. Many other cultures have far more relaxed attitudes toward time and punctuality. In many South American countries, it's not impolite to come late to meetings or classes, and it's not assumed that people will leave at the scheduled ending time. Whether time is treated casually, or closely watched and measured out, reflects larger cultural attitudes toward living.

The amount of time we spend with different people reflects our priorities. A manager spends more time with a new employee who seems to have executive potential than with one who seems less impressive. A speaker spends more time responding to a question from a high-status member of the audience than to a person of lower status. We spend more time with people we like than with those we don't like.

Paralanguage

Paralanguage is vocal communication that does not involve words. It includes sounds, such as murmurs and gasps, and vocal qualities, such as volume, rhythm, pitch, and inflection. Our voices are versatile instruments that tell others how to interpret us and what we say. Vocal cues signal others to interpret what we say as a joke, threat, statement of fact, question, and so forth. Vocal cues also express irritation. Effective public speakers know how to modulate inflection, volume, and rhythm to enhance their verbal messages.

We use our voices to communicate feelings. Whispering, for instance, often signals secrecy, and shouting conveys anger. Depending on the context, sighing may communicate empathy, boredom, or contentment. Research indicates that tone of voice is a powerful clue to feelings between marital partners. Negative vocal tones are among the most important symbols of marital dissatisfaction (Gottman, 1994b). Negative intonation may also signal dissatisfaction or disapproval in work settings. The reverse is also true: A warm voice conveys liking, and a playful lilt suggests friendliness.

We use our voices to communicate how we see ourselves and wish to be seen by others. For instance, we use a firm, confident voice in job interviews or when

paralanguage Vocal communication that does not include actual words; for example, sounds, vocal qualities, accents, and inflection.

Communication Highlight

Sounding Like a (Wo)man

Deciding to transition from one sex to the other involves more than hormonal therapy and surgeries. It also requires retraining the voice to sound like that of the new sex. Richard Adler, Sandy Hirsch, and Michelle Mordaunt (2012) are clinicians who specialize in voice therapy for transgender people. From their work with transgender clients, they have developed evidence-based protocols for retraining the voice in the areas of pitch, intonation, volume, rate, articulation, language, resonance, and other facets of nonverbal communication.

Men who transition to women have to learn to use a higher pitch, more inflection, more pauses, and lower volume. They may also learn to cant their heads, hold more eye contact when speaking to others, and cross their legs knee over knee. For women who transition to men, the nonverbal challenges are to speak at a lower pitch, increase volume, decrease inflection, hold the head straight, use infrequent eye contact, and cross legs ankle over knee.

explaining why we deserve a raise. We also know how to make ourselves sound apologetic, seductive, or angry when it suits us. People who speak at a slow-to-moderate rate are perceived as having greater control over interaction than people who speak rapidly (Tusing & Dillard, 2000).

> **RAYNA**   *When I first moved to the United States, I didn't understand many words and idioms. I did not understand that "A bird in the hand is worth two in the bush" meant it is smart to hold on to what is sure. I did not understand that "hang a right" meant to turn right. So when I did not understand, I would ask people to explain. Most times they would say the very same thing over, just louder and more slowly, like I was deaf or stupid. I felt like saying to them in a very loud, slow voice, "I am Indian, not stupid. You are stupid."*

We use paralanguage to perform gender. To perform masculinity, men use strong volume, low pitch, and limited inflection, all of which conform to cultural prescriptions for men to be assertive and emotionally controlled. To perform femininity, women tend to use higher pitch, softer volume, and more inflection. We also perform class by our pronunciation of words, our accents, and the complexity of our sentences.

Silence

A final type of nonverbal behavior is **silence,** which can communicate powerful messages. The assertion "I'm not speaking to you" actually speaks volumes. We use silence to communicate different meanings. For instance, silence indicates contentment when intimates are so comfortable they don't need to talk. Silence can also communicate awkwardness, as you know if you've ever had trouble keeping conversation going with a new acquaintance. We feel pressured to fill the void.

Silence can also disconfirm others. In some families, children are disciplined by being ignored. No matter what the child says or does, parents refuse to acknowledge his or her existence. In later life, the silencing strategy may also surface. You know how disconfirming silence can be if you've ever said hello to someone and gotten no reply. Even if the other person didn't deliberately ignore you, you felt slighted. In some military academies, such as West Point, silencing is a recognized method of stripping a cadet of personhood if he or she is perceived as having broken the academy code. Whistle-blowers and union-busters are often shunned by peers. Similarly, the Catholic Church excommunicates people who violate its canons.

The complex system of nonverbal communication includes kinesics, haptics, physical appearance, artifacts, proxemics, environmental features, chronemics, paralanguage, and silence. We use these nonverbal behaviors to announce our identities and to communicate how we feel about relationships with others.

Digital Media and Nonverbal Communication

As is the case with every aspect of communication, nonverbal behavior is connected to digital media. Perhaps the most obvious issue is that nonverbal communication is more restricted in digital and online communication than in face-to-face interaction. Words in an email, tweet, or text don't tell us whether the person who wrote

---

Review It!

Types of Nonverbal Communication:

- Kinesics
- Haptics
- Physical Appearance
- Artifacts
- Proxemics
- Environmental Factors
- Chronemics
- Paralanguage
- Silence

silence The lack of verbal communication or paralanguage. Silence is a type of nonverbal communication that can express powerful messages.

them is serious, sarcastic, or playful. The need to signal others how to interpret our words and to understand how we should interpret their words compelled invention of emoticons such as

(::[ ]::) = band aid to symbolize comfort
;)   = smile + wink to symbolize playfulness
=^.^= = cat to symbolize friskiness
<3 = heart

But emoticons aren't expressive enough for some people, which led to the development of stickers, which are cartoon-like icons that people send to replace text messages. First used in Japan, stickers are gaining popularity among Westerners, who find words and even emoticons insufficient for what they want to express. Now that stickers have caught on, the race for super-cute is on, with startups trying to come up with the cutest stickers. Path offers Willa, a playful wombat; Facebook offers Pusheen, a cat that sometimes presents herself as a unicorn, and Napoli, a very emotional ice cream cone (Rusli, 2013). Facebook founder Mark Zuckerberg sends a blue thumbs up sign to symbolize approval. An undergraduate sends a sleepy bunny cartoon to signal that she's tired (Rusli, 2013). And stickers don't need translating when shared between users who have different languages. Emoji soon followed as yet another way to symbolize emotions in digital communication.

Second, as we noted earlier in this chapter, digital communication can compete with, and sometimes interfere with, face-to-face communication. Do you send or check texts while talking with others face-to-face? (And don't think people don't notice just because you have eye contact while texting!) If so, does that convey the level of responsiveness you want to convey? Dual perspective might lead you to think about the person with whom you are in face-to-face contact. Is he or she

ArtWell/Shutterstock.com

Based on nonverbal cues, what can you infer about these two children's relationship?

someone who is as wired to social media as you? If not, you might want to focus on the face-to-face interaction.

The presence of social media in our lives has not been lost on furniture manufacturers. Traditional home offices are out and chairs and chaises specifically designed for mobile computing are in (Hrabi, 2013). Dubbed the lifestyle work-at-home collection, this furniture has wide arms for laptops and allows people to adjust them infinitely. Conversely, office designers should rethink the open-plan workspace that relies on cubicles. People who work in cubicles are interrupted 29% more often than people who work in private offices, and interruptions are not just irritating; they are costly: They increase workers' exhaustion, error rates, and stress-related illnesses (Shellenbarger, 2013).

Guidelines for Improving Nonverbal Communication

Nonverbal communication, like its verbal cousin, can be misinterpreted. You can reduce the likelihood of misunderstandings in nonverbal communication by following two guidelines.

Monitor Your Nonverbal Communication

The monitoring skills we have stressed in other chapters are also important for competent nonverbal communication. Think about the ways we use nonverbal behaviors to announce our identities. Are you projecting the image you desire? Do your facial and body movements represent how you see yourself and how you want others to perceive you? Do people ever tell you that you seem uninterested when they are talking to you? If so, you can monitor your nonverbal actions and modify them to more clearly communicate involvement and interest. You can also set up your spaces to invite the kind of interaction you prefer.

Interpret Others' Nonverbal Communication Tentatively

In this chapter, we've discussed findings about the meanings people tend to attach to nonverbal behaviors. It's important to realize that these are only generalizations about how we interpret nonverbal communication. We cannot state what any particular behavior means to specific people in a particular context. For instance, we've said that people who like each other tend to be physically closer when interacting. However, sometimes people prefer autonomy and want personal space. In addition, someone may maintain distance because she or he has a cold and doesn't want a partner to catch it. Also, the generalizations we've discussed may not apply to people from non-Western cultures. Ethical communicators qualify their interpretations of nonverbal behavior by considering personal and contextual considerations.

Personal Qualifications   Nonverbal patterns that accurately describe most people may not apply to particular individuals. Although eye contact generally indicates responsiveness, some people close their eyes to concentrate when listening. In such cases, it would be inaccurate to conclude that a person who doesn't look at us isn't listening. Similarly, people who cross their arms and condense into a tight posture may be expressing hostility or lack of interest in interaction. However, the same behaviors might mean a person is cold. Most people use less inflection, fewer gestures, and a slack posture when they're not really interested in what they're talking about. However, fatigue can result in the same behaviors.

To avoid misinterpreting others' nonverbal communication, you can check perceptions and use *I*-language, not *you*-language, which we discussed in Chapter 5. You can check perceptions to find out whether the way you interpret another's nonverbal behavior is what that other person means: "I sense that you're not really involved in this conversation; is that how you feel?" In addition, you can rely on *I*-language. *You*-language might lead us to inaccurately say of someone who doesn't look at us, "You're communicating lack of interest." A more responsible statement would use *I*-language to say, "When you don't look at me, I feel you're not interested in what I'm saying." Using *I*-language reminds us to take responsibility for our judgments and feelings. In addition, it reduces the likelihood that we will make others defensive by inaccurately interpreting their nonverbal behavior.

Contextual Qualifications   Like the meaning of verbal communication, the significance of nonverbal behaviors depends on the contexts in which they occur. Most people are more at ease on their own turf than on someone else's, so we tend to be more friendly and outgoing in our homes than in business meetings and public spaces. We also dress according to context. When I am on campus or in business meetings, I dress professionally, but at home, I usually wear jeans or running clothes.

In addition to our immediate settings, nonverbal communication reflects cultures. We are likely to misinterpret people from other cultures if we impose the norms and rules of our culture on them. An Arab who stands practically on top of others to talk with them is not being rude, according to his culture's standards, although Westerners might interpret him as such.

> **ELENI**   *I have been misinterpreted very much in this country. In my first semester here, a professor told me he wanted me to be more assertive and to speak up in class. I could not do that, I told him. He said I should put myself forward, but I have been brought up not to do that. In Taiwan, that is very rude and ugly, and we are taught not to speak up to teachers. Now that I have been here for 3 years, I sometimes speak in classes, but I am still quieter than Americans. I know my professors think I am not so smart because I am quiet, but that is the teaching of my country.*

Even within a single culture, different social communities have distinct rules for nonverbal behavior. A man who doesn't make "listening noises" may be listening intently according to the rules of masculine speech communities. Similarly, when women nod and make listening noises while another is talking, men may misperceive them as agreeing. According to the rules typically learned in feminine social communities, ongoing feedback is a way of signaling interest, not necessarily agreement. We should adopt dual perspective when interpreting others, especially when they belong to cultures or communities that are different from ours.

Chapter Summary

In this chapter, we've explored the world beyond words. We learned that there are similarities and differences between nonverbal communication and verbal communication. Next, we noted that nonverbal communication supplements or replaces verbal messages, regulates interaction, reflects and establishes relationship-level meanings, and expresses cultural membership.

We discussed nine types of nonverbal communication: kinesics, haptics, physical appearance, artifacts, proxemics, environmental features, chronemics, paralanguage, and silence. Each form of nonverbal communication reflects cultural understandings and values and also expresses our personal identities and feelings toward others. We then considered how nonverbal communication operates in the realm of digital communication.

Because nonverbal communication, like verbal communication, is symbolic, it has no inherent, universal meaning. Instead, we construct meaning as we notice, organize, and interpret nonverbal behaviors.

MindTap° ## Experiencing Communication in Our Lives

CASE STUDY: Nonverbal Cues

Apply what you've learned in this chapter by analyzing the following case study, using the accompanying questions as a guide. These questions and a video of the case study are also available online with your MindTap Speech for *Communication in Our Lives*.

A project team is meeting to discuss the most effective way to present its recommendations for implementing a flextime policy on a trial basis. Members of the team are Jason Brown, team leader; Erika Filene; Victoria Lawrence; Bill Williams; and Jensen Chen. They are seated around a rectangular table with Jason at the head.

JASON: So we've decided to recommend trying flextime for a 2-month period and with a number of procedures to make sure that people's new schedules don't interfere with productivity. There's a lot of information to communicate to employees, so how can we do that best?

VICTORIA: I think it would be good to use PowerPoint to highlight the key aspects of the new procedures. People always seem to remember better if they see something.

BILL: Oh, come on. PowerPoint is so overused. Everyone is tired of it by now. Can't we do something more creative?

VICTORIA: Well, I like it. It's a good teaching tool.

BILL: I didn't know we were teaching. I thought our job was to report recommendations.

VICTORIA: So what do you suggest, Bill? (*She nervously pulls on her bracelet as she speaks.*)

BILL: I don't have a suggestion. I'm just against PowerPoint. (*He doesn't look up as he speaks.*)

JASON: Okay, let's not bicker among ourselves. (*He pauses, gazes directly at Bill, then continues.*) Lots of people like PowerPoint, lots don't. Instead of arguing about its value, let's ask what it is we want to communicate to the employees here. Maybe talking about our goal first will help us decide on the best means of achieving it.

ERIKA: Good idea. I'd like us to focus first on getting everyone excited about the benefits of flextime. If they understand those, they'll be motivated to learn the procedures, even if there are a lot of them.

JENSEN: Erika is right. That's a good way to start. Maybe we could create a handout or PowerPoint slide—either would work—to summarize the benefits of flextime we've identified in our research.

JASON: Good, okay now we're cooking. Victoria, will you make notes on the ideas as we discuss them?

Victoria opens a notebook and begins writing notes. Noticing that Bill is typing into his PDA, Jason looks directly at Bill and speaks.

JASON: Are you with us on how we lead off in our presentation?

BILL: Sure, fine with me. (*He puts the PDA aside but keeps his eyes on it.*)

ERIKA: So maybe then we should say that the only way flextime can work is if we make sure that everyone agrees on procedures so that no division is ever missing more than one person during key production hours.

JENSEN: Very good. That would add to people's motivation to learn and follow the procedures we've found are effective in other companies like ours. I think it would be great if Erika could present that topic because she did most of the research on it. (*He smiles at Erika, and she pantomimes tipping her hat to him.*)

JASON: (*He looks at Erika with a raised brow, and she nods.*) Good. Okay, Erika's in charge of that. What's next?

VICTORIA: Then it's time to spell out the procedures and . . .

BILL: You can't just spell them out. You have to explain each one—give people a rationale for them—or they won't follow them.

Victoria glares at Bill, then looks across the table at Erika, who shrugs as if to say, "I don't know what's bothering Bill today."

JASON: Bill, why don't you lead off, then, and tell us the first procedure we should mention and the rationale we should provide for it.

BILL: (*Looks up from his PDA, which he's been using again, and shrugs.*) Just spell out the rules, that's all.

VICTORIA: Would it be too much trouble for you to cut off your gadget and join us in this meeting, Bill?

BILL: Would it be too much trouble for you to quit hassling me?

JASON: (*He turns his chair to face Bill squarely.*) Look, I don't know what's eating you, but you're really being a jerk. If you've got a problem with this meeting or someone here, put it on the table. Otherwise, be a team player.

QUESTIONS FOR ANALYSIS AND DISCUSSION

1. Identify nonverbal behaviors that regulate turn taking within the team.

2. Identify nonverbal behaviors that express relational-level meanings of communication. What aspects of team members' nonverbal communication express liking or disliking, responsiveness or lack of responsiveness, and power?

3. How do artifacts affect interaction between members of the team?

4. If you were the sixth member of this team, what kinds of communication might you enact to help relieve tension in the group?

MindTap®

Use flashcards to learn key concepts and take a quiz to test your knowledge.

Key Concepts

artifacts	kinesics	physical appearance
environmental factors	nonverbal communication	proxemics silence
haptics	paralanguage	

Sharpen Your Skill

1. Communicating Closeness

What do nonverbal behaviors say about how intimate people are? To find out, observe (a) a couple who you know are very close, (b) a clerk and a shopper in a store, and (c) a teacher and student who are talking. How closely do the people sit or stand to each other? How do their postures differ? What facial expressions and eye contact do they use in each situation?

2. Environmental Awareness

Think of one place where you feel rushed and one where you linger. Describe the following about each place:

How is furniture arranged?
What kind of lighting is used?
What sort of music is played, and what other sounds are there?
How comfortable is the furniture for sitting or lounging?
What colors and art are there?

Based on your observations, can you make generalizations about environmental features that promote relaxation and ones that do not?

For Further Reflection and Discussion

1. Attend a gathering of people who belong to a social community different from yours. Observe nonverbal behaviors of the people there: How do they greet one another, how much eye contact accompanies interaction, and how close to one another do people stand and sit?

2. Visit restaurants near your campus. Describe the kinds of seats, lighting, music (if any), and distance between tables. Do you find any connections between nonverbal patterns and expensiveness of restaurants?

3. Describe the spatial arrangements in the home of your family of origin. Was there a room in which family members interacted a good deal? How was furniture arranged in that room? Who had separate space and personal chairs in your family? What do the nonverbal patterns reflect about your family's communication style?

4. What ethical issues are entailed in interpreting others' nonverbal communication? What would be ethical and unethical interpretations?

Beyond the Classroom

Let's take the material in this chapter beyond the classroom by thinking about how what you've learned about nonverbal communication might apply to the workplace, ethical choices, and engagement with the broader world.

1. **Workplace.** Visit a workplace of the type you imagine working in after you've completed your education. Analyze nonverbal communication and notice what it tells you about this particular workplace. How is space arranged? Are there individual offices or workstations that aren't isolated? If there are both, who gets the private offices? How do employees dress? How much do employees rely on nonverbal communication such as touch and eye contact to signal friendliness?

2. **Ethics.** Ethical issues surround space and who does and doesn't have access to particular spaces. Some managers of stores do not want homeless citizens in their places of business. They think that these citizens' presence would hurt business by discouraging other citizens from patronizing their stores. Yet advocates for homeless citizens say that businesses are places that are open to the public, and business owners and managers can't allow only some of the public to enter their establishments. What do you think is the most ethical way to address the issue of whether businesses should allow homeless citizens into their establishments?

3. **Engagement.** Attend a gathering of people from a culture different from yours. It might be a meeting at a Jewish temple if you're Christian, a black church if you are white, or a meeting of Asian students if you are Western. Observe nonverbal behaviors of the people there: How do they greet one another? How much eye contact accompanies interaction? How close to one another do people sit? Can you make inferences about cultural values based on nonverbal communication that you observe?

Photolibrary/Getty Images

7

We love because
it's the only true
adventure.

Nikki Giovanni

Communication in Personal Relationships

LEARNING OBJECTIVES

After studying the topics in this chapter, you should be able to:

1. Examine one of your own current or former friendships by applying each of the five features of personal relationships to it.

2. Provide an example of each of the three relationship dialectics.

3. Name the three factors most strongly associated with choice of romantic partners.

4. Explain how communication patterns shift as a relationship begins, grows, endures, declines, and ends.

5. Identify benefits and risks of online relationships.

6. Apply this chapter's guidelines to improve your ability to build and maintain healthy relationships

What is the single most important quality you look for in a close friend?

MindTap

Review the chapter's learning objectives and **start** with a quick warm-up activity.

Robin Dunbar (2012) studies the science of human love. As much as Dunbar tries to reduce love to scientific principles, he admits he can't explain why we yearn for the people we love or why thinking of a beloved makes us happy. Dunbar is one of the latest in a long line of scholars who have tried and failed to unravel the mysteries of human love and longing. Although science can't fully explain personal relationships, it has produced much useful knowledge about them.

I n this chapter, we focus on communication in two special types of personal relationships: friendships and romantic relationships. To launch the discussion, we'll define personal relationships. Next, we'll consider how communication guides the development of friendships and romances over time. Third, we will discuss some of the ways that digital communication affects personal relationships. Finally, we'll identify guidelines that should help you meet the challenges to personal relationships in our era.

Defining Personal Relationships

Personal relationships are unique commitments between irreplaceable individuals who are influenced by rules, relational dialectics, and surrounding contexts. We'll discuss each part of this definition.

Uniqueness

Most of our relationships are social, not personal. In social relationships, participants adhere to social roles rather than interacting as unique individuals. For instance, you might exchange class notes with a classmate, play racquetball each week with a neighbor, and talk about politics with a coworker. In each case, the other person could be replaced by someone else taking the same role. The value of social relationships lies more in what participants do than in who they are because a variety of people could fulfill the same functions.

In personal relationships, however, the particular people—who they are and what they think, feel, and do—define the connection. When one person in a personal relationship leaves the relationship or dies, that relationship ends. We may later have other intimates, but a new romantic partner or best friend will not replace a former one.

Commitment

For most of us, passion is what first springs to mind when we think about intimacy. **Passion** involves intensely positive feelings and desires for another person. The sparks and the emotional high of being in love or discovering a new friend stem from passion. It's why we feel "butterflies in the stomach" and fall "head over heels." Despite its excitement, passion isn't the primary building block of long-lasting personal relationships.

Passion is a feeling based on the rewards of involvement with a person. **Commitment**, in contrast, is a decision to remain in a relationship in spite of troubles, disappointments, sporadic boredom, and lulls in passion. The hallmark

personal relationship A relationship defined by uniqueness, rules, relational dialectics, and commitment and affected by contexts. Personal relationships, unlike social ones, are irreplaceable.

passion Intensely positive feelings and desires for another person. Passion is based on the rewards of involvement and is not equivalent to commitment.

commitment A decision to remain with a relationship. One of three dimensions of enduring romantic relationships, commitment has more impact on relational continuity than does love alone.

of commitment is the intention to share the future. Committed partners are unlikely to bail out if the going gets rough. Instead, they weather bad times (Badiou, 2012; Le & Agnew, 2003; Lund, 1985).

Commitment grows out of **investments,** or what we put into relationships that we could not retrieve if the relationship were to end. When we care about another person, we invest material things, such as money and possessions. Even more important, we invest time, energy, trust, and feelings. In doing this, we invest *ourselves.* For good or ill, the more we invest in a relationship, the more difficult it is to end it (Guerrero, Andersen, & Afifi, 2008).

Relationship Rules

All relationships have **rules** that guide how partners interact. As in other contexts, relationship rules define what is expected, what is not allowed, and when and how to do various things. As you may recall from our discussion in Chapter 5, two kinds of rules guide our communication. *Constitutive rules* define the meaning of various types of communication in personal relationships. For instance, women friends often count listening to problems as demonstrating care, whereas many men are more likely to count doing things together as showing care (Metts, 2006; Wood, 1998, 2005). Couples work out constitutive rules to define what counts as loyalty, support, rudeness, love, joking, and so forth.

Regulative rules influence interaction by specifying when and with whom to engage in various kinds of communication. For example, some friends have a regulative rule that says it's okay to criticize each other in private but not okay to do so in front of others. Some romantic partners limit physical displays of affection to private settings.

Affected by Contexts

Personal relationships are not isolated from the social world. Friendships and romances are affected by social circles, family units, and society as a whole. For instance, families may approve or disapprove of our choices of intimates or friends. Our social circles have norms of the appropriateness of activities such as recreation, community service, and religious engagement.

Laurence Monneret/Riser/Getty Images

MindTap® Which dialectic has been most challenging in one of your long-term relationships?

investments Something put into a relationship that cannot be recovered should the relationship end. Investments, more than rewards and love, increase commitment.

rules Patterned ways of behaving and interpreting behavior; all relationships develop rules.

> **KAYA** *I had never drunk much until I started going out with Steve. He was 10 years older than me. We usually spent time with his friends, who were also older and in business. All of them drank—not like a whole lot or anything, but several drinks a night. Pretty soon, I was doing that too—it was just part of the relationship with Steve.*

Changes in society and social norms go hand in hand with changes in the forms that relationships take. Compared to earlier eras, current Western society has increasing numbers of single parent families, gay and trans families, and blended families. Today, nearly 60% of couples who marry live together first (Jensen, 2014; Stobbe, 2012), and 15% of new marriages are between people of different races (Jordan, 2012). Further, 74% of women in the United States are in the paid labor force and nearly half of all households in the United States have a woman who is the primary or exclusive breadwinner (Edwards, 2015).

The growing number of dual-career couples is revising traditional expectations about how much each partner participates in earning income, homemaking, and child care (Choose Your Parents, 2014; Coontz, 2014; Miller, 2014; Pedulla & Thébaud, 2015) and how much organizations are supposed to accommodate working parents (Wood & Dow, 2010; Wood & Fixmer-Oraiz, 2017). In all of these ways, our social circles and the larger society as well are contexts that influence the relationships we form and how we communicate within them.

Relational Dialectics

A final feature of personal relationships is **relational dialectics**, which are opposing and continual tensions that are normal in personal relationships. Scholars have identified three relational dialectics (Baxter, 1990, 1993; Baxter & Montgomery, 1996; Erbert, 2000).

relational dialectics Opposing forces or tensions that are normal parts of all relationships. Three relational dialectics are autonomy/connectedness, novelty/predictability, and openness/closedness.

neutralization One of four responses to relational dialectics; involves balancing or finding a compromise between two dialectical poles.

Autonomy/Connection   In most close relationships there is frequent friction arising from the contradictory impulses for autonomy and connection. Because we want to be deeply linked to intimates, we cherish sharing experiences, thoughts, and feelings. At the same time, each of us needs some independence. We don't want our individuality to be swallowed up by relationships, so we sometimes seek distance, even from the people we love most. Friends and romantic partners may go for vacation together and be with each other almost all the time for a week or more. Yet the intense closeness leads them to crave time apart once the vacation ends. Both autonomy and closeness are natural human needs. The challenge is to preserve individuality while also creating intimacy.

STANLEY   *For a long time, I've been stressed about my feelings. Sometimes I can't get enough of Annie, and then I feel crowded and don't want to see her at all. I never understood these switches, and I was afraid I was unstable or something. Now I see that I'm pretty normal after all.*

separation One of four responses to relational dialectics, in which friends or romantic partners assign one pole of a dialectic to certain spheres of activities or topics and the contradictory dialectical pole to distinct spheres of activities or topics.

segmentation One of four responses to relational dialectics. Segmentation responses meet one dialectical need while ignoring or not satisfying the contradictory dialectical need.

Novelty/Predictability   The second dialectic is the tension between wanting familiar routines and wanting novelty. We like a certain amount of routine to provide security and predictability in our lives. Friends often have standard times to get together, and they develop preferred interaction routines (Braithwaite & Kellas, 2006). Romantic couples develop preferred times and places for going out, and they establish patterns for interacting. Families have rituals to mark holidays (Bruess, 2015; Bruess & Hoefs, 2006). Yet too much routine is boring, so friends occasionally explore a new restaurant, romantic couples periodically do something spontaneous to introduce variety into their customary routines, and families change established rituals.

Openness/Closedness   The third dialectic is the tension between a desire for openness and a desire for privacy. We want to share our inner selves with our intimates, yet there are times when we don't feel like sharing and topics that we don't want to talk about. All of us need some privacy, and our partners need to respect that (Petronio & Caughlin, 2006).

Managing Dialectics   Leslie Baxter (1990) identifies four ways intimates deal with dialectical tensions. One response, called **neutralization,** negotiates a compromise in which each dialectical need is met to an extent but neither is fully satisfied. A couple might agree to be somewhat open but not intensely so. The **separation** response favors one need in a dialectic and ignores the other. For example, friends might agree to make novelty a priority and suppress their needs for routine. Separation also occurs when partners cycle between dialectical poles to favor each pole alternately. For example, friends may get together on weekends and have little contact during the week.

A third way to manage dialectics is **segmentation** in which partners assign each need to certain spheres, issues, activities, or times. For instance, friends might be open about many topics but not discuss politics or religion.

> **MARIANNE**   *Bart and I used to be spontaneous all the time. There was always room for something unexpected and unplanned. That changed when we had the twins last year. Now our home life is totally regulated, planned to the last nanosecond. If we get off schedule in getting the boys dressed and fed in the morning, then we're late getting to day care, which means we have to talk with the supervisor there, and then we're late getting to work. We try to have some spontaneity times when Bart's folks take the boys for a weekend, but it's a lot harder now that the boys are in our life.*

The final method of dealing with dialectics is **reframing.** This is a complex strategy that redefines apparently contradictory needs as not really in opposition. My colleagues and I found examples of reframing in a study of romantic partners (Wood, Dendy, Dordek, Germany, & Varallo, 1994). Some of the couples said that their autonomy enhanced closeness because knowing they were separate in some ways allowed them to feel safer being connected. Instead of viewing autonomy and closeness as opposing, these partners transcended the apparent tension between the two to define the needs as mutually enhancing.

Research suggests that the least satisfying way to manage dialectical tension is separation in which only one need is fulfilled (Baxter, 1990). Separation is unsatisfying because repressing any natural human impulse diminishes us. The challenge is to find ways to honor and satisfy the variety of needs that humans have. Understanding that dialectics are natural and constructive allows us to accept and grow from the tensions they generate.

The Evolutionary Course of Personal Relationships

Each relationship develops in unique ways. Yet there are commonalities in how personal relationships tend to progress. We'll explore typical patterns for the evolution of friendships and romances.

Tatyana Vyc/Shutterstock.com

Novelty provides vitality to relationships.

Friendships

Although friendships sometimes blaze to life quickly, usually they unfold through a series of fairly predictable stages (Rawlins, 1981, 1994). We meet a new person at work, in class, on an athletic team, in a club, or online. During initial face-to-face encounters, we rely on standard social rules and roles, and we tend to be careful about what we disclose. In the early stage of online relationships, people often venture into more personal, self-disclosing communication than they would at a similar stage of face-to-face acquaintance.

JOSH   *I met Stan over the Internet. We were both in the same chat room, and it was like we were on the same wavelength, so we started emailing each other privately. After a couple of months, it was like I knew Stan better than any of my close friends here, and he knew me, too—inside and out. It seemed safer or easier to open up online than in person. Maybe that's why we got so close so fast.*

Review It!

Features of Personal Relationships:

- Uniqueness
- Committed
- Guided by Rules
- Affected by Contexts
- Influenced by Relational Dialectics

If both people are interested, they communicate to learn whether they have shared interests and whether they enjoy interacting. . As people discover shared interests, they generally spend more time together and are more relaxed. To signal that we're interested in being friends, we could introduce a more personal topic than any we've discussed so far. People who have gotten to know each other online may arrange a face-to-face meeting. As people interact more personally, they begin to form a foundation for friendship.

At some point, people begin to think of themselves as friends. When this happens, social norms and roles become less important, and friends begin to work out their own private ways of relating. Some friends settle into patterns of getting together for specific things (e.g., watching games, discussing books, exercising, shopping). A friend and I catch up during our 2-hour walks three times a week.

When friends feel established in each other's lives, friendship stabilizes. As trust and knowledge of each other expand, friends become more deeply woven into each other's life. Stabilized friendships may continue indefinitely.

While some friendships last for years or even lifetimes, not all do. Sometimes friends drift apart because each is pulled in a different direction by personal or career demands (Grayling, 2013). In other cases, friendships deteriorate because they've become boring. Breaking relationship rules can also end friendships. Telling a friend's secrets to a third person or being dishonest may violate the rules

of the friendship. Even when serious violations occur between friends, relationships can sometimes be repaired. For this to happen, both friends must be committed to rebuilding trust and talking openly about their feelings and needs.

When friendships deteriorate, communication changes in predictable ways. The most obvious changes are reductions in frequency and intimacy of communication. In some cases, defensiveness and uncertainty rise, causing people to be more guarded and less open.

Romantic Relationships

Like friendships, romances also have a typical—but not a universal—evolutionary path. For most of us, romance progresses through the stages of escalation, navigation, and deterioration.

Escalation Before a romantic relationship begins, there are individuals who have particular needs, goals, experiences, and qualities that affect what they want in others and relationships. Individuals have learned constitutive and regulative communication rules that affect how we interact with others and how we interpret their communication.

Romantic relationships usually start with predictable social interaction. The meaning of early communication is found on the relational level of meaning, not the content level. The content level of meaning of "Do you like jazz?" is unimportant. But on the relationship level of meaning, the comment says "I'm available and possibly interested. Are you?"

Out of all the people we meet, we are attracted romantically to only a few. The three greatest influences on initial attraction are self-concept, proximity, and similarity. Our self-concept affects our choices of candidates for romance. Sexual orientation, for example, is a primary influence on our consideration of potential romantic partners.

In addition to self-concept, proximity influences initial attraction. We can interact only with people we meet, whether in person or virtually. Consequently, the places in which we live, work, and socialize, as well as online communities in which we participate, constrain the possibilities for relationships. Some contexts, such as college campuses, promote meeting potential romantic partners, whereas other contexts are less conducive to meeting and dating.

Similarity is also important in romantic relationships. In the realm of romance, "birds of a feather flock together" seems truer than "opposites attract" (Samp & Palevitz, 2009). Most of us are attracted to people whose values, attitudes, and lifestyles are similar to ours and to people who are about as physically attractive as we are.

If early interaction increases attraction, then we may increase the amount and intimacy of interaction. During this phase, partners spend more and more time together, and they rely less on external events such as concerts or parties. Instead, they immerse themselves in the budding relationship and may feel they can't be together enough. Additional and more personal disclosures are exchanged, and partners increasingly learn how the other feels and thinks. Increasingly, people develop relationships online. As caring develops, physical desirability increases—in other words, as people get to know and like each other, they perceive each other as more physically attractive (Tierney, 2015). Compared to face-to-face relationships, online relationships tend to form more rapidly and tend to involve greater idealization in which partners have overly positive perceptions of one another.

At some point, partners consider whether they want the relationship to be permanent or at least extended. For most of America's history, a majority of citizens

SHARPEN YOUR SKILL

At the end of this chapter, refer to the Sharpen Your Skill feature, Faded Friendships, to apply concepts from Chapter 7.

have married. This is no longer the case. In 1950, only 4 million Americans lived alone; in 2012, 32 million did (Ansari, 2015). In 1960, 72% of American adults were married whereas only 50% were in 2012 (Edwards, 2015). Between 1996 and 2012, cohabitation in the United States rose 170% to 7.8 million couples (Angier, 2013).

Partners who do want to stay together may cohabit or marry. Either way, they will work through any problems and obstacles to long-term viability. In same-sex relationships, partners often have to resolve differences about openness regarding their sexual orientations and acceptance by families. Couples may also need to work out differences in religions and conflicts in locations and career goals.

KYLE   *When Todd and I got together, I knew he was the one for me—the man I wanted to spend the rest of my life with. But we had a huge problem. He is totally out, and I'm not. If I came out at my job, I'd be off the fast track immediately, and I'd probably be fired. It was a huge issue between us because he wanted me to be as out as he is—like to take him with me to the holiday parties at my company. I can't do that. It's still a real tension between us.*

Communication Highlight

How Do I Love Thee?

MindTap®

"How do I love thee? Let me count the ways." In opening one of her best-known poems with these lines, Elizabeth Barrett Browning foresaw what social scientists would later discover: that there are many ways of loving (Swidler, 2001). Just as people differ in their tastes in food and styles of dress, we differ in how we love. Researchers have identified six different styles of loving, each of which is valid in its own right, although not all styles are compatible with one another (Hendrick & Hendrick, 1996; Hendrick, Hendrick, Foote, & Slapion-Foote, 1984; Lee, 1973, 1988). See whether you can identify your style of loving in the descriptions given in Figure 7.1.

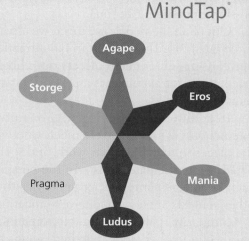

FIGURE 7.1
The Colors of Love

Eros is a style of loving that is passionate, intense, and fast moving. Not confined to sexual passion, eros may be expressed in spiritual, intellectual, or emotional ways.

Storge (pronounced "store-gay") is a comfortable, best-friends kind of love that grows gradually to create a stable and even-keeled companionship.

Ludus is a playful, sometimes manipulative style of loving. For ludic lovers, love is a challenge, a puzzle, a game to be relished but not one to lead to commitment.

Mania is a style of loving marked by emotional extremes. Manic lovers often are insecure about their value and their partners' commitment.

Agape is a selfless kind of love in which a beloved's happiness is more important than one's own. Agapic lovers are generous, unselfish, and devoted.

Pragma is a pragmatic and goal-oriented style of loving. Pragmas rely on reason and practical considerations to select people to love.

As you might expect, during this phase of romance, communication often involves negotiation and even conflict. Issues that aren't problems in a dating relationship may have to be resolved to allow a long-term future. Some couples find they cannot resolve problems. It is entirely possible to love a person with whom we don't want to share our life.

Commitment is a decision to stay with a relationship permanently. This decision transforms a romantic relationship from one based on past and present experiences and feelings into one with a future.

Navigation   In long-term relationships, the longest span of time is navigation, which is the ongoing process of communicating to sustain intimacy in the face of changes in oneself, one's partner, the relationship, and surrounding contexts. Couples continuously work through new issues, revisit old ones, and accommodate changes in their individual and joint lives. To use an automotive analogy, navigating involves both preventive maintenance and periodic repairs (Galvin & Braithwaite, 2015; Stafford, 2009). Navigating communication aims to keep intimacy satisfying and healthy and to deal with problems and tensions. Couples who talk issues through and make decisions thoughtfully have higher quality relationships than couples who are less communicative (Parker-Pope, 2014). The later years in very long-term marriages can be the happiest, in part because couples have learned to focus on what matters and not to sweat the small stuff. Other research (Parker-Pope, 2009b) confirms the finding that many couples find the "empty nest years" the happiest in their marriages because there are fewer stresses and more couple time.

The nucleus of intimacy is **relational culture,** a private world of rules, understandings, meanings, and patterns of interacting that partners create for their relationship (Wood, 1982). Relational culture includes how couples manage relational dialectics. Relational culture also includes communication rules, usually unspoken, about how to express anger, love, sexual interest, and so forth. Especially important in navigation is small talk, through which partners weave together the fabric of their history and their current lives, experiences, and dreams.

Not all intimately bonded relationships endure. Nearly half of first marriages end within 20 years (Tobbe, 2012). Tensions within a relationship, as well as pressures and problems in surrounding contexts, may contribute to declines in intimacy.

Deterioration   Deterioration often begins when one or both partners reflect and sometimes brood about dissatisfaction with the relationship. It's easy for this process to become a self-fulfilling prophecy: As gloomy thoughts snowball and awareness of positive features of the relationship ebbs, partners may actually talk themselves into the failure of their relationship.

There are some general sex and gender differences in what generates dissatisfaction (Barstead, Bouchard, & Shih, 2013; Burchell & Ward, 2011; Duck & Wood, 2006). For women, unhappiness most often arises when communication declines in quality or quantity. Men are more likely to be dissatisfied by specific behaviors or the lack of valued behaviors or by having domestic responsibilities that they feel aren't a man's job. Because many women are socialized to be sensitive to interpersonal nuances, they are generally more likely than men to notice tensions and early symptoms of relationship problems.

If unchecked, dissatisfaction tends to lead to the breakdown of established patterns, understandings, and rules that have been part of the relationship. Partners may stop talking after dinner, no longer bother to call when they are running late,

SHARPEN YOUR SKILL

At the end of this chapter, refer to the Sharpen Your Skill feature, Private Language, to apply concepts from Chapter 7.

relational culture A private world of rules, understandings, and patterns of acting and interpreting that partners create to give meaning to their relationship; the nucleus of intimacy.

Communication Highlight

The Four Horsemen of the Apocalypse

Psychologist John Gottman has spent more than 20 years studying marriages and counseling couples (Gottman, 1994a, 1994b, 1999; Gottman & Silver, 1994). He concludes that there is no difference in the amount of conflict between happily married couples and couples who divorce or have unhappy marriages.

Healthy and unhealthy marriages do differ in two important respects. First, partners who are unhappy together and who often divorce tend to engage in what Gottman calls "corrosive communication patterns." Gottman views these destructive communication practices as "the four horsemen of the apocalypse":

complaint and criticism

defensiveness and denial of responsibility

expressions of contempt

stonewalling

These "four horsemen of the apocalypse" foster negative feelings: anger, fear, sadness, and dissatisfaction. Often these destructive communication patterns are evident in extensive nagging, which can profoundly sour marriages, according to Dr. Howard Markman, who directs the Center of Marital and Family Studies (Bernstein, 2012).

Gottman thinks the most corrosive of the four is **stonewalling**, which is refusing to discuss issues that are causing tension in a relationship. When people stonewall, they block the possibility of resolving conflicts. In addition, on the relationship level of meaning they communicate that problems in the relationship aren't worth dealing with.

The second major difference between marriages that succeed and those that fail is not bad moments but a predominance of good moments. Happy couples have as many conflicts and tensions as unhappy ones, but they have more enjoyable times together. Says Gottman, a positive balance is everything.

stonewalling Refusal to discuss issues that are creating tension in a relationship. Stonewalling is especially corrosive in relationships because it blocks the possibility of resolving conflicts.

and in other ways depart from rules and patterns that have defined their relational culture. As the relational culture weakens, dissatisfaction mounts.

Conflict, which is normal in all enduring relationships, may escalate when a relationship is deteriorating. In addition, partners may feel less motivated to manage conflict constructively, so it can become increasingly hurtful and unproductive, which may accelerate relational decline. The communication highlight on this page identifies key aspects of conflict that can kill relationships.

Whether a relationship survives at this juncture depends on how committed partners are, whether they perceive attractive alternatives to the relationship, and whether they have the communication skills to work through problems constructively.

LUKE   *I'd been with Maggie for nearly a year when our relationship ended. Things had been a little rough, but I thought that was natural in long-distance relationships. I found out it was over when I saw her status update on Facebook!*

If partners lack commitment or the communication skills they need to restore intimacy, they often begin to tell others about problems in the relationship and to seek support from others. Friends and family members can provide support by being available and by listening. Although self-serving explanations of breakups are common, they aren't necessarily constructive. We have an ethical responsibility to monitor communication during this period so that we don't say things we'll later regret.

When an important relationship ends, each partner works individually to make sense of what it meant, why it failed, and how it affected him or her. Typically, partners mourn the failure to realize that which once seemed possible. Yet mourning and sadness may be accompanied by other, more positive outcomes from breakups. People report that breaking up gives them new insights into themselves, improved family relationships, and gave them more clear ideas about future partners (Tashiro & Frazier, 2003).

Digital Media and Personal Relationships

In the foregoing pages, we have already noted some of the ways in which digital media affect personal relationships. One major impact of social media is the expansion of possible friends and romantic partners. Before digital media existed, our choices of friends and romantic partners were largely limited to the people we encountered face-to-face. Today, 38% of Americans who are single and looking for a partner have used an online dating site. And these people are not all twenty-somethings. Baby boomers too are using online dating sites. Nearly 25% of people who date online find long-term partners that way (Rudder, 2015).

Social media are especially valuable to people who have strict criteria for relationship partners. Within your existing social circles, you might have trouble finding partners who are under 35 years old, Indian, and not interested in having children. However, you can specify those criteria on a dating site and find people who meet them (Ansari, 2015).

At the same time, social media have some downsides. Ironically, the advantage of having many choices is also a disadvantage of online match making. The existence of seemingly endless choices may encourage us to be dissatisfied with very good options (Ansari with Klinenberg, 2015). We want the best and may assume whatever profile we are looking at is not as good as one that we haven't yet seen. A second downside is that both sexes tend to misrepresent themselves when posting online profiles (Hall, Park, Song, & Cody, 2010). People may give false information about their physical attractiveness, and people who are less attractive are more likely to embellish their photographs and self-descriptions (Toma & Hancock, 2010).

Another concern about social media is the potential for cyberstalking. Former boyfriends and girlfriends may monitor your online communication and harass you or interfere with your communication with other people. In addition, someone you meet online can become obsessed with you and, in extreme cases, can engage in stalking you online, following your every move and imposing himself or herself into your life.

Guidelines for Maintaining Healthy Personal Relationships

We'll consider ways to deal with four common challenges that friends and romantic partners face.

Manage Distance

One of the greatest problems for long-distance commitments is inability to share small talk face-to-face and to engage in daily routines. Unlimited calling plans are a great way to stay in touch about the day-to-day stuff in your lives.

A second common problem for long-distance relationships is unrealistic expectations for time together. Because long-distance friends and partners have so little time together physically, they may feel that there should be no conflict and that they should be with each other during the time they are together. Yet this is an unrealistic expectation. Conflict and needs for autonomy are natural in all relationships. They may be even more pronounced in long-distance relationships because friends and partners are used to living alone and have established independent rhythms that may not mesh well.

The good news is that these problems don't necessarily sabotage long-distance romance. Many people maintain satisfying commitments despite geographic separation. Go to the book's online resources for this chapter to learn more about long-distance relationships and ways to connect with people who are in them.

Create Equitable Romantic Relationships

On the job, we expect equity: to be treated the same as other employees at our level. If we are asked to do more work than our peers, we can appeal to a manager or supervisor. In romantic relationships, however, there is no supervisor to ensure equity. Researchers report that the happiest dating and married couples believe both partners invest equally (DeMaris, 2007; Pedulla & Thébaud, 2015). When we think we are investing more than our partner is, we tend to be resentful. When it seems our partner is investing more than we are, we may feel guilty (Guerrero, La Valley, & Farinelli, 2008).

Traditionally, women were assigned care of the home and family because men were more likely to be the primary or only wage earners. That is no longer true. Today, nearly two thirds of women in the U.S. work outside of the home (Peters & Wessel, 2014), and many women in heterosexual partnerships earn more money than their male partners (Adams, 2014; Ream, 2012). Unfortunately, divisions of family and home responsibilities inadequately reflect changes in employment. Even when both partners in heterosexual relationships work outside the home, women typically do most of the child care and homemaking (Bianchi, Sayer, Milkie, & Robinson, 2012). Gay and lesbian couples report a greater desire for shared power and decision-making than do heterosexual couples (Hunter, 2012).

Although few partners demand moment-to-moment equality, most of us want our relationships to be equitable over time (Wood, 2011). Equity has multiple dimensions. We may evaluate the fairness of financial, emotional, physical, and other contributions to a relationship. One area that strongly affects satisfaction of spouses and cohabiting partners is equity in housework and child care. Inequitable division of domestic obligations fuels dissatisfaction and resentment, both of which harm intimacy (Alberts, Tracy, & Trethewey, 2011; Coontz, 2013, 2014).

As a rule, women assume **psychological responsibility** for relationships, which involves remembering, planning, and coordinating domestic activities (Hochschild with Machung, 2003). Parents may take turns driving children to the doctor, but it is often the mother who remembers when check-ups are needed, makes appointments, and reminds the father to take the child. Both partners may sign birthday cards, but women typically remember birthdays and buy cards and gifts. Successful long-term relationships in our era require partners to communicate collaboratively to design equitable divisions of responsibility.

psychological responsibility The responsibility for remembering, planning, and coordinating domestic work and child care. In general, women assume the psychological responsibility for child care and housework even if both partners share in the actual tasks.

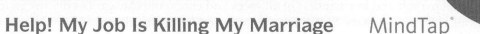

Help! My Job Is Killing My Marriage MindTap

Millennial men (those aged 18 to early 30s) want egalitarian relationships. Compared to men just a few years older, millennials see women as equals, gender roles as old-fashioned, and parenting as a shared responsibility.

A mere 35% of employed millennial men think men should be breadwinners and females should be caregivers, and 24% of millennial men without children anticipate being the primary caregiver once they have children (Miller, 2015). However, only 8% of millennial men with children are doing a majority—or even half—of parenting (Miller, 2015). What explains the discrepancy between these figures?

Careers. More specifically, institutional rules and structures that do not accommodate today's families. Most professions continue to follow policies that were developed when men were the primary breadwinners and women were the primary caregivers. Institutions have failed to adapt to the reality of two-earner families. When institutions won't bend, parents have to. Women are more likely than men to downsize careers when children are born or adopted because institutions are more inclined to offer benefits such as parental leave to women than men. Also, informal networks often devalue men who prioritize family (Miller, 2015; Pedulla & Thébaud, 2015).

MOLLY *It really isn't fair when both spouses work outside of the home but only one of them takes care of the home and kids. For years, that was how Sean's and my marriage worked, no matter how much I tried to talk with him about a more fair arrangement. Finally, I had just had it, so I quit doing everything. Groceries didn't get bought, laundry piled up and he didn't have clean shirts, he didn't remember his mother's birthday (and for the first time ever, I didn't remind him), and bills didn't get paid. After a while, he suggested we talk about a system we could both live with.*

Blend Images/Shutterstock.com

Equitable participation in domestic responsibilities enhances partners' satisfaction.

Resist Violence and Abuse Between Intimates

Intimate partner violence is experienced and perpetrated by both sexes and by gays, lesbians, straights, and transgender people (Douglas, 2012). It is also experienced and perpetrated by members of all races and economic classes. Twenty-five percent of U.S. women have been violently attacked by husbands or boyfriends, and one U.S. woman dies every 6 hours from a partner's violence (Kristof, 2014). Worldwide, at least 30% of women have been victims of intimate partner violence (Prevalence of Domestic Violence, 2013). Violence is high not only in marriages but also in dating and cohabiting relationships (Hoffman, 2012). In addition to physical abuse, verbal and emotional brutality poison altogether too many relationships.

A rising form of intimate partner violence is stalking, which is repeated, intrusive behavior that is uninvited and unwanted, that seems obsessive, and that makes the target afraid or concerned for her or his safety. Stalking is particularly easy on campuses because it isn't difficult to learn others' routines. Social networking sites such as Snapchat and Facebook give stalkers more ways to learn about (potential) victims' habits and patterns (Spitzberg & Cupach, 2014).

Intimate partner violence tends to follow a predictable cycle: Tension mounts in the abuser, the abuser explodes by being violent, the abuser then is remorseful and loving, the victim feels loved and reassured that the relationship is working, and then tension mounts anew and the cycle begins again. Too often, people don't leave abusive relationships because they feel trapped by economic pressures or by relatives and clergy who counsel them to stay (Foley, 2006; Jacobson & Gottman, 1998). Without intervention, the cycle of violence is unlikely to stop. Abusive relationships are unhealthy for everyone involved. They violate the trust that is a foundation of intimacy, and they jeopardize the comfort, health, and sometimes the lives of victims of violence.

Communication is related to intimate partner violence in two ways. Most obviously, patterns of communication between couples and the intrapersonal communication of abusers can fuel tendencies toward violence. Some partners deliberately annoy and taunt each other. Also, the language abusers use to describe physical assaults on partners includes denial, trivializing the harm, and blaming the partner or circumstances for "making me do it" (notice this is a form of *you-language*). These intrapersonal communication patterns allow abusers to deny their offenses, justify violence, and cast responsibility outside themselves.

Violence is highly unlikely to stop on its own. The cycle shown in Figure 7.2 is self-perpetuating. Further, violence that begins in the home may precede violent

Review It!

Stages in Cycle of Violence
- Tension
- Explosion
- Remorse
- Honeymoon

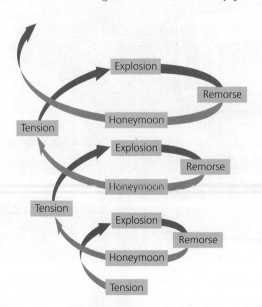

FIGURE 7.2
The Cycle of Abuse

crime outside of the home. As two people who work with intimate partner violence phrase it, "Women and children are target practice, and the home is the training ground for men's later actions" (Shifman & Tillet, 2015, p. A21).

Violent relationships are not the fault of victims. If you know or suspect that someone you care about is a victim of abuse, don't ignore the situation, and don't assume it's none of your business. It is an act of friendship to notice and offer to help. Victims of violence must make the ultimate decision about what to do, but the support and concern of friends can help them.

Negotiate Safer Sex

In our era, sexual activities pose serious, even deadly, threats to people of all sexual orientations. Each year in the United States, 18,000 people die of AIDS, and 56,000 people are diagnosed as HIV positive (Collins & Fauci, 2010). The cumulative numbers are grim: In the United States, more than one million people are living with HIV today, and over 500,000 people have died of HIV (Centers for Disease Control and Prevention, 2009, 2011).

HIV is not the only sexually transmitted disease (STD). Over 65 million Americans are currently living with one or more STDs, and 15 million new cases are diagnosed each year (Centers for Disease Control and Prevention, 2009; Dennis & Wood, 2012). Because STDs often have no symptoms, they are often undiagnosed and untreated. The long-term effects of untreated STDs can be severe: infertility, blindness, liver cancer, increased vulnerability to HIV, and death.

Despite the real dangers of unsafe sex, many people find it awkward to ask partners direct questions (i.e., "Have you been tested for HIV?" "Are you having sex with anyone else?") or to make direct requests to partners (i.e., "I want you to wear a condom," "I would like you to be tested for STDs before we have sex"). Naturally, it's difficult to talk explicitly about sex and the dangers of STDs. However, it is far more difficult to live with a disease or the knowledge that you have infected someone else.

A second reason some people don't practice safer sex is that they hold erroneous and dangerous misperceptions. Among these are the assumptions that you are safe if you and your partner are monogamous, the belief that you can recognize "the kind of person" who might have an STD, and the idea that planning for sex destroys the spontaneity. These are dangerous, false beliefs that can put you and your partners at grave risk. Another reason people sometimes fail to practice safer sex is that their rational thought and control are debilitated by alcohol and other drugs.

Discussing and practicing safer sex may be awkward, but there is no sensible alternative. Good communication skills can help you negotiate safer sex. It is more constructive to say, "I feel unsafe having unprotected sex" than "Without a condom, you could give me AIDS." (Notice that the first statement uses *I*-language, whereas the second one relies on *you*-language.) A positive communication climate is fostered by using relational language, such as *we, us,* and *our relationship,* to talk about sex.

Chapter Summary

In this chapter, we've explored communication in personal relationships, which are defined by uniqueness, commitment, relational dialectics, relationship rules, and interaction with surrounding contexts. We traced the typical evolutionary paths of friendships and romances by noting how partners communicate as relationships develop, stabilize, and sometimes decline.

In the final section of the chapter, we considered four challenges that friends and romantic partners face. The communication principles and skills we have discussed in this and previous chapters help us meet the challenges of sustaining intimacy across geographic distance, creating equitable relationships, resisting violence, and negotiating safer sex. Good communication skills enable us to meet these challenges so that our relationships survive and thrive over time.

MindTap® **Experiencing Communication in Our Lives**

CASE STUDY: Growing Together

Apply what you've learned in this chapter by analyzing the following case study, using the accompanying questions as a guide. These questions and a video of the case study are also available online with your MindTap Speech for *Communication in Our Lives.*

Max and Tara are preparing dinner together. Max has just finished a certificate program at college and informed Tara that he's thinking about continuing coursework in the fall for a bachelor's degree in engineering.

TARA: If you're keeping your project management job, why would you need a bachelor's in engineering? You're not an engineer.

MAX: Not now anyway. But I think I might like to be one.

TARA: When did this happen?

MAX: Since taking these classes. I didn't realize how interesting it is. Sometimes I get really bored at my job and I think about trying something else.

TARA: So our life is boring now?

MAX: I didn't say that. I said my job can be boring.

TARA: Mine can too – do you think I enjoy updating charts all day? That's how jobs are. But *I* still want to see you at night.

MAX: It's not about us.

TARA: How is this not about us if you're deciding to spend four nights a week in classes instead of with me? And how are we going to afford classes? Your job isn't going to pay for this.

MAX: No, it won't. The money will be an issue to discuss. But I'm pretty sure I can get some grants, And we'll figure out how to make more time for us – maybe do more lunches together during the week? Our jobs aren't that far apart.

TARA: I'm just confused. I thought we liked our life the way it is. Now it seems like you want to be someone else. Is this not enough for you anymore? Now you need to be some big man on campus?

MAX: I love our life. And I'd hardly be the big man on campus. I know this was a lot for me to throw at you. I just wanted to tell you what I was thinking – we can keep talking about it. I'm not doing anything without you. And I certainly don't want to be someone new. Maybe just someone with a new job. Ok?

TARA: Ok. I guess there are ways to make this work if it's what you really want. I just hope you won't think less of me once you're a big college man.

MAX: You're better at your job than any college man or woman could ever be. I respect that.

QUESTIONS FOR ANALYSIS AND DISCUSSION

1. What love styles do you think Max and Tara have? What cues in dialogue lead you to identify each person's love style?

2. Based on the dialogue, how would you judge Tara and Max's levels of commitment to the relationship?

3. If Max decides to pursue college classes in the fall, what suggestions for maintaining contact in long-distance relationships might be applied to this couple?

Key Concepts

commitment
investments
neutralization
passion
personal relationship

psychological
   responsibility
 reframing
relational culture
relational dialectics

rules
segmentation
separation
stonewalling

MindTap

Use flashcards to learn key concepts and take a quiz to test your knowledge.

Sharpen Your Skill

1. Faded Friendships

Remember three friendships that were once very close but have faded away. Describe the reasons they ended. How did boredom, differences, external circumstances, or violations contribute to the decay of the friendships? How did communication patterns change as the friendships waned?

2. Private Language

Private language between intimates heightens partners' sense of themselves as a special couple. Partners make up words and nicknames for each other, and they develop ways to send private messages in public settings.

What are the special words and nonverbal codes in a close relationship of yours? Do you have a way to signal each other when you're bored at a party and ready to leave? Do you use nicknames and private words? Would you feel any loss if you had no private language in your relationship?

For Further Reflection and Discussion

1. Think about the distinction between passion and commitment in personal relationships. Describe relationships in which commitment is present but passion is not. Describe relationships in which passion exists but not commitment. What can you conclude about the values of each?

2. Are you now or have you been involved in a long-distance friendship or romance? How did you communicate to bridge the distance? Do your experiences parallel the chapter's discussion of challenges in long-distance relationships?

3. Does a person who wants to end a serious romantic relationship have an ethical responsibility to talk with his or her partner about why he or she is no longer interested in maintaining the relationship? Under what conditions are we ethically obligated to help a partner through a breakup?

Beyond the Classroom

Let's take the material in this chapter beyond the classroom by thinking about how what you've learned about communication in personal relationships might apply to the workplace, ethical choices, and engagement with the broader world.

1. **Workplace.** Apply the idea of investments and commitments to the employment context. Review the jobs that you have had in your life. Which ones did you invest most heavily in? Were you more committed to those jobs than ones in which you invested less?

2. **Ethics.** This chapter cites substantial research that shows equity between partners in romantic relationships is linked to satisfaction and relationship longevity. The chapter also notes that men and women in heterosexual relationships are not contributing equitably. Are inequitable relationships unethical? Is it right or fair for one partner to do more of the work required to keep a relationship going? If not, what ways can you think of to change the long-standing pattern whereby women do more of the work involved in maintaining relationships?

3. **Engagement.** Talk with someone who was raised in a culture different from the one in which you were raised. Ask him or her what he or she considers the most important qualities in a friend and in a romantic partner. Reflect on similarities and differences in his or her answers and the answers you would give.

Corepics VOF/Shutterstock.com

8

Never doubt that
a small group
of thoughtful
committed citizens
can change the
world; indeed, it's
the only thing that
ever has.

Margaret Mead

Communication in Groups and Teams

LEARNING OBJECTIVES

After studying the topics in this chapter, you should be able to:

1. Apply the definition of a small group to a situation to determine whether it constitutes a group.

2. Distinguish between a group and a team, using your personal experience as support.

3. Determine whether a past (or future) project was (or will be) well suited to group work based on your knowledge of the limitations and strengths of small group work.

4. Examine your past experience in small groups by considering each of the five features of small groups.

5. Identify at least three strategies to maximize performance of virtual groups.

6. Apply chapter guidelines to improve your interactions in small groups.

How many groups do you currently belong to?

MindTap®

Review the chapter's learning objectives and **start** with a quick warm-up activity.

- *"Teams take too much time to decide anything."*
- *"Working in groups increases creativity."*
- *"Groups suppress individuality."*
- *"Teams make better decisions than individuals."*

You probably agree more with some of these statements than others. Actually, there's some truth to each statement. Groups generally do take more time to reach decisions than individuals, yet group decisions often are superior to those made by one person. Although group interaction stimulates creativity, it may also suppress individual opinions.

Communication is a major influence on whether groups and teams are productive and enjoyable or inefficient and unpleasant. Communication in groups and teams calls for many of the skills and understandings that we've discussed in previous chapters. For example, constructive group communication requires that members express themselves clearly, check perceptions, and listen mindfully. This chapter will increase your understanding of how groups work and enhance your ability to participate in and lead groups and teams effectively.

The chapter opens by defining groups and teams and identifying potential weaknesses and strengths of collective work. We then examine features of small groups. The third section of the chapter focuses digital media and group communication. In the final section, we discuss guidelines for effective participation and leadership.

Understanding Groups and Teams

Pick up any newspaper or surf the Internet and you will see announcements and advertisements for social groups, volunteer service committees, personal support groups, health teams, focus groups sought by companies trying out new products, and political action coalitions.

The tendency toward group work is especially pronounced in the workplace (Barge, 2009; Beebe & Masterson, 2011; Rothwell, 2015). Whether you are an attorney working with a litigation team, a medical technician who participates in a health delivery team, or a middle manager on a team assigned to find ways to increase productivity, working with others probably will be part of your career. In fact, some medical schools rely on admissions procedures specifically designed to weed out applicants who lack skill in teamwork (Harris, 2011).

What are groups and teams? Are six people standing together on a street corner waiting to cross the street a group? Are five people studying independently in a library a group? Are four students standing in line to buy books a group? The answer is *no* in each case. These are collections of individuals, but they are not groups.

For a group to exist, there must be interaction and interdependence between individuals, a common goal, and shared rules of conduct. Thus, we can define a **group** as three or more people who interact over time, depend on one another, and follow some shared rules of conduct to reach a common goal. To be a group, members must perceive themselves as interdependent—as somehow needing one another (Adams & Galanes, 2011; Harris & Sherblom, 2010).

group Three or more people who interact over time, are interdependent, and follow shared rules of conduct to reach a common goal. The team is one type of group.

team A special kind of group characterized by different and complementary resources of members and a strong sense of collective identity. All teams are groups, but not all groups are teams.

Teamwork Lacking in the OR

Reports of errors in surgery are not uncommon. Have you ever wondered how a sponge could be left inside a patient or how surgery could be performed on the wrong knee? One contributor to surgical errors is poor teamwork among those working in the operating room. A survey of more than 2,100 surgeons, anesthesiologists, and nurses at 60 hospitals showed that many teams suffer from weak teamwork (Nagourney, 2006). Doctors' disregard for nurses' expertise was one of the most commonly cited dynamics that undermined effective teamwork.

A **team** is a special kind of group that is characterized by different and complementary resources of members and a strong sense of collective identity. Like all groups, teams involve interaction, interdependence, shared rules, and common goals. Yet a team is distinct in two respects. First, teams consist of people with diverse skills and experience. Whereas group members may have similar backgrounds and abilities, a team consists of people who have different resources. Second, teams tend to develop greater interdependence and a stronger sense of collective identity than other groups (Lumsden & Lumsden, 2009).

Because groups consist of individuals who are interdependent and who interact over time, groups develop rules that members understand and follow. You'll recall from previous chapters that constitutive rules state what counts as what. For example, in some groups, disagreement counts as a positive sign of involvement, whereas other groups regard disagreement as negative. Regulative rules regulate how, when, and with whom we interact. For instance, a group might have regulative rules stipulating that members don't interrupt each other and that it's okay to be a few minutes late but more than 10 minutes is a sign of disregard for other group members. Groups generate rules over time in the process of interacting and figuring out what works for them.

Groups also have shared goals. Citizens form groups to accomplish political goals, establish social programs, protest zoning decisions, and protect the security of neighborhoods. Workers form teams to protect their benefits, develop and market products, evaluate and refine company programs, and improve productivity. Other groups form around goals such as promoting personal growth (therapy groups), sharing a life (families), socializing (singles clubs), having fun and fitting in (peer groups), or participating in sports (intramural teams).

David K Purdy/Getty Images Sport/Getty Images

Interaction between team members often heightens commitment to collective goals.

As Mieko explains in her commentary, without a common goal, a group doesn't exist. Groups end if the common objective has been achieved or if it ceases to matter to members. To better understand small groups, we'll now consider their potential values and limits, features that affect participation, and the influence of culture on group communication.

> **MIEKO**   *When I first came here to go to school, I felt very alone. I met some other students from Japan, and we formed a group to help us feel at home in the United States. For the first year, that group was most important to me and the others because we felt uprooted. The second year, it was good but not so important because we'd all started finding ways to fit in here, and we felt more at home. When we met the first time of the third year, we decided not to be a group anymore. The reason we wanted a group no longer existed.*

Potential Limitations and Strengths of Groups

Researchers have compared individual and group decision making. As you might expect, the research identifies both potential weaknesses and potential strengths of groups.

Potential Limitations of Groups

Three significant disadvantages of group discussion are the time needed for the group process and the potential for pressure to conform; both can interfere with high-quality work from groups. A third potential problem is reduced individual responsibility.

Time   From your own experience, you know that groups take longer to decide something than individuals. Operating solo, an individual can think through ideas efficiently and choose the one she or he considers best. In group discussion, however, all members must have an opportunity to voice their ideas and to respond to the ideas others put forward. In addition, groups need time to deliberate about alternative courses of action. Thus, group discussion probably is not a wise choice for routine policy making or emergency tasks. When creativity and thoroughness are important, however, the values of groups may outweigh the disadvantage of time.

Conformity Pressures   Groups also have the potential to suppress individuals and encourage conformity. This can happen in two ways. First, conformity pressure may exist when a majority of members has an opinion different from that of a minority of members or a single member. It's hard to hold out for your point of view when most of your peers have a different one.

Second, conformity pressures may arise when one member is extremely charismatic, powerful, or prestigious. Even if that person is all alone in a point of view, he or she may have sufficient status to sway others. Sometimes a high-status member doesn't intend to influence others and may not overtly exert pressure.

In effective groups, all members understand and resist conformity pressures. They realize that a high-status member isn't necessarily smarter than others, that the majority is sometimes wrong, and that the minority, even a minority of one, is sometimes right.

LANCE   *I used to belong to a creative writing group where all of us helped each other improve our writing. We were all equally vocal, and we had a lot of good discussions and even disagreements when the group first started. But then one member of the group got a story of hers accepted by a big magazine, and all of a sudden we thought of her as a better writer than any of us. She didn't act any different, but we saw her as more accomplished, so when she said something, everybody listened and nobody disagreed. It was like a wet blanket on our creativity because her opinion just carried too much weight once she got published.*

Reduced Individual Responsibility   A third potential disadvantage of group work is the possibility of **social loafing**, which exists when members of a group exert less effort than they would if they worked alone (Hoon & Tan, 2008). If an individual is charged with a task and the task doesn't get done, the individual can be held accountable. When a group is charged with a task, however, members may have less of a sense of accountability for the end product.

Potential Strengths of Groups

Groups also have noteworthy advantages. In comparison to individuals, groups generally have greater resources, are more thorough and more creative, and generate greater commitment to decisions.

Greater Resources   A group obviously exceeds any individual member in the number of ideas, perspectives, experiences, and expertise it can bring to bear on solving a problem. The diversity on teams means that one member knows the technical aspects of a product, another understands market psychology, a third has expertise in cost analysis, and so forth (Fujishin, 2014).

Greater Thoroughness   Groups also tend to be more thorough than individuals, probably because members act as a check-and-balance system for each other (Rothwell, 2015). The parts of an issue one member doesn't understand, another person does; the details of a plan that bore one person interest another; and the holes in a proposal that one member overlooks are recognized by others. The greater thoroughness of groups isn't simply the result of more people. The discussion process promotes more critical and more careful analysis because members propel each other's thinking. **Synergy** is a special kind of collaborative vitality that enhances the efforts, talents, and strengths of individual members (Furnham & Xenikou, 2013; Rothwell, 2015).

Greater Creativity   The third value of groups is that they are generally more creative than individuals. Any individual eventually runs out of new ideas, but groups seem to have almost infinite generative ability. As members talk, they build on each other's ideas, refine proposals, see new possibilities in each other's comments, and so forth. Often, the result is a greater number of ideas and more creative final solutions.

Review It!

Potential Limitations
of Groups:
- Time
- Conformity Pressures
- Reduced Individual
  Responsibility

**SHARPEN
YOUR SKILL**

At the end of this chapter, refer to the Sharpen Your Skill feature, Group Creativity, to apply concepts from Chapter 8.

social loafing Exists when members of a group exert less effort than they would if they worked alone.

synergy Collaborative vitality that enhances the efforts, talents, and strengths of individual members.

LAURA   *The first time I heard about brainstorming was on my job, when the supervisor said all of us in my department were to meet and brainstorm ways to cut costs for the company. I thought it was silly to take time to discuss cost saving when each person could just submit suggestions individually. But I was wrong. When my group started, each of us had one or two ideas—only that many. But the six of us came up with more than 25 ideas after we'd talked for an hour.*

Communication
Highlight

Einstein's Mistakes   MindTap

That's the title of a book by Hans Ohanian (2009). As brilliant as Einstein may have been, he didn't make his great discoveries alone. He is most famous for $E = mc^2$, the equation expressing the law of relativity. However, his proof of the law contained a number of mathematical errors. Another physicist, Max Von Laue, worked out a complete and correct proof, at which point $E = mc^2$ was on scientifically solid ground.

The myth of the individual genius is popular in Western societies, in part because they place high value on individualism. However, great innovations, discoveries, and inventions usually reflect the work of many people (Rae-Dupree, 2008). In his book *Group Genius,* Sawyer (2008) shows that most creativity is the product of groups and teams. One person may get the credit—the raise, the patent, or the Nobel Prize— but it takes many to do the work.

Review It!

Potential Strengths of Groups:

- Resources
- Thoroughness
- Creativity
- Commitment

Greater Commitment   Finally, an important strength of groups is their potential to generate stronger commitment to decisions. The greater commitment fostered by group discussion arises from two sources. First, participation in the decision-making process enhances commitment to decisions, which is especially important if members are to be involved in implementing the decision. Second, because groups have greater resources than an individual decision maker, their decisions are more likely to take into account the points of view of various people whose cooperation is needed to implement a decision. This is critical because a decision can be sabotaged if the people it affects dislike it or believe their perspectives weren't considered.

MindTap   How does communication in groups affect members' commitment to group decisions?

Yellow Dog Productions/Photodisc/Getty Images

Greater resources, thoroughness, creativity, and commitment to group goals are powerful values of group decision making. To realize these values, however, members must be aware of the trade-off of time needed for group discussion and must resist pressures to conform, or to induce others to conform, without critical thought.

Features of Small Groups

The group strengths we've identified are realized only if members participate effectively. Thus, we need to know what influences communication in small groups. We'll consider five features of small groups that directly affect participation.

Cohesion

Cohesion is the degree of closeness, esprit de corps, and group identity. In highly cohesive groups, members see themselves as linked tightly together and unified in their goals. This increases members' satisfaction with the group and, in turn, their productivity (Forsyth, 2009).

Communication can enhance cohesion in three ways. First, communication that emphasizes the group or team and the common objectives of all members builds cohesion. Second, cohesion is fostered by communication that highlights similarities between members. A third way to enhance cohesion is by talking in ways that allow all members to feel valued and part of the group.

Cohesion and participation influence each other reciprocally. Cohesion is promoted when all members participate. At the same time, because cohesion generates a feeling of identity and involvement, once established, it fosters participation. Encouraging all members to be involved and attending responsively to everyone's contributions generally foster cohesion and continued participation.

Although cohesion is important for effective group communication, too much cohesion can cause problems. When members are extremely close, they may be less critical of each other's ideas and less willing to engage in the analysis and arguments necessary for the best outcomes. When groups are too cohesive, they may engage in **groupthink**, a process in which members cease to think critically and independently about ideas generated by the group. Groupthink has occurred in such high-level groups as presidential advisory boards and national decision-making bodies (Janis, 1989; Young, Wood, Phillips, & Pedersen, 2001). Members perceive their group so positively that they share the illusion that it cannot make bad decisions. Consequently, they are less careful in evaluating ideas, which can result in inferior group outcomes.

Group Size

The sheer number of people in a group affects the amount of communication. The greater the number of people in a group, the fewer the contributions any individual may make. Because participation is linked to satisfaction and commitment, larger groups may generate less satisfaction and commitment to decisions than smaller ones. Groups with nine or more members may form cliques and may be less cohesive than smaller ones (Benenson, Gordon, & Roy, 2000).

Groups can be too small as well as too large. With too few members, a group has limited resources, which eliminates one of the primary advantages of groups. Also, in very small groups, members may be unwilling to disagree or criticize each other's ideas because alienating one person in a three- or four-person group would

cohesion Closeness among members of a group; esprit de corps.

groupthink The cessation of critical, independent thought on the part of a group's members about ideas generated by the group.

dramatically diminish the group. Five to seven members seems to be the ideal size for a small group (Lumsden & Lumsden, 2009).

> **MOLLY**   *The worst group I was ever in had three members. We were supposed to have five, but two dropped out after the first meeting, so there were three of us to come up with proposals for artistic programs for the campus. Nobody would say anything against anybody else's ideas, even if we thought they were bad. For myself, I know I held back from criticizing a lot of times because I didn't want to offend either of the other two. We came up with some really bad ideas because we were so small we couldn't risk arguing.*

Power Structure

Power structure is a third feature that influences participation in small groups. Power is the ability to influence others (Rothwell, 2015; Young et al., 2001). There are different kinds of power, or ways of influencing others.

Power over is the ability to help or harm others. This form of power usually is expressed in ways that highlight the status and visibility of the person wielding influence. A group leader might exert positive *power over* a member by providing mentoring, positive reports to superiors, and visibility in the group. A leader could also exert negative *power over* a member by withholding these benefits, assigning unpleasant tasks, and responding negatively to the member's communication during group meetings.

Power to is the ability to empower others to reach their goals. *Power to* is expressed in creating opportunities for others, recognizing achievements and facilitating others in accomplishing their goals (Conrad & Poole, 2012). Group members use *power to* foster a win–win group climate in which each member's success is seen as advancing collective work.

power The ability to influence others; a feature of small groups that affects participation.

power over The ability to help or harm others. Power over others usually is communicated in ways that highlight the status and influence of the person using the power.

> **STANLEY**   *The different kinds of power we discussed make me think of my high school. The principal came over the intercom to make announcements or lecture us on improper behaviors and threaten us about what was going to happen if we misbehaved. The teachers were the ones with power to. Most of them worked to empower us. They were the ones who gave us encouragement and praise. They were the ones who helped us believe in ourselves and reach our goals.*

power to The ability to empower others to reach their goals. People who use power to help others generally do not highlight their own status and influence.

The power structure of a group refers to the distribution of power among various members. If all members of a group have equal power, the group has a *distributed power structure*. On the other hand, if one or more members have greater power than others, the group has a *hierarchical power structure*. In some cases, hierarchy takes the form of one person who is more powerful than all others, who are equal in power to each other. In other cases, hierarchy may be more complicated, with more than two levels of power. A leader might have the greatest power, three others might have power equal to each other's but less than the leader's, and two other members might have little power.

Communication Highlight

Five Bases of Power

What is power? How does a person get it? There is more than one answer to each of these questions because there are different sources of power (Arnold & Feldman, 1986).

Reward power	The ability to give people things they value, such as attention, approval, public praise, promotions, and raises
Coercive power	The ability to punish others through demotions, firing, and undesirable assignments
Legitimate power	The organizational role, such as manager, supervisor, or CEO, that results in others' compliance
Expert power	Influence derived from expert knowledge or experience
Referent power	Influence based on personal charisma and personality

How is power related to participation? First, members with high power tend to be the centers of group communication: They talk more, and others talk more to them. **Social climbing** is the attempt to increase personal status in a group by winning the approval of high-status members. If social climbing doesn't work to increase the status of the climber, he or she may become a marginal participant in the group. In addition, members with a great deal of power often have greater influence on group decisions. Not surprisingly, high-power members tend to find group discussion more satisfying than members with less power (Young et al., 2001). This makes sense because those with power get to participate more and get their way more often.

Power not only influences communication but also is influenced by communication. In other words, how members communicate can affect the power they acquire. People who demonstrate expertise in the group's task and who help build group cohesion tend to acquire power quickly.

Interaction Patterns

Another important influence on participation is the group's interaction patterns. Some groups are centralized so that most or all communication is funneled through one or two people (Figure 8.1). Other groups have decentralized patterns, in which communication is more balanced and thus more satisfying to everyone. As you might suspect, the power of individual members and the power structure of the group often affect interaction patterns. If one or two members have greater power than others, a centralized pattern of interaction is likely to emerge. Decentralized patterns are more typical when members have relatively equal power.

Group Norms

A final small-group feature that affects communication is **norms**. Norms are standardized guidelines that regulate how members act and how they interact with each other. Our definition of a small group, in fact, emphasizes that individuals must

social climbing The attempt to increase personal status in a group by winning the approval of high-status members.

norms Informal rules that guide how members of a group or culture think, feel, act, and interact. Norms define what is normal or appropriate in various situations.

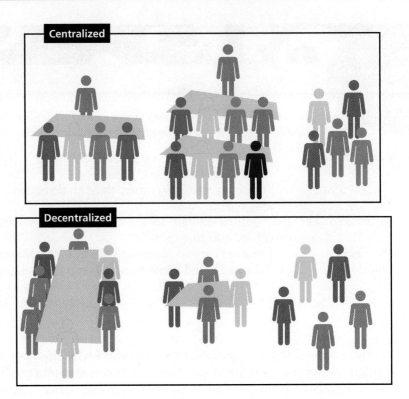

FIGURE 8.1
Group Interaction Patterns

share understandings about their conduct. Like rules in relationships, a group's norms define what is allowed, what is not allowed, and what kind of participation is rewarded.

Group norms regulate all aspects of a group's life, from the trivial to the critical. Fairly inconsequential norms may regulate whether members take breaks and eat during meetings. More substantive norms govern how carefully members prepare for meetings, how critically they analyze ideas, how well they listen to one another, and how they deal with differences and conflict.

Norms grow directly out of interaction. For example, at a group's initial meeting, one person might dismiss another's idea as dumb, and several members might not pay attention when others are speaking. If this continues for long, a norm of disrespect will develop. On the other hand, when one member says an idea is dumb, another person might counter by saying, "I don't think so. I think we ought to consider the point." If others then do consider the idea, a norm of respectful communication may develop.

Because norms become entrenched, it's important to pay attention to them from the outset of a group's existence. By noticing patterns and tendencies, you can exert influence over the norms that take hold in groups.

Digital Media and Group Communication

Whereas physical copresence was once required for groups and teams to exist and work together, that is no longer the case. Today, groups may operate through virtual conferences or through computer networking. In fact, one report found that 46% of people who work on virtual teams have never met face-to-face ("Virtual Team Challenges," n.d.). It's easy to understand why virtual teams have soared in

Review It!

Features of Groups that Affect Communication:

- Cohesion
- Size
- Power Structure
- Interaction Patterns
- Norms

popularity. They save the cost of flights for members who live in different locations, they don't require physical meeting space, and they save members' time by not requiring packing and travel. Yet, virtual teams also pose challenges. To be effective, virtual teams must adapt to the computer-mediated communication (CMC) environment in which they operate. In other words, effective leadership and participation in virtual teams requires adjustments from face-to-face style.

The two greatest challenges for virtual teams are limited nonverbal cues and constraints on building relationships and group climate (Virtual Team Challenges, n.d.). Many of the nonverbal cues we take for granted in face-to-face interaction are absent or limited in virtual groups. How do members know when it's their turn to speak? How do they know how others interpret their ideas? How do they know whether others are listening? Missing also are some of the informal interactions that build relationships among members of face-to-face groups. There is no water cooler where people get comfortable with each other through casual conversations. The literal pat on the back or smile that build report may not be possible in virtual groups.

Those who have studied best practices in virtual groups recommend the following strategies for meeting the key challenges of virtual groups (Harvard Business Press, 2010; Kurtzberg, 2014; Virtual Team Challenges, n.d.):

1. Have regular (weekly or monthly) nontask meetings. These allow members to get to know each other and build a group climate.
2. Establish a rule against multitasking during group meetings. This increases the likelihood that members are attending to group discussion and listening to one another.
3. Use multiple forms of CMC to connect. Email, tweets, skyping, and individual conversations with group members build rapport.
4. Post information about all members on a group site so that each member's accomplishments and expertise are highlighted and so that members become familiar with each other.
5. Take time zones into account when scheduling meetings. When it is 9 a.m. Eastern Daylight Saving Time, it is 6 a.m. in California, and 10 p.m. in Tokyo.
6. If at all possible, arrange for occasional face-to-face meetings. Especially when starting a group, an opportunity for members to see, hear, and be with each other is important.

Guidelines for Communicating in Groups and Teams

To realize the strengths of group work and avoid its potential weaknesses, members must participate constructively, provide leadership, and manage conflict so that it benefits the group and its outcomes.

Participate Constructively

Because communication is the heart of all groups, the ways members communicate are extremely important to the effectiveness of group process. There are four kinds of communication in groups (Table 8.1). The first three—*task communication, procedural communication,* and *climate communication*—are constructive

Table 8.1	Types of Communication in Groups

Task Communication	Climate Communication
Initiates ideas	Establishes and maintains healthy climate
Seeks information	Energizes group process
Gives information	Harmonizes ideas
Elaborates ideas	Recognizes others
Evaluates and offers critical analysis	Reconciles conflicts
	Builds enthusiasm for group

Procedural Communication	Egocentric Communication
Establishes agenda	Aggresses toward others
Provides orientation	Blocks ideas
Curbs digressions	Seeks personal recognition (brags)
Guides participation	Dominates interaction
Coordinates ideas	Pleads for special interests
Summarizes others' contributions	Confesses, self-discloses, and seeks personal help unrelated to the group's focus
Records group progress	Disrupts tasks
	Devalues others
	Trivializes group and its work

because they foster good group processes and outcomes. The fourth kind of communication is *egocentric*, or *dysfunctional, communication*. It tends to detract from group cohesion and effective decision making.

Task Communication   **Task communication** focuses on the problems, issues, or information before a group. It provides ideas and information, ensures members' understanding, and uses reasoning to evaluate ideas and information. Task contributions may initiate ideas, respond to others' ideas, or provide critical evaluation of information before the group. Task contributions also include asking for ideas and evaluation from others. Task comments emphasize the content of a group's work.

Procedural Communication   If you've ever participated in a disorganized group, you understand the importance of **procedural communication**, which helps a group get organized and stay on track. Procedural contributions establish an agenda, coordinate the comments of different members, and record group progress. In addition, procedural contributions may curb digressions and tangents, summarize progress, and regulate participation so that everyone has opportunities to speak and nobody dominates.

Climate Communication   A group is more than a task unit. It also includes people who are involved in a relationship that can be more or less pleasant and open.

task communication One of three constructive forms of participation in group decision making; focuses on giving and analyzing information and ideas.

procedural communication One of three constructive ways of participating in group decision making. Procedural communication orders ideas and coordinates the contributions of members.

climate communication One of three constructive forms of participation in group decision making. Climate communication focuses on creating and sustaining an open, engaged atmosphere for discussion.

Climate communication focuses on creating and maintaining a supportive climate that encourages members to contribute cooperatively and evaluate ideas critically (Fujishin, 2014). Climate comments emphasize a group's strengths and progress, encourage cooperative interaction, recognize others' contributions, reconcile conflicts, and build enthusiasm for the group and its work.

Egocentric Communication   The final kind of group communication is not recommended but does sometimes occur in groups. **Egocentric communication**, or dysfunctional communication, is used to block others or to call attention to oneself. It detracts from group progress because it is self-centered rather than group centered. Examples of egocentric talk are devaluing another member's ideas, trivializing the group's efforts, aggressing toward other members, bragging about one's own accomplishments, dominating, disrupting group work, and pleading for special causes that aren't in a group's interest. Another form of egocentric communication is making cynical remarks that undermine group cohesion and enthusiasm.

Task, procedural, and climate communication work together to foster productive, organized, and comfortable group discussion. Egocentric communication, on the other hand, can sabotage a group's climate and hinder its progress. Communicating clearly that egocentric behavior will not be tolerated in your group fosters norms for effective interaction.

van Hunter/Jupiter images

Effective teams have good climate communication, along with task and procedural communication.

Figure 8.2 provides an excerpt from a group discussion will give you concrete examples of each type of group communication. Each comment is coded as one of the four types of communication we have identified. This excerpt includes all four kinds of communication that we've discussed. Notice how skillfully Ann communicates to defuse tension between Bob and Jan before it disrupts the group. You might also notice that Ed provides the primary procedural leadership for the group, and Bob is effective in interjecting humor.

In effective group discussion, communication meets the task, procedural, and climate demands of teamwork and avoids egocentrism that detracts from group progress and cohesion. By understanding how varied types of communication affect collective work, you can decide when to use each type of communication in your own participation in groups. Although you may not be proficient in all three valuable kinds of group communication right now, with commitment and practice you can develop the skill.

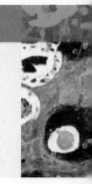

SHARPEN YOUR SKILL

At the end of this chapter, refer to the Sharpen Your Skill feature, Your Communication in Groups, to apply concepts from Chapter 8.

egocentric communication
An unconstructive form of group contribution that blocks others or calls attention to oneself.

ED: We might start by discussing what we see as the goal of this group. *(procedural)*

JAN: That's a good idea. *(climate)*

BOB: I think our goal is to come up with a better meal plan for students on campus. *(task)*

ED: What do you mean by "better"? Do you mean cheaper or more varied or more tasteful? *(task)*

ANN: I think we need to consider all three. *(task)*

ED: Well, we probably do care about all three, but maybe we should talk about one at a time so that we can keep our discussion focused. *(procedural)*

BOB: Okay, I vote we focus first on taste—like it would be good if there were some taste to the food on campus! *(task and climate [humor])*

JAN: Do you mean taste itself or quality of food, which might also consider nutrition? *(task)*

BOB: Pure taste! When I'm hungry, I don't think about what's good for me, just what tastes good. *(task)*

JAN: Well, maybe that's a reason why we might want the food service to think about nutrition—because we don't. *(task)*

BOB: If you're a health food nut, that's your problem. I don't think nutrition is something that's important in the food service on campus. *(task; possibly also egocentric if his tone toward Jan was snide)*

ED: Let's do this: Let's talk first about what we would like in terms of taste itself. *(procedural)* Before we meet next time, it might be a good idea for one of us to talk with the manager of the cafeteria to see whether they have to meet any nutritional guidelines in what they serve. *(task)*

ANN: I'll volunteer to do that. *(task)*

ED: Great. Thanks, Ann. *(climate)*

BOB: I'll volunteer to do taste testing! *(climate [humor])*

JAN: With your weight, you'd better not. *(egocentric)*

BOB: Yeah, like you have a right to criticize me. *(egocentric)*

ANN: Look, none of us is here to criticize anyone else. We're here because we want to improve the food service on campus. *(climate)* We've decided we want to focus first on taste *(procedural)*, so who has an idea of how we go about studying that? *(task)*

FIGURE 8.2
Excerpt of Group Communication

Review It!

Types of Group Communication
- Task
- Procedural
- Climate
- Egocentric

Provide Leadership

All groups need leadership. However, leadership is not necessarily one individual. Instead, leadership is a set of behaviors that helps a group maintain a good climate and accomplish tasks in an organized way. Sometimes one member provides guidance on task and procedures, and another member focuses on building a healthy group climate by recognizing and responding to members' ideas and feelings (Covey, 2012) as well as by encouraging cohesion. It's also not uncommon for different people to provide leadership at different times in a group's life. The person who guides the group at the outset may not be the one who advances the group's work in later phases. Even when an official leader exists, other members may contribute much of the communication that provides the overall leadership of a group.

Leadership is maintaining set of communication functions that establishes a good working climate, organizes group processes, and ensures that discussion is substantive. Whether a group has one or multiple leaders, the primary responsibilities of leaders are to organize discussion, to ensure sound research and reasoning, to promote norms for mindful listening and clear verbal and nonverbal communication, to create a productive climate, to build group morale, and to discourage egocentric communication that detracts from group efforts. Krystal's commentary provides an example of effective shared leadership.

> **KRYSTAL** *The most effective group I've ever been in had three leaders. I was the person who understood our task best, so I contributed the most to critical thinking about the issues. But Belinda was the one who kept us organized. She really knew how to see tangents and get us off of them, and she knew when it was time to move on from one stage of work to the next. She also pulled ideas together to coordinate our thinking. Kevin was the climate leader. He could always tell a joke if things got tense, and he was the best person I ever saw for recognizing others' contributions. I couldn't point to any one leader in that group, but we sure did have good leadership.*

In sum, whether provided by one member or several, effective leadership involves communication that advances a group's task, organizes deliberations, builds group morale, controls disruptions, and fosters a constructive climate.

Manage Conflict Constructively

Conflict is natural in groups and it can be productive. Conflict stimulates thinking, helps members consider diverse perspectives and avoid groupthink, and enlarges members' understanding of issues involved in making decisions and generating ideas (Rothwell, 2015). To achieve these goals, however, conflict must be managed skillfully. Although many of us may not enjoy conflict, we can nonetheless recognize its value—even its necessity—for effective group work.

leadership Set of communicative functions that assists groups in accomplishing tasks efficiently, staying organized, and maintaining a good climate.

Effective leadership encourages all members to participate constructively.

Emotionally Intelligent Leadership

MindTap

Psychologist Daniel Goleman (1995, 1998, 2007) asserts that standard IQ tests don't measure *emotional intelligence,* which is the ability to recognize which feelings are appropriate in which situations and the ability to communicate those feelings effectively.

Substantial research now indicates that emotionally intelligent people are more effective leaders (Ciarrochi & Mayer, 2007; Goleman, 1998; Goleman, McKee, & Boyatzis, 2002; Niedenthal, Krauth-Gruber, & Ric, 2006). They have keen awareness of their own feelings and can recognize and respond to the feelings of others. Thus, they are both self-confident and sensitive—a winning combination in leaders. Does this mean we have finally found a leadership "trait"? No. Goleman maintains that emotional intelligence is learned through commitment and practice.

Disruptive Conflict   Effective members promote conflict that is constructive for the group's tasks and climate and discourage conflict that disrupts healthy discussion. Conflict is disruptive when it interferes with effective work and a healthy communication climate. Typically, disruptive conflict is marked by egocentric communication that is competitive as members vie with each other to wield influence and get their way. Accompanying the competitive tone of communication is a self-interested focus in which members talk about only their own ideas, solutions, and points of view. The competitive and self-centered communication in disruptive conflict fosters diminished cohesion and a win–lose orientation to conflict.

Group climate deteriorates during disruptive conflict. Members may feel unsafe volunteering ideas because others might harshly evaluate or scorn them. Personal attacks may occur as members criticize one another's motives or attack one another personally. Recall the discussion in Chapter 7 about communication that fosters defensiveness; we saw that defensive climates are promoted by communication that expresses evaluation, superiority, control orientation, neutrality, certainty, and closed-mindedness. Just as these forms of communication undermine healthy climates in personal relationships, they also interfere with group climate and productivity (Fujishin, 2014).

Constructive Conflict   Constructive conflict occurs when members understand that disagreements are natural and can help them achieve their shared goals. Communication that expresses respect for diverse opinions reflects this attitude. Members also emphasize shared interests and goals. The cooperative focus of communication encourages a win–win orientation. Discussion is open and supportive of differences, and disagreements focus on issues, not personalities.

To encourage constructive conflict, communication should demonstrate openness to different ideas, willingness to alter opinions when good reasons exist, and respect for the integrity of other members and the views they express. Also, keep in mind that conflict grows out of the entire system of group communication. Thus, constructive conflict is most likely to occur when members have established a supportive, open climate of communication. Group climate is built throughout the life of a group, beginning with the first meeting. It is important to communicate in ways that build a strong climate from the start so that it is already established when conflict arises.

Chapter Summary

In this chapter, we've considered what small groups are and how they operate. We identified potential weaknesses and strengths of groups and discussed features of groups that affect group process. We then considered how to maximize the potential of digital communication in group contexts. Guidelines for group work are to participate effectively, provide leadership, and manage conflict.

Experiencing Communication in Our Lives

MindTap°

CASE STUDY: The Class Gift

Apply what you've learned in this chapter by analyzing the following case study, using the accompanying questions as a guide. These questions and a video of the case study are also available online with your MindTap Speech for *Communication in Our Lives.*

Andy, Erika, Camilla, Vernon, and Jenn are in charge of deciding what their graduating class will give to their university as the class gift. This is the second meeting of their group.

VERNON (*looking around at the other members*): Hey, hey—good to see you all again.

CAMILLA: The most awesome group on campus!

ANDY: We're looking fine, for sure.

VERNON (*glances at watch*): Okay, all of you fine-looking people (smiles at Andy), it's 10 minutes after. Has anyone heard from Jenn?
    Erika, Camilla, and Andy shake their heads and shrug.

VERNON: Okay, well, let's get started and hope she joins us in a couple of minutes. I want to get rolling on this project!

ERIKA: Hear, hear! I'm really psyched about doing this. We have the coolest class ever, and I want us to come up with a gift that's as cool as we are.

ANDY: That would have to be waaaaaaaaaaaay cool!
    The four slap hands, laugh, and chorus: Waaaaaaaaaaaaaay cool!!

VERNON: Okay, since we're so cool, what are our cool ideas for our class gift? Anybody have a suggestion?

CAMILLA: When we met last week, one idea we all kind of liked was giving a sculpture— you know, an outdoor one that could go in the main quad where everyone would see it.

ANDY: Yeah, I agree; that's the best idea we came up with.

CAMILLA: The image I have is a sculpture of a student studying—like maybe reading a book.

ERIKA: Hold on. Studying is not waaaaaaaaaaaay cool.

ANDY: Definitely not. Maybe we could have a sculpture of players on our basketball team. Now *that* would be cool!

ERIKA: Oh, please, that's even worse.
    Jenn walks in and pulls a chair into the circle with the others. Erika and Vernon smile at her as she joins them. Camilla gives her a quick hug.

ANDY: Hey, Jenn. Glad you made it.

JENN: Sorry I'm late. I was meeting with a study group for my Econ exam tomorrow.

CAMILLA (*smiling mischievously*): I rest my case. Jenn was studying, which *is* what students do!

ERIKA: Yeah, but it's not waaaaaay cool.

VERNON: Wait a minute, let's give Camilla's idea a chance. A sculpture. I kind of like the idea of a sculpture.

JENN: That would be unique. I don't think any other class has given a sculpture.

ERIKA: I'm not against a sculpture. I just don't think a student studying is the most exciting thing.

VERNON: Maybe not the most exciting, but it really gets at what being at this school is about.

ANDY: I'm beginning to agree. I mean, the sculpture should celebrate this school and its values.

VERNON: What about you, Erika. Is this idea working for you yet?

ERIKA: Personally, I'm not wild about a sculpture of a student studying. But the most important thing is that we come up with something we can all support, and the other four of you seem to like this idea.

CAMILLA: I don't think any of us is settled on the idea yet. We may come up with a different kind of sculpture that we'd all love. Does anyone have a different idea for the sculpture?
    Erika, Vernon, and Andy shrug no.

JENN: How about a sculpture of a student in regalia—as if the student is graduating? Isn't that the goal of being here?

ERIKA: That's interesting—instead of symbolizing studying to get to the goal, we could symbolize achieving it.

ANDY: I don't know. Those regalia are pretty weird looking, and they're not what students wear, except for one day. I don't think students would identify with that as much as a sculpture of a student in regular dress, like we're wearing.

JENN: Good point. You could be right.

CAMILLA: Yeah, but we do identify with the goal that the regalia symbolize. I don't know that students wouldn't identify with a sculpture of a student wearing the regalia.

VERNON: I think they might.

ERIKA: I'm not convinced.

CAMILLA: We're just speculating and stating our own opinions. Let's do some research to find out what students think. Why don't we do a couple of sketches—one of a student studying and one of a student in regalia—and poll students as to which they like better?

JENN: Good idea, but let's not move to that just yet. We might come up with more ideas for the sculpture if we talk longer.

QUESTIONS FOR ANALYSIS AND DISCUSSION

1. Apply material from this chapter to analyze the features of this small group.

2. How effective is the climate communication in this group?

Key Concepts

climate
communication
cohesion
egocentric
    communication
group
groupthink

leadership
norms
power
power over
power to
procedural
    communication

social climbing
social loafing
synergy
task communication
team

MindTap

Use flashcards to learn key concepts and take a quiz to test your knowledge.

Sharpen Your Skill

1. Group Creativity

Test the claim that groups tend to be more creative than individuals. Ask five students individually to write down all the ways they can think of to improve Facebook. When they have run out of ideas, ask them to form a group and generate as many improvements for Facebook as they can. Did the individuals or the group produce more ideas?

2. Your Communication in Groups

Draw on your own perceptions to answer the following four questions. After you have responded, ask one or two people who have worked with you in groups to answer these questions about your participation.

1. Observe yourself in a small group setting, and record the focus of your comments.

    _____

2. Do you specialize in task, procedural, or climate communication?

    _____

3. Which kinds of group communication do you do well? In which areas do you want to develop greater skill?

    _____

For Further Reflection and Discussion

1. Interview a professional in the field you hope to enter after college. Ask him or her to identify the different work groups and teams he or she has been part of in the past year. How many of the types of groups and teams described in this chapter do your interviewee name?

2. What ethical responsibilities accompany having power in a group? What are ethical and unethical uses of power in group and team situations?

3. Observe a group discussion on your campus or in your town. Record members' contributions by classifying them as task, climate, procedural, or egocentric. Does the communication you observe explain the effectiveness or ineffectiveness of the group?

4. Go to the book's online resources for this chapter to learn more about groupthink.

5. Go to the book's online resources for this chapter to view an article on team cohesion among athletes.

Beyond the Classroom

Let's take the material in this chapter beyond the classroom by thinking about how what you've learned about the foundations of group and team communication might apply to the workplace, ethical choices, and engagement with the broader world.

1. **Workplace.** Interview a professional in the field you hope to enter after college. Ask him or her to identify how various groups and teams discussed in this chapter are used on the job. If you are already employed in a career, reflect on your experiences with groups on the job.

2. **Ethics.** Is it ethical for a group member with high prestige to press her or his opinion when she or he knows others are likely to defer?

3. **Engagement.** This chapter points out that groups exist within cultural contexts that affect how they operate. Talk with classmates or other students who were raised in a non-Western culture. Ask them what values of their home culture are reflected in the ways groups operate.

StockLite/Shutterstock.com

Find a job you like and you add five days to every week.

H. Jackson Brown, Jr.

Communication in Organizations

LEARNING OBJECTIVES

After studying the topics in this chapter, you should be able to:

1. Consider how the three features of organizations have influenced your experience in your college or university.

2. Explain the reciprocal relationship between an organization's communication and its culture.

3. Examine an organization's website for evidence of its organizational values.

4. Draw on personal experience to provide examples of organizational communication, such as rites, rituals, stories, and structures.

5. Evaluate the advantages and disadvantages of technology on organizational communication.

6. Apply chapter guidelines to improve your effectiveness when communicating in and with organizations.

Should employers monitor employees' use of digital media during work hours?

MindTap

Review the chapter's learning objectives and **start** with a quick warm-up activity.

A patient dies after what should have been routine surgery. His is one of the 100,000–200,000 deaths that result from preventable medical errors in U.S. hospitals each year (Gupta, 2012). As soon as the patient is pronounced dead, the blame game begins. The doctor in charge of the case claims the nurse was not monitoring vital signs. The nurse insists that she noted drops in the patient's blood pressure on the chart, but the doctor didn't pay attention. The doctor says the nurse should have told him about the drop, not just made a note on the chart. The nurse replies that the doctor has yelled at her when she's called his attention to patient information in the past. Both the nurse and the doctor seem more interested in defending themselves than figuring out what went wrong. That's almost inevitable in a culture of blame.

When assigning blame is a priority, staff may hide errors rather than report them and protect themselves and their friends rather than talk honestly about what—not who—is the problem (Domrose, 2010; Palmieri, Peterson, Pesta, Flit, & Saettone, 2010). Evidence that a culture of blame can be counterproductive has convinced many health care organizations to cultivate a culture of safety to reduce risks and improve care for patients (Clancy, 2011). A safety culture exists when management and employees share a strong commitment to ensuring the safety of the work environment and to making safety of patients and employees paramount. In a safety culture, employees at all ranks feel free to report errors and near misses without fear of being reprimanded or punished. open communication increases awareness of challenges to safety and enables teamwork in overcoming them.

To assess their culture, many hospitals rely on a survey that asks staff to rate their organization's emphasis on teamwork, openness in communicating about errors, and freedom to question actions and decisions, including those of staff with higher authority. Hospitals with more open communication have a stronger safety culture, which studies show means better patient care (Clancy, 2011).

Communication is central to cultivating a safety culture—or any other kind of organizational culture. It is communication—upward, downward, lateral, internal, and external—that defines an organization's identity, guides its actions, and specifies members' roles and responsibilities.

Communication in organizations is the topic of this chapter. In the first section, we identify key features of organizational communication. Next, we discuss the overall culture of the organization, which establishes the context for communication among members of the organization. In the third section of the chapter, we consider the impact of digital media's increasing presence in organizational contexts. Finally, we discuss three guidelines for communicating in organizations in our era.

Key Features of Organizations

Much of what you've learned in previous chapters applies to communication in organizations. For instance, effective communication on the job requires listening, verbal and nonverbal competence, appreciation of cultural differences, and the ability to work well on teams. To build on what you've already learned, we'll discuss three features of organizations: structure, communication networks, and links to external environments.

Structure

Structure orders activity in organizations. It is a set of procedures, relationships, and practices that provides predictability for members of an organization so that they understand roles, procedures, and expectations related to doing work.

Most modern organizations rely on a hierarchical structure, which assigns different levels of power and status to different members and specifies who is to communicate with whom about what. Rigidly hierarchical organizations have strict rules about following the chain of command. In more loosely structured organizations, members may communicate more openly with their own peers and with peers of their supervisors.

Communication Networks

A second characteristic of organizational communication is that it occurs in **communication networks**, which are formal and informal links between people (Modaff, Butler, & DeWine, 2011). In most organizations, people belong to multiple networks. For example, faculty belong to social networks that include colleagues; task networks consisting of people with whom they discuss teaching, research, and departmental and university issues; and ad hoc networks that arise to respond to specific crises or issues. Overlaps among networks to which we belong ensure that faculty will interact with many people in a university.

In addition to networks physical networks, virtual networks are common in most professions (Kurtzberg, 2014; Rothwell, 2015). Virtual networks are essential for employees who telecommute. An estimated 3.3 million U.S. employees telecommute half of the time, and an estimated 25 million telecommute part of the

structure In an organization, the set of procedures, relationships, and practices that provides predictability for members so that they understand roles, procedures, and expectations and so that work gets done.

communication networks Formal and informal links between members of organizations.

Virtual networks are essential in professional life.

AntonioDiaz/Shutterstock.com

time. This is an 80% increase since 2005 (Global Analytics, n.d.). Using computers, smart phones, tablets, faxes, and other devices, telecommuters do their work and maintain contact with colleagues and clients without being at a central, physical workplace. As we noted in Chapter 8, virtual workplaces pose challenges, but the benefits are substantial.

Links to External Environments

Like other communication systems, organizations are embedded in contexts that affect how they work and whether they succeed or fail (Siebold, Hollingshead, & Yoon, 2013). In other words, an organization's operation cannot be understood simply by looking only within the organization. We must also grasp how it is related to and affected by the larger environment.

Consider the impact of recession that began in 2008 on a few U.S. organizations:

As companies' profits tumbled, they laid off workers.

- Faced with unemployment, former workers scaled back spending. They drove less, which affected companies that sell and repair cars, sell gasoline, and host tourists.

- As unemployment stretched from months to years, homeowners could not pay mortgages, so homes were foreclosed.

- As foreclosed homes flooded markets at bargain prices, fewer new homes were built, taking a bite out of the construction industry.

- Workers in construction and tourism were laid off.

- And on and on.

Although internal factors may have contributed to particular businesses' troubles, clearly many organizations suffered because of factors outside their organizational boundaries. When external conditions are good, even mediocre companies survive. When external conditions are bad, even good companies can be hurt or driven out of business.

Organizational Culture

Organizational culture consists of ways of thinking, acting, and understanding work that are shared by members of an organization and that reflect an organization's distinct identity.

Just as ethnic cultures consist of meanings shared by members of the ethnic groups, organizational cultures consist of meanings shared by members of organizations. Just as new members of ethnic cultures are socialized into preexisting meanings and traditions, new members of organizations are socialized into preexisting meanings and traditions (Argyris, 2012; Eisenberg, Goodall, & Trethewey, 2013; Miller, 2014). Just as a culture's way of life continues even though particular people leave or die, an organization's culture persists despite turnover.

The relationship between communication and organizational culture is reciprocal: Communication between members of an organization creates, sustains, and sometimes alters the culture. At the same time, organizational culture influences patterns of communication. Four kinds of communication that are particularly important in developing, expressing, and sustaining organizational culture are vocabularies, stories, rites and rituals, and structures.

Review It!

Features of
Organizations:

- Structure
- Communication
  Networks
- Links to External
  Environment

---

organizational culture
Ways of thinking, acting, and understanding work that are shared by members of an organization and that reflect an organization's distinct identity.

Caution: Work May Be Hazardous to Your Health

MindTap

What makes jobs stressful? Big issues such as harassment and incompetent leadership are surely stressful, but the biggest stressor may be the continuous stream of uncivil, rude behavior from bosses and coworkers. Georgetown University's McDonough School of Business Professor Christine Porath (2015) identifies common rude behaviors that take a daily toll on employees:

- Interruptions
- Walking away from a conversation
- Answering calls in the middle of meetings
- Taking credit for wins but blaming others for losses
- Not saying please and thank you
- Swearing
- Putting others down

But employees who complain about the above rude behaviors admit to engaging in some pretty uncivil actions themselves:

- Hibernating into e-gadgets
- Ignoring invitations
- Not listening
- Emailing/texting during meetings
- Belittling others nonverbally
- Not saying please and thank you

The costs of incivility are significant. Intermittent stressors such as the above behaviors compromise the immune system and can lead to serious health conditions including ulcers and heart problems. In addition, uncivil work environments are linked to missing information and reduced cognitive processing.

Vocabularies

Just as the language of an ethnic culture reflects and expresses its history, norms, values, and identity, the *vocabulary* of an organization reflects and expresses its history, norms, values, and identity.

Hierarchical Language   Many organizations and professions have vocabularies that distinguish levels of status among members. The military, for example, relies on language that continually acknowledges rank (i.e., *Yes, sir, chain of command*), which reflects the close ties between rank, power, and privilege. Salutes, as well as stripes and medals on uniforms, are part of the nonverbal vocabulary that emphasizes rank and honors.

"I've never actually seen a corporate ladder before."

From *The Wall Street Journal.* Reprinted by permission of Cartoon Features Syndicate.

Unequal terms of address also communicate rank. For instance, the CEO may use first names ("Good morning, Bob") when speaking to employees. Unless given permission to use the CEO's first name, however, lower status members of an organization typically use *Mr., Ms., Sir,* or *Ma'am* to address the CEO. Colleges and universities use titles to designate faculty members' rank and status: instructor, assistant professor, associate professor, full professor, and distinguished (or chaired) professor. Faculty generally use students' first names, whereas students tend to use titles to address their teachers: Dr. Armstrong or Professor Armstrong, for example.

Masculine Language   Because organizations historically have been run by men, it's not surprising that many organizations have developed and continue to use language more related to men's traditional interests and experiences than to women's (Ashcraft & Mumby, 2004; Mumby, 2006a, 2006b). Consider the number of phrases in the working world that are taken from sports (i.e., home run, ballpark estimate, touchdown, develop a game plan, be a team player, take a time out, the starting lineup), from military life (i.e., battle plan, mount a campaign, plan of attack, under fire, get the big guns, defensive move, offensive strike), and from male sexual parts and activities (i.e., a troublesome person is a *prick*; you can *hit* on a person, *screw* someone, or *stick it to* them; bold professionals have *balls*).

Less prevalent in most organizations is language that reflects traditionally feminine interests and experiences (i.e., put something on the back burner, percolate an idea, stir the pot, give birth to a plan, nurse an idea along). Whether intentional or not, language that reflects traditionally masculine experiences and interests can bind men together while prompting some women to feel excluded.

Similarly, many organizations in the United States reflect Caucasian and Christian values and experiences more than those of other ethnic and religious

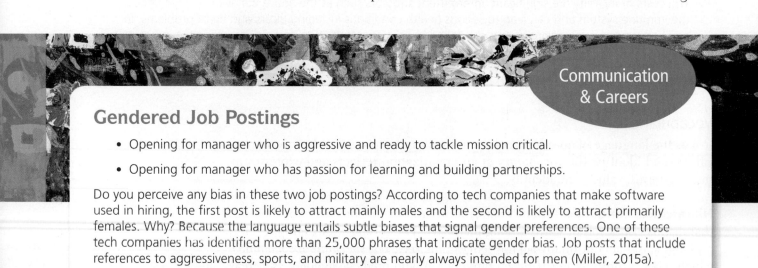

Communication & Careers

Gendered Job Postings

- Opening for manager who is aggressive and ready to tackle mission critical.

- Opening for manager who has passion for learning and building partnerships.

Do you perceive any bias in these two job postings? According to tech companies that make software used in hiring, the first post is likely to attract mainly males and the second is likely to attract primarily females. Why? Because the language entails subtle biases that signal gender preferences. One of these tech companies has identified more than 25,000 phrases that indicate gender bias. Job posts that include references to aggressiveness, sports, and military are nearly always intended for men (Miller, 2015a).

Language in Left Field

The prevalence of sports-related terms in U.S. business culture can pose challenges for international business conversations. Consider these foul balls that only Americans understood (Jones, 2007):

While at a global leadership meeting in Italy, William Mitchell, CEO of Arrow Electronics, wanted to change the agenda, so he said, "I'm calling an audible."

At a meeting with Indian executives, Alan Guarino, CEO of Cornell International, tried to change a contractual clause by demanding "a jump-ball scenario."

AFLAC CEO Dan Amos baffled Japanese executives when he told them that using the AFLAC duck for ads in Japan would be a "slam dunk."

groups (Allen, 2006). For instance, most portraits are of white people, usually males; official holidays generally include Christmas but not Kwanzaa or Hanukkah. Such biases may be unconscious and unintended, but they can nonetheless make organizations feel more comfortable to some people and unwelcoming to others (Miller, 2015a).

Stories

Scholars of organizational culture recognize that humans are storytellers by nature. In professional life, the stories we tell do some real work in establishing and sustaining organizational cultures. In a classic study, Michael Pacanowsky and Nick O'Donnell-Trujillo (1983) identified three kinds of stories within the organizational context.

Corporate Stories   Corporate stories convey the values, style, and history of an organization. Just as families have favorite stories about their histories and identities that they retell often, organizations have favorite stories that reflect their collective visions of themselves (Mumby, 2006a; Pacinowski & O'Donnello-Trujillo, 1983).

One important function of corporate stories is to socialize new members into the culture of an organization. Newcomers learn about the history and identity of an organization by listening to stories of its leaders as well as its trials and triumphs. For example, both Levi Strauss and Microsoft are known for their informal style of operation. Veteran employees regale new employees with tales about the laid-back founders of the companies. These stories socialize new employees into the cultures of the companies.

When retold among members of an organization, stories foster feelings of connection and vitalize organizational culture. As long-term members of organizations rehash pivotal events—crises, successes, and takeovers—in the organization's history, they cement bonds among them and their identification with the organization. Jed's commentary provides an example of how stories express and reinforce organizational culture.

JED   *I sing with the Gospel Choir, and we have a good following in the Southeast. When I first joined the group, the other members talked to me. In our conversations, what I heard again and again was the idea that we exist to make music for God and about God, not to glorify ourselves. One of the choir members told me about a singer who had gotten on a personal ego trip because of all the bookings we were getting, and he started thinking he was more important than the music. That guy didn't last long with the group.*

Review It!

Organizational Stories:
* Corporate
* Personal
* Collegial

SHARPEN YOUR SKILL

At the end of this chapter, refer to the Sharpen Your Skill feature, Noticing Stories and the Work They Do, to apply concepts from Chapter 9.

Personal Stories   Members of organizations also tell stories about themselves. Personal stories are accounts that announce how people see themselves and how they want to be seen by others (Cockburn-Wootten & Zorn, 2006). For example, if Sabra perceives herself as a team player, she could simply tell new employees "I am a person who believes in teamwork." On the other hand, she could define her image by telling a story: "When I first started working at this clinic, most folks were operating in isolation, and I thought a lot more could be accomplished if we collaborated. Let me tell you something I did to make that happen. After I'd been on staff for 3 months, I was assigned to work up a plan for downsizing our billing department. Instead of just developing a plan on my own, I talked with other managers, and then I met with people in accounting to get their ideas. The plan we came up with reflected all of our input." This narrative gives a concrete, coherent account of how Sabra sees herself and wants others to see her.

Collegial Stories   The third type of organizational story is accounts of other members of the organization. When I first became a faculty member, a senior colleague took me out to lunch and told me anecdotes about people in the department and the university. At the time, I thought he was simply sharing some interesting stories. Later, however, I realized he had told me who the players were so that I could navigate my new context.

Collegial stories told by coworkers tell us what to expect from whom. "If you need help getting around the CEO, Jane's the one to see. A year ago, I couldn't finish a report by deadline, so Jane rearranged his calendar so he thought the report wasn't due for another week." "Roberts is a real stickler for rules. Once when I took an extra 20 minutes on my lunch break, he reamed me out." Whether positive or negative, collegial stories assert identities for others in an organization. They are part of the informal network that teaches new workers how to get along with others in the organization.

Rites and Rituals

Rites and rituals are verbal and nonverbal practices that express and reproduce organizational cultures. They do so by providing standardized ways of expressing organizational values and identity.

Rites   Rites are dramatic, planned sets of activities that bring together aspects of an organization's culture in a single event. Harrison Trice and Janice Beyer (1984) identified six kinds of organizational rites. Rites of passage are used to mark membership in different levels or parts of organizations. For example, a retirement is often symbolized by a lunch or dinner, acknowledging the retiring employee's contributions. A desk plaque with a new employee's name and title is a rite that

rites Dramatic, planned sets of activities that bring together aspects of an organization's culture in a single event.

acknowledges a change in identity. *Rites of integration* affirm and enhance the sense of community in an organization. Examples are holiday parties, annual picnics, and retreats.

Organizational cultures also include rites that blame or praise people. Demotions and firings are blaming rites. The counterpart is enhancement rites, which praise individuals and teams that embody the organization's goals and self-image. Campuses bestow awards on faculty who are especially gifted teachers and chaired professorships on outstanding scholars. Many sales companies give awards for productivity (i.e., most sales of the month, quarter, or year). Audrey describes an enhancement rite in her sorority.

AUDREY *In my sorority, we recognize sisters who make the dean's list each semester by putting a rose on their dinner plates. That way everyone realizes who has done well academically, and we can also remind ourselves that scholarship is one of the qualities we all aspire to.*

Renewal rites aim to help organizations manage change. Training workshops serve this purpose, as do meetings at which new leaders are introduced and their visions are explained. Organizations also develop conflict resolution rites to deal with differences and discord. Examples are HR counseling, grievance, arbitration, collective bargaining, mediation, executive fiat, and ignoring or denying problems.

Rituals Rituals are the forms of communication that occur regularly and that members of an organization perceive as familiar and routine parts of organizational life. Rituals differ from rites in that rituals don't necessarily bring together a number of aspects of organizational ideology into a single event. Rather, rituals

rituals Forms of communication that occur regularly and that members of an organization perceive as a familiar and routine part of organizational life.

Michaeljung/Shutterstock.com

Organizational rites often honor those who exemplify what an organization stands for.

are repeated communication performances that communicate a particular value or role definition.

Organizations have personal, task, and social rituals. *Personal rituals* are routine behaviors that individuals use to express their organizational identities. In their study of organizational cultures, Pacanowsky and O'Donnell-Trujillo (1983) noted that Lou Polito, the owner of a car company, opened all the company's mail every day. Whenever possible, Polito hand-delivered mail to the divisions of his company to communicate his openness and his involvement with the day-to-day business.

Social rituals are standardized performances that affirm relationships between members of organizations (Mokros, 2006; Mumby, 2006a). Some organizations have a company dining room to encourage socializing among employees. In the United Kingdom and Japan, many businesses have afternoon tea breaks. Many employees develop griping rituals in which the purpose is to complain about problems, not to solve them. Sharon provides an example of an office griping ritual.

SHARON   *Where I work, we have this ritual of spending the first half-hour or so at work every Monday complaining about what we have to get done that week. Even if we don't have a rough week ahead, we go through the motions of moaning and groaning. It's kind of like a bonding ceremony for us.*

SHARPEN YOUR SKILL

At the end of this chapter, refer to the Sharpen Your Skill feature, Noticing Rituals in Your Organization, to apply concepts from Chapter 9.

Task rituals are repeated activities that help members of an organization perform their jobs. Common task rituals are forms and procedures that members of organizations are expected to use to do various things. These forms and procedures standardize task performance in a manner consistent with the organization's view of itself and how it operates. In their study of a police unit, Pacanowsky and O'Donnell-Trujillo (1983) identified the routine that officers are trained to follow when they stop drivers for violations. The questions officers are taught to ask ("May I see your license, please?" "Do you know why I stopped you?" "Do you know how fast you were going?") allow them to size up traffic violators and decide whether to give them a break or a closer look.

Structures

Organizational cultures are also represented through structural aspects of organizational life. As the term implies, structures organize relationships and interaction between members of an organization. We'll consider four structures that express and uphold organizational culture: roles, rules, policies, and communication networks.

Roles Roles are responsibilities and behaviors that are expected of people because of their specific positions in an organization. Most organizations formally define roles in job descriptions:

Training coordinator: Responsible for assessing needs and providing training to Northwest branches of the firm; supervises staff of 25 professional trainers; coordinates with director of human relations.

A role is not tied to any particular person. Rather, it is a set of functions and responsibilities that could be performed by any number of people who have

roles The collection of responsibilities and behaviors associated with and expected of a specific position in an organization.

particular talents, experiences, and other relevant qualifications. If one person quits or is fired, another can be found as a replacement. Regardless of who is in the role, the organization will continue with its structure intact. The different roles in an organization are a system, which means they are interrelated and interacting. Each role is connected to other roles within the system. Organizational charts portray who is responsible to whom and clarify the hierarchy of power among roles in the organization.

Rules   Rules, which we discussed in Chapter 5, are patterned ways of interacting. Rules are present in organizational contexts just as they are in other settings of interaction. As in other contexts, organizational rules may be formal (in the contract or organizational chart) or informal (norms for interaction).

Within organizations, constitutive rules specify what various kinds of communication mean. Socializing with colleagues after work may count as showing team spirit. Participating in training sessions and dressing like upper management may communicate ambition.

Regulative rules specify when, where, and with whom communication occurs. Organizational charts formalize regulative rules by showing who reports to whom. Other regulative rules may specify that problems should not be discussed with people outside the organization and that personal communication with people outside the organization is (or is not) permitted during working hours. Lyle's commentary points out what counted as violating the chain of command in his company.

> **LYLE**   *I found out the hard way that a company I worked for was dead serious about the organizational chart. I had a problem with a coworker, so I talked with a guy in another department I was friends with. Somehow my supervisor found out, and he blew a gasket. He was furious that I had "gone outside of the chain of command" instead of coming straight to him.*

Policies   Policies are formal statements of practices that reflect and uphold the overall culture of an organization. Most organizations codify policies governing such aspects of work life as hiring, promotion, benefits, grievances, and medical leave. The content of policies in these areas differs among organizations in ways that reflect the distinct cultures of diverse work environments.

Organizational policies also reflect the larger society within which organizations are embedded. For example, as public awareness of sexual harassment has increased, most organizations have developed formal policies that prohibit sexual harassment and detail the procedure for making complaints. The prevalence of dual-career couples has prompted some organizations to help place the spouses of people they want to hire.

Communication Networks   As we noted previously in this chapter, communication networks link members of an organization together through formal and informal forms of interaction and relationship. These networks play key roles in expressing and reinforcing the culture of an organization.

Job descriptions and organizational charts, which specify who is supposed to communicate with whom about what, are formal networks. They define lines of upward communication (i.e., subordinates to superiors: providing feedback, reporting results), downward communication (i.e., superiors to subordinates: giving

policies Formal statements of organizational practices. An organization's policies reflect and uphold the overall culture of the organization.

orders, evaluating job performance, establishing policies), and horizontal communication (i.e., peer to peer: coordinating between departments).

The informal communication network is more difficult to describe because it is neither formally defined nor based on fixed organizational roles. Friendships, alliances, car pools, and adjoining work spaces can create informal networks through which a great deal of information flows. Most professionals have others within their organization with whom they regularly check perceptions and past whom they run certain ideas.

Communication outside the formal channels of an organization is sometimes called the *grapevine*, a term that suggests its free-flowing quality. Grapevine communication, although continual in organizational life, tends to be especially active during periods of change. This makes sense because we engage in communication to reduce our uncertainty and discomfort with change. New information (a fresh rumor) activates the grapevine.

Review It!

Organizational
Structures:
• Roles
• Rules
• Policies
• Networks

Digital Media and Organizational Communication

It is not an exaggeration to state that technologies have revolutionized how organizations operate. We'll discuss six of the many ways that digital media have changed the workplace.

First, digital media have the potential to increase productivity and efficiency. We count on email, tweets, and texts with coworkers to keep us informed, expect material we need to come to us as attachments or scans, and assume computers will do the majority of calculating and record keeping. Virtual conferences are increasingly preferred to more costly and time-intensive physical meetings. Much of the information we need—from company reports to research in libraries—is available online, saving our time in tracking it down. These and other time savers mean that digital media can boost productivity (Kendrick & Sooknanan, 2014; Rice & Leonardi, 2013).

Second, technologies increase organizational flexibility. As we noted in Chapter 8, technologies allow people to work in places other than brick and mortar offices and at times other than 9 to 5. Most professionals have computers, smart phones, and scanner/printers, and often fax machines in their homes. For many jobs, that's all the equipment that's needed to conduct business. Employees who experience temporary mobility limitations from surgery or accidents may be able to meet all of their job requirements without leaving their homes. Similarly, if a child is ill, a nanny is sick, or a day care center closes, employees may be able to stay home with a child while still doing their work.

Third, digital media enlarge the range of professional contacts. LinkedIn began as a tool to link entrepreneurs and has expanded to be a networking hub for professionals in many fields. In addition, professional networks are increasingly used for job-seeking and job recruiting. Active job-seekers may survey job opportunities posted on these sites. Recruiters pay LinkedIn for the privilege of trawling the network to find professionals suited to jobs they are trying to fill. Before deciding where to locate new offices, some companies review profiles on LinkedIn to see where qualified workers are grouped (Workers of the World, 2014).

Fourth, digital media increase an organization's marketing reach and strength (Quesenberry, 2015). Using Twitter and Instagram and websites lets organizations gather information about potential or actual customers and clients, listen and

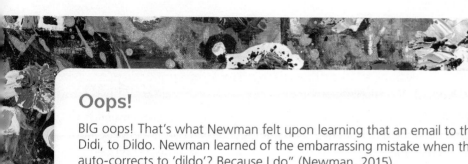

Oops!

BIG oops! That's what Newman felt upon learning that an email to the boss, Didi Gluck, auto corrected Didi, to Dildo. Newman learned of the embarrassing mistake when the boss said, "Did you know 'Didi' auto-corrects to 'dildo'? Because I do" (Newman, 2015).

Lesson: Always proofread content and addressees to make sure you are sending what you intend to whom you intend.

respond to stakeholders, create demand for products, and build and reward loyalty. Touching thousands of people costs almost nothing and is instant—quite a change from sending letters via mail or paying operators to make calls (Coombs, Falkheimer, Heide, & Young, 2016; Luttrell, 2014).

But digital media in the workplace are not always beneficial. Social media can be a powerful distraction from work. We all know how tempting it is to post updates on our lives, look at Facebook and LinkedIn for updates in our social networks, tweet friends, shop, watch videos, and play games. And those actions can cause problems. The most obvious is that all of these activities interfere with our productivity and, ultimately, our job performance and success. A second problem is that, unless there is a policy allowing personal media, it's unethical to engage in personal communication via your computer, tablet, or phone during the time that your employer is paying you a salary. Employers are becoming increasingly intolerant of employees who engage in personal and social communication via digital media during work hours. As the COMMUNICATION HIGHLIGHT on next page indicates, many employers rely on sophisticated systems to monitor employees' use of digital media.

The final impact of digital media that we will note is related to the prior one. Employers want to benefit from the fact that employees are wired. A recent Gallop poll found that nearly one third of workers say they are expected to check email and be in touch with the office after working hours (Streitfeld, 2015). Some employees report that their companies require them to download an app that monitors where they are 24 hours a day (Streitfeld, 2015).

Guidelines for Effective Communication in Organizations

We'll discuss two guidelines that are particularly relevant to organizational communication in our era.

Balance Investments in Work and the Rest of Your Life

None of us is only a career person. We are also parents and citizens and people who have responsibilities and passions outside of the workplace. Each of us needs to balance our investments in our work and in other aspects of life, including family, recreation, civic engagements, and community involvement.

Keeping Track of Employees

MindTap

A majority of today's employers monitor their employees. Two-thirds of employers monitor their employees' website visits and 43% monitor email, sometimes with dire consequences: 28% of employers have fired workers for email misuse (Staples, 2014; Workplace Privacy, 2011). Here are a few facts to keep in mind:

- In most cases, employers have the right to monitor employees' computer screens while they are working and to see what is stored in computers terminals and hard disks.

- Employers have the right to monitor employees' Internet usage, including email.

- In most cases, employers have the right to monitor employees' phone calls and to obtain records of calls made. Personal calls are an exception; employers are supposed to cease monitoring if they realize a call is personal.

- In most cases, employers have the right to videotape employees. Videotaping is not allowed in bathrooms, locker rooms, and other places where courts have ruled it would be intrusive.

- A 2010 legal ruling broadened employers' rights. This ruling states that an employer's policy regarding monitoring need not specify every means of communication subject to the policy. In other words, employees should assume they, as well as their phones and computers, are subject to monitoring.

Many workplaces do not make it easy to have a life outside of work. In a survey of people who work outside of their homes, 48% of women and 39% of men said the demands of work interfered with their personal lives too often (June, 2012). Some employees even put off child bearing because of work demands: Almost 40% of women and 27% of men said they had done this (June, 2012).

The United States is the only Western country and one of only three countries in the world that do not provide paid family leave to all workers. Of 185 countries in the U.N.'s most recent study, 182 offer some level of financial support to new mothers on maternity leave. The three that do not are Oman, Papau New Guinea, and the United States (Rowe-Finkbeiner, 2014; Zarocostas, 2014). Further, at least 70 countries provide paid leave to fathers (Coontz, 2013; Weber, 2013; Zarocostas, 2014). In addition to institutional barriers, social norms can also constrain efforts to balance work and life. Some men subscribe to traditional views of masculinity and are unwilling to let family responsibilities affect their careers, which often means a female partner's career suffers from her commitment to family. Men who would like to take family leave often do not because they fear that doing so would reduce their status at work (Miller, 2015b; Parker & Wang, 2013; Weber, 2013).

Organizations with the best chance of thriving in the future will adapt to the realities of contemporary workers and their families (Buzzanell & Kirby, 2013; Williams, 2013). Recognizing this, many organizations are becoming more flexible and generous in supporting employees' nonwork commitments. Doing so reduces turnover and increases employees' commitment to organizations.

Manage Personal Relationships on the Job

A second challenge of organizational life involves relationships that are simultaneously personal and professional. You will probably be involved in a number of such relationships during your life. Although management has traditionally discouraged personal relationships, particularly romantic ones, between employees, they develop anyway. The goal, then, is to understand these relationships and manage them effectively.

Friendships between coworkers or supervisors and subordinates often enhance job commitment and satisfaction (Allen, 2006; Mokros, 2006; Mumby, 2006a). Yet workplace friendships also have drawbacks. On-the-job friendships may involve tension between the role expectations for friends and for colleagues. A supervisor may have difficulty rendering a fair evaluation of a subordinate who is also a friend. The supervisor might err by overrating the subordinate friend's strengths or might try to compensate for personal affection by being especially harsh in judging the subordinate friend. Also, workplace friendships that deteriorate may create stress and job dissatisfaction (Sias, Heath, Perry, Silva, & Fix, 2004).

Stockbyte/Getty Images

MindTap® Have you ever had a personal relationship with a coworker?

ANNA   *It's hard for me now that my best friend has been promoted over me. Part of it is envy, because I wanted the promotion too. But the hardest part is that I resent her power over me. When Billie gives me an assignment, I feel like as my friend she shouldn't dump extra work on me. But I also know that as the boss she has to give extra work to all of us sometimes. It just doesn't feel right for my best friend to tell me what to do and evaluate my work.*

Romantic relationships between people who work together are also increasingly common. Most women and men work outside the home, sometimes spending more hours on the job than in the home. In Chapter 8, we learned that proximity is a key influence on the formation of romantic relationships. It's no surprise, then, that people who interact almost daily sometimes find themselves attracted to each other. Workplace romances involve many of the same tensions that operate in friendships between supervisors and subordinates. In addition, romantic relationships are especially likely to arouse coworkers' resentment (Sias, 2013). Romantic breakups also tend to be more dramatic than breakups between friends. Go to the book's online resources for this chapter to learn more about personal relationships in the workplace.

EUGENE   *Once, I got involved with a woman where I was working. We were assigned to the same team and really hit it off, and one thing led to another, and we were dating. I guess it affected our work some, since we spent a lot of time talking and stuff in the office. But the real problem came when we broke up. It's impossible to avoid seeing your "ex" when you work together in a small office, and everyone else acted like they were walking on eggshells around us. She finally quit, and you could just feel tension drain out of everyone else in our office.*

It's unrealistic to assume that we can avoid personal relationships with people on the job. The challenge is to manage those relationships so that the workplace doesn't interfere with the personal bond, and the intimacy doesn't jeopardize professionalism. Friends and romantic partners may need to adjust their expectations and styles of interacting so that personal and work roles do not conflict. It's also advisable to make sure that on-the-job communication doesn't reflect favoritism and privileges that could cause resentment in coworkers. It's important to invest extra effort to maintain an open communication climate with other coworkers.

Chapter Summary

The culture of an organization is created, sustained, and altered in the process of communication between members of an organization. As they talk, interact, develop policies, and participate in the formal and informal networks, they continuously weave the fabric of their individual roles and collective life. We also discussed the role of digital media in organizational life.

Organizations, like other contexts of communication, involve a number of challenges. To meet those challenges, we discussed two guidelines. One is to find ways to balance commitments to work and other spheres of your life. A second guideline is to manage personal relationships in the workplace so that professionalism and intimacy do not conflict. The communication skills we've discussed throughout this book will help you navigate the tensions and challenges of close relationships on the job.

Experiencing Communication in Our Lives   MindTap®

CASE STUDY: Ed Misses the Banquet

Apply what you've learned in this chapter by analyzing the following case study, using the accompanying questions as a guide. These questions and a video of the case study are also available online with your MindTap Speech for *Communication in Our Lives*.

Ed recently began working at a new job. Although he's been in his new job only for 5 weeks, he likes it a lot, and he's told you that he sees a real future for himself with this company. But last week, a problem arose. Along with all other employees, Ed was invited to the annual company banquet, at which everyone socializes and awards are given for outstanding performance. Ed's daughter was in a play the night of the banquet, so Ed chose to attend his daughter's play rather than the company event. The invitation to the banquet had stated only, "Hope to see you there" and contained no RSVP, so Ed didn't mention to anyone that he couldn't attend. When he arrived at work the next Monday morning, however, he discovered he should have rearranged his plans to attend or, at the very least, should have told his supervisor why he would not be at the event. That Monday, Ed talked with several coworkers who had been around a few years, and he discovered that top management sees the annual banquet as a "command performance" that signifies company unity and loyalty. Later in the day, Ed had the following exchange with his manager.

ED'S MANAGER: You skipped the banquet last Saturday. I had really thought you were committed to our company.

ED: My daughter was in a play that night.

ED'S MANAGER: I don't care why you didn't come. We notice who is really with us and who isn't.

QUESTIONS FOR ANALYSIS AND DISCUSSION

1. How does the concept of constitutive rules, which we first discussed in Chapter 5, help explain the misunderstanding between Ed and his manager?

2. How might Ed use the informal network in his organization to learn the normative practices of the company and the meanings they have to others in the company?

3. How do the ambiguity and abstraction inherent in language explain the misunderstanding between Ed and his manager?

4. How would you suggest that Ed repair the damage done by his absence from the company banquet? What might he say to his manager? How could he use *I*-language, indexing, and dual perspective to guide his communication?

5. Do you think the banquet is a ritual? Why or why not?

MindTap

Use flashcards to learn key concepts and take a quiz to test your knowledge.

Key Concepts

communication	policies	roles
networks	rites	structure
organizational culture	rituals	

Sharpen Your Skill

1. Noticing Stories and the Work They Do

Think about an organization to which you belong, perhaps one in which you have worked or one that you have had many opportunities to observe. Identify corporate, personal, and collegial stories you were told when you first entered the organization. How did these stories shape your understandings of the organization?

2. Noticing Rituals in Your Organization

Think of an organization to which you belong. It could be your school or a more specific group such as a sports team, club, or workplace. Describe one ritual (i.e., personal, social, or task) and explain what it does for the organization and its members. What would be missing if this ritual were abandoned?

For Further Reflection and Discussion

1. Think about a group to which you belong. It may be a work group or a social group, such as a fraternity or interest club. Describe some common rites and rituals in your group. What do these rites and rituals communicate about the group's culture?

2. One of the best ways to learn about social and organizational trends that are reshaping the world of work is to read online magazines. *Entrepreneurial Edge* discusses emerging trends and resources for entrepreneurs. Another savvy site is an idea café created by business owners, where you'll find advice on starting and running a business, using technologies, and networking.

3. How can organizational rites and rituals normalize discrimination against particular groups? Identify examples of organizational rites and rituals that encourage or allow unequal treatment based on factors such as race, sex, ethnicity, sexual orientation, or economic class. When, if ever, are such uses of rites and rituals ethical?

Beyond the Classroom

Let's take the material in this chapter beyond the classroom by thinking about how it might apply to the workplace, ethical choices, and engagement with the broader world.

1. **Workplace.** Think about the place where you work or a place you worked in the past. What stories—collegial, personal, and corporate—did you hear during the initial stage of your employment? How did those stories shape your early understandings of that workplace and your understandings of what was expected of you as an employee?

2. **Ethics.** In recent years, we've discovered instance after instance of egregiously unethical behavior by leaders of organizations. Between 2006 and 2008, loan officers in banks were told to sign people up for mortgages they didn't understand and couldn't afford. As a result, many of these people lost their homes to foreclosure. Bernie Madoff lied to thousands of people, taking their money in a giant Ponzi scheme that left many penniless. Incidents such as these have led some to recommend that ethical training of some sort be required for all professionals. Do you think ethics should be part of the curriculum in business and law schools?

3. **Engagement.** Watch the film *Remember the Titans*. It provides a dramatic account of a man who was assigned to coach a group of football players in a recently integrated high school. The players didn't work together well, largely because of ethnic differences and ethnocentric attitudes. This film provides rich insights into leadership and the development of a cohesive organizational culture for the team.

10

Preservation of one's own culture does not require contempt or disrespect for other cultures.

César Chavez

Patrick Eckersley/arabianEye/Getty Images

Communication and Culture

To what extent is your identity individual and to what extent is it based on groups you belong to?

MindTap

Review the chapter's learning objectives and **start** with a quick warm-up activity.

LEARNING OBJECTIVES

After studying the topics in this chapter, you should be able to:

1. Give examples to illustrate the premise that cultures are systems.

2. Recall and explain the five dimensions of culture.

3. Reflect on a social community or coculture to which you belong and explore how its communication practices differ from those of the dominant culture.

4. Explain the dual role communication plays in cultural change.

5. Point out values as well as dangers of digital media for cultural groups and social communities.

6. Identify which of the five responses to diversity you experience when encountering situations that challenge your own cultural values.

Our era is one of global connectivity. More than ever in history, people from different cultures interact, work together, and live side by side. Further, events in one part of the world reverberate around the globe. When Nepal was devastated by earthquakes in 2015, people all over the world sympathized and offered support. When Greece was on the brink of economic collapse in 2012 and again in 2015, financial markets around the world quavered.

The most culturally diverse nation that exists, the United States becomes home to more immigrants every year than any other nation (Qin, 2014). To participate effectively in the United States and to be part of the global society, we need to understand and adapt to the communication to people of varied cultural backgrounds. The competitive and direct style of negotiation customary among Westerners may offend Korean business people (Kim & Meyers, 2012). Friendly touches that are comfortable to most U.S. citizens may be perceived as rude and intrusive by Germans or suggestive by Ugandans (Muwanguzi & Musambira, 2013). In some cultures, direct eye contact is interpreted as honesty, whereas in other cultures it is interpreted as disrespect.

MindTap®

Read, highlight, and take notes online.

In this chapter, we explore relationships between communication and culture. First, we'll define culture and discuss the intricate ways it is entwined with communication. Then, we'll focus on guidelines for increasing the effectiveness of communication between people of different cultures.

Understanding Culture

Although the word **culture** is part of our everyday vocabulary, it's difficult to define. Culture is part of everything we think, do, feel, and believe, yet we can't point to a thing that is culture. Most simply defined, culture is a way of life. It is a system of ideas, values, beliefs, structures, and practices that is communicated by one generation to the next and that sustains a particular way of life. To understand cultures more fully, we now consider four key premises about them.

Cultures Are Systems

The first premise about cultures is that they are systems. A culture is not a random collection of ideas, beliefs, values, and customs; rather, it is a coherent system of understandings, traditions, values, communication practices, and ways of living. As anthropologist Edward T. Hall noted years ago, "You touch a culture in one place and everything else is affected" (1977, p. 14).

Culture is one of the most important systems within which communication occurs. We are not born knowing how close to stand to others, how to express disagreement politely, or how much personal information to reveal to friends. We learn our culture's rules for these behaviors as we interact with others. For each of us, our culture directly shapes how we communicate, teaching us how much eye contact is polite, and whether argument and conflict are desirable in groups and personal relationships, and how much disclosure is appropriate.

You'll recall from our previous discussion of systems that the parts of a system interact and affect one another. Because cultures are systems, aspects of a

culture Beliefs, understandings, practices, and ways of interpreting experience that are shared by a number of people.

What's Your CQ?

MindTap

You've heard of IQ and maybe even EQ (emotional intelligence), but have you heard of CQ? CQ is **cultural intelligence**, which includes motivational, cognitive, and behavioral abilities to understand and adapt to a range of contexts, people, and patterns of interaction (Livermore, 2015). CQ has four components:

- *Drive*—extent of motivation for and confidence in interacting with people from other cultures.

- *Knowledge*—extent of understanding of religion, values, norms, and languages in other cultures.

- *Strategy*—ability to predict how interaction should unfold in unfamiliar cultural settings, yet to be open to changing plans if necessary.

- *Action*—capacity to adapt behavior to particular situations by drawing on a broad repertoire of behaviors.

CQ is required for leadership in an era when Coca-Cola sells more beverages in Japan than in the United States, negotiations typically involve people from different cultures, and organizations increasingly have production facilities in multiple countries. The ability to recognize, respect, and adapt to varying norms of doing business and diverse patterns of thought and action is critical to professional success in international organizations.

Go to the book's online resources for this chapter to learn more about CQ and the tests for measuring it.

culture are interrelated and work together to create a whole. For example, one of the major changes in Western society was the Industrial Revolution. Before the mid-1800s, most families lived and worked together in one place. In agricultural regions, women, men, and children worked together to plant, tend, harvest, and store crops and to take care of livestock. In cities, family businesses were common. This preindustrial way of life promoted cooperative relationships and family togetherness. The invention of fuel-powered machines led to mass production in factories, where workers spent 8 or more hours each day. In turn, this activated competition among workers to produce and earn more, and on-the-job communication became more competitive and individualistic. As men were hired for industrial jobs, women assumed primary responsibilities in the home, and men's roles in family life diminished. Thus, a change in work life produced reverberations throughout the culture.

The technological revolution that began in the 1970s and continues today has also had multiple and interrelated repercussions in cultural life. The Internet and smartphones allow people to form and maintain relationships over great distances and to stay in nearly constant touch with friends and family members. Computer networking, virtual conferencing, and virtual offices allow many people to work at home. New technologies change how, where, and with whom we communicate, just as they change the boundaries we use to define work and personal life. Because cultures are holistic systems, no change is ever isolated from the overall system.

Cultures Vary on Five Dimensions

Geert Hofstede (1991, 2001; Hofstede et al., 2010), a Dutch anthropologist and social psychologist, provided insight into defining features of cultures. Before becoming a faculty member, Hofstede trained managers and supervised personnel research at IBM. In that job, Hofstede surveyed more than 100,000 IBM employees in countries all over the world. He noticed that there were clear differences among IBM employees in different cultures. Intrigued by his findings, Hofstede left IBM to study cultural differences. His program of research identified five key dimensions that vary among cultures.

Individualism/Collectivism   The first dimension on which cultures vary is **individualism/collectivism,** which refers to the extent to which members of a culture understand themselves as part of and connected to their families, groups, and cultures. In cultures high in collectivism (e.g., Pakistan, China), people's identity is deeply tied to their groups, families, and clans (Luhrmann, 2014; Neuliep, 2014). In cultures high in individualism (e.g., United States, Australia), people tend to think of themselves as individuals who act relatively independently.

Communication scholar Stella Ting-Toomey has studied cultural differences in what she calls face, which includes individual and cultural facets of identity. For instance, individual facets of your identity include your major or profession and your achievements, whereas cultural facets of your identity include your membership in your family, your work and social networks, and your location in a specific collective society. Ting-Toomey (2005) reports that in collectivist cultures, group identity is more important than individual identity, or face. In individualist cultures, individual identity is more important than group identity.

Uncertainty Avoidance   The second dimension of cultural variation is **uncertainty avoidance,** which refers to the extent to which people try to avoid ambiguity and vagueness. In some cultures (e.g., Poland, South Korea), people like to have everything spelled out very explicitly in order to avoid misunderstandings. Yet, in other cultures (e.g., Hong Kong, Sweden), uncertainty is more tolerated and expectations are more flexible.

Power Distance   The third dimension of cultural variation is **power distance**, which refers to the size of the gap between people with high and low power and the extent to which that gap is regarded as normal. In some cultures (e.g., India, China), the distance between high and low power is great and is often inherited. Significant power differences that are passed on in families cultivate a society in which people respect the powerful, and there is low expectation of movement between classes, castes, or levels. In cultures where power distance is small (e.g., New Zealand, Norway), people tend to assume that those in power have earned it, rather than simply gaining power by virtue of being in powerful families.

Cultural differences in power relations may lead to misunderstandings. A Ugandan immigrant to the United States interpreted the relatively casual and egalitarian relationships between professors and students as rudeness by the students. The immigrant commented that, "The students drink, eat in class, talk back to professors . . . all this is unacceptable behavior in Uganda. No wonder Americans are losing their jobs to outsourcing because they are not respectful" (Muwanguzi & Musambira, 2013, n.d.).

individualism/collectivism One of five dimensions of variation among cultures, this refers to the extent to which members of a culture understand themselves as part of and connected to their families, groups, and cultures.

uncertainty avoidance One of five dimensions of variation among cultures, this refers to the extent to which people try to avoid ambiguity and vagueness.

power distance One of five dimensions of variation among cultures, this refers to the size of the gap between people with high and low power and the extent to which that gap is regarded as normal.

Masculinity/Femininity   The fourth dimension of cultural variation is **masculinity/femininity**. This dimension refers to the extent to which a culture values aggressiveness, competitiveness, looking out for yourself, and dominating others and nature (considered masculine orientations) versus gentleness, cooperation, and taking care of others and living in harmony with the natural world (considered feminine orientations). In cultures that are higher in femininity (e.g., the Netherlands, Norway), men and women are more gentle, cooperative, and caring. In cultures that are higher in masculinity (e.g., Japan, Germany), however, men are more aggressive and competitive. In highly masculine cultures, women may also be competitive and assertive, but generally they are less so than men.

Long-Term/Short-Term Orientation   The final dimension was not included in Hofstede's original work, but he added it later when it became clear to him that cultures varied how long-term their orientations are. **Long-term/short-term orientation** refers to the extent to which members of a culture think about and long term (history and future) versus short term (present). Long-term planning, thrift, and industriousness and respect for elders and ancestors are valued in cultures with a long-term orientation (e.g., Japan, Korea). In contrast, living for the moment, not saving for a rainy day, and not having as much respect for elders and ancestors are more likely to be found in cultures with a short-term orientation (e.g., Australia, Germany). The long-term end of the continuum is associated with what are sometimes called Confucian values, although cultures not historically connected with this influence can also have a long-term orientation. This value is not just about future—it is also about respect for one's ancestors and plans and hopes for those who follow.

Cultures Are Dynamic

The third principle of cultures is that they are **dynamic**, which means they evolve and change over time. Scholars (Samovar et al., 2015, 2017) have identified four primary sources of change in cultural life. The first is *invention*, which is the creation of tools, ideas, and practices. The classic example of a tool is the wheel, which had far-reaching implications. Not only did its invention alter modes of transportation, but it is also the foundation of many machines and technologies. Other inventions that have changed cultural life are medical devices such as pacemakers, the computer, and the automobile.

Cultures also invent ideas that alter social life. For example, the United States was founded on the concept of *democracy,* which influenced laws, rights, and responsibilities. Another concept that has changed Western life is environmental awareness. Information about our planet's fragility has infused cultural consciousness. Terms such as *environmental responsibility* and *environmental ethics* have entered our everyday vocabularies, reshaping how we understand our relationship with the environment.

A second source of cultural change is *diffusion*, which involves borrowing from other cultures. What we call English includes a number of words imported from many cultures: *brocade, touché,* and *yin and yang*. U.S. businesses adopt best practices from businesses in other countries just as those countries adopt best practices developed in the United States.

A third source of cultural change is *calamity,* which is adversity that brings about change in a culture. For example, war may devastate a country, destroying

---

Review It!

Dimensions of Cultural Variation:

- Individualism/ Collectivism
- Uncertainty Avoidance
- Power Distance
- Masculinity/Femininiity
- Long-Term/Short-Term Orientation

masculinity/femininity One of five dimensions of variation among cultures, this refers to the extent to which a culture values aggressiveness, competitiveness, looking out for yourself, and dominating others and nature (considered masculine orientations) versus gentleness, cooperation, and taking care of others and living in harmony with the natural world (considered feminine orientations).

long-term/short-term orientation One of five dimensions of variation among cultures, this refers to the extent to which members of a culture think about and long term (history and future) versus short term (present).

dynamic Evolving and changing over time.

land and people alike. Cultural calamity may also involve disasters such as hurricanes, volcanic eruptions, and plagues.

A fourth source of cultural change is *communication*. A primary way in which communication propels change is by naming things in ways that shape how we understand them. For instance, the term *date rape* was coined in the late 1980s. Although historically, many women had been forced to have sex by men they were dating, until recently there was no term that named what happened as a violent invasion and a criminal act (Wood, 1992). Similarly, the term *sexual harassment* names a practice that is certainly not new but only lately has been labeled and given social reality (Wood, 1994c). As a primary tool of social movements, communication impels significant changes in cultural life. Thirty years ago, the civil rights movement in the United States used communication to transform laws and views of blacks. Powerful leaders such as the Reverend Martin Luther King Jr., and Malcolm X raised blacks' pride in their identity and heritage and inspired them to demand their rights in United States. Simultaneously, black leaders used communication to persuade the nonblack citizens to rethink their attitudes and practices.

In addition to bringing about change directly, communication also accompanies other sources of cultural change. Inventions such as antibiotics had to be explained to medical practitioners and to a general public that believed infections were caused by fate and accident, not viruses and bacteria. Ideas and practices borrowed from other cultures similarly must be translated into the language and culture of a particular society. Cultural calamities, too, must be defined and explained: Did the volcano erupt because of pressure in the earth or because of the anger of the gods? Did we lose the war because we had a weak military or because our cause was wrong? The ways a culture defines and communicates about calamities establish what these events mean and imply for future social practices and social life.

Invention, diffusion, calamity, and community ensure that cultures are highly dynamic—always changing in subtle and not-so-subtle ways.

Multiple Social Communities Coexist Within a Single Culture

The fourth principle about cultures is that they may include multiple social communities, which are also called cocultures. When we speak of different cultures, we often think of geographically distinct regions. For instance, India, South America, Africa, and Europe are separate cultures. Yet geographic separation isn't what defines a culture. Instead, a culture exists when a distinct way of life shapes what a group of people believes, values, and does, as well as how they understand themselves. Even within a single country, there are numerous social communities with distinct ways of life.

Social communities, or cocultures, are groups of people who live within a dominant culture, yet also are members of another group that is not dominant in that culture. For example, immigrants may identify with both the culture to which they have moved and the culture of their homeland. Social communities are distinct from dominant culture although not necessarily opposed to or entirely outside of it. Since the colonial days, mainstream Western culture has reflected the values and experiences of Western, heterosexual, young and middle-aged, middle- and upper-class, able-bodied white men who are Christian, at least in heritage if not in actual practice.

Yet Western culture includes many groups that do not identify exclusively with the mainstream. Gay men, lesbians, bisexuals, and trans people experience difficulty in a society that includes many people who do not respect them.

> **Review It!**
>
> Sources of Cultural Change:
> - Invention
> - Diffusion
> - Calamity
> - Communication

> **social communities**
> Groups of people who live within a dominant culture yet who also have common distinctive experiences and patterns of communicating.

Communication Highlight

Life on the Color Line

Gregory Howard Williams began life as the white son in a middle-class family in Virginia. At age 10, however, he became a black living in Muncie, Indiana. His father, James Anthony "Buster" Williams, was an olive-skinned man with some African ancestry. Buster wanted desperately to escape racism and gain the privileges that whites have as a birthright. His son, Gregory, has pale skin, thin lips, and straight hair, which allowed others to perceive him as White.

In his autobiography, *Life on the Color Line: The True Story of a White Boy Who Discovered He Was Black* (1995), Gregory Williams provides a stunning account of the differences in how he was treated when he was considered white and black.

iStockphoto.com/abalcazar

Members of some social communities may find it difficult to navigate mainstream culture.

high-context communication style The indirect and undetailed communication favored in collectivist cultures.

low-context communication style The direct, precise, and detailed communication favored in individualistic cultures.

People who have disabilities encounter problems as they attempt to live and work in a society that is made for able-bodied people. Muslims in the United States grapple with a culture that, in many ways, doesn't accommodate or value their traditions.

Mainstream ideology is evident in nonverbal communication. For example, Western culture often conveys the message that people with disabilities don't matter. Notice how many buildings have no ramps and how many public presentations don't include signers for people with impaired hearing. Most campus and business buildings feature portraits of white men, leaving people of color and women unrepresented.

Dimensions of cultural variation, which we discussed earlier in this chapter, apply to social communities. Collectivist cultures and social communities regard people as deeply connected to their families, groups, and communities. Thus, priority is given to harmony, group welfare, and interdependence (Jandt, 2012; Samovar et al., 2015, 2017). Collectivist cultures and social communities tend to rely on a **high-context communication style**, which is indirect and undetailed. Because it is assumed that people are deeply interconnected, people do not feel the need to spell everything out in explicit detail (Jandt, 2012).

Individualistic cultures and social communities regard each person as distinct from others; individuality is more prominent than membership in groups, families, and so forth. Priority is given to personal freedom, independence, and individual rights. Members of individualist cultures and social communities generally use a **low-context communication style**, which is explicit, detailed, and precise. The emphasis on individuality means that communicators cannot presume others share their meanings and values (Jandt, 2012).

SABRINA *I get hassled by a lot of white girls on campus about being dependent on my family. They say I should grow up and leave the nest. They say I'm too close to my folks and my grandparents, aunts, uncles, and cousins. But what they mean by "too close" is that I'm closer with my family than most whites are. It's a white standard they're using, and it doesn't fit most blacks. Strong ties with family and the black community have always been our way.*

When people from different cultures and social communities interact, their different ways of communicating may cause misunderstandings. For instance, traditional Japanese people don't touch or shake hands to greet. Instead, they bow to preserve each person's personal space, which is very important in that culture. In Greece, however, touching is part of being friendly and sociable.

Gender as a Social Community   Of the many social communities that exist, gender has received particularly intense study. Because we know more about it than about other social communities, we'll explore gender to illustrate how a social community shapes members' communication.

You may have noticed that, despite many similarities, there are some fairly common differences in women's and men's communication. For instance, women's talk generally is more expressive and focused on feelings and relationships, whereas men's talk tends to be more instrumental and competitive (Kimbrough, Guadagno, Muscanell, & Dill, 2013; Rudman & Glick, 2010; Terlecki, Brown, Harner-Steciw, Irvin-Hannum, Marchetto-Ryan, Ruhl, & Wiggins, 2011; Wood & Fixmer-Oraiz, 2015; Ye & Palomares, 2013).

Another general difference lies in what each gender regards as the primary basis of relationships. Many men develop friendships by doing things together (i.e., working on cars, watching sports) (Inman, 1996; Metts, 2006a; Swain, 1989; Wood & Inman, 1993). Women more often build relationships primarily by talking about feelings, personal issues, and daily life (Braithwaite & Kellas, 2006; Duck & Wood, 2006; Johnson, 1996; Metts, 2006a).

Given the differences between how women and men, in general, use communication, it's hardly surprising that misunderstandings occur. One clash between gendered communication styles occurs when women and men discuss problems. When women talk about something that is troubling them, they are often looking first for empathy and connection. Yet, masculine socialization teaches men to use communication instrumentally, so they often offer advice or solutions. Thus, women sometimes interpret men's advice as a lack of personal concern. On the other hand, men may feel frustrated when women offer empathy and support instead of advice for solving problems.

Perhaps the most common complication in communication between women and men occurs when a woman says, "Let's talk about us." To men, this often means trouble because they interpret the request as implying there is a problem in a relationship. For women, however, this is not the only—or even the main—reason to talk about a relationship. Within feminine social communities, talking is a primary way to celebrate and increase closeness. The instrumental focus of masculine social communities teaches that talking about a relationship is useful only if there is some problem to be resolved.

Yuri Arcurs/Dreamstime.com

MindTap®   Do the men in this photo appear to be communicating in ways consistent with research on masculine social communities?

> **LARRY**   *Finally, I see what happens between my girlfriend and me. She always wants to talk about us, which I think is stupid unless we have a problem. I like to go to a concert or do something together, but then she says that I don't want to be with her. We speak totally different languages.*

Other Social Communities   Gender isn't the only social community, and communication between men and women is not the only kind of interaction that may be plagued by misunderstandings. Research indicates that communication patterns vary between social classes. For example, working-class people tend to stay closer to and rely more on extended family than do middle- and upper-class Americans (Bornstein & Bradley, 2003; Cancian, 1987). Working-class men also tend to see physical strength and practical skills as more central to masculinity than middle- and upper-class men (Mumby, 2006a).

Racial and ethnic social communities may also have distinct communication patterns. For example, research indicates that African Americans generally communicate more assertively than European Americans (Gonzalez, Houston, & Chen, 2011; Orbe & Harris, 2015). What some African Americans consider authentic, powerful exchanges may be perceived as antagonistic by people from different social communities. As a rule, African Americans also communicate more interactively than European Americans. This explains why some African Americans call out responses such as "Tell it," "That's right," and "Keep talking" during speeches, church sermons, and other public presentations. What many Caucasians regard as interruptions, some African Americans perceive as constructive participation in communication and community.

Notice that in discussing social communities and their communication patterns, I use qualifying words. For instance, I note that *most* women behave in certain ways and that *as a rule* blacks *tend to* communicate more interactively than many whites. This is to remind us that not all members of a social community behave in the same way. Although generalizations are useful and informative, they should not mislead us into thinking that all members of any social community think, feel, and communicate alike. We engage in stereotyping and uncritical thinking when we fail to recognize differences between individual members of social groups.

In this section, we have discussed four key premises about cultures. First, cultures are systemic. Second, there are five dimensions that distinguish cultures. Third, we noted that cultures are dynamic, continuously. Finally, we saw that multiple social communities with distinct norms, values, and practices may coexist within a single culture. With these understandings of culture in mind, let's now elaborate the connections between cultures and communication.

> **Review It!**
>
> Premises About Cultures:
> - They Are Systems
> - They Vary Along Five Dimensions
> - They Are Dynamic
> - They May Include Multiple Social Communities

Communication's Relationship to Culture and Social Communities

As our discussion so far suggests, communication and culture influence each other. Culture is reflected in communication practices; at the same time, communication practices shape cultural life. We'll discuss two principles that illuminate the intimate relationship between communication and social communities and cultures.

Communication Expresses and Sustains Cultures

Patterns of communication reflect cultural values and perspectives. For example, many Asian languages include numerous words to describe specific relationships (grandmother's brother, father's uncle, youngest son, oldest daughter). This reflects the cultural emphasis on family relationships (Ferrante, 2009). There are fewer English words to describe precise kinship bonds.

The respect of many Asian cultures for elderly people is reflected in language. "I will be 60 tomorrow" is an Asian saying that means, "I am old enough to deserve respect." In contrast, Western cultures tend to prize youth and to have many positive words for youthfulness (*young in spirit, fresh*) and negative words for seniority (*has-been, outdated, old-fashioned, over the hill*) (Ferrante, 2009).

> **SHARPEN YOUR SKILL**
>
> At the end of this chapter, refer to the Sharpen Your Skill feature, Communicating Culture, to apply concepts from Chapter 10.

Pontino/Alamy Stock Photo

Understandings of family differ from culture to culture.

In the process of learning language, we also learn our culture's values. The importance that most Asian cultures attach to age is structured into Asian languages. For instance, the Korean language makes fine distinctions between different ages, and any remark to another person must acknowledge the other's age

Communication Highlight

Proverbs Express Cultural Values   MindTap®

Here are examples of sayings that reflect the values of particular cultures (Gudykunst & Lee, 2002; Samovar et al., 2017).

- "It is the nail that sticks out that gets hammered down." This Japanese saying reflects the idea that a person should not stand out from others but instead should conform.

- "No need to know the person, only the family." This Chinese axiom reflects the belief that individuals are less important than families.

- "A zebra does not despise its stripes." Among the African Masai, this saying encourages acceptance of things and oneself as they are.

- "The child has no owner." "It takes a whole village to raise a child." These African adages express the cultural beliefs that children belong to whole communities and that rearing and caring for children are the responsibility of all members of those communities, not just the children's biological parents.

Go to the book's online resources for this chapter to learn proverbs in other countries such as Turkey and Palestine.

(Ferrante, 2009). Eastern cultures also tend to place greater emphasis on family and community than on individuals. If I were a Korean, I would introduce myself as Wood Julia to communicate the greater value placed on familial than personal identity. It's unlikely that an Eastern textbook on human communication would even include a chapter on self, which is standard in Western textbooks. Calendars reflect cultural traditions and values by designating significant days as holidays that should be recognized and honored. In the United States, the Fourth of July commemorates the U.S. independence from Britain; Eastern societies have a day each year to honor the elderly people. In this way, calendars tell us who is in the mainstream in a given society and who is not.

RACHAEL *It is hard to be Jewish in a Christian society, especially in terms of holidays. For me, Rosh Hashanah and Yom Kippur are high holy days, but they are not holidays on the calendar. Some of my teachers give me grief for missing classes on holy days, and my friends don't accept that I can't go out on Saturday, which is our sacred day. At my job, they act like I'm being a slouch and skipping work because my holidays aren't their holidays. They get Christmas and New Year's Day off, but I celebrate Hanukkah and Rosh Hashanah. And I don't have to tell you why making Easter a national holiday offends Jewish people.*

We Learn Culture in the Process of Communicating

We learn a culture's views and patterns in the process of communicating. As we interact with others, we come to understand the beliefs, values, norms, and language of our culture. By observing how others communicate, we learn language (*dog*) and what it means (i.e., a pest, a pet, a work animal, or food to eat). This allows us to participate in a social world of shared meanings.

SHARPEN YOUR SKILL

At the end of this chapter, refer to the Sharpen Your Skill feature, Your Culture's Sayings, to apply concepts from Chapter 10.

Both verbal and nonverbal communication reflect cultural teachings. Here, an elder and a young boy wear traditional yarmulkes and partake of unleavened bread and wine as part of Passover Seder.

Bill Aron/PhotoEdit

From the moment of birth, we begin to learn the beliefs, values, norms, and language of our society. We learn our culture's values in a variety of communication contexts. We learn to respect our elders, or not to, by how we see others communicate with older people and by what we hear others say about elders. We learn what body shape is valued by what we see in media and how we hear others talk about people of various physical proportions. By the time we are old enough to appreciate the idea that culture is learned, our beliefs, values, languages, and practices are already thoroughly woven into who we are and are almost invisible to us.

In sum, we've seen that communication is a primary way in which cultures are expressed and sustained and that communication is a primary way that each of us learns our culture's codes so that we can participate effectively in it.

Digital Media, Cultures, and Social Communities

One of the more obvious connections between digital media and cultures and social communities is that digital technologies allow access to and interaction among members of different cultures and social communities. Just a few clicks on your computer yield a wealth of websites that provide you with information on any religion, sexual orientation, gender identity, race, or ethnicity. You can learn a great deal about other cultures and social communities by visiting online websites. Computer technology also allows us to interact with members of other cultures and social communities.

Digital media also have a dark side related to cultures and social communities. The virtual world provides a home for **hate groups**, which are collections of people that advocate and engage in hatred, aggression, or violence toward members of a particular race, ethnicity, gender, sexual orientation, gender identity, religion, or any other selected segment of society. Hate groups stoke stereotypes, ethnocentrism, and violence. These groups specialize in degrading social communities and cultures that they dislike. They also encourage hateful attitudes and, in some cases, violence toward members of particular communities and cultures. In the United States, the FBI follows hate groups, and two organizations have taken the lead in monitoring online hate groups: The Anti-Defamation League and the Southern Poverty Law Center. This chapter's online resources provide links to both of these groups so that you may learn about the work they do.

Guidelines for Improving Communication Between Cultures and Social Communities

You have already encountered a number of people from cultures and social communities different than your own. In the years to come, you will continue to do so. Let's consider two principles for enhancing communication between members of different cultures and social communities.

Resist the Ethnocentric Bias

Most of us unreflectively use our home culture as the standard for judging other cultures. Some Japanese may regard many European Americans as rude for maintaining direct eye contact, whereas some European Americans may perceive traditional Japanese as evasive for averting their eyes (Jandt, 2012; Samovar et al., 2017). Many Westerners' habitual self-references may appear egocentric to some Koreans, and many Koreans' unassuming style may seem passive to some Westerners.

hate groups Collections of people that advocate and engage in hatred, aggression, or violence toward members of particular groups.

How we view others and their communication depends more on the perspective we use to interpret them than on what they say and do.

Ethnocentrism is the use of one's own culture and its practices as the standard for interpreting the values, beliefs, norms, and communication of other cultures. Literally, ethnocentrism means to put our own ethnicity (*ethno*) at the center (*centrism*) of the universe. Ethnocentrism fosters negative judgments of anything that differs from our own ways. In extreme form, ethnocentrism can lead one group of people to think it has the right to dominate and exploit other groups and to engage in genocide.

To reduce our tendencies to be ethnocentric, we should first remind ourselves that culture is learned. What is considered normal and right varies between cultures. In place of ethnocentrism, we can adopt the perspective of cultural relativism, which recognizes that cultures vary in how they think, act, and behave as well as in what they believe and value. Cultural relativism reminds us that something that appears odd or even wrong to us may seem natural and right from the point of view of a different culture. That awareness facilitates understanding among people of different cultures and cocultures.

Recognize That Interacting with Diverse People Is a Process

We don't move suddenly from being unaware of how people in other cultures communicate to being totally comfortable and competent interacting with them. Dealing with diversity is a gradual process that takes time, experience with a variety of people, and a commitment to learning about a range of people and communication styles. We will discuss five responses to diversity, ranging from rejection to complete acceptance.

Resistance A common response to diversity is resistance, which occurs when we attack the cultural practices of others or proclaim that our own cultural traditions are superior. Without education or reflection, many people deal with diversity by resisting the practices of cultures and social communities different from their own. Some people think their judgments reflect universal truths about what is normal and right. They aren't aware that they are imposing the arbitrary yardstick of their own particular social communities and culture and ignoring the yardsticks of other cultures and social communities.

ethnocentrism The tendency to regard ourselves and our way of life as superior to other people and other ways of life.

cultural relativism The idea that cultures vary in how they think, act, and behave as well as in what they believe and value; not the same as moral relativism.

resistance A response to cultural diversity in which the cultural practices of others are attacked or the superiority of one's own cultural traditions is proclaimed.

BRENDA   *I overheard three of my classmates complaining about all of the mess and noise in the building where we have a class. They were saying what an inconvenience it is. The construction is to install an elevator in the building so that students like me, who are in wheelchairs, can take classes in classrooms on the second and third floor. I don't think my classmates are mean, but I do think they've never put themselves in my shoes—or my wheelchair! Every semester they pick classes according to what they want to take and when they want to take it. My first criterion is finding classes that I can get to—either first floor or in buildings that are wheelchair accessible.*

Resistance may be expressed in many ways. It fuels racial slurs, anti-Semitic messages, and homophobic attitudes and actions. Resistance may also motivate members of a culture or social community to associate only with each other and to resist recognizing any commonalities with people from other cultures or social communities.

Interacting with those who differ from us enlarges our understanding of people and communication.

Members of a culture or social community may resist their own group practices in an effort to fit into the mainstream. **Assimilation** occurs when people give up their own ways and adopt those of the dominant culture. For many years, assimilation was the dominant response of immigrants who came to the United States. The idea of the United States as a "melting pot" encouraged newcomers to melt into the mainstream by abandoning anything that made them different from native-born Americans. More recently, Reverend Jesse Jackson used the metaphor of a family quilt, which portrays the United States as a country in which people's unique values and customs are visible, as are the individual squares in a quilt; at the same time, each group contributes to a larger whole, just as each square in a quilt contributes to its overall beauty.

Tolerance   A second response to diversity is **tolerance**, the acceptance of differences even though we may not approve of or even understand them. Tolerance involves respecting others' rights to their own ways even though we perceive their ways are wrong, inferior, or offensive. Judgment still exists, but it's not actively imposed on others.

Understanding   A third response to diversity involves **understanding** that differences are rooted in cultural teachings and that no customs, traditions, or behaviors are intrinsically better than any others. This response grows out of cultural relativism, which we discussed previously. Rather than assuming that whatever differs from our ways is a deviation from a universally right standard (ours), we realize that diverse values, beliefs, norms, and communication styles are rooted in distinct cultural perspectives. A person who responds to diversity with understanding might notice that a Japanese person doesn't hold eye contact, but he or she wouldn't assume that the Japanese person was deceitful. Instead, he or she would try to learn what eye contact means in Japanese society to understand the behavior in its native cultural context. Curiosity, rather than judgment, dominates in this response to cultural diversity.

assimilation The giving up of one's own culture's ways for those of another culture.

tolerance A response to diversity in which one accepts differences even though one may not approve of or even understand them.

understanding A response to cultural diversity in which it is assumed that differences are rooted in cultural teachings and that no traditions, customs, and behaviors are intrinsically more valuable than others.

Respect   Once we move beyond judgment and begin to understand the cultural basis for practices that diverge from our own, we may come to **respect** differences. We can appreciate the value of placing family above self, of arranged marriage, and of feminine and masculine communication styles. We don't have to adopt others' ways to respect them on their own terms. Respect allows us to acknowledge differences yet remain personally anchored primarily in the values and customs of our own culture.

Participation   A final response to diversity is **participation**, in which we incorporate some of the practices and values of other groups into our own lives. More than other responses, participation encourages us to develop new skills and perspectives and to nurture a civic culture that celebrates both differences and commonalities.

Participation calls for us to be **multilingual**, which means we are able to speak and think in more than one language. Members of many social communities already are at least bilingual: Many blacks know how to operate in mainstream white society and in traditional black communities (Orbe & Harris, 2015). Most women know how to communicate in both feminine and masculine ways, and they adapt their style to the people with whom they interact. Bilingualism is also practiced by many Asian Americans, Hispanics, lesbians, gay men, and members of other groups that are simultaneously part of a dominant culture and minority communities.

In the course of our lives, many of us move in and out of various responses as we interact with people from multiple cultures and social communities. Most of us will discover that our responses change over time.

> **Review It!**
> ....
> • Responses to Diversity:
>   • Resistance
>   • Tolerance
> • Understanding
>   • Respect
> • Participation

respect A response to cultural diversity in which one values others' customs, traditions, and values, even if one does not actively incorporate them into one's own life.

participation A response to cultural diversity in which people incorporate some practices, customs, and traditions of other groups into their own lives.

multilingual Able to speak and think in more than one language.

Communication Highlight

Learning Bias

Is racial bias still a problem in America? According to ABC News and *Washington Post* poll reported in January 2009, that depends on whom you ask. Twice as many blacks as whites think racism is still a problem, whereas twice as many whites as blacks think racial equality has been achieved (Blow, 2009).

What can explain the major discrepancy between blacks' and whites' views? One explanation is that most whites believe they are not racially biased but still hold implicit biases. That's the idea behind Project Implicit, a virtual lab managed by scholars at Harvard, the University of Virginia, and the University of Washington. After 6 years of testing people's biases, the findings are clear: 75% of whites have an implicit pro-white/antiblack bias. While some blacks also harbor implicit racial biases—some pro-black and some pro-white—blacks are the least likely of all races to have any racial bias (Blow, 2009).

Another question studied by scientists at Project Implicit is when racial prejudice starts. According to Mahzarin Banaji, a professor at Harvard, it starts at much earlier ages than most of us think. Banaji has devoted her career to studying hidden and often subtle biases and attitudes. According to Banaji's research, children as young as 3 years old have the same level of bias as adults (Fogg, 2008).

Chapter Summary

In this chapter, we've learned about the close connections between communication and cultures. Our communication reflects our culture's values and norms; at the same time, our communication sustains those values and norms and the perception that they are natural and right. We also discussed the importance of learning to communicate effectively in a multicultural society and ways in which digital media can assist us in learning about and interacting with people different from us. Moving beyond ethnocentric judgments based on our own culture allows us to understand, respect, and sometimes to participate in a diverse world and to enlarge ourselves in the process.

But differences between us are only part of the story. It would be a mistake to be so aware of differences that we overlook our commonalities. We all have feelings, dreams, ideas, hopes, fears, and values. Our common humanness transcends many of our differences.

MindTap®

Experiencing Communication in Our Lives

CASE STUDY: The Job Interview

Apply what you've learned in this chapter by analyzing the following case study, using the accompanying questions as a guide. These questions and a video of the case study are also available online with your MindTap Speech for *Communication in Our Lives*.

Mei-ying Yung is a senior who has majored in computer programming. Mei-ying's aptitude for computer programming has earned her much attention at her college. She has developed and installed complex new programs to make advising more efficient and to reduce the frustration and errors in registration for courses. Although she has been in the United States for 6 years, in many ways Mei-ying reflects the Chinese culture into which she was born and in which she spent the first 15 years of her life. Today Mei-ying is interviewing for a position at New Thinking, a fast-growing tech company that specializes in developing programs tailored to the needs of individual companies. The interviewer, Barton Hingham, is 32 years old and a native of California, where New Thinking is based. As the scenario opens, Ms. Yung walks into the small room where Mr. Hingham is seated behind a desk. He rises to greet her and walks over with his hand stretched out to shake hers.

HINGHAM: Good morning, Ms. Yung. I've been looking forward to meeting you. Your résumé is most impressive.

Ms. Yung looks downward, smiles, and limply shakes Mr. Hingham's hand. He gestures to a chair, and she sits down in it.

HINGHAM: I hope this interview will allow us to get to know each other a bit and decide whether there is a good fit between you and New Thinking. I'll be asking you some questions about your background and interests. And you should feel free to ask me any questions you have. Okay?

YUNG: Yes.

HINGHAM: I see from your transcript that you majored in computer programming and did very well. I certainly didn't have this many As on my college transcript!

YUNG: Thank you. I am very fortunate to have good teachers.

HINGHAM: Tell me a little about your experience in writing original programs for business applications.

YUNG: I do not have great experience, but I have been grateful to help the college with some of its work.

HINGHAM: Tell me about how you've helped the college. I see you designed a program for advising. Can you explain to me what you did to develop that program?

YUNG: Not really so much. I could see that much of advising is based on rules, so I only need to write the rules into a program so advisors could do their jobs better.

HINGHAM: Perhaps you're being too modest. I've done enough programming myself to know how difficult it is to develop a program for something with as many details as advising. There are so many majors, each with different requirements and regulations. How did you program all of that variation?

YUNG: I read the handbook on advising and the regulations on each major and then programmed decision trees into an advising template. Not so hard.

HINGHAM: Well that's exactly the kind of project we do at New Thinking. People come to us with problems in their jobs, and we write programs to solve them. Does that sound like the kind of thing you would enjoy doing?

YUNG: Yes. I very much like to solve problems to help others.

HINGHAM: What was your favorite course during college?

YUNG: They are all very valuable. I enjoy all.

HINGHAM: Did you have one course in which you did especially well?

YUNG: (*blushing, looking down*) I would not say that. I try to do well in all my courses, to learn from them.

　　Later, Barton Hingham and Molly Cannett, another interviewer for New Thinking, are discussing the day's interviews over dinner.

CANNETT: Did you find any good prospects today?

HINGHAM: Not really. I thought I was going to be bowled over by this one woman— name's Mei-ying Yung—who has done some incredibly intricate programming on her own while in college.

CANNETT: Sounds like just the kind of person we're looking for.

HINGHAM: I thought so too, until the interview. She just didn't seem to have the gusto we want. She showed no confidence or initiative in the interview. It was like the transcript and the person were totally different.

CANNETT: Hmmm, that's odd. Usually when we see someone who looks that good on paper, the interview is just a formality.

HINGHAM: Yeah, but I guess the formality is more important than we realized—Yung was a real dud in the interview. I still don't know what to make of it.

QUESTIONS FOR ANALYSIS AND DISCUSSION

1. How does Mei-ying Yung's communication reflect her socialization in Chinese culture?

2. How could Mei-ying be more effective without abandoning the values of her native culture?

3. What could enhance Barton Hingham's ability to communicate effectively with people who were raised in non-Western cultures?

MindTap

Use flashcards to learn key concepts and take a quiz to test your knowledge.

Key Concepts

Assimilation
cultural intelligence
cultural relativism
culture
dynamic
ethnocentrism
high-context
   communication
   style

individualism/
   collectivism
long-term/short-term
   orientation
low-context
   communication style
masculinity/femininity
multilingual
participation

power distance
resistance
respect
social communities
tolerance
uncertainty avoidance
understanding

Sharpen Your Skill

1. Communicating Culture

Locate a standard calendar and an academic calendar used on your campus. Check each calendar to determine which of the following holidays of different cultural groups are recognized on the calendars and which are declared as holidays by suspension of normal operations in communities and on campuses:

Christmas
Hanukkah
Kwanzaa
Elderly Day
Passover
Easter
Yom Kippur
Ramadan
Hegira
Rosh Hashanah
Saka
Martin Luther King Jr. Day

2. Your Culture's Sayings

What do common sayings and proverbs in the United States tell us about cultural values? What cultural values are expressed by the following sayings?

"You can't be too rich or too thin."
"A stitch in time saves nine."
"What goes around comes around."
"A watched pot never boils."
"Penny wise, pound foolish."
"You can't take it with you."
"You've made your bed, now you have to lie in it."
What other sayings can you think of that express key Western values?

For Further Reflection and Discussion

1. Some scholars claim that there are many distinct social communities in the United States. Examples are deaf people, people with disabilities, and elderly people. Do you agree that these groups qualify as distinct social communities? What is needed for a group to be considered a specific and distinctive social community?

2. Continue the exercise started on page 198 by listing common sayings or adages in your culture and social communities. Decide what each saying reflects about the beliefs, values, and concerns of your culture.

3. Are the different styles of communication typical of distinct social communities evident in online interaction? For instance, do you see patterned differences between messages written by women and men? If you see differences, are they consistent with the generalizations about gendered social communities that we discussed in this chapter?

4. Think critically about how you do and do not fit generalizations about your racial or ethnic group. Identify three ways in which you reflect what is generally true of your group. Identify three ways in which you personally diverge from generalizations about your group. Extend this exercise by thinking critically about how people in racial or ethnic groups other than your own do and do not fit generalizations about their group.

5. Reflect on the different responses to diversity that we discussed in the last section of this chapter. What ethical values do you perceive in each response?

Beyond the Classroom

Let's take the material in this chapter beyond the classroom by applying it to the workplace, ethical choices, and engagement with the broader world.

1. **Workplace.** Go to an office building (it could be one on your campus) and make note of the culture and social communities that it reflects. If there are portraits on the walls, what are the sexes, races, and nationalities of the subjects? How accessible is the building to people with mobility limitations?

2. **Ethics.** This chapter encourages people to resist the ethnocentric bias, but doesn't offer a specific plan or set of guidelines for reaching that ethical goal. Based on what you've learned in Chapters 1–9, as well as your life experiences, what can you suggest as concrete steps people can take to resist or at least reduce the tendency to judge other cultures by the norms and values of their home culture?

3. **Engagement.** Check your campus calendar for meetings of various groups and select an event sponsored by an ethnic group other than your own. Attend the event and pay attention not only to the event itself but to the verbal and nonverbal communication patterns, including protocols for greeting, parting, and introducing speakers (if there is one or more).

11

Television and the Internet are the most powerful socializing and enculturating forces in society.

Arthur Asa Berger

Media and Media Literacy

LEARNING OBJECTIVES

After studying the topics in this chapter, you should be able to:

1. Explain three key ways in which social media differ from traditional mass media.

2. Discuss three theories of mass media: uses and gratification, agenda setting, and cultivation.

3. Provide examples of media acting as gatekeepers and discuss the effects on public opinion.

4. Describe two ways in which mass media cultivate a particular worldview.

5. Discuss the impact of social media hyperconnectivity.

6. Apply chapter guidelines to improve your media literacy.

In an average day, how much time do you spend using digital media?

MindTap®

Review the chapter's learning objectives and **start** with a quick warm-up activity.

- Young people who grow up connected to the digital world will be nimble, analytic thinkers who connect easily with others.
- The hyperconnectivity of today's youth will make them unable to think in depth and unskilled in face-to-face relationships.

Which of these two predictions seems more likely to you? Are our ever-present, always-on devices making us smarter, more engaging, and more socially skilled or just the reverse? Whichever prediction you believe, you're in good company.

When the Pew Research Center polled people who are Internet experts, 55% said they believed that being electronically connected would make today's youth more capable than their predecessors of managing complex tasks and relating to others. On the other hand, 40% of the Internet experts believed that the extensive connectedness of young people would undermine their abilities for deep thinking and making meaningful relationships with others (Gregory, 2012). Despite their different overall predictions, the Internet experts did agree on one issue: Either you control your engagement with media, or the media will control you.

The goal of this chapter is to increase your understanding of the media you use so that you control them. In the most media-saturated and media-engaged era in history, we should think carefully about how our intense engagement with media affects our lives. How do we use media to develop and negotiate identity, participate in relationships, and form opinions and perspectives, and participate in civic life? These are questions we'll consider in this chapter. We begin by defining and distinguishing between mass media and social media. Next, we explore how mass media and social media affect our lives. The last part of this chapter focuses on media literacy, a critical skill for living in today's world.

The Nature and Scope of Media

Media is a broad term that includes both mass media and social media. In this section, we define and distinguish between mass media and social media.

Mass Media

Mass media are electronic or mechanical channels of delivering one-to-many communication—in other words, they are means of transmitting messages to large audiences. Mass media broadcast messages to a large group of people who generally are not in direct contact with the sources of the messages. Mass media include television, newspapers, magazines, radios, books, and so forth. Television programs such as *The Office*, *Big Bang*, and *Empire* attract millions of viewers; advertisements on television and the Web and in magazines and newspapers reach millions of people each week; newspapers and the Web provide news updates to vast numbers of people. Each of these media reaches a mass audience.

Social Media

Social media are the means of connecting and interacting actively. Social media include emails, tweets, instagrams, texts, and postings that rely on smartphones

mass media Channels of mass communication, such as television and radio.

social media Computer-mediated tools that allow people and organizations to create, and share photos, videos, and information for personal, social, political, and professional reasons.

Communication Highlight

Generations Online

Many people think that new technologies are favored far more by younger than older people. Surveys of actual users, however, suggest the generational divide is not so great (Dijck, 2013; Hill, 2011; Luttrell, 2014; Snider, 2012):

- People between the age of 18 and 34 years account for only 23% of the U.S. population, but make up 39% of the smartphone owners and 33% of the tablet owners.

- People between the age of 35 and 49 years compose 21% of the U.S. population and account for 30% of those using smartphones and 28% of those visiting social networks, blogs, and online videos.

- Both teens and people aged 18–32 years go online for videos, games, virtual worlds, and music downloads.

- Baby boomers now represent about 20% of the online daters.

- Sixty-seven percent of the 33- to 44-year-olds bank online.

and droids; iPads and iPods; MP3s; websites on the Web. Social media allow us to interact actively, collaborate, and participate in self-organizing, fluid communities. Social media are seamlessly integrated into our routines and identities (Bohil, Owen, Jeong, Alicea, & Bocca, 2009; Dijck, 2013; Luttrell, 2014; Potter, 2009; Styer, 2012; Turkle, 2011).

The primary difference between mass media and social media is digitalization. Three key implications of digitization are ease of manipulation, convergence, and speed (Steele, 2009; Turow, 2008). Manipulation is not new; it was possible with analog film and video and film photography. For instance, a photo could be retouched and video could be edited. However, manipulating analog media took a high level of skill that few people had. In contrast, most people who have grown up using digital media know how to manipulate them—for instance, Photoshop's clone stamping and Despeckle filter allow a person to alter a photo. The line that divided production and consumption of media in the analog era is blurred, if not erased in the digital era.

Digital media also cultivate convergence. Just a few years ago, it was very difficult and expensive to have a voice-over Internet phone call. Today, soldiers stationed overseas routinely skype with their families at home as do students on study abroad programs. This is possible because the technology for transmitting sound and the technology for transmitting visual images are both digital, and thus, they can be managed on a single network.

A third feature of digital media is nearly instant speed. With digital photography, you don't need to wait for photos to be developed. With texting, you are in immediate contact with another person or at least that person's smartphone. There's little, if any, pause between production of a message or photo and its consumption by others or us. That can lead to problems since we can't undo what we do in cyberspace. Anyone can do a screen capture of a photo you send on impulse and then share it with the world.

Interpersonal   Mass

FIGURE 11.1   Telephone   IM   PDA   Email   Twitter   Instagram   Listservs   Facebook   Blogs   YouTube   TV
The Media Continuum   and   and
                      Smartphone   LinkedIn

> RICH   *Before I became a full-time student here, I took three online courses. It was great to be able to do the classes at home when I could make time. But the content of the class was only part of the experience. What I really loved was talking with other students who were also taking the class online. We set up discussion boards, and some of us put each other on our IM lists so we could talk even when we weren't on the course website. I really loved the interaction with other students.*

The lines between social and mass media are not as clear cut as the foregoing discussion may suggest. For instance, if you send a video to a friend who then posts it on YouTube, is the video personal communication or mass communication or both? It is more appropriate to think of media as a continuum that ranges from clearly interpersonal, on one end, to clearly mass, on the other end, with a lot of mediated communication between those two ends (Figure 11.1).

Understanding How Media Work

In this section of the chapter, we'll first consider the ways we use mass media and social media and the ways they affect us.

Understanding Mass Media

Researchers have spent decades studying and theorizing about mass media. From their work, we can identify four key ways in which mass media influence—or *attempt* to influence—our lives.

Mass Media Provide Gratification   Think about the last time you watched a film. Did you choose it because the story mattered to you? Were you using the movie to escape from problems and worries? Did you watch because it featured stars you like? According to **uses and gratification theory**, we choose mass communication to gratify ourselves (Reinhard & Dervin, 2009). If you are bored and want excitement, you might watch an action film, whereas if you are stressed, perhaps you choose a lighthearted comedy or fantasy film. Uses and gratification theory says we use mass media to fulfill our needs and desires.

This theory assumes that we are active agents who deliberately choose media to gratify ourselves. We use media to gain information, to alleviate loneliness, to divert us from problems, and so forth. As we look at the next theory, we'll see that not everyone agrees that people are active, deliberate consumers of mass communication.

uses and gratification theory The theory that people choose to attend to mass communication in order to fulfill personal needs and preferences.

Mass Media Set Agendas   Mass media spotlight some issues, events, and people and downplay others. This affects our perceptions of what is (and is not) happening in the world and what is (and is not) important. **Agenda setting** is selecting and calling to the public's attention some and not other ideas, events, people, and perspectives (Bryant & Oliver, 2008; McCombs, Ghanem, & Chernov, 2009; Robinson, 2009).

Mass media exercise considerable control over the events, people, and issues that reach the public. For instance, television and newspaper reports make us aware of the sexual activities (real or rumored) of public figures. Historical accounts document the extramarital sexual activities of many past presidents, but at the time, those activities were not put on the public agenda. In our era, mass media call the sexual lives of public figures to our attention, making the public more aware of this issue than in previous times. Mass media also give prominence to celebrities;

Mass media set agendas by highlighting some, and not other, issues and perspectives.

anyone who reads a newspaper or watches television or surfs the Web gets updates on Taylor Swift, real or suspected steroid use by athletes, and Justin Bieber's latest antics.

Within agenda-setting theory, **gatekeeper** is a key concept. A gatekeeper is a person or group that decides which messages pass through the gates of media to reach consumers. Gatekeepers—producers, editors, Webmasters, and so forth—shape our perceptions of what is happening and what is and is not significant. Which stories make the front page of a newspaper, which are placed on a back page of Section C, and which are not covered at all? Which stories are covered by online newspapers and aggregators such as the *Huffington Post*? When a controversial issue is covered, do spokespeople for all sides get opportunity to present their points of view, or are spokespeople for some points of view given more or all of the time and space? Each of these gatekeeping decisions shapes what we perceive to be significant and the information to which we do and do not have access. The media have many gatekeepers:

- Reporters and program hosts decide whose perspectives on a story to present and whose to ignore.

- Editors of newspapers, books, and magazines screen the information that gets to readers and decide where to place stories (cover, front page, back page).

- Owners, executives, and producers filter information for radio and television programs.

- Government agencies may put pressure on the press and television and radio stations not to broadcast certain information.

Advertisers and political groups may influence which messages get through Gatekeepers of mass media underrepresent and often negatively portray women and minorities. Although women outnumber men in the population, media do not give them equal visibility. When women characters are in films and television shows, the majority are depicted in interpersonal and secondary roles

agenda setting Mass media's ability to select and call to the public's attention ideas, events, and people.

gatekeeper A person or group that decides which messages pass through the gates of media that control information flow to consumers.

(Butsch, 2011; Merskin, 2011; Ross, 2013; Sharp, 2011). Interestingly, films with strong female characters gross more than those that marginalize women; recent examples include the *Hunger Games* series and Disney's *Frozen* (Dewey, 2014; Hickey, 2014).

Minorities are also underrepresented and negatively portrayed in mass media. In the 500 top-grossing films between 2007 and 2012, 76.3% of the speaking characters were white, 10.8% were black, 5% were Asian, 4.2% were Hispanic, and 3.6% were from other or mixed race ethnicities (Smith, Choueiti, & Pieper, 2013). Researchers also found that Hispanic women were most likely to be shown with little or no clothing, and Black men are least likely to be portrayed as fathers or in committed relationships. Media depict Asians and Asian Americans in stereotypical ways as well—for example, Asian women are often portrayed as silent and exotic or as ruthless and evil while Asian men are typically portrayed as asexual and subordinate or villainous (Balaji & Worawongs, 2010; Zhang, 2010).

Historically, gays and lesbians have been virtually invisible in mass media. In recent years, we have seen an increase in the presence of gays, lesbians, and trans people who are portrayed positively on some prime-time shows and major films.

Mass Media Cultivate Worldviews   Cultivation theory claims that television promotes a worldview that is inaccurate but that viewers nonetheless assume reflects real life. This theory is concerned exclusively with television, which it claims shapes heavy viewers' perspectives and beliefs about the world (Gerbner, 1990; Shanahan & Jones, 1999; Signorielli, 2009).

Cultivation is the cumulative process by which television shapes beliefs about social reality. According to this theory, television fosters particular and often unrealistic understandings of the world as more violent and dangerous than statistics on actual violence show it is. Thus, goes the reasoning, watching television promotes distorted views of life. The word *cumulative* is important to understanding cultivation. Researchers don't argue that a particular program has a significant effect on viewers' beliefs. However, they claim that watching a lot of television over a long period of time affects viewers' overall views of the world. By extension, the theory claims that the more television people watch, the more distorted their views of the world are likely to be. Simply put, the theory claims that television cumulatively cultivates a synthetic worldview that heavy viewers are likely to assume represents reality.

Cultivation theorists identify two means by which cultivation occurs: *mainstreaming* and *resonance*. **Mainstreaming** is a process by which mass communication stabilizes and homogenizes social perspectives. For example, if commercial programming consistently portrays Hispanics as unambitious, African Americans as criminals and uneducated, and European Americans as upstanding citizens, viewers may come to accept these representations as factual. If television programs, from Saturday morning cartoons to prime-time dramas, feature extensive violence, viewers may come to believe that violence is more common than it actually is.

The second explanation for television's capacity to cultivate worldviews is **resonance**, the extent to which media representations are congruent with personal experience. For instance, a person who has been robbed or assaulted is likely to identify with televised violence when watching shows that feature it. When media representations correspond with our personal experiences, we are more likely to assume that they accurately represent the world in general.

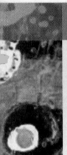

SHARPEN YOUR SKILL

At the end of this chapter, refer to the Sharpen Your Skill feature, Media Literacy in Action, to apply concepts from Chapter 11.

cultivation theory The theory that television promotes an inaccurate worldview that viewers nonetheless assume reflects real life.

cultivation The cumulative process by which television fosters beliefs about social reality.

mainstreaming The process by which mass communication stabilizes and homogenizes social perspectives; a concept in cultivation theory.

resonance The extent to which media representations are congruent with personal experience.

> **KELLY**   *I didn't think much about sex and violence on television until my daughter was old enough to watch. When she was 4, I found her watching an MTV program that was absolutely pornographic. What does seeing that do to the mind of a 4-year-old girl? We don't let her watch television now unless we can monitor what she sees.*

The high incidence of violence in news programming reflects in part the fact that the abnormal is more newsworthy than the normal. It isn't news that most couples either get along or work out their problems in nonviolent ways; it is news when one spouse kills another. Simply put, violence is news.

Perhaps you are thinking that few people confuse what they see on television with real life. Research indicates that this may not be the case. Investigations have shown that both males and females who watch sexually violent MTV are more likely to regard sexual violence as normal in relationships (Weimann, 2000). Children who watch a lot of violence on television tend to be less sensitive to actual violence than children who do watch less (Sparks, 2006). It's also the case that children who watch a lot of television violence score higher on measures of personal aggression than children who watch less television violence (Huesmann, Moise-Titus, Podolski, & Eron, 2003). Go to the book's online resources for this chapter to read a study of violence on children's TV.

> **Review It!**
>
> Cultivation Processes:
> - Mainstreaming
>   - Resonance

> **KASHETA**   *To earn money, I babysit two little boys 4 days a week. One day they got into a fight, and I broke it up. When I told them that physical violence isn't a good way to solve problems, they reeled off a list of television characters that beat up on each other. Another day, one of them referred to the little girl next door as a "ho." When I asked why he called her that, he started singing the lyrics from an MTV video he'd been watching. In that video women were called "hos." It's scary what kids absorb.*

Mass Media Exercise Ideological Influence   Because individuals and groups that have benefited from the existing social structure tend to control mass media, they have a vested interest in promoting their own views and values. Thus, it's not surprising that mass media, where gatekeepers are largely those who have done well in the status quo, are more likely to portray whites and middle- and upper-class people good, powerful, and successful than they are to describe minority people or lower- and working-class people in those ways (Hesmondhaigh, 2007; Kendall, 2011).

We've considered four perspectives on how mass media affect us. Probably each view has some validity. Surely, we make some fairly conscious choices about how to use mass media, as uses and gratification theory claims. At the same time, mass media probably influence us in ways we don't notice, as agenda setting and cultivation theories assert. And mass media clearly support dominant ideologies to a significant extent.

> **SHARPEN YOUR SKILL**
>
> At the end of this chapter, refer to the Sharpen Your Skill feature, Detecting Dominant Values in Media, to apply concepts from Chapter 11.

Understanding Social Media

Theories that emphasize mass media's ability to set agenda, cultivate worldviews, and maintain ideological control do not easily apply to social media. There is no mainstream view that dominates the Web; there is no single form of music or broadcast that people load onto iPods; there is not one privileged group that controls content on the Internet or blogs.

Yet one theory about mass media, uses and gratification theory, does seem applicable to social media. In fact, social media offer us considerably more options for gratifying ourselves than mass media do. With social media, we have nearly infinite choices for pleasure, competition, information, conversation, and collaboration. We can load our iPods with the songs and podcasts that we like, post and read friends' posts on Facebook, and participate in communities that gratify our various needs and desires.

SKINNYGIRL   *Skinnygirl was the name I used when I belonged to a pro-ana blog. When I was anorexic I couldn't get any support or understanding from my family or ftf friends. It was only when I joined the pro-ana blog that I found people who were like me and who accepted me as I was. A lot of people say pro-ana websites are bad because they encourage girls to be unhealthy, but that's not true. The one I belonged to gave me support when I was anorexic and also when I decided I wanted to get better. It was a safe space to work out who I was and to evolve at my own pace.*

Four principles of social media help us understand how they fit into our lives and how they may change those lives.

Social Media Blur Production and Consumption   Unlike mass media, social media are increasingly produced and consumed by the same people, and most of them are not media executives. Rather, they are ordinary people who get to know social media by participating in their actual construction. Rather, the lines between them have become blurred as people create personal blogs and podcasts, record their daily activities on LiveJournal, and post videos they've made (Dijck, 2013; Luttrell, 2014).

Social Media Alter Conceptions of Space   Social media change how we create and participate in communities by redefining our sense of space. Prior to the invention of computers, we understood space as an inert container that was distinct from the people, objects, and events within it. It was something we could enter, send messages through, and put things into. It was something that existed independent of our actions.

Cyberspace ushers in new understandings of space as a set of relations that is produced through the process of interacting. Rather than an empty container, cyberspace is a fluid, emergent process of connecting that grows out of interactions, not merely the context in which they occur. Cyberspace is a social space in which dynamic actions and interactions actually constitute the environment. In other words, cyberspace is not something that exists prior to our interactions. It is not "out

MindTap®   How often do you attempt to multitask?

there" awaiting us. Instead, it comes into being only as a result of what we do. It is what we do in cyberspace that defines space—the space is produced by what we do.

Consider how you produce the spaces (and the possibilities of relations) in which you interact online. When you use Facebook, you enter into a set of relations, a community that changes as you friend and unfriend people. Once you do that, you produce a different community—a different space and new set of relations. The space that you are in is produced—brought into being—by what you do.

Social Media Invite Supersaturation   Today's social media give us unprecedented access to information. We are saturated with information; at times we may feel overwhelmed and stressed by the information available to us, even as we increasingly believe Google should answer all of our questions (Coombs et al., 2016; Hillis, Petit, & Jarrett, 2012).

But it's not just information that saturates us—it's also people. Social media allow nearly instant contact with other people. At the same time, these media give others greater access to us than ever before (Staples, 2014). Although students are continuously engaged with digital media, they aren't wholly positive about it. A 2011 report (Levy, Nardick, Turner, & McWatters, 2011) noted that more than half of college students surveyed were concerned about being their immersed in technology. After college doesn't look much better: 62% of workers say they are so overloaded with information that it hampers the quality of their work (Schumpeter, 2011).

STELLA   *I totally count on iPhone to stay in touch with friends. We text all the time, like nonstop. As much as I love staying connected to everyone, I sometimes feel like it's not a choice anymore, like I can't cut off the phone. If I did, all my friends would be really upset and think I was mad or something. It's not okay to just want to be offline.*

Communication Highlight

What's Lost with Perpetual Connection?   MindTap

We know what we get from being continuously connected, but do we know what we lose? Recent studies raise concerns about three potential losses.

One cost may be emotional health. Girls are particularly vulnerable because their emotional health tends to be established by age 12, whereas boys' emotional health develops over a longer span (Nass, 2012). Tween girls who spend a lot of time interacting socially online feel less normal than girls who spend less time interacting online (Nass, 2012). Research also shows that students who are the heaviest users of technology have the highest levels of anxiety and depression (Rice, 2011). Researchers think the reasons for this may be that online socializing is often done while also engaging in other activities so users are less attentive to relationship levels of meaning and that online interaction doesn't help us develop skill in responding immediately to others' emotions.

Self-esteem may also suffer if children perceive their parents find digital devices more interesting than them. Parents who are texting, checking messages, and so forth may not engage their children fully. One young girl said, "I feel like I'm just boring. I'm boring my dad because he will take any text, any call, any time" (Brody, 2015, p. D7).

Another cost may be conversational skill. The Pew Internet and American Life Project reports that many people today prefer texting to phone calls and face-to-face contact. People whose main form of social engagement is texting may be less likely to make eye contact when they talk with others and may be less skillful in the give and take of conversation (Irvine, 2012). We also have more control over text and online interactions, which may mean we develop less skill in dealing with people and situations that are not within our control (Baron, 2010).

One more cost is sleep. Many young people sleep with their phones on and wake up to respond to texts. Many report they feel compelled to answer messages immediately. One study found that students lose an average of 45 minutes sleep each week because cell phones wake them up. In addition, they may get less of the deep REM sleep that makes us feel rested (Rice, 2011).

Our 24/7 mobile means we can practically leave the physical world of face-to-face relationships and live in the virtual world of online contacts. MIT professor Sherry Turkle (2011, 2015) asserts that our ability to stay connected with many people all the time poses a paradox: It provides the illusion of intimacy without the responsibilities of intimacy. On the one hand, we can and do interact with more people more often. On the other hand, online connections allow us to control the amount and degree of closeness. Turkle calls this "connection made to measure," which is radically different from relationships in which we sometimes spend more time and deal with more intimacy than we like because the other person needs us and we're committed to her or him.

The impact of hyperconnectivity is not limited to adults. Children are also affected in at least two ways. First, when they engage in extensive digital communication, their emotional and intellectual growth may be impaired (Brody, 2015; Turkle, 2015). Second, they may suffer from parents' involvement with digital media. Children may perceive their parents as more interested in digital devices than in them when parents are constantly talking or texting rather than engaging children.

Using Social Media to Improve Health Care

What do social media have to do with health care? A lot, according to recent research (Eytan, Benabio, Golla, Parikh, & Stein, 2011). Consider these advantages of active participation in social media by health care systems:

- coaching patients in making healthy life choices
- assisting patients in managing chronic conditions
- providing timely information to patients in a medium they use
- allowing patients to provide timely information to health care providers about changes or needs
- facilitating online support groups
- recruiting new patients through Twitter and other tools that accelerate dissemination of messages

Social Media Encourage Multitasking   Multitasking is doing multiple tasks at the same time. During classes, you may take notes while also texting and checking favorite websites. Many people play games while shopping and responding to texts. But are these really multitasking?

Despite widespread use of the term *multitasking*, people do not really do multiple tasks at once. Neither do computers, for that matter—they do one task at a time; they just do each one very, very quickly. A slow computer can implement a million instructions in less than a second (Harmon, 2002), but it executes each one individually, in sequence.

On the Job Netiquette   MindTap

When sending texts and tweets, many people are informal and somewhat careless. They use abbreviations (srsly for seriously, imho for in my humble opinion), forego capitalization (so I becomes i), and don't check spelling, grammar, and punctuation. For the most part, friends don't use salutations (Dear Emmons) or closings (Best, Vanessa).

That's fine for texting and tweeting between friends, but it's not advisable for on-the-job communication. When using media to interact with coworkers, bosses, and staff, always use a salutation and closing and proofread to make sure your grammar, punctuation, and spelling are correct. Care in communicating, whether face-to-face or via digital technology, is an earmark of professionalism (Helmrich, 2015; Lublin, 2010).

Bizarro

Do you mind if I strap your PDA to my forehead so I can pretend you're looking at me when I talk?

BIZARROCOMICS.COM

cartoonistgroup.com

Dan Piraro/The Cartoonist Group

What about humans? Can we multitask? Probably not. Neuroscientist Jordan Grafman says that people who try to do multiple tasks simultaneously tend to do all of them superficially and they still do them sequentially (Aratani, 2007). Studies show that extensive use of computers (including smartphones, droids, and tablets) remaps our neural circuitry. For instance, people who spend a lot of time online are likely to skim, scroll, and focus on hypertexted words rather than to read material in its entirety and with concentrated attention (Carr, 2011; Styer, 2012). This may explain why one former Microsoft and Apple executive refers to multitasking as "continuous partial attention" (Levy, 2006). There's also evidence that people who attempt to do several things at once make more mistakes and actually take longer than people who do one task at a time (Freeman, 2009; Jackson, 2009).

Communication Highlight

Do u text while driving?

Early one morning, Jim Furfaro and Keith O'Dell, both scientists, got in a Saturn and took off for morning commute to work. At about the same time, 19-year-old Reggie Shaw got behind the wheel and did what he always did when he was driving through Utah's mountains. He started texting to pass the time. And that's when he clipped the Saturn, causing it to spin out of control and killing Furfaro and O'Dell (Richtel, 2015). Evidence later showed that Shaw had sent 11 texts in the minutes before the tragedy.

Despite the mounting toll of highway deaths caused by using smartphones, some people continue to insist that using a phone doesn't interfere with their driving. At first, those who want to talk and text while driving argued that talking on a cell was no different than talking to a passenger. Once that argument was discredited, the new defense was that it was safe to drive and talk if you used a handsfree cell. Now that argument was also refuted by research. The problem isn't that "your hands aren't on the wheel. It's that your mind isn't on the road" (Parker-Pope, 2009a, p. D5). But perhaps technology will save us from itself. Sebastian Thrun (2011), Google Fellow at Stanford, spends his time developing a self-driving car. According to Thrun, "Our cars use specialized lasers, radar, and cameras to analyze traffic at a speed faster than the human brain can process" (p. D4). His model self-driving cars have driven 200,000 miles and counting.

Guidelines for Enhancing Your Effectiveness with Mass and Digital Media

Because mass and social media pervade our lives, we need to be responsible and thoughtful about how we use them—and how they use us. This requires us to develop **media literacy**, which is the ability to understand the influence of mass media and to access, analyze, evaluate, and respond actively to mass media in informed, critical ways. Figure 11.2 shows the components of media literacy. Just as it takes effort to become literate in written and oral communication, it takes effort to develop literacy in interacting with media. How media literate you are depends on the extent to which you work to develop and apply critical skills.

Understand the Influence of Media

Media literacy begins with understanding the extent to which social and mass media influence us. Do they determine individual attitudes and social perspectives, or are they two of many influences on individual attitudes and social perspectives? The first view is both naive and overstated. It obscures the complex, multiple influences on how we think as individuals and how we organize social life. It also assumes that media are linear—that we passively receive whatever mass media's gatekeepers send us and that we don't exercise thought as we engage in communication via social media.

The second view represents a thoughtful, qualified assessment of the influence of media and our ability to exercise control over their effects. Media, individuals, and society interact in complex ways. We are not unthinking sponges that absorb whatever is poured on us. Instead, we can interact thoughtfully and critically with media to mediate how they affect our identities and what they encourage us to believe, think, feel, and do.

If we choose to interact thoughtfully with media to control their impact on us, then we embrace questions about access to media and deliberate choices of how to engage them.

Access to Media

Access is the capacity to own and use televisions, tablets, computers, smartphones, and so forth. You may be thinking that access is not an issue. After all, you probably have and regularly use four or more personal media as well as engaging with mass media. But not everyone does.

media literacy The ability to understand the influence of mass media and to access, analyze, evaluate, and respond to mass media in informed, critical ways.

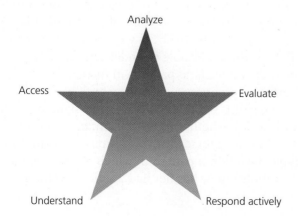

FIGURE 11.2
The Components of Media Literacy

Democratic Access   The term **digital divide** refers to the gap between people and communities with access to media, especially social media, and people and communities with less or no access. Some media scholars (Doyle, 2008; McChesney, 2008) believe that an information elite already exists because access to media, especially social media, requires both knowledge and resources that not everyone has.

If access to technologies is limited to individuals and groups that are already privileged by their social, professional, and economic status, we will see an increasing chasm between the haves and the have-nots. In the short run, it would be expensive to provide access and training for people who cannot afford to purchase it for themselves. In the long run, however, it might be far less costly than the problems of a society in which a small technology elite is privileged and many citizens are excluded from full participation.

People who can afford the newest technology will be the first to own multiple computerized devices, some of which will soon be connected to each other (e.g., when your computerized alarm clock rings, your computerized coffeemaker will start, and adjust the temperature in your home) and all of which will be linked to the Internet (e.g., the Internet will automatically reset your alarm clock and all other timing devices when you go on and off daylight savings time or after a power outage). If access is based on wealth, **convergence**—the integration of mass media, computers, and telecommunications—will increase the divide between haves and have-nots.

Expose Yourself to a Range of Media Sources   In addition to the issue of democratic access to mass communication, each of us faces a personal challenge in deciding what we attend. Many people access only media that support the views they already hold. For instance, if you are conservative politically, you might visit politically conservative blogs and websites, follow conservative commentators on Twitter, and listen to conservative television programs. The problem with that is that you don't expose yourself to criticisms of conservative policies and stances, and you don't give yourself the opportunity to learn about more liberal policies and positions. The same is true if you are politically liberal—you cannot be fully informed if you engage only media that share your liberal leanings. To be truly informed about any issue, you must attend to multiple, and even conflicting, sources of information and perspective.

Analyze Media

When we are able to analyze something, we understand how it works. If you aren't aware of the grammatical structure and rules of the English language, you can't write, read, or speak English effectively. If you are unaware of the patterns that make up basketball, you will not be able to understand what happens in a game. In the same way, if you don't understand patterns in media, you can't understand fully how blogrings, advertising, programming, and so forth work.

James Potter (2009) points out that there are a few standard patterns that media use repeatedly. Most stories, whether in print, film, or television, open with some problem or conflict that progresses until it climaxes in final dramatic scenes. Romance stories typically follow a pattern in which we meet a main character who has suffered a bad relationship or has not had a serious relationship. The romance

digital divide The gap between people and communities with access to media, especially social media, and people and communities with less or no access.

convergence The integration of mass media, computers, and telecommunications.

pattern progresses through meeting Mr. or Ms. Right, encountering complications or problems, resolving the problems, and living happily ever after.

Just as media follow a few standard patterns for entertainment, they rely on basic patterns for presenting news. There are three distinct but related features by which media construct the news.

- Selecting what gets covered: Only a minute portion of human activity is reported in the news. Gatekeepers in the media decide which people and events are newsworthy. By presenting stories on these events and people, the media make them newsworthy.

- Choosing the hook: Reporters and journalists choose how to focus a story, or how to "hook" people into a story. In so doing, they direct people's attention to certain aspects of the story. For example, in a story about a politician accused of sexual misconduct, the focus could be the charges made, the politician's denial, or the increase in sexual misconduct by public figures.

- Choosing how to tell the story: In the aforementioned story, media might tell it in a way that fosters sympathy for the person who claims to have been the target of sexual misconduct (i.e., interviews with the victim, references to other victims of sexual misconduct); or media might tell it in a way that inclines people to be sympathetic toward the politician (i.e., shots of the politician with his or her family, interviews with colleagues who proclaim the politician's innocence). Each way of telling the story encourages people to think and feel distinctly about the story.

Critically Evaluate Media Messages

When interacting with mass communication, you should think critically to assess what is presented. Rather than accepting news accounts unquestioningly, you should be thoughtful and skeptical. It's important to ask questions such as these:

- Why is this story getting so much attention? Whose interests are served, and whose are muted?

- What is the source of the statistics and other forms of evidence? Are the sources current? Do the sources have any interest in taking a specific position? (e.g. tobacco companies have a vested interest in denying or minimizing the harms of smoking.)

- What's the hook for the story, and what alternative hooks might have been used?

- Are stories balanced so that a range of viewpoints are given voice? For example, in a report on environmental bills pending in Congress, do news reports include statements from the Sierra Club, industry leaders, environmental scientists, and so forth?

It's equally important to be critical in interpreting other kinds of mass communication, such as music, magazines, newspapers, and billboards. When listening to a piece of popular music, ask what view of society, relationships, and so forth it portrays, who and what it represents as normal, and what views of relationships it fosters. Raise the same questions about the images in magazines and

Puffery: The Very Best of Its Kind!

One of the most popular advertising strategies is **puffery**, superlative claims that seem factual but are actually meaningless. For instance, what does it mean to state that a particular juice has "the most natural flavor"? Most natural in comparison to what? Other juices? Other drink products? Who judged it to have the most natural flavor: The corporation that produces it? A random sample of juice drinkers? What does it mean to say a car is "the new benchmark"? Who decided this was the new benchmark? To what is this car being compared? It's not clear from the ad, which is only puffery.

Recently, researchers tested the advertising claims for dozens of fitness products such as sports drinks, oral supplements, footwear, and wrist bands. The researchers could not find valid scientific support for a single claim. In fact, the products that were carefully tested "appear to have no effect on strength, endurance, speed or reduced muscle fatigue" (Bakalar, 2012, p. D5). All of the claims are puffery. Media-literate people don't buy the claims or the products.

on billboards. When considering an ad, ask whether it offers meaningful evidence or merely groundless claims for a product's superiority. Asking questions such as these allows you to be critical and careful in assessing what mass communication presents to you.

You should also keep a critical eye on claims that look or sound like facts. Tim Clydesdale (2009) says claims and reports grounded in fact appear side by side with opinions those that have no basis. Communication professor Rayford Steele (2009) extends this thinking one step further. He believes that newer media tempt people to rely on peer opinion rather than expert authority. In the online world, everyone may state opinions, make claims, and so on. The problem is that not everyone is equally qualified, and not every opinion is equally well grounded. When we don't think critically about sources and their qualifications, we impede our ability to make reasoned judgments about which opinions really are supported and good.

The popular online encyclopedia, Wikipedia, illustrates both the advantages and drawbacks of open-source architecture on the Internet. The good news is that anyone can add, delete, or edit entries in Wikipedia. The bad news is that anyone can add, delete, or edit entries in Wikipedia—yep, in this case, the bad news is the same as the good news. You or I can access Wikipedia and edit entries on cyberspace, baseball, or paragliding, regardless of whether we have any expertise on those topics. When anyone can contribute to a website, we need to exercise more than usual critical thinking about what we find on that website.

Respond Actively

puffery In advertising, superlative claims for a product that seem factual but are actually meaningless.

People may respond actively or passively to mass and social media. If we respond passively, we mindlessly consume messages and the values implicit in them. On the other hand, if we respond actively, we recognize that the worldviews presented in mass communication are not unvarnished truth but partial, subjective perspectives that serve the interests of some individuals and groups while disregarding or mis-representing the interests of others. Responding actively to mass communication includes choosing consciously how and when to use it, questioning what is presented, and involving yourself in controversies about media, particularly the newer technological forms. Responding actively to social media requires us to use our devices deliberately, choosing when to text and when to talk face-to-face, when to be online and when not to.

Participate in Decision Making about Media   Responding actively is not just looking out for ourselves personally. It also requires us to become involved in thinking about how media influence cultural life and how, if at all, media should be regulated. We've already discussed the escalation of violence in media and the digital divide. But there are other issues, particularly in the context of the Internet and the Web. What guidelines are reasonable? What guidelines infringe on freedom of speech and the press? We need to think carefully about what kinds of regulations we want and how to implement them.

Privacy is a key issue for those interested in regulation of social media. Many online advertisers rely on *cookies*, small electronic packets of information about users that the advertisers store in users' personal browsers. *Spyware* is a means by which a third party (neither you-the-user nor the website you are visiting) tracks your online activity and gains personal information about you. Because spyware is implanted on users' computers, it can monitor a range of online activities in which users engage. Should cookies, spyware, and similar tools be regulated? Should users have the right to control who monitors their online communication and with whom it is shared?

Much of the media, particularly social media, remains unregulated. We have an ethical responsibility to become involved in questions of whether regulations should be developed and, if so, who should develop and implement them.

Review It!

Elements of
Media Literacy:

• Understanding

• Access

• Critical Analysis

• Evaluation

• Active Response

Communication Highlight   **Responding Actively**

If you want to learn more about gender and media, or if you want to become active in working against media that foster views of violence as normal, girls and women as subordinate, and buying as the route to happiness, visit these websites:

Action Coalition for Media Education: http://www.acmecoalition.org
Center for Media Literacy: http://www.medialit.org
Children Now: http://www.childrennow.org
Media Watch: http://www.mediawatch.com
National Association for Family and Community Education: http://www.nafce.org
TV Parental Guidelines Monitoring Board: http://www.tvguidelines.org

Chapter Summary

In this chapter, we have examined mass and social media. We've explored ways in which these media influence our lives. They affect what we know and think about the world around us, and they affect how we think and act in our lives, both online and offline.

The second section of the chapter focused on developing media literacy so that we can be informed, critical, and ethical citizens in a media-saturated world. To be responsible participants in social life, we need to think critically about what is included—and what is made invisible—in mass and social media.

Media-literate people do not accept media messages unthinkingly. Instead, they analyze and evaluate the messages and respond actively by participating thoughtfully in considerations about the extent of regulation of media and the people who should exercise that regulation.

Perhaps a good way to end this chapter is by returning to the opening observation that media, both mass and social, are not inherently good or bad. Michael Rich (2012), a pediatrician who directs the Center on Media and Child Health, reminds us, "It's what we do with the tools that decides how they affect us and those around us" (p. D5).

MindTap°

Experiencing Communication in Our Lives

CASE STUDY: Online Relationships

Apply what you've learned in this chapter by analyzing the following case study, using the accompanying questions as a guide. These questions and a video of the case study are also available online with your MindTap Speech for *Communication in Our Lives*.

Christina is visiting her family for holidays. One evening after dinner, her mother comes into her room, where Christina is typing at her computer. Her mother sits down, and the following conversation takes place.

MOM: Am I disturbing you?

CHRIS: No, I'm just signing off on email.

MOM: Emailing someone?

CHRIS: Just a guy.

MOM: Someone you've been seeing at school?

CHRIS: Not exactly.

MOM: (Laughs) Well, either you are seeing him or you're not, honey. Are you two dating?

CHRIS: Yeah, you could say we're dating.

MOM: (Laughs) What's he like?

CHRIS: He's funny and smart and easy to talk to. We're interested in the same things, and we share so many values. Brandon's just super. I've never met anyone like him.

MOM: When do I get to meet him?

CHRIS: Well, not until I do. (Laughs) We met online, and we're just starting to talk about getting together in person.

MOM: Online? You act as if you know him!

CHRIS: I do know him, Mom. We've talked a lot—we've told each other lots of stuff.

MOM: How do you know what he's told you is true? For all you know, he's a 50-year-old mass murderer!

CHRIS: You've been watching too many movies on Lifetime, Mom. Brandon's 23, he's in college, and he comes from a family like ours.

MOM: How do you know that? He could be lying.

CHRIS: So? A guy I meet at school could lie, too.

MOM: Haven't you read about all the weirdos that go to these online matching websites?

CHRIS: Mom, Brandon's not a weirdo, and we didn't meet in a matching website. We met in a chat room where people talk about politics.

MOM: Chris, you can't be serious about someone you haven't met.

CHRIS: I have met him, Mom, just not face to face. I know him better than lots of guys I've dated for months.

MOM: This makes me really nervous, honey. Please don't meet him by yourself.

CHRIS: Mom, you're making me feel sorry I told you how we met. This is why I didn't tell you about him before. Nothing I say is going to change your mind about dating online.

MOM: (Pauses) You're right. I'm not giving him—or you—a chance. Let's start over. Tell me what you like about him.

CHRIS: Well, he's thoughtful.

MOM: Thoughtful? How so?

CHRIS: If I say something one day, he'll come back to it a day or so later, and I can tell he's thought about it, like he's really interested in what I say.

MOM: So he really pays attention to what you say?

CHRIS: Exactly. So many guys I've dated don't. They never return to things I've said. And when I come back to things he's said with ideas I've thought about, he really listens.

MOM: Like he values what you think and say?

CHRIS: Exactly! That's what's so special about him.

QUESTIONS FOR ANALYSIS AND DISCUSSION

1. Identify examples of ineffective and effective listening on the part of Chris's mother.

2. What do you perceive as the key obstacle to listening for Chris's mom during the early part of this conversation?

3. Identify specific listening skills that Chris's mother uses once she chooses to listen mindfully.

4. Is Chris's mother being unethical by not continuing to state her concerns about Chris's safety?

Key Concepts

agenda setting	gatekeeper	resonance
convergence	mainstreaming	social media
cultivation	mass media	uses and gratification
cultivation theory	media literacy	theory
digital divide	puffery	

Sharpen Your Skill

1. Media Literacy in Action

In this chapter, you have learned about some of the ways that gatekeepers shape understanding, perspectives, and attitudes. Apply what you've learned by identifying ways that I, as the author of this chapter, shaped the information presented to you.

- *Gatekeeping*: Whose points of view do I emphasize in discussing mass communication and media literacy? Are there other involved groups that I neglect or ignore?
- *Agenda setting*: Which aspects of mass communication did I call to your attention? Which aspects of mass communication did I not emphasize or name?

2. Detecting Dominant Values in Media

Watch 2 hours of prime-time commercial television. Pay attention to the dominant ideology that is represented and normalized in the programming. Who are the good and bad characters? Which personal qualities are represented as admirable, and which are represented as objectionable? Who are the victims and victors, the heroes and villains? What goals and values are endorsed?

For Further Reflection and Discussion

1. Would it be ethical to exercise control over the violence presented in media? Do you think viewers, especially children, are harmed by the prevalence of violence in media? If you think there should be some controls, what groups or individuals would you trust to exercise them?

2. Susan Crawford is a legal scholar with particular expertise on Internet law and issues of privacy, intellectual property, and advertising. Her blog gives her opinions on a range of legal issues entailed by cyberspace. Go to the book's online resources for this chapter to read her blog.

Beyond the Classroom

Let's take the material in this chapter beyond the classroom by thinking about how what you've learned about the media might apply to the workplace, ethical choices, and engagement with the broader world.

1. **Workplace.** How have technologies altered the operation of groups in the workplace? Reflect on your own experience or talk with others who have belonged to work groups that operate face-to-face and to work groups that operate virtually. Are the two types of groups equally effective? Do they cultivate equal commitment from group members? Are there particular advantages and disadvantages of each type?

2. **Ethics.** Increasingly everything from attending school to communicating with coworkers to maintaining ties with friends and family depends on technologies of communication. Does the increasing importance of these technologies mean that we should ensure that everyone has equal access to them? Is there an ethical responsibility to prevent the digital divide?

3. **Engagement.** Technologies of communication have vastly increased our ability to learn about and even participate in cultures other than our own. Identify an issue that interests you—the election and voting process, a human rights issue, education—and use technologies such as PDA or computer to learn about that issue in the context of a specific culture other than your own.

12

> There are three things to aim at in public speaking: first, to get into your subject, then to get your subject into yourself, and finally, to get your subject into the heart of your audience.
>
> **Alexander Gregg**

Pojoslaw/Shutterstock.com

Planning Public Speaking

How many speeches have you given in the past 5 years?

LEARNING OBJECTIVES

After studying the topics in this chapter, you should be able to:

1. Explain ways in which public speaking is similar to everyday conversation.

2. List four considerations of choosing a topic for a public presentation.

3. Distinguish between a speech's general purpose and its specific purpose and provide an example of each.

4. Summarize what is meant by the terms demographic analysis and situational analysis.

5. Recall four criteria for evaluating online research.

6. Apply chapter guidelines to improve your ability to plan a public presentation.

- Hank is a commercial artist at a public relations firm. On Thursday, Hank's supervisor asks him to prepare a 10-minute presentation for a client whose million-dollar account the firm hopes to get.
- Bonnie's first performance review is scheduled for next week. She knows her supervisor always asks employees he reviews what they think they have brought to the company, and she wants to have a smart, confident answer.
- Juan is the best man at his friend's wedding. He knows it is traditional for the best man to give a toast to the newly married couple, and he wants his remarks to be really meaningful.
- At the first meeting of class, the professor asks each person to "say a few words" to introduce himself or herself. Brittany wants to make a good impression on her peers with her self-introduction.

Although these people aren't professional speakers, each of them is called on to speak. Competence in public speaking increases your chances of advancing professionally. In addition, you expand your impact in social situations and your ability to have a voice in community and civic affairs. Expressing ideas is so basic to a democratic society that it is the very first amendment to the Constitution.

MindTap®

Read, highlight, and take notes online.

The role of speaking in professional life is more obvious in some occupations than in others. If you plan to be an attorney, a politician, a salesperson, or an educator, it's easy to see that speaking in public will be a routine part of your life. The importance of public speaking is less obvious, yet also present, in other careers. In fact, you're likely to find that speaking to small and large groups is part of everyday life in the workplace, such as giving a report, presenting an idea to coworkers, making a proposal to a client, informing a patient about a procedure, or explaining a play to teammates. The ability to present ideas effectively in public situations will also enhance your influence in civic, social, and political contexts. You'll have opportunities to voice your ideas at zoning meetings, political events, and school boards. Although some people may have more experience and perhaps more aptitude for public speaking than others, everyone can learn to make effective presentations. As we will see, many of the skills we've discussed in the previous chapters are relevant to effective public communication.

This chapter and the four that follow lead you through the process of planning, developing, and presenting informative and persuasive speeches. In this chapter, we'll first note similarities between public speaking and other kinds of communication we've studied. Next, we'll discuss foundations of effective public speaking: selecting and limiting topics, defining a general purpose and a specific purpose, and developing a thesis statement. The third section of the chapter emphasizes adapting speeches to particular speaking occasions and to particular listeners' orientations to topics and speakers. The final section of the chapter identifies ways that digital media can assist you in planning a speech.

The next four chapters build on material presented in this one. Chapter 13 identifies types of support for public speeches and discusses methods of conducting research. In Chapter 14, we'll learn about ways to organize and present public speeches, and we'll discuss ways to increase your confidence as a public speaker. Chapter 15 focuses on informative public speeches, and Chapter 16 focuses on persuasive public speeches. After reading these five chapters, you should be able to plan, develop, and present an effective speech.

MindTap®   Does this speaker appear to be effective?

Public Speaking Is Enlarged Conversation

Years ago, James Winans (1938), a distinguished professor of communication, remarked that effective public speaking is really enlarged conversation. Winans meant that the skills of successful public speaking are not so different from those we use in everyday conversations.

Public communication is also like conversation in a second way. It occurs naturally in everyday life. Public speaking is not just giving a long speech in front of a crowd. More often, it is speaking for 5 or even 2 minutes to fewer than 20 people. It happens in meetings, hallways, and receptions. It happens at retreats and workshops. It happens in boardrooms and ballrooms.

Effective public communication uses and builds on skills and principles we've discussed in the previous chapters. Whether we are talking with a couple of friends or speaking to an audience of 500, we need to consider listeners' perspectives, adapt to the situation, express our ideas clearly, organize what we say so that others can follow our thinking, explain and support our ideas, and be personally engaging. In public speaking, as in everyday conversation, these are the skills of effective communication.

CHLOE   *I had a great history teacher last year. We met twice a week for 75 minutes, so I was prepared for serious boredom. But it never seemed like he was "lecturing." It was more like he was talking with us—telling interesting stories and asking what we thought about stuff. The 75 minutes just flew by every time.*

Communication Highlight

The First Amendment: Freedom of Religion, Speech, and Press

"Congress shall make no law respecting an establishment of religion, or prohibiting the free exercise thereof; or abridging the freedom of speech, or of the press; or the right of people peaceably to assemble, and to petition the Government for a redress of grievances."

—Amendment I, The Constitution of the United States

Choose and Refine a Topic

When people think of public speaking, they often focus on the delivery. However, 90% of a speech happens before it is delivered. The choices you make in planning your speech are the foundation of your effectiveness.

A well-crafted speech begins with a thoughtfully selected topic, a clear purpose, and a concise thesis statement that listeners grasp quickly and retain.

Choose Your Topic

The first step in preparing a public speech is to select a topic. Often the topic is selected for you. For instance, your supervisor might ask you to brief a team on some issue or to give a report on a training program you attended. In other cases, you will prepare remarks for an occasion that constrains what you should say. For example, if you are asked to present an award, the occasion demands that you talk about what the award means and the accomplishments of the recipient.

For the class you are taking, you may have the opportunity to select your own topic. If you don't already have a topic in mind, you might consult newspapers and news magazines, current events programs on television, and online news websites. Go to the book's online resources for this chapter to visit online websites.

Select a Topic That Matters to You   When you care about your topic, you already know something about it. In addition, personal interest in the subject will make your delivery more engaging and more dynamic. Maybe you have strong beliefs about the death penalty, funding of college athletics, or environmental responsibility. In cases where your topic is assigned to you—for instance, your supervisor might tell you to make a report—then your challenge is to find something in the topic with which you can connect personally.

Select a Topic Appropriate to the Speaking Occasion   You should also consider the expectations, demands, and constraints of particular speaking situations (Ferguson, 2008). Some contexts virtually dictate speech topics. For example, a rally for a political candidate demands speeches that praise the candidate and a ceremony honoring a person requires speakers to pay tribute to the person.

> **PAT**   *When we had our Phi Beta Kappa induction last spring, we had a very well-known scholar give the speech. He began by talking about how great our basketball team is and how we may win the championship this year. He talked about the team for about 5 minutes before he said anything else. It's not like I'm against sports or anything. I mean, I go to games and I think our team is way cool. But Phi Beta Kappa is the highest academic honor society on campus. It didn't seem the right situation to be leading a rally for the team.*

Physical setting is also part of the speaking occasion. You know what your classroom is like and the time of day you will speak. In other speaking situations, you should familiarize yourself with the physical setting. Is the room in which you will speak large or small? Is it well lit or dim? Are chairs comfortable or not? Will you present your speech at 10 a.m., after a heavy lunch, or in the evening? Will listeners have sat through a long day of meetings and speeches? Each of these factors influences listeners' ability to listen and pay attention.

If you are not familiar with the speaking context, try to check the room in advance. You might be able to control some possible hindrances, such as temperature or seating arrangement. If undesirable aspects of the setting are beyond your control (i.e., uncomfortable seating, speaking after listeners have had a big meal), you must do your best to compensate for them. A dynamic and engaging delivery can do much to surmount listeners' lethargy or discomfort.

Sometimes, you won't know the physical setting in advance or won't be able to control it. In that case, you must adapt as best you can on the spot. Once, my partner, Robbie, was asked to give a keynote speech after dinner at a meeting of the Student Sierra Club. In the past, he had given many keynote speeches at Sierra Club meetings. Based on past events, Robbie assumed that the dinner would be in a banquet room and that people would be dressed somewhat formally. He prepared a 30-minute speech, which he planned to deliver from a speaking podium. He dressed in a good suit and tie. When he got to the meeting, he discovered that the dinner was a cookout—certainly appropriate for a Sierra Club group, but not what he was expecting!

Robbie quickly adapted his appearance by taking off his jacket and tie and rolling up his shirtsleeves. He then adapted the content of his speech and his delivery to the informal speaking situation in which he found himself. He decided to eliminate some of the quotations from environmental leaders because the light from the campfire would not be sufficient for him to read the quotations from note cards, and he didn't want to risk misquoting sources. And he adapted his planned, forceful, podium delivery to a more conversational, storytelling style. Robbie would have been ineffective had he not adapted to the physical setting.

Select a Topic Appropriate to Your Audience   Effective speakers also select topics that will appeal to the needs, interests, and situations of listeners. A speech is not primarily a chance to showcase yourself by showing how smart, clever, funny, or knowledgeable you are. Rather, it is first and foremost a chance to affect others— that's the reason for speaking. And if you want to affect others, you begin thinking about them in the first stages of planning a speech.

In selecting a topic or thinking about one assigned to you, ask how the topic is or can be relevant to your listeners, what knowledge they have, and what experiences and concerns they are likely to share with you. Later in this chapter, we'll discuss in depth how you can take listeners into consideration.

Communication Highlight

Connecting Yourself with Your Topic

One of the most powerful ways for speakers to enhance impact is to demonstrate personal involvement with their topics. Some good examples of speakers who show their personal involvement with topics come from acceptance speeches at Academy Awards ceremonies (Robinson, 2001). When Tom Hanks won the best actor award for his portrayal of an attorney with AIDS in the film, "Philadelphia," he used his speech to honor the millions of people who have died of HIV-related illnesses. He also paid tribute to a former teacher who was gay and who inspired his performance. That same year, Gerda Weisman Klein won an award for her documentary film about the Holocaust, *One Survivor Remembers*. Accepting the award, Weisman said, "I've been in a place for 6 incredible years where winning meant a crust of bread and to live another day" (p. 16).

Narrow Your Topic   Effective speakers limit their speeches to a manageable focus (McGuire, 1989). If you're interested in the general topic of health care reform, you might narrow that to reducing the costs of drugs or increasing preventive medicine (wellness). You can't cover the broad topic of health care reform in a single speech, but you can cover a particular aspect of it.

Another way to narrow your speaking purpose is to use a *mind map* (Jaffe, 2016). A **mind map** is a holistic record of information on a topic, which many visual thinkers prefer to an outline. You create a mind map by free-associating ideas in relation to a broad area of interest. For example, perhaps you want to speak on the general topic of the environment. To narrow that broad topic to a manageable focus for a single speech, you could brainstorm issues related to the topic. Figure 12.1 shows many specific issues that might occur to someone who creates a mind map on the topic of environment. If you would like to use a software program to map your ideas, go to the book's online resources for this chapter.

Define Your General and Specific Purposes in Speaking

The second step in designing an effective speech is to define your purpose for speaking. This involves two steps. First, decide on your general purpose. Second, refine your general purpose into a specific purpose.

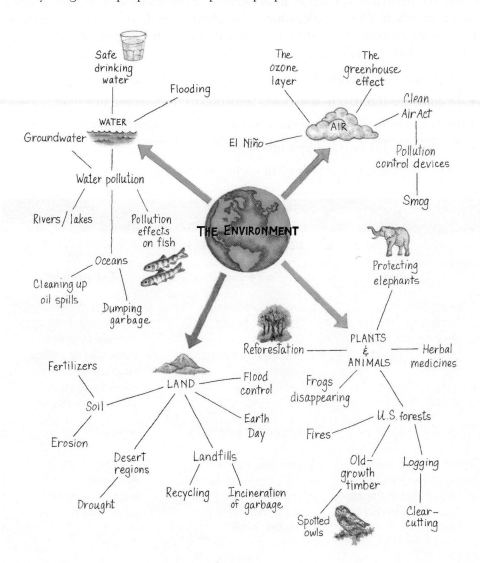

FIGURE 12.1
A Mind Map

Review It!

Choose a Topic That:

- Matters to You
- Is Appropriate to the Occasion
- Is Appropriate to the Audience
- Is Narrowed

---

mind map A holistic record of information on a topic. Mind mapping is a method that can be used to narrow speech topics or to keep track of information gathered during research.

SHARPEN YOUR SKILL

At the end of this chapter, refer to the Sharpen Your Skill feature, Selecting and Narrowing Your Topic, to apply concepts from Chapter 12.

General Purposes of Speaking   Traditionally, three general speaking purposes have been recognized: informing, persuading, and entertaining (Table 12.1). You probably realize that these purposes often overlap. For example, informative speeches routinely include humor or stories that aim to keep listeners interested. Speeches intended to inform may also persuade listeners to adopt new beliefs, attitudes, or actions. Although speeches often involve more than one general purpose, usually one purpose is primary.

Speeches to inform have the primary goal of increasing listeners' understanding, awareness, or knowledge about some topic. When you speak to inform, your goal is to tell listeners something they don't already know.

Consider several purposes for informative speaking:

- to teach listeners how to do something
- to correct listeners' misconceptions
- to make listeners aware of a problem
- to describe a new procedure or policy

Speeches to persuade aim to change or reinforce people's attitudes, beliefs, or behaviors or to motivate people to act. Persuasive goals are to influence attitudes, change practices, alter beliefs, and to motivate action. Rather than an entertainer or teacher, the persuasive speaker is an advocate who argues for a cause, issue, policy, attitude, or action. To persuade, a speech must do more than provide information, although information typically is part of persuasive speaking as well. Persuasive purposes include the following:

- To convince listeners to do something they are not currently doing
- To convince listeners to stop doing something they are currently doing
- To motivate listeners to support a specific policy, law, or candidate
- To convince listeners to buy a product
- To inspire listeners to give time or money to a worthy cause

speech to inform A speech, the primary goal of which is to increase listeners' understanding, awareness, or knowledge of some topic.

speech to persuade A speech, the primary goal of which is to change listeners' attitudes, beliefs, or behaviors or to motivate listeners to action.

Table 12.1	Speaking Purpose		
GENERAL PURPOSES			
	To Inform	**To Persuade**	**To Entertain**
	Speaking to define, instruct, explain, clarify, demonstrate, teach, or train	Speaking to influence attitudes, beliefs, or actions; to convince, motivate to action, inspire, or sell	Speaking to create interest, amusement, warm feelings; to celebrate, remember, or acknowledge others or events; to create or fortify ties between people
SPECIFIC PURPOSES			
	To help listeners understand the balloting procedure used in the 2000 presidential elections in Florida	To persuade listeners to sign a petition demanding new voting systems for all districts in the United States	To have listeners laugh at my jokes in the after-dinner speech at the retreat

In speeches to entertain, the primary objective is to interest, amuse, or please listeners. You might think that speeches to entertain are presented only by accomplished comics and performers. Actually, in the course of our lives, many of us will be involved in speaking to entertain. You might be asked to give an after-dinner speech, to present a toast at a friend's wedding, or to make remarks at a retirement party for a colleague. In each case, the primary goal is to entertain, although the speech might include information about the occasion, the couple being married, or the colleague who is retiring.

Even when your primary purpose in speaking is not to entertain, you'll want to interest listeners whom you intend to inform or persuade. If you want to include some entertainment in your speech, it's a good idea to test your jokes or amusing comments in advance. Don't assume that others will find humor in something you think is funny, and don't rely exclusively on close friends' judgment; after all, friends often think alike and have similar senses of humor.

Humor isn't the only means of entertaining. We also entertain by telling stories to share experiences, build community, pass on history, and teach lessons. Storytelling is prominent in cultures that emphasize oral, more than written, communication. In some countries and in some social communities in the United States, individual and collective histories are kept alive through storytelling (Einhorn, 2000; Fitch, 2000; Schram & Schwartz, 2000). In traditional West African culture, storytellers, who are called griots, tell stories that blend words, song, and dance, and audience members respond as a chorus (Cummings, 1993).

Specific Purposes of Speaking   Once you have decided on your general speaking purpose, you will want to define a **specific purpose**, which is a behavioral objective or observable response that will indicate that you achieved your communication goal. Here are some examples of specific speaking purposes:

- I want 25% of listeners to sign up to donate blood.

- I want a majority of listeners to be able to give correct answers to questions about how HIV is and is not spread.

- I want listeners to know this candidate's stand on free trade.

Develop a Thesis Statement

Once you have selected and narrowed your speaking topic and defined your general and specific purpose, you're ready to develop the thesis statement for your speech. A **thesis statement** is the main idea of an entire speech. It should capture the heart of your speech in a short, precise sentence that listeners can remember easily (Table 12.2).

A good thesis statement is one that listeners grasp at the beginning of your talk and remember after you have finished. They may forget the specific details and evidence you present, but you want them to remember the main idea. Outline Builder, accessed through MindTap includes a section on developing thesis statements that are appropriate and effective for the type of speech you're preparing.

Review It!

Three General
Purposes of Speaking:

- To Inform

- To Persuade

- To Entertain

speech to entertain A speech, the primary goal of which is to amuse, interest, or engage listeners.

specific purpose A behavioral objective or observable response that a speaker specifies as a gauge of effectiveness; reinforces a speaker's more general speaking goals.

thesis statement The main idea of an entire speech. It should capture the key message in a concise sentence that listeners can remember easily.

Storytelling is a powerful way to pass on history and strengthen community bonds. It plays a central role in oral cultures.

The Elevator Speech

MindTap

Communication & Careers

- You hop on an elevator and press the button for the 12th floor. The door closes and another passenger says to you, "I've seen you in this building before. Where do you work?"

- You are at a community fund-raiser dinner. As the salads are served, the person seated to your right asks, "What do you do?"

- You are on a flight to a conference. As the plane takes off, your seatmate says, "Hi, I'm Sam" and waits for you to say something.

The "elevator speech" is how you present yourself in 30 seconds to 2 minutes—the time it takes an elevator to travel several flights in an elevator. Think of it as your oral business card. It's essential for effective networking, so savvy professionals spend time preparing whip smart elevator speeches.

Table 12.2   Sample Thesis Statements

INEFFECTIVE	EFFECTIVE
Think twice before you decide you're for gun control.	Gun control jeopardizes individuals' rights and safety.
Vegetarianism is a way of life.	Vegetarian diets are healthful and delicious.
Big business should get breaks.	Tax breaks for businesses are good for the economy.

Table 12.3   Steps in Planning Public Speaking

STEP	EXAMPLE
1. Identify the broad topic.	Education
2. Narrow the topic.	Continuing education
3. Define a general purpose.	To persuade
4. Determine a specific purpose.	To motivate listeners to take courses after graduating from college
5. Develop a thesis statement.	"Taking courses after you graduate can enrich your personal life and your professional success."

SHARPEN YOUR SKILL

At the end of this chapter, refer to the Sharpen Your Skill feature, Defining Your Purpose and Thesis Statement, to apply concepts from Chapter 12.

In sum, the first steps in planning a public speech are to select and narrow a topic, define your general and specific speaking purposes, and develop a clear, concise thesis statement (Table 12.3). Now we're ready to consider the key process of adapting your speaking goals, content, and delivery to specific listeners and speaking contexts.

Analyze Your Audience

A student named Jake gave a persuasive speech to convince listeners to support affirmative action. His ideas were well organized, and his delivery was dynamic. The only problem was that his audience had little background on affirmative action, and he didn't explain exactly what it does and does not involve. Jake mistakenly assumed listeners understood how affirmative action works, and he focused on its positive effects. His listeners weren't persuaded because he failed to give them information they needed. This example also illustrates the point that speeches often combine more than one speaking purpose; in this case, giving information was essential to Jake's primary goal of persuading listeners.

Another student named Christie spoke passionately about vegetarianism. She provided dramatic evidence of the cruelty animals suffer as they are raised and slaughtered. When we polled listeners after her speech, only 2 of 30 had been persuaded to consider vegetarianism. Why was Christie ineffective? Because she didn't recognize and address listeners' beliefs that vegetarian foods are tasteless. Christie's listeners weren't about to consider a diet that they thought was unappetizing.

Christie and Jake made the mistake of not adapting to their audiences. Speakers need to know what listeners already know and believe as well as what reservations they might have about a topic (Coopman & Lull, 2013; Griffin, 2015; McGuire, 1989). To paraphrase the advice of an ancient Greek rhetorician, "The fool persuades me with his or her reasons, the wise person with my own." That is, effective speakers work with listeners' reasons, values, knowledge, and concerns.

Demographic Audience Analysis

Demographic audience analysis identifies general features common to a group of listeners. Demographic characteristics include age, sex, religion, cultural heritage, race, occupation, political allegiances, and educational level. Demographic information is useful in two ways.

First, demographic information can help you adapt your speech to your listeners. For example, if you know the age or age range of listeners, you know what experiences are likely to be part of their history. You could assume that 60-year-old listeners know a fair amount about the Vietnam War but that 20-year-olds might not. You can assume that 60-year-olds remember the Vietnam War and Martin Luther King, Jr., but that 18- to 22-year-old listeners do not. In speaking situations with listeners of different ages, either restrict your references to the ones that will be familiar to listeners of all ages or explain any references that might not be understood by some listeners.

demographic audience analysis A form of audience analysis that seeks information about the general features of a group of listeners.

Communication Highlight

What Do People Think About . . .?   MindTap

Speakers often want to know what the general public thinks about issues related to their topics. Tracking down information on opinions about specific issues can be time consuming, but there's a shortcut. The People & the Press website, sponsored by the Pew Charitable Trusts, presents the results of public opinion surveys on a variety of topics, such as the present administration, national health care, and biological warfare. To check it out, go to the book's online resources for this chapter.

Age is also linked to persuadability. In general, as people age, they are less likely to change their attitudes, perhaps because they've held their attitudes longer than younger people or because they've acquired knowledge that supports their attitudes (Meyers, 1993). Thus, it's generally reasonable to expect to move older listeners less than younger listeners toward new beliefs, attitudes, or actions.

Other demographic information can also guide speakers in preparing presentations that will interest and involve particular listeners. Because we live in a multicultural world, effective speakers must be careful not to use examples that exclude some groups. For instance, the use of generic male language (*chairman*, the pronoun *he* to refer to a doctor) is likely to offend some listeners. Similarly, referring to the winter break from school as "the Christmas holiday" may be perceived as ignoring listeners who are not Christian. Although many women work outside the home, not all do, so an audience of women should not be addressed as if no homemakers were present. Similarly, speakers shouldn't stereotype an audience of men as uninterested in child care because many men are involved parents.

Speakers also use demographic information to make inferences about listeners' likely beliefs, values, and attitudes. For example, assume you plan to give a speech on the general topic of health care reform. If your listeners' average age is 68 years, they are likely to be more interested in options for long-term care of older adults than in methods of birth control. Listeners with an average age of 21 years, on the other hand, would be likely to perceive birth control as more immediately relevant than ensuring reasonable options for long-term care.

Knowing something about the general characteristics of listeners may also suggest what type of evidence and which authorities will be effective. Statistics bore many listeners, especially if presented in a dull manner, but they might be interesting to an audience of economists or mathematicians. A quotation from Barack Obama is more likely to be effective with a Democratic audience than with a Republican one. Citing Justice Sonja Sotomayor might impress a group of women attorneys more than citing Clarence Thomas would. Speakers may also draw on demographic information to create connections with their listeners. Politicians create points of identification with voters in diverse regions. In the South, a candidate

Communication & Careers

Adapting to Listeners

Professionals are sometimes called upon to speak at press conferences, which Dr. Dong Kim discovered on Saturday, January 8, 2011, when Jared Lee Loughner shot Representative Gabrielle Giffords of Arizona in the head during Giffords' meeting with constituents. Miraculously, she survived the head wound.

Her doctors held a press conference to inform the public of her status. Dr. Dong Kim, the Chair of Neurosurgery at UT Health where Giffords was treated, demonstrated how to adapt highly technical medical information to listeners without medical expertise. He told viewers that Giffords had mild hydrocephalus. Since many in his audience wouldn't know the term *hydrocephalus*, Dr. Kim translated it by saying, it's like "water in the head." He went on to explain that patients with brain injury often have difficulty absorbing fluid in the head, which he compared to "having a partially clogged drain." Again, Dr. Kim used something laypeople are familiar with (a clogged drain) to make his communication understandable. The entire press conference is available on the book's online resources for this chapter.

might tell stories about growing up in a Southern town; in New England, the candidate might reminisce about college years at Harvard; in the Midwest, the candidate might speak about friends and family who live there. It is unethical for a speaker to disguise or distort his or her background, ideas, or positions to build common ground with listeners. However, understanding the demographic characteristics of listeners helps a speaker decide which aspects of his or her life and interests to emphasize in particular situations.

LAMONT *A big filmmaker came to talk to our class, and I figured he was in a world totally different from ours. I mean, the man makes multimillion-dollar movies and knows all the big stars. But he started his talk by telling us about when he was in college, and he talked about his favorite classes, about a bar he went to on Fridays, and about the special friends he'd made at college. I felt like he understood what my life is about, like he wasn't so different from me after all.*

Situational Audience Analysis

A second method of audience analysis is **situational audience analysis,** which seeks information about listeners that relates directly to the speaker's topic and purpose. Situational audience analysis allows a speaker to discover what listeners already know and believe about a topic, speaker, and occasion so that the speaker can adapt to his or her listeners.

Listeners' Orientation Toward the Topic Speakers want to begin by piquing listeners' interest. How does the topic affect their lives? Why should they care about what you have to say? Emma, a student of mine, began an informative speech about breast cancer this way: "Think about 8 women who matter to you. According to statistics, 1 of those 8 women will develop breast cancer."

You also want to analyze listeners' knowledge about your topic so that you can adapt appropriately. What do they already know about the topic? How much information (or misinformation) do they have? Once you have assessed listeners' knowledge about your topic, you can decide how much information to provide.

Finally, in assessing your listeners' orientation toward your topic, you want to know what attitudes they hold. If they already favor something you are proposing, you don't need to persuade them to adopt a positive attitude. Instead, you may want to move them to action—to motivate them to act on what they already favor. On the other hand, if your listeners are against or indifferent to something you are proposing, your persuasive goal is to convince them to consider your point of view.

Listeners' Orientation Toward the Speaker Listeners' perceptions of a speaker shape how they respond to the message. Do the listeners already know who you are? Do they respect your expertise on the topic? Do listeners believe you care about what is good for them? If not, you need to give listeners reasons to trust your expertise and to believe that you are interested in their welfare.

If you are not an expert on a topic, you will want to demonstrate to listeners that you know what you are talking about. Describe your experiences with the topic. Include research that shows you are knowledgeable. Because a speaker's credibility is critical to effectiveness, we'll return to this topic when we discuss using evidence (Chapter 13), building a strong introduction to a speech (Chapter 14), and increasing credibility (Chapter 16).

situational audience analysis A method of audience analysis that seeks information about specific listeners that relates directly to a topic, speaker, and occasion.

Listeners' Orientation Toward the Speaking Occasion   In the fall of 2002, Paul Wellstone, a Democratic senator from Minnesota, was killed in a plane crash. In addition to grieving for his tragic loss, Democrats were worried about the elections coming up in just a month. Wellstone had seemed assured of reelection. His sudden death meant that the Republican candidate might win his seat in the United States Senate. After late-night strategy sessions, the Democrats announced that Walter Mondale, a former vice president from Minnesota, was the Democratic candidate and would carry on Wellstone's legacy.

The nationally televised memorial service for Senator Wellstone and those of his family who also died in the plane crash began with speeches honoring the fallen senator, as was expected on this occasion. However, after the opening speeches, the memorial service turned into a political rally for Mondale, the new Democratic candidate. Many viewers were shocked and offended by what they perceived as disrespect for Wellstone and his family and a blatant exploitation of a memorial service for political purposes. Mondale was defeated, and most political analysts cited the voting public's negative reaction to the political rally displacing the memorial service as the key reason.

Whereas politicians and corporations can afford to conduct sophisticated polls to discover what people know, want, think, and believe, most of us don't have the resources to do that. So how do ordinary people engage in situational audience analysis? You may gather information about listeners through conversations, interviews, or surveys. You might conduct a survey to learn about your classmates' knowledge of and attitudes toward your thesis statement. The results of your survey should give you sufficient insight into the opinions of students on your campus to enable you to adapt your presentation to the students in your class.

Demographic and situational audience analysis provides you with direct knowledge of listeners and information from which you can draw additional inferences. Taking listeners into consideration allows you to build a speech that is adapted to your particular listeners and thus likely to have impact.

Review It!

Types of Audience Analysis:
- Demographic
- Situational

Digital Media and Planning Public Speaking

Digital media can assist speakers in planning public presentations. Broad search engines such as Google can provide general information on virtually any topic. In fact, the number of hits produced in response to a Google search can be overwhelming. More specialized search engines such as Google Scholar provide fewer and often more reliable hits. You may also use online databases such as LexisNexis Academic and Academic Search Complete.

When conducting research online, you have a special responsibility to evaluate information critically. As you know, anyone can post anything online, so there are no guarantees of reliability or validity. Ask questions such as the following:

- Is the website signed?

- Is the author qualified to know about this topic (search the author separately)?

- Is the information current? If the date is not posted at the bottom of the website, use the Tools menu to learn when the post was last modified.

- Is the information trustworthy? Verify information on the website by checking it on other websites.

Chapter Summary

In this chapter, we considered the first steps in designing effective presentations. Planning includes selecting and limiting your topic, defining your general and specific purposes, and developing a clear thesis statement. In addition, designing an effective presentation requires consideration of listeners. Effective speakers take into account what listeners know, believe, value, think, and feel about the topic, speaker, and occasion. When a speaker adapts to listeners, they are likely to be more receptive to the speaker's ideas. Online search engines and databases can help you research topics, but exercise critical thinking about information you find online.

In the next chapter, we'll discuss ways to conduct research and use research in public speaking. Building good arguments increases a speaker's credibility and enhances the power of ideas presented. Before proceeding to Chapter 13, complete the checklist to make sure you've done the preliminary work to create a strong foundation for your speech.

Checklist for Planning a Public Speech

MindTap

You may want to use Outline Builder, which you can access through MindTap.

My speech topic is _____

My general purpose is _____

My specific purpose is _____

My thesis statement is _____

1. I know the following demographic information about the people who will listen to my speech:
   Age: _____
   Education: _____
   Political position: _____
   Sex ratio: _____
   Ethnicities: _____
   Other: _____

2. I know the following information about my particular listeners:
   Listeners' interest in my topic: _____

   Listeners' knowledge about my topic: _____

   Listeners' personal experience with my topic: _____

   Listeners' beliefs about my topic: _____

Listeners' attitudes toward my thesis: _____

Listeners' expectations of the speaking occasion: _____

Listeners' orientation toward me as a speaker: _____

MindTap

Experiencing Communication in Our Lives

CASE STUDY: A Model Speech of Introduction

Apply what you've learned in this chapter by analyzing the following case study, using the accompanying questions as a guide. These questions and a video of the case study are also available online with your MindTap Speech for *Communication in Our Lives*.

Dan's assignment was to present a speech of introduction in which he introduces his classmates to Dr. Evelyn Horton. Dr. Horton is a doctor who specializes in family medicine, the profession that Dan hopes to enter.

"If you don't listen to your patients, you'll never be able to provide them with good medical care." That was the first thing Dr. Evelyn Horton said to me when I asked her what kinds of communication are essential to her work. Last Monday, I interviewed her because I hope one day to be a doctor. I want to introduce you to Dr. Horton and to describe the role of communication in her work as a doctor. I'll focus on the importance of two communication skills that Dr. Horton emphasized: listening and building a supportive, trusting relationship.

The first communication skill that Dr. Horton emphasized is listening. She told me that one of the reasons she wanted to become a doctor is that she had encountered too many doctors who didn't listen to her when she was a patient. "How can a doctor treat you if he or she doesn't listen to you?" asked Dr. Horton. Dr. Horton isn't alone in feeling that many doctors don't listen. The *Journal of the American Medical Association* reported last year that patients' biggest dissatisfaction with doctors is that they don't listen.

I asked Dr. Horton to explain what was involved in effective listening. She said, and I quote, "To be a good listener, I have to let my patients know I really want to hear what's going on with them. I have to give them permission to tell me how they are feeling and if anything is bothering them." Some of the ways that Dr. Horton does this are to repeat what patients tell her so that they will elaborate, and to keep eye contact with them when they are speaking.

So focusing on patients and encouraging them to talk openly with her are the keys to effective listening in Dr. Horton's practice. The second communication skill that Dr. Horton emphasized is building a supportive, trusting relationship with her patients. She told me about one of her patients who had an eating disorder. Dr. Horton suspected the problem, but she couldn't do much to treat it until her patient, a 19-year-old woman, was willing to admit she had a problem.

How did Dr. Horton gain the patient's trust? She told me that she showed the patient she wasn't going to judge her—that it was okay to say anything, and it would be confidential. When the patient made a small disclosure about being afraid of gaining weight, Dr. Horton recalled, and I quote, "I told her many women have that fear, and there are healthy ways to control weight." Later, the patient told her that sometimes she skipped meals. Dr. Horton responded, and again I quote her, "That's an understandable thing to do when you're afraid of gaining weight, but there are healthier ways to maintain a good weight." As Dr. Horton responded without judgment to the patient, the young woman gradually opened up and told Dr. Horton about her excessive dieting and exercise. Together, they worked out a better plan for managing the patient's weight.

Being nonjudgmental, then, is a key to building a trusting doctor–patient relationship. Now you've met Dr. Evelyn Horton, a doctor who knows the importance of communication to her work. For her, listening and building a supportive, trusting relationship with patients are the keys to being a good doctor. Let me close with one last statement Dr. Horton made. She told me, "To treat people, you have to communicate well with them."

QUESTIONS FOR ANALYSIS AND DISCUSSION

1. Does Dan's speech give you a sense of who Dr. Horton is?

2. Did Dan's introduction catch your attention and give you a road map of what he would cover in his speech?

3. How did Dan move you from one part of his speech to the next?

4. How did quotes and examples from Dr. Horton add to the speech?

5. Was Dan's conclusion effective?

6. Which model of communication presented in Chapter 1 best describes Dr. Horton's communication with patients?

Key Concepts

demographic audience
    analysis
mind map
situational audience
    analysis

specific purpose
speech to entertain
speech to inform

speech to persuade
thesis statement

MindTap

Use flashcards to learn key concepts and take a quiz to test your knowledge.

Sharpen Your Skill

1. Selecting and Narrowing Your Topic

Identify three broad topics or areas that you care about.

Topic 1: _____

Topic 2: _____

Topic 3: _____

Now list three subtopics for each one. The subtopics should be narrow enough to be covered well in a short speech.

Topic 1: 1. _____

　　　　　2. _____

　　　　　3. _____

Topic 2: 1. _____

       2. _____

       3. _____

Topic 3: 1. _____

       2. _____

       3. _____

Select one of the nine subtopics for your upcoming speech.

2. Defining Your Purpose and Thesis Statement

Write out the general purpose of your speech.
I want my speech to _____

_____

Define the specific purpose of your speech by specifying the observable response that will indicate you have succeeded:
At the end of my speech, I want listeners to _____

_____

Does your specific purpose require you to meet subordinate goals, such as including information in a persuasive speech?
To achieve my specific purpose I need to [entertain, inform, and/or persuade]. _____

_____

For Further Reflection and Discussion

1. Think about one presentation that you recently attended—perhaps a lecture in a class or a speech at a campus event. To what extent did the speaker seem to take the audience into consideration? Identify specific factors that affect your perception of the speaker's knowledge of you and other listeners. Did this make a difference in the speaker's effectiveness?

2. In this chapter, we discussed the importance of adapting to particular listeners. What ethical considerations apply to the process of adapting speeches to particular listeners? Is it ethical for a speaker not to disclose certain experiences with a topic? Is it ethical for a speaker to leave out evidence that is contrary to his or her speaking goal?

3. Check two databases for sources on a topic that interests you. Track down two sources from each database to read in detail.

4. Go to the book's online resources for this chapter to review commonly believed myths about public speaking.

Yuri Arcurs/Dreamstime.com

13

Handle them carefully, for words have more power than atom bombs.

Pearl Strachan

Researching and Developing Support for Public Speeches

LEARNING OBJECTIVES

After studying the topics in this chapter, you should be able to:

1. List four types of research that are useful in preparing a speech.

2. List five kinds of evidence used by effective public speakers.

3. Identify three kinds of examples a speaker might use in preparing a speech and provide an example of each.

4. Analyze a quotation to see if it meets the three criteria for ethical use in a speech.

5. Determine the appropriate number of visual aids to use in a classroom speech.

6. Use the checklist at the end of this chapter to validate your research for an upcoming speech.

What type of evidence do you find most compelling?

MindTap®

Review the chapter's learning objectives and **start** with a quick warm-up activity.

- Guns kill too many people.
- Guns have killed 1,516,863 Americans.
- Since 1968, guns have killed more Americans than have died in all of the wars America has fought.

Which of the aforementioned statements do you find most interesting and most persuasive (Jacobson, 2015)? If you are like the most people, the third statement is most compelling. The first statement is a weak generalization. The second gives a concrete number that is stunning, but the statistic is not related to anything. The third statement offers a comparison that puts gun deaths in a broader perspective. This illustrates the difference that strong evidence can make in a speech. It also shows that evidence is not only a matter of facts and statistics, but also of a speaker's imagination and effort to make it meaningful.

A speaker's success is tied directly to whether listeners understand, believe, and accept what he or she says. In this chapter, you will learn how to conduct research and weave it into your speech so that listeners understand and believe in you and your message. You will also learn how digital media can assist you in conducting research for your speech. Throughout the process of researching and building support for a speech, it's important to conduct research and select evidence adapted to particular listeners.

Conducting Research

Research is essential to a sound informative or persuasive speech. We'll discuss four types of research: online research, library research, interviews, and surveys.

Online Research

Online search engines such as Yahoo and Google are often the first step in researching a topic. They are fast and convenient and they often provide lots of material. However, the material's quality is not assured. It may be highly credible or may be junk. Most print magazines and newspapers have fact checkers who check all information in articles before they go to press. In contrast, as we noted in Chapter 12, the accuracy of information posted on the Internet is not assured. People who create or contribute to websites may not have evidence for their claims. They may have vested interests in particular viewpoints. Information you find online should be verified. Thus, although you may start with online research, that should not be your sole or primary means of gathering sound information about your topic.

Library Research

Libraries hold a wealth of information that can help you develop and support the ideas in your speech. Begin your research by paying a visit to the reference librarian at your library. Describe your speech topic to your reference librarian, and ask for suggestions on relevant print and electronic sources of information.

The librarian will probably direct you to the online catalogue, which lists holdings by author, title, and subject. The online catalogue will help you find reference

FIGURE 13.1
Online Research
Includes Websites,
such as the U.S.
Census Bureau, which
Provides Information on
Demographics and Many
Facets of American Life
Reprinted by permission
of www.Virtual Library,
http://vlib.org.

works that can provide background information on people whom you cite in your
speech: *Who's Who in America, Who's Who in American Women, Biography Index,*
and *Directory of American Scholars.* The catalogue will also let you search periodi-
cals (print materials that are published periodically) for very current information on
your topic (see Figure 13.1).

Libraries also have databases that have high subscription fees and so are not
available to most of us (see Figure 13.2). As we noted in Chapter 12, databases

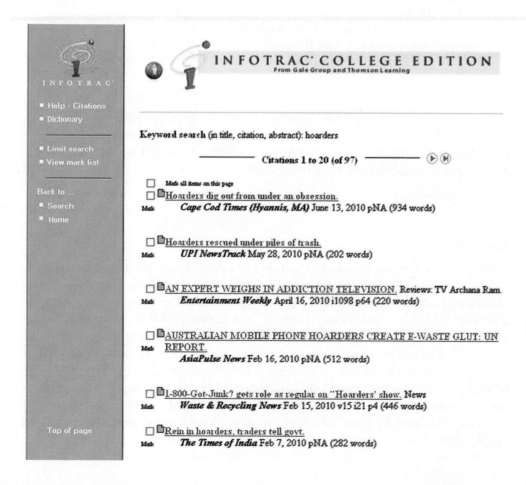

FIGURE 13.2
Using an Online
Database to Research
Your Speech Topic
Source: From InfoTrac
College Edition by Gale.
Reprinted with permission
of Gale a division of
Cengage Learning. www.
cengage.com /permissions

give you access to popular and academic publications and news services. Two other superior information retrieval systems are Bibliographic Retrieval Service (BRS) and Wilsonline.

Interviews

Interviews allow you to gather information, to check the accuracy of ideas you have, and to understand the perspective of people who are experts or who have special experience with your topic.

You need to plan ahead for interviews. When you call or email to request an interview, identify yourself, explain the purpose of the interview, and state the approximate length of time you expect the interview to take. Prepare a list of questions in advance to ensure that you don't forget important questions.

In addition to questions you prepare, you'll want to invite interviewees to initiate ideas. As experts, they may be aware of information and dimensions of a topic that haven't occurred to you. If an interviewee gives permission, it's acceptable to take notes or tape during interviews. However, you should be careful to keep your primary attention on the interviewee.

Quoting interviewees shows that you invested personal effort in researching a topic. To maximize the impact of testimony, you should explain why sources are qualified as experts. You may credit your sources in several ways:

> "After 10 years in the position of chief of campus police, Chris Brenner says, . . ."
>
> "In an interview I conducted with Chris Brenner, longtime chief of campus police, he told me that. . ."
>
> "To find out about crime on our campus, I interviewed the chief of campus police. According to Chief Brenner, . . ."

COLE *It was really effective when Joel told us he had interviewed police officers to find out their views about drivers who use cell phones. He had lots of good information from other sources, but what really impressed me was that he took time to talk with police officers himself. I felt like that showed he cared enough to really learn about his topic in a personal way.*

Surveys

survey research Research that involves asking a number of people about their opinions, preferences, actions, or beliefs.

Survey research involves asking a number of people about their opinions, views, values, actions, or beliefs. Surveys are useful in two situations. First, sometimes there's no published research on something important to your speech. Yumiko, a student taking his first speaking course, was concerned that many of his peers at the university had misperceptions about Japanese people and their traditions. He decided to use his speech as an opportunity to correct misperceptions. After 2 weeks of research, he was discouraged because he couldn't find any studies of U.S. college students' views of Japanese people. We developed a short questionnaire on views of Japanese people that he handed out to 100 students on campus. This gave Yumiko some information about local students' perceptions (Table 13.1).

Table 13.1	Guidelines for Constructing Surveys

The following guidelines will help you construct a survey that will provide you with solid information.

1. Respondents should be chosen to reflect the population (or larger group) whose opinions you seek to understand. (Students may reflect students' opinions. However, students generally would not reflect homeowners' opinions.)

2. Respondents should be qualified to answer the questions. (Only people who are informed about inflation and living expenses have the information to answer this question: "How much should the cost-of-living adjustment be for Social Security recipients?")

3. Questions should be worded to avoid bias. ("You favor gun control, don't you?" is a leading question that biases respondents toward answering affirmatively. The question "Do you favor gun control?" is not biased. You will get different responses if you ask people if they favor "helping the poor" and if they favor "welfare.")

4. Each question should focus on only one issue. ("Do you favor Medicare and Medicaid?" asks respondents' opinions on two distinct issues. This question should be split into two separate questions.)

5. Questions should allow for all possible responses. (It would not be accurate to ask respondents whether they are Democrats or Republicans because those two responses don't include other possible choices, such as Libertarians and Independents.)

6. Questions should rely on language that will be clear to respondents. (For years, the U.S. Bureau of the Census asked people whether they worked "full time," which the bureau defined as 35 hours a week or more. However, many respondents interpreted "full time" to mean 40 hours a week or more. The bureau revised the wording of the question to remove the ambiguity.)

7. Avoid negative language in survey items; it tends to be confusing. (Respondents are likely to misunderstand the question "Do you agree or disagree that the United States should not have socialized medicine?" The question is clearer when phrased this way: "Do you agree or disagree that the United States should have socialized medicine?")

Second, sometimes you can directly survey your listeners. Although this isn't always feasible, when possible, a survey helps you find out what listeners know. Based on what you learn, you can include information they don't have and avoid boring them by telling them what they already know. Surveys of listeners also allow you to discover what personal experience they have pertinent to your topic. Attitudes based on direct experience are more difficult to change (Wu & Shaffer, 1988).

Audience surveys can also help you learn what attitudes your listeners hold. At a minimum, you'll want to know whether your listeners agree or disagree with your position and how strong their attitudes are. If you want to argue for more severe sentences for convicted felons, and your listeners are strongly against that, then you might choose to limit your persuasive goal to reducing the strength of listeners' resistance to stronger sentencing. On the other hand, if they already agree with your position, you might try to move them toward action by asking them to write letters to senators or to vote for candidates who share their attitudes. What you can achieve in a given speech depends to a large extent on the starting beliefs and knowledge of your listeners (Wu & Shaffer, 1988).

Review It!

Types of Research:
- Online
- Library
- Interviews
- Surveys

SHARPEN YOUR SKILL

At the end of this chapter, refer to the Sharpen Your Skill feature, Background on Experts, to apply concepts from Chapter 13.

Now that we have discussed ways to conduct research, we're ready to consider specific forms of support, or evidence.

Using Evidence to Support Ideas

Evidence is material used to support claims a speaker makes. Evidence serves a number of important functions in speeches. First, it can be used to make ideas clearer, more compelling, and more interesting. Second, evidence fortifies a speaker's opinions. Finally, evidence heightens a speaker's credibility. Speakers who use good evidence show that they are informed and prepared.

> **MARTEL**   *We had a guest speaker in my econ class. He quoted Nobel Prize–winning economists and the findings of a report that was just done and hasn't even been published yet. All of us felt he was highly informed and credible.*

Five forms of support are widely recognized. Before including any form of evidence in a speech, the speaker should check the accuracy of the material and the credibility of the source. When presenting evidence to listeners, speakers have an ethical responsibility to give credit to the source (an oral footnote).

Statistics

Statistics are numbers that summarize many individual cases or demonstrate relationships between phenomena. Including statistics can enhance speaker credibility (Crossen, 1997). For example, a speaker could demonstrate the prevalence of injuries caused by drivers who are under the influence of alcohol by stating, "According to the American Automobile Association, one in four people injured in traffic accidents is the victim of a driver who had been drinking." Statistics can also be used to document connections between two or more things. For instance, a speaker could tell listeners, "According to the Highway Patrol, you are 50% more likely to have an accident if you drink before driving."

Statistics aren't boring, but they can be poorly presented. Effective speakers translate statistics into information that is meaningful to listeners (see Table 13.2).

evidence Material used to support claims. Types of evidence are statistics, examples, comparisons, and quotations. Visual aids may be used to represent evidence graphically.

statistics A form of ev idence that uses numbers to summarize a great many individual cases or to demonstrate relationships between phenomena.

Cartoon by Signe Wilkinson. Reprinted by permission of Cartoonists & Writers Syndicate/cartoonweb.com

Table 13.2	Guidelines for Using Statistics Effectively

Used unimaginatively, statistics are likely to bore listeners. To avoid this fate when you are speaking, follow these guidelines for using statistics effectively.

- Limit the number of statistics you use in a speech. A few well-chosen numbers mixed with other kinds of support can be dramatic and persuasive, whereas a laundry list of statistics can be monotonous and ineffective.
- Round off numbers so that listeners can understand and retain them. We're more likely to remember that "approximately a million Americans are homeless" than that "987,422 Americans are homeless."
- Select statistics that are timely. Occasionally, an old statistic is still useful. For example, the number of people who died in the Great Plague is not likely to change over the years. In most cases, however, the most accurate statistics are recent. Remember that statistics are a numerical picture of something at a specific time. But things change, and speakers should get new snapshots when they do.
- Make statistics interesting to listeners by translating statistics into familiar and relevant information.

SHARPEN YOUR SKILL

At the end of this chapter, refer to the Sharpen Your Skill feature, Bringing Statistics Alive, to apply concepts from Chapter 13.

To describe a million homeless people in terms listeners will immediately understand, a student speaker said, "That's 50 times the number of students on our campus." Here's how another student speaker translated the statistic that one in four college-age women will be raped in her lifetime: "Of the seventeen women students in this room today, four will probably be raped sometime during their lives."

Examples

Examples are single instances used to make a point, dramatize an idea, or personalize information. There are three types of examples that have different uses for speakers.

Undetailed Examples When speakers want to make a point quickly, undetailed examples are useful. These are brief references that quickly recount specific

examples Forms of evidence; single instances that make a point, dramatize an idea, or personalize information. The four types of examples are undetailed, detailed, hypothetical, and anecdotal.

What Is a Flame?

MindTap

Communication & Careers

The Flame Challenge is an annual conference in which science students offer understandable explanations of complex phenomena. The first contest, held in 2009, asked "What is a flame?"

The Flame Contest is sponsored by the Alan Alda Center for Communicating Science at Stony Brook University's School of Journalism. The Center aims to teach scientists how to communicate complex, technical information in ways that are understandable to nonscientists. Well-known actor, Alan Alda, has a passion for teaching scientists how to present their research to the public. Using improvisational acting workshops and group techniques, Alda mentors scientists in effective public communication (Chang, 2015).

Go to the book's online resources for this chapter to find information on the Flame Contest, including winners for each year.

instances of something. One student opened a speech on the costs of textbooks by saying, "Remember standing in the long lines at the bookstore and paying for more than your tuition at the start of this term?" His listeners immediately identified with the topic of the speech.

Detailed Examples   Detailed examples provide more elaborate information than undetailed ones, so they are valuable when listeners aren't familiar with an idea. A student included this detailed example in her speech on environmental justice:

> *Most of you haven't lived near a toxic waste dump, so you may not understand what's involved. In one community, the incidence of cancer is 130% higher than in the country as a whole. The skin on one man's hands was eaten away when he touched the outside of a canister that stored toxic waste. His skin literally dissolved when it came in contact with the toxin.*

Detailed examples create vivid pictures that can be moving and memorable. However, because they take time to present, they should be used sparingly.

Stories or anecdotes are a type of detailed example. Presidents routinely include stories in their speeches to personalize their ideas and create identification with listeners. Religions rely on stories—parables in Christianity, *teichos* in Buddhism—to teach values and persuade people to follow them. Attorneys rely on stories to persuade judges and jurors, taking all the known facts in a case and weaving them together in a way that makes sense and supports their clients' accounts of events. The attorneys with whom I consult tell me that the key challenge in trial court is to create a story that covers all the facts and is more believable than the story created by the opposing counsel.

Speakers often tell a story to personalize abstract issues. To help middle-class listeners understand the personal meaning of poverty, a student told this story about a woman he interviewed to prepare his speech:

> *To start her day, Annie pours half a glass of milk and mixes it half and half with water so that the quart she buys each week will last. If she finds day-old bread on sale at the market, she has toast, but she can't afford margarine. Annie coughs harshly and wishes this throat infection would pass. She can't afford to go to a doctor. Even if she could, the cost of drugs is beyond her budget. She shivers, thinking that winter is coming. That means long days in the malls so that she can be in heated places. It's hard on her and the kids, but the cost of heat is more than she can pay. Annie is only 28 years old, just a few years older than we are, but she looks well into her forties. Like you, Annie grew up expecting a pretty good life, but then her husband left her. He doesn't pay child support, and she can't afford a detective to trace him. Her children, both under 4, are too young to be left alone, so she can't work.*

The story about Annie puts a human face on poverty. A story that has depth takes time, so speakers have to consider whether the point they want to make justifies the time a story will take.

Review It!

Types of Examples:
- Undetailed
- Detailed
- Hypothetical

Hypothetical Examples   Sometimes a speaker has no real example that adequately makes a point. In such cases, a speaker can create a hypothetical example, which is not factual but can add clarity and depth to a speech. To be effective, hypothetical examples must be realistic illustrations of what you want to exemplify.

Diamond Images/Getty Images

Communication Highlight

The Typical American Family

John F. Kennedy was a powerful public speaker. He wove many kinds of support into his speeches to strengthen his credibility and increase the impact of his ideas.

On May 19, 1962, President John F. Kennedy used the following hypothetical example in his speech at the rally for the National Council of Senior Citizens at Madison Square Garden.

Let's consider the case of a typical American family—a family which might be found in any part of the United States. The husband has worked hard all of his life, and now he has retired. He might have been a clerk or a salesman or worked in a factory. He always insisted on paying his own way. This man, like most Americans, wants to care for himself. He has raised his own family, educated his children, and he and his wife are drawing Social Security now. Then his wife gets sick, not just for a week, but for a very long time. First the savings go. Next, he mortgages his home. Finally, he goes to his children, who are themselves heavily burdened. Then their savings begin to go. What is he to do now? Here is a typical American who has nowhere to turn, so he finally will have to sign a petition saying he's broke and needs welfare assistance.

Hypothetical examples often are used to portray average cases rather than to represent a single person or event. If you use a hypothetical example, you have an ethical responsibility to inform listeners that it is not a factual example.

Comparisons

Comparisons are associations between two things that are similar in some important way or ways. **Similes** are explicit comparisons that typically use the words *like* or *as* to link two things: "A teacher is like a guide." "Service is like paying dues for membership in a community." **Metaphors** are implicit comparisons that suggest likeness between two things that have something in common: "A teacher is a guide," "Service is the dues you pay for belonging to a community."

Quotations

Quotations, or testimony, are statements made by others. If someone has stated a point in an especially effective manner, then you may want to quote that person's words. Quotations may also be used to substantiate ideas. Using an expert's testimony may be persuasive to listeners, but only if they respect the expert who is quoted. Thus, it's important to provide "oral footnotes" in which you identify the name, position, and qualifications of anyone you quote, as well as the date of the quoted statement. For example, in a speech advocating tougher laws for driving under the influence, you might say, "Speaking in 2016, our senior state senator, Ben Adams, observed that if we had enacted the proposed law 3 years ago, 23 people killed by drunk drivers would be alive today."

comparisons Forms of evidence that use associations between two things that are similar in some important way.

similes Direct comparisons that typically use the words *like* or *as* to link two things.

metaphors Implicit comparisons of two different things that have something in common.

quotations Forms of evidence that use exact citations of statements made by others. Also called *testimony*.

Communication Highlight

I Have a Dream

In 1963, Reverend Martin Luther King Jr. delivered his moving speech, "I Have a Dream" to more than 200,000 people gathered on the National Mall in front of the Lincoln Memorial. In it, he compared the unfulfilled promises of the United States to African American citizens to an unpaid check. He said that the nation's founders had guaranteed rights to citizens and that those rights were a check for which payment was due. Comparing promises due to all citizens to a check was a compelling metaphor.

Go to the book's online resources for this chapter to search for more information about Martin Luther King Jr.'s "I Have a Dream" speech.

AP Images/Anonymous

Whenever you quote another person, you are ethically obligated to give credit to that person, just as you credit the sources of all forms of evidence. This can be done by changing your tone of voice after stating an authority's name, or by telling listeners, "John Smith stated that. . . ." It is also acceptable to say "quote" at the beginning of a quotation and "end quote" at the end of it, although this method of citing sources becomes boring if it is used repeatedly in a speech.

Effective and ethical quotations meet three criteria. First, as we've already noted, sources should be people whom listeners know and respect or whom they will respect once you identify the source's credentials (Cooper & Lull, 2013; Olson & Cal, 1984). Michael Phelps is an awesome athlete. However, his swimming skill has no relevance to Subway sandwiches, which he endorses in ads. Subway is counting on the **halo effect**, the tendency to assume that an expert in one area is also an expert in other areas. Although some people may fall prey to the halo effect, discerning listeners will not. Ethical speakers rely on authorities who are qualified, and they identify authorities' qualifications.

Ethical quotations must also meet the criterion of accuracy. For instance, you should respect the context in which comments are made. It is unethical to take a statement out of context to make it better support your ideas. Also, it's unethical to alter a direct quotation by adding or deleting words. Sometimes, writers omit words and indicate the omission with ellipses: "Noted authority William West stated that 'there is no greater priority . . . than our children.'" In oral presentations, however, it is difficult to indicate omitted words smoothly. When using quotations, speakers have an ethical responsibility to be accurate and fair in representing others and their ideas.

Finally, quotations should come from unbiased sources. It's hardly convincing when scientists paid by the tobacco industry tell us cigarettes don't cause cancer. Likewise, thoughtful listeners may not believe the CEO of a coal mining company who states that mining causes no environmental damage. Whether or not the statement is true, listeners are likely to think the CEO has a vested interest that makes him or her less than trustworthy.

halo effect The tendency to assume that an expert in one area is also an expert in other unrelated areas.

Communication Highlight

Avoiding Plagiarism   MindTap

The word *plagiarism* comes from the Latin word *plagiare*, which means "to kidnap." Plagiarism is the unattributed use of the language or ideas of another person. If you use the actual words or ideas of someone else, you must give credit to that person. Also, if you only slightly modify another's words or ideas, you must attribute the words or ideas to that person.

There is a distinction between paraphrasing and plagiarism. Paraphrasing is putting another person's ideas in your own words. Paraphrasing does not mean changing a word or two in someone else's sentence, changing the sentence structure while maintaining the original words, or changing a few words to synonyms. If you are tempted to rearrange a sentence in any of these ways, you are writing too close to the original. That's plagiarizing, not paraphrasing.

In the academic world, plagiarism by students is a very serious academic offense that can result in punishments such as a failing grade on the particular assignment, a failing grade for the course, suspension, or even expulsion from school. Go to the book's online resources for this chapter to learn more about what plagiarism is and how to avoid it.

Visual Aids

Visual aids are unlike the other types of evidence we have discussed. They do not prove claims with data. They do, however, clarify claims and make them accessible and memorable, which supports an overall presentation. **Visual aids** are charts, graphs, photographs, transparencies, computer graphics, and physical objects. Visual aids can increase listeners' understanding and retention of ideas presented in a speech (Hamilton, 2015; Hamilton & Parker, 2001). Visual aids also tend to increase listeners' interest in a presentation because they add variety to the message (Hamilton, 2015; Hamilton & Parker, 2001).

Visual aids can be used either to reinforce ideas presented verbally or to provide information. For example, Figure 13.3 is a bar graph that could effectively strengthen statistics on juvenile reform. Pie charts can forcefully emphasize contrasts and proportions (Figure 13.4). You can also use technologies to create visual

visual aids Presentation of evidence by such visual means as charts, graphs, photographs, and physical objects to reinforce ideas presented verbally or to provide information.

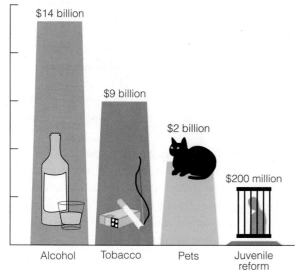

FIGURE 13.3
Bar Graphs Dramatize Statistics

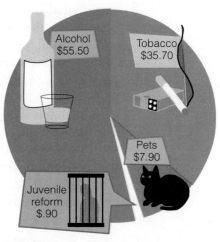

FIGURE 13.4
Pie Charts Clarify Proportions

Syracuse Newspapers/Dick Blume/The Image Works

MindTap

Is this speaker
using his visual aid
effectively?

aids. You may want to use part of a film or create a videotape to dramatize a point in your speech. A student speaker showed parts of the Disney film *Pocahontas* to support her claim that the main character was different from the historical figure.

Diagrams or models help speakers explain complex concepts and unfamiliar topics. Especially in speeches of demonstration, a model or physical diagram can be useful. Photographs can reinforce verbal messages, or they can be messages in their own right. To fortify her argument that development is eroding coastal land, a student showed enlarged pictures of an island community before development, when healthy sand dunes existed, and after development, when the dunes had eroded.

Handouts are also useful visual aids. Because listeners can take handouts with them, they are particularly valuable when a speaker wants information to remain with listeners. After a speech encouraging students to vote for a bill currently under consideration by the state legislature, a student gave every listener a handout with the names, addresses, and phone numbers of their representatives. This was effective because it avoided breaking up a speech to pass out paper and listeners reading the handout while the speaker was talking.

Visual aids don't need to be complex to have impact. Even simple ones can be effective. For example, President Reagan often held up letters from which he reads to audiences. He could have simply summarized what the letter said, but he added force by holding the actual sheet of paper (Spaeth, 1996).

Guidelines for Using Visual Aids   For visual aids to be effective, speakers should observe several guidelines (Williams, 1994). First, a visual aid should be large enough and clear enough to be seen clearly by all listeners. As obvious as this advice is, speakers routinely violate it by showing photographs, graphs, or slides that can be seen only by listeners close to the speaker. Make sure that letters in main headings are at least 3 inches high and that letters in subpoints are at least 2 inches high.

Second, visuals should be simple and uncluttered. Visuals with a great deal of information are more likely to confuse than clarify. Especially if you are presenting a series of slides (computerized or not), simplicity is important. You can create effective slides by following the guidelines in Table 13.3.

Many visual aids are verbal texts—main ideas of a speech, major points in a policy, or steps to action. When visual texts are used, certain guidelines apply. As a general rule, a visual text should have no more than six lines of words, should use phrases more than sentences, and should use a simple typeface. A good basic rule is to use visual aids to highlight key information and ideas, not to summarize all content.

Third, visual aids should be safe and nondistracting. Some visual aids are not appropriate for use in any circumstances. For example, a real, functional firearm is dangerous. In addition to the fact that "there's no such thing as an unloaded gun," firearms may frighten listeners, distracting them from listening to the speech. Other visual aids that are risky and should be avoided include live animals, illegal substances, and chemicals that could react with one another. It's also unwise to use

Table 13.3	Guidelines for Using Slides in a Speech

To create effective slides, including PowerPoint presentations for speeches, follow these guidelines:

1. Each slide should focus on a single concept or point and key information to support that concept or point (phrases or keywords generally are preferable to whole sentences or lengthy text).

2. Fonts should be large enough to be read by listeners at the back of the speaking room. Generally, main points should appear in 36-point type, supporting ideas should appear in 24- or 28-point type, and text should appear in type no smaller than 18 points.

3. Typefaces should be clean and clear. Avoid script styles, *overuse of italics*, or TRENDY TYPEFACES. They are distracting and can detract from clarity.

4. Mix uppercase and lowercase lettering. ALL CAPITAL LETTERS CAN BE HARD TO READ.

5. Use art to provide visual relief from text and enhance interest. If using a computerized presentation program, consider using clip art or pictures imported from the Web.

6. Use one design consistently. Computerized programs such as PowerPoint have design templates. Stick with one design to provide visual continuity and transitions.

7. Select a color scheme that is visually strong but not overpowering. Especially if you are showing a series of slides, avoid glaring colors that can tire listeners. Occasionally, you may violate this guideline to adapt to your particular listeners. For instance, if you are speaking at the banquet of a company whose logo is teal and white, you might want a teal and white color scheme.

8. Use special effects sparingly. It may be effective to have text zoom in from the right with a blaring sound on one slide, but it would be tiring and ineffective for text to zoom in on slide after slide.

9. Use visual highlighting sparingly. It can be effective to **boldface** or highlight one particularly important idea. However, the impact of visual highlighting is lost when it is overdone.

10. Give credit to those who created material you use. Acknowledge authors of quotations or other material. You should also get permission to use any materials that are not in the public domain.

11. Don't sacrifice content for flashy visuals. Visual aids, including computerized ones, should enhance your content, not substitute for it.

12. Make slides bright enough that you do not have to darken the room fully.

visual aids that might seriously upset or disgust listeners. The purpose of visuals is to enhance your speech, not to be so sensational that they take attention away from your ideas.

Although visual aids can be effective, it's possible to have too much of a good thing. As a guideline for deciding how many visuals to use in a speech, Cheryl Hamilton (2015) suggests this formula:

$$\frac{\text{Length of speech}}{2} + 1 = \text{Maximum number of visuals}$$

If you are preparing a 10-minute speech, you should include no more than six visual aids (10/2 + 1 = 6). Note that each slide in a series of slides counts as one visual aid.

There are also some mechanical guidelines for using visual aids effectively. First, remove or cover visual aids before and after you use them. A visual aid that's strong enough to be effective will distract listeners' attention from what you are saying if it is left in view when not in use. Also, maintain visual contact with listeners when using visual aids. Novice speakers often make the mistake of facing their charts or pictures when discussing them. This breaks the connection between speaker and listeners.

It's a good idea to keep an ongoing record of evidence you discover during the research process. There are two ways to do this. The traditional method is to write out each piece of evidence and save the file. In Chapter 12, we discussed mind maps as a way to narrow the focus of a broad topic. The same method can also help you record information. To construct a mind map for your speech, begin by writing the subject of your presentation in the center of a blank page. Then, draw a line from the center to each piece of evidence that you discover as you conduct your research. Once you have a complete record of information you've gathered, you can decide which evidence to include in your presentation. Figure 13.5 shows a mind map record of information for a speech on Hawaiian sovereignty.

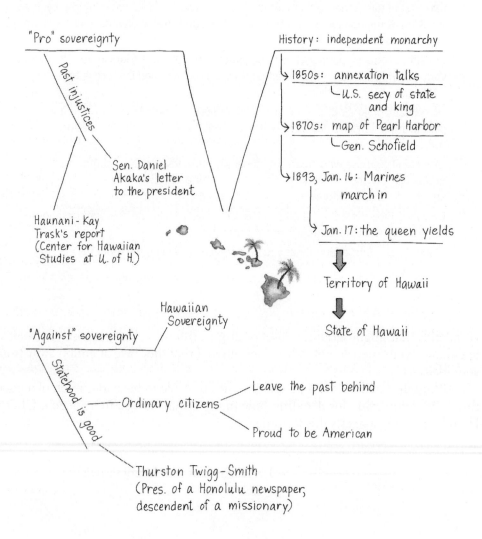

FIGURE 13.5

Mind Map of Evidence

Source: Jaffe, C. (2007). Public Speaking: Concepts and Skills for a Diverse Society, Fifth Edition, Belmont, CA: Wadsworth.

Table 13.4	Testing Evidence

Five questions help speakers test whether evidence is ethical and effective. Each question addresses a specific criterion for assessing the worth of evidence:

1. Is there enough evidence to support a claim? (sufficiency)
2. Is the evidence accurately presented—quotations are verbatim, nothing is taken out of context? (accuracy)
3. Does the evidence relate directly to the claim it is intended to support? (relevance)
4. Is the evidence appropriately timely—are statistics, quotations, examples, and comparisons current or appropriate for the time discussed? (timeliness)
5. Is the evidence free of biases such as vested interest? (impartiality)

Whereas evidence such as statistics, examples, and quotations can provide strong logical support, visual aids and analogies often are more powerful in adding clarity, interest, and emotional appeal to a speech. All forms of evidence, when carefully chosen and ethically used, tend to increase the credibility listeners confer on a speaker and the extent to which they retain the speaker's ideas (Table 13.4).

Digital Media and Researching and Developing Speeches

We have already mentioned ways that digital media will assist you in researching your speech. Online search engines and databases provide a treasure trove of material on topics. They also allow you to learn about the credentials of sources you will cite so that you can inform your listeners of qualifications that give weight to your sources' ideas. Just remember to critically evaluate any material that you find online. Although much online material is sound, some is not. It is your responsibility to make sure that what you present to listeners is valid and reliable.

We can also note that interviews and surveys may be conducted using digital media. Video systems such as Skype and Facetime allow you to conduct interviews without having to travel and find a place to meet face-to-face with sources. Surveys can be accessed online (Survey Money, for example) or can be emailed to respondents.

Digital media may also be used to create and present visual aids. PowerPoint slides, for example, provide visual information as do digitally produced graphs, photos, and so forth. The MindTap resources that accompany this text allow you to see effective and ineffective slides, and Outline Builder allows you to select the amount and type of evidence you need for your speech.

Evaluating Online Sources for Speeches

Material found online is not necessarily trustworthy. Anyone can set up a website, and anyone can make claims on the Internet. Because Internet content is unregulated, you should be especially critical while evaluating it. To assess information found on the Internet, begin by applying the five standard tests for evidence summarized in Table 13.4 on page 261. In addition, ask the following questions:

1. Can you verify the material independently (by checking another source or consulting an expert)?

2. Does the source have the experience, position, or other credentials to be an authority?

3. Does the source have any vested interest in making the claim or presenting the alleged information?

4. Does the source acknowledge other sources, including ones that advance different points of view?

If you decide the online material is sound, you should cite it in your bibliography as well as your text, using the following format:

Hulme, M. & Peters, S. (2001). *Me, my phone, and I: The role of the mobile phone.* Workshop: Mobile communications: Understanding users, adoption, and design, Seattle WA. Retrieved January 3, 2002, from http://www.cs.colorado.edu/~palen/chi_workshop.

Go to the book's online resources for this chapter to find basic principles for evaluating material found on the Web, as well as links to multiple websites that discuss the credibility of the Web information.

Chapter Summary

The process of researching a speech includes interviewing experts who can expand your insight into the subject, searching online for relevant material, scouting libraries for evidence, and conducting surveys to find out about others' beliefs, practices, and knowledge relevant to your topic. It isn't unusual for speakers to revise the focus of a speech in the course of conducting research. This is appropriate when information you discover modifies or alters your knowledge or even your position.

Research for a speech provides speakers with different kinds of evidence that they can use to clarify, dramatize, and energize a speech. The five types of support we discussed are statistics, examples, comparisons, quotations, and visual aids. Each of these is effective when used thoughtfully and ethically and when adapted to the interests, knowledge, attitudes, and experiences of listeners.

Now that you've gone through the phases of planning, researching, and finding support for speeches, we're ready to consider the final steps in designing effective presentations. Chapter 14 explains how to organize and present public speeches. Before you move on to Chapter 14, take a moment to fill in this chapter's checklist for researching and supporting your speech.

Checklist for Researching and Supporting a Public Speech   MindTap

1. I conducted the following research:

    A. Review of my personal experience showed that _____

    _____

    B. I interviewed (name/title): _____

    _____

    (name/title): _____
    (name/title): _____

    C. I checked these three indexes: _____

    _____

    D. I checked these three online sources: _____

    _____

    E. I surveyed on the following issues: _____

    _____

2. I found the following key evidence for my speech:
    A. Statistics: _____
    B. Authorities I will quote: _____
    C. Examples: _____
    D. Comparisons: _____
    E. Visual aids: _____

3. I have all the information to identify my sources appropriately and to explain why they are qualified and relevant to the ideas I will present.

MindTap

Experiencing Communication in Our Lives

CASE STUDY: Understanding Hurricanes

Apply what you've learned in this chapter by analyzing the following case study, using the accompanying questions as a guide. These questions and a video of the case study are also available online with your MindTap Speech for *Communication in Our Lives.*

Think about a time you've been absolutely terrified—whether it was by a person, event, or situation, and all you wanted to do was go home and be with your family and friends.

Now imagine the feeling you might have if you were that afraid, but you had no idea if your home would even be there when you arrived. This is the reality for many people living on the coastlines of the United States. Hurricanes affect the lives of those living in their direct paths, but they can also affect the entire country.

I have lived about 45 minutes from the Gulf Coast of Texas my entire life and have seen and experienced the destruction caused by hurricanes first hand, especially in the past 3 years. (*Slide 1: Picture of hurricane that hit my hometown last year.*) This is a picture of my hometown when a hurricane hit it last year.

Today, I'd like to speak with you about the way hurricanes work, the ways they affect our whole country and, most importantly, the toll they have on the people who live in their direct paths.

To begin, let's discuss how hurricanes form and the varying degrees of intensity of them so we can be better informed when we watch news broadcasts and read newspaper reports about them.

Several basic conditions must be present for a hurricane to form. According to award-winning Discovery Communications website, HowStuffWorks.com, hurricanes form "when an area of warm low-pressure air rises and cool, high pressure seizes the opportunity to move in underneath it." This causes a center to develop. This center may eventually turn into what is considered a hurricane. The warm and moist air from the ocean rises up into these pressure zones and begins to form storms. As this happens, the storm continues to draw up more warm moist air and a heat transfer occurs because of the cool air being heated causing the air to rise again. "The exchange of heat creates a pattern of wind that circulates around a center," (the eye of the storm), "like water going down a drain." The "rising air reinforces the air that is already" being pulled up from the surface of the ocean, "so the circulation and speeds of the wind increase."

Classifications of these types of storms help determine their intensity so we can prepare properly for them. Winds that are less than 38 miles per hour are considered tropical depressions. Tropical storms have winds that range from 39 to 73 miles per hour. And lastly, hurricanes are storms with wind speeds of 74 miles per hour and higher.

When storms become classified as a *hurricane*, they become part of another classification system that is displayed by the Saffir–Simpson Hurricane Scale. Hurricanes are labeled as categories 1–5 based on their wind intensity level or speed. (*Slide 2: Hurricane scale chart*) Hurricane Ike was labeled differently at different places. (*Slide 3: Map showing the different places Ike was labeled in the different categories*)

Knowing how and where hurricanes occur help us determine how our daily lives, even here in Kentucky, may be affected when one hits.

A hurricane can affect more than just those living in its direct path and these effects can actually be seen across the country in terms of the environment and the economy.

Hurricanes affect wildlife in negative ways. According to the Beaumont Enterprise on October 7, 2008, Christine Rappleye reported that the storm surge, which is basically a wall of water, Hurricane Ike brought in across some parts of Southeast Texas—about 14 feet in some places—swept dolphins inland with the surge and then, when the waters flowed back out to sea, dolphins were left stranded in the marsh. Some were rescued, but not all. This dolphin was rescued from a ditch. (*Slide 4: Dolphin being rescued*)

Hurricanes also affect the economy. Prices climb close to all-time highs when hurricanes hit. According to economist Beth Ann Bovino, quoted in the September 29, 2005, issue of the *Washington Post*, gas prices skyrocket when a hurricane like Katrina, Rita, or Ike hits. Paul Davidson said, in a September 12, 2008, article in *USA Today*, that in the anticipation of Hurricane Ike, 12 refineries in Texas were shut down. "This is 17% of the U.S. refining capacity" he said. That's why even residents here in Lexington saw a dramatic spike in gas prices immediately following Ike's landfall.

Energy costs to heat and cool our homes also rise. When consumers have to pay more to heat and cool our homes, we also have less to spend eating out at restaurants. And we have less to spend on nonessentials at the mall. So, economically we all feel the ripple effect when hurricanes hit.

So, yes, we all feel the effects of hurricanes, but we should not overlook the dramatic ways in which people who live in the direct path of a hurricane are affected.

When a hurricane hits, many of these people become homeless, at least for a while, and suffer emotionally and financially as they evacuate to places all over the country, including Kentucky!

People who go through hurricanes suffer extreme emotional effects. Evacuation is stressful because people have to pack up what they can and have no way of knowing if their home will still be standing or inhabitable when they return (*Slides 5 and 6: Before and after pictures from Hurricane Ike*).

Even returning home is emotionally taxing because returning home means rebuilding homes, neighborhoods, and even memories. Though we try to get back to a "normal" life, it can never really be the same as it once was. Instead, it's what Silicon Valley venture capitalist and investor, Roger McNamee, calls the "new normal" in his book, *The New Normal: Great Opportunities in a Time of Great Risk*.

Because they have to rebuild their homes and lives, people also go through financial difficulties. People battle with insurance companies about whether a home has wind or water damage as they seek financial assistance. Insurance companies will often claim that it is the one (wind or water) the homeowner is uninsured for.

Price gouging is another financial challenge hurricane victims face. When families and businesses begin the process of rebuilding, people come from outside areas to help with labor and materials and will charge exorbitant fees. An example of this is when my father needed people to help remove two trees from our home in September 2005 after Hurricane Rita.

To close, I'd like to remind you that hurricanes affect victims who live in their direct path and the country as a whole. To understand some of these effects, we talked about how hurricanes work, how they affect our country and daily lives, and the impacts they have on the lives of people who live through them. Maybe knowing some of these facts will help each of us appreciate our homes and our families just a little bit more. *(Handout: Hurricane tracking charts)*

References

Associated Press. (2008, October 8). Windstorm costs insurers $550M. *Newark Advocate*, p. x.

Bovino, B. A. (2005, September 29). Hurricanes impact national economy. *Washington Post*, Retrieved online at: http://washingtonpost.com/wp-dym /content/discussion/2005/09/28 /D12005092801431.html

Davidson, P. (2008, September 12). Ike blows gasoline prices higher. *USA Today*, p. x.

Marshall, B., Freudenrich, C., & Lamb, R. How hurricanes work. Retrieved October 8, 2008, from http://www.howstuffworks.com /hurricanes.htm

McNamee, R. (2004). *The new normal: Great opportunities in a time of great risk.* New York: Penguin.

Rappleye, C. (2008, October 7). Hurricane strands marine mammals, damages facility for the stranded. *Beaumont Enterprise.*

QUESTIONS FOR ANALYSIS AND DISCUSSION

1. Identify the types of evidence that the speaker used to develop the point in this excerpt from a speech.

2. Was the evidence effective? Did it meet the five tests for evidence?

3. Was the evidence ethical?

MindTap

Use flashcards to learn key concepts and take a quiz to test your knowledge.

Key Concepts

comparisons
evidence
examples
halo effect

metaphors
quotations
similes
statistics

survey research
visual aids

Sharpen Your Skill

1. Background on Experts

Research the credentials of three authorities you plan to cite in your speech. Below, write important information that contributes to their credibility.

1. _____ holds the following titles: _____ and has the following experiences and qualifications: _____

2. _____ holds the following titles: _____ and has the following experiences and qualifications: _____

3. _____ holds the following titles: _____ and has the following experiences and qualifications: _____

2. Bringing Statistics Alive

Practice translating statistics into interesting and meaningful information. Here's an example.

Statistic: Americans annually spend $14 billion on alcohol, $9 billion on tobacco, $2 billion on pets, and $200 million on juvenile reform.

Translation: For every $1 spent on juvenile reform in the United States, $70 are spent on alcohol, $45 on tobacco, and $10 on pets.

Statistic: Children under 10 watch television an average of 50 hours each week.

Translation: _____

Statistic: The Stealth bomber program cost $40 billion and produced a total of 20 aircraft.

Translation: _____

Statistic: The number of working poor, people who make $13,000 or less a year, rose from 12% of the workforce in 2000 to 18% in 2013.

Translation: _____

Now, apply what you've learned to your own speech. Select three statistics you could use in your speech, and translate them into meaningful, interesting terms.

Statistic 1: _____

can be translated this way _____

Statistic 2: _____

can be translated this way _____

Statistic 3: _____

can be translated this way _____

For Further Reflection and Discussion

1. After you've interviewed two experts on your topic, reflect on what you learned. What did they explain, reveal, or show you that added to your knowledge of the topic?

2. How did the process of researching your speech affect your understandings, beliefs, and speaking goal? Explain what changed and why.

3. Use an online database to find current evidence to support your speech. If you plan to speak on a health-related topic, use publications such as *World Health, Health News,* or *Healthfacts.* If you plan to speak on a public policy issue, check out publications such as *Public Welfare, Weekly Compilation of Presidential Documents,* and *Public Interest.* Type in the keywords relevant to your topic.

4. Pay attention to evidence in a speech on campus. Evaluate the effectiveness of evidence. Are visuals clear and uncluttered? Does the speaker explain the qualifications of sources cited, and are those sources adequately unbiased? What examples and comparisons are presented, and how effective are they? Evaluate the ethical quality of the evidence used. Did the speaker provide enough information for you to assess the expertise of any sources cited? Did the speaker show that the sources were not biased?

5. Experiment with PowerPoint or other computerized software. Notice how different designs, colors, and special effects affect the clarity and impact of your slides.

14

As long as there are human rights to be defended; as long as there are great interests to be guarded; as long as the welfare of nations is a matter for discussion, so long will public speaking have its place.

William Jennings Bryan

Organizing and Presenting Public Speeches

LEARNING OBJECTIVES

After studying the topics in this chapter, you should be able to:

1. List and explain the three ways in which oral communication differs from written communication.

2. Distinguish between working outlines, formal outlines, and key word outlines used in public speaking.

3. Identify seven common organizational patterns used in speeches.

4. Name the four elements of a speech introduction and the two elements of a speech conclusion.

5. Recall tips for understanding and managing speech anxiety.

6. Use the recommendations in this chapter to effectively practice an upcoming speech.

What aspects of delivery are most important to you when you are listening to a speech?

MindTap®

Review the chapter's learning objectives and **start** with a quick warm-up activity.

- Millions of people have back problems in this country. It's hard to recover from back problems, particularly ruptures of discs. A lot of problems result from strains caused by lifting heavy objects. People could save themselves a lot of pain if they avoided doing things that hurt their backs. It's important to take care of your back because a disc rupture can immobilize you for up to 2 weeks. Another way discs rupture is from unhealthy everyday habits such as sitting too long in one position or not using chairs that provide good support.
- Millions of people in this country who suffer from back problems could save themselves a lot of pain by avoiding the two primary causes of back injury. One major cause is excessive strain, for example, from lifting heavy objects. A second cause is unhealthy everyday habits, such as sitting too long in one position. Avoiding strain and unhealthy habits can save weeks of recuperation.

Which of these paragraphs was easier for you to understand and follow? Which one made more sense to you? If you're like most people, the second paragraph seemed more logical and coherent. The content of the two paragraphs is the same. What differs is how they are organized. In the first paragraph, the speaker doesn't tell us that he or she is going to focus on two causes of back problems. Instead, the speaker wanders from discussing one cause (strain) of back problems, to noting the length of recuperation time, and then back to discussing a second cause (unhealthy habits) of back problems.

In contrast, in the second paragraph the speaker tells us that there are two primary causes of back problems, so we're prepared at the outset to learn about two categories. The speaker next explains both causes, and only then does the speaker discuss the recuperation time we're in for if we don't take care of our backs. The organization of the second paragraph makes it easier to follow and retain the information presented.

This chapter guides you through the process of organizing your speech and practicing your delivery. In the pages that follow, we'll consider alternative ways to organize ideas, styles of delivery, and ways to practice effectively. We will also discuss ways that digital media can assist you in organizing and presenting speeches.

Organizing Speeches

Organization increases speaking effectiveness for several reasons. First, people like structure, and they expect ideas to come to them in an orderly way. Second, listeners can understand and remember content that is well organized because they grasp connections between ideas. Third, listeners find an organized speech more persuasive than a disorganized one. Finally, good organization enhances a speaker's credibility because it reflects well on a speaker's preparation and respect for listeners.

Organizing an effective speech is not the same as organizing a good paper, although the two forms of communication benefit by some similar structural principles. Effective organization for oral communication differs from organization for written communication in three key ways:

1. **Oral communication requires more explicit organization.**
2. **Oral communication benefits from greater redundancy within the message.**
3. **Oral communication should rely on less complex sentence structures.**

Unlike readers, listeners can't refer back to a previous passage if they become confused or forget a previous point. To increase listeners' comprehension and retention, speakers should use simple sentences, provide signposts to highlight organization, and repeat key ideas (Woolfolk, 1987). Consistent with the need for redundancy in oral communication, good speeches follow the form of telling listeners what you're going to tell them, presenting your message, then reminding them of your main points. This translates into preparing an introduction, a body, and a conclusion for an oral presentation.

Effective organization begins with a good outline. We'll discuss different kinds of outlines and how each can help speakers organize their ideas. Next, we'll focus on organizing the body of a speech because that is the substance of a presentation. Finally, we'll discuss how to build an introduction and a conclusion and how to weave in transitions to move listeners from one point to another.

Outlining Speeches

An outline helps you organize your ideas and make sure that you have enough evidence to support your claims. An outline also provides you with a safety net in case you forget what you intend to say or are interrupted by a question or a disturbing noise. There are three kinds of outlines: working, formal, and key word.

The Working Outline   Speakers usually begin organizing their ideas by creating a **working outline** to give themselves a basic map of the speech. The working outline is just for the speaker; it is his or her sketch of the speech. In it, the speaker usually jots down main ideas to see how they fit together. Once the ideas are laid out in a basic structure, the speaker can tell where more evidence is needed, where ideas don't seem well connected, and so forth. Working outlines usually evolve through multiple drafts as speakers see ways to improve their speeches. Because working outlines aren't meant for others' eyes, they often include abbreviations and shorthand that make sense only to the speaker.

The Formal Outline   A **formal outline** includes all main points and subpoints, supporting materials, and transitions, along with a bibliography of sources. It should not be the whole speech unless you are giving a manuscript speech, which we will discuss later in this chapter.

An effective formal outline has main headings for the introduction, body, and conclusion. Under each main point are subpoints, references to support each subpoint, and abbreviated transitions. If your speech includes quotations, statistics, or other evidence that must be presented with absolute accuracy, you should write the evidence in full, either in your outline, on separate index cards, or on a digital tablet you will use when speaking. Your written evidence should include the source and date of the evidence so that you can provide oral footnotes to listeners. Full references should be listed as your bibliography, or **Works Cited**. Table 14.1 presents guidelines for constructing formal outlines. Figure 14.1 (pages 273–275) shows a sample formal outline prepared by a student.

Review It!

Oral Communication:
- Requires Explicit Organization
- Benefits from Redundancy
- Relies Less on Complex Sentences

working outline A sketch of main ideas and their relationships; used by and intended only for the speaker.

formal outline A complete outline of a speech, including the parts of a speech, main points, supporting material, transitions, and citations for sources.

works cited A list of sources used in preparing a speech.

Table 14.1	Principles for Preparing a Formal Outline

1. Use full sentences for each point.

2. Each point or subpoint in a speech should have only one idea.

3. Use standard symbols and indentation for outlines.

   I. Roman numerals are used for main points.

     A. Capital letters are used for subpoints that support main points.

        1. Arabic numbers are used for material that supports subpoints.

           a. Lowercase letters are used for material that amplifies supporting material.

4. A point, subpoint, or supporting material should never stand alone. If you have a point I, you must have a point II (and possibly III). If you have a subpoint A, there must be a subpoint B (and possibly C). Outlines show how ideas are developed and related. If there is only one subpoint, you don't need to outline it—it's the main point.

5. Strive for parallelism when wording main points and subpoints. This adds to the coherence of a speech and makes it easier for listeners to follow. Here's an example of parallel wording of main and subpoints in a speech:

   I. Poor advising diminishes students' academic experiences.

     A. Students lose out by taking courses that don't interest them.

     B. Students lose out by missing courses that would interest them.

   II. Poor advising delays students' graduation.

     A. Some students have to return for a fifth year to graduate.

     B. Some students have to take extension courses to graduate.

     C. Some students have to attend summer school to graduate.

6. Include all references in your outline. These should be written as full citations according to the guidelines of a standard style manual, such as those published by the Modern Language Association (MLA) or the American Psychological Association (APA), or *The Chicago Manual of Style*. Your instructor may specify the style guidelines that you should follow.

7. Cite sources using accepted style guidelines for research reports. Three widely used systems for citing sources in papers and speech outlines are APA, MLA, and Council of Biology Editors (CBE). You can learn how to cite your sources using each set of guidelines by visiting these websites:

APA: http://owl.english.purdue.edu/handouts/research/r_apa.html

MLA: http://library.osu.edu/sites/guides/mlagd.php

CBE: http://library.osu.edu/sites/guides/cbegd.html

Review It!

Three Kinds of Outlines:

- Working
- Formal
- Key Word

key word outline An abbreviated speaking outline that includes only key words for each point in a speech. The key words trigger the speaker's memory of the full point.

The Key Word Outline   Some speakers prefer a less detailed formal outline, called a **key word outline**. As the term implies, a key word outline includes only key words for each point. The speaker uses words that will jog her or his memory of each idea in the speech. Figure 14.2 (page 276) shows a key word outline for a student speech.

Organizing the Body of a Speech

The body of a speech develops and supports the central idea, or thesis statement, by organizing it into several points that are distinct yet related. In short speeches of 5–10 minutes, no more than three points can be developed well, and two are often adequate. In longer speeches of 11–20 minutes, more points can be developed.

I. Introduction
   A. **Attention:** Would you vote for a system in which half
      of us work only one job, the other half of us work two
      jobs, and everyone gets equal rewards? No? Well that's
      the system that most families in this country have today.
   B. **Thesis statement:** Women's double shift in the paid labor
      force and the home has negative effects on them
      personally and on marriages.
   C. **Preview:** In the next few minutes, I will show that the
      majority of married women work two jobs: one in the paid
      labor market and one when they get home. I will then
      trace the harmful effects of this inequitable division of
      labor.
II. Body
   A. The majority of married women today work two jobs: one
      in the paid labor market and a second one when they get
      home each day.
      1. Most families today have two wage earners.
         a. Only 17% of contemporary families have one
            earner.
         b. As married women have taken on full-time jobs
            outside of the home over the past three decades,
            husbands of working wives have increased the
            amount of housework and child care they do from
            20% to 30%.
      2. Working wives do more "homework" than working
         husbands.
         a. Research shows that husbands tend to do the less
            routine chores while wives do most of the daily
            chores.

(continued)

FIGURE 14.1
A Formal Outline

We'll discuss seven organizational patterns. As we discuss each pattern, you'll have the opportunity to think about how you might use it in your speech. In Chapter 16, we'll discuss one additional pattern that can be especially effective for persuasive speaking.

The Temporal Pattern   Temporal patterns (also called time and chronological patterns) organize ideas on the basis of temporal relationships. Listeners find it easy to follow a time pattern because we often think in terms of temporal order: what follows what, what comes first, and what comes next.

Time patterns are useful for describing processes that take place over time, explaining historical events, and tracing sequences of action. Time patterns are also effective for presentations that create suspense and build to a climax. One student speaker led his listeners through the detective work of pharmaceutical research to develop a new drug for treating mood disorders.

> *Thesis:* Our campus has changed over time.
> *Main Point 1:* Our school was founded in 1895 as a private academy for
>   young men.
> *Main Point 2:* In 1928, the school was reorganized as a public university.
> *Main Point 3:* In 1960, the school began admitting women as well as men.

b. Husbands' reasons for not doing more work in the home are that they are tired after work, they don't feel men should do many home chores, and their wives don't expect them to help out more.

3. Working wives tend to do more homemaking and child care chores, regardless of which spouse earns more in the job outside the home.

a. Consider Jeremy and Nancy. She earns 65% of the family's income, and she does 80% of the child care and home chores.

b. Sociologist Arlie Hochschild found that 2 out of 10 husbands in two-worker families do 50% of the work involved in homemaking and child care.

Transition: Now that we've seen what the double shift is, let's consider its effects.

B. The double shift harms women's health and creates marital stress.

1. The double shift harms women's physical and psychological health.

a. Research shows that women who work outside of the home and do most of the homemaking and child care suffer sleep deprivation, reduced immunity to infections, and increased susceptibility to illnesses.

b. A recent study by the American Medical Association found that working women who do the majority of "homework" are more stressed, depressed, and anxious.

2. The double shift also erodes marital satisfaction.

a. Women resent husbands who don't contribute a fair share to home life.

FIGURE 14.1
A Formal Outline
(*Continued*)

(continued)

The Spatial Pattern Spatial patterns organize ideas according to physical relationships. This structure is especially appropriate for speeches that describe or explain layouts, geographic relationships, or connections between objects or parts of a system.

Spatial patterns can be used to structure both informative and persuasive speeches. Student speakers have successfully used spatial patterns to inform listeners about the relationships between components of nuclear reactors and the four levels of forest vegetation. In persuasive speeches, students have relied on spatial patterns to argue that urban sprawl is increasing in the United States and that global climate change will have devastating effects on the Antarctic, Africa, and Asia.

Thesis: Our campus includes spaces for learning, socializing, and living.

Main Point 1: At the center of our campus are the classroom buildings.

Main Point 2: Surrounding the classroom buildings are places for students to eat and socialize.

Main Point 3: The south part of campus consists of dormitories and apartments for students with families.

b. Inequitable division of "homework" is linked to separations and divorces.

Transition: Let me now pull together what the double shift is and how it harms women and marriages.

III. Conclusion

A. **Summary:** I've shown you that the majority of wives today work a double shift while their husbands do not. This is not only unfair, it is also harmful to women's health and to marriages.

B. **Final appeal:** Each of us who chooses to marry can create an equitable marriage. As I've shown you, the reward for making that choice is healthier wives and happier, more enduring marriages. That's a pretty good return on the investment of creating an equitable marriage.

FIGURE 14.1
A Formal Outline
(*Continued*)

The Topical Pattern   Topical patterns order a presentation into several categories, classes, or areas of discussion. The classification pattern is appropriate when your topic breaks down into two or three areas that aren't related temporally, spatially, causally, or otherwise. Although topical patterns don't have the organic power of structures that highlight relationships, they can effectively order points in a speech.

Topical patterns are appropriate for informative speeches on the three branches of government, the social and academic activities funded by student fees, and the contributions of students, faculty, and staff to campus life.

Topical patterns can also be effective for persuasive speeches. In a speech urging students to vote for a candidate, one student focused on the candidate's personal integrity, experience in public service, and commitment to the community. Another student designed a persuasive speech that extolled the benefits of student fees.

Thesis: Student fees fund extracurricular, intellectual, and artistic activities on campus.

Main Point 1: Fully 40% of student fees is devoted to extracurricular organizations.

Main Point 2: Another 30% of student fees pays for lectures by distinguished speakers.

Main Point 3: The final 30% of fees supports concerts and art exhibits.

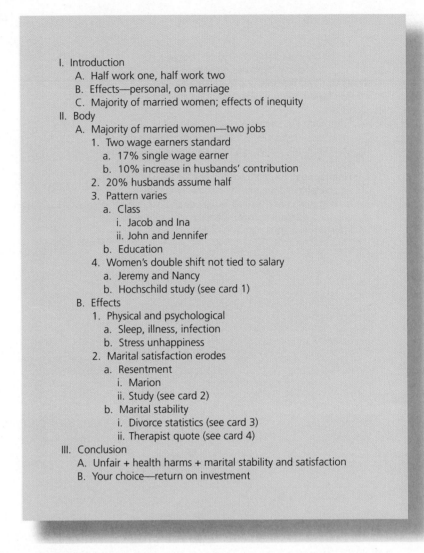

I. Introduction
    A. Half work one, half work two
    B. Effects—personal, on marriage
    C. Majority of married women; effects of inequity
II. Body
    A. Majority of married women—two jobs
        1. Two wage earners standard
            a. 17% single wage earner
            b. 10% increase in husbands' contribution
        2. 20% husbands assume half
        3. Pattern varies
            a. Class
                i. Jacob and Ina
                ii. John and Jennifer
            b. Education
        4. Women's double shift not tied to salary
            a. Jeremy and Nancy
            b. Hochschild study (see card 1)
    B. Effects
        1. Physical and psychological
            a. Sleep, illness, infection
            b. Stress unhappiness
        2. Marital satisfaction erodes
            a. Resentment
                i. Marion
                ii. Study (see card 2)
            b. Marital stability
                i. Divorce statistics (see card 3)
                ii. Therapist quote (see card 4)
III. Conclusion
    A. Unfair + health harms + marital stability and satisfaction
    B. Your choice—return on investment

FIGURE 14.2
A Key Word Outline

The Star Pattern   The star pattern is a variation on the topical structure (Jaffe, 2016). A standard topical organization has two or three points that a speaker covers in the same order and to the same extent each time the speech is given. With a star pattern, however, a speaker might start with different points and give more or less attention to specific points when speaking to different audiences.

One of the more common uses of the star pattern is in political speeches. Most candidates for office have a standard stump speech that includes their key positions and proposals. The order in which a candidate presents points and the extent to which each point is developed vary from audience to audience. For example, a candidate's platform might include strong support for the environment, enhancing the fiscal security of the United States, and ensuring adequate care for elderly citizens. When the candidate speaks to environmental activists, he or she would lead with the stand on the environment and elaborate it in detail. When the candidate speaks to older citizens, he or she would begin by emphasizing his or her commitment to their health and to strengthening Medicare and Medicaid. When the candidate speaks to young and middle-aged audiences, the first point would be ensuring the fiscal security of the United States so young people aren't strapped with debt. Using the star pattern, the candidate could adapt the order of points and the emphasis placed on each one. It would not be ethical to misrepresent positions to suit different audiences, but it is both ethical and effective to adapt the order and emphasis on points.

Similarly, a star pattern can be used to describe the ways in which different groups contribute to campus life, and the order of points could vary for audiences of students, staff, and faculty.

> *Thesis:* Our campus reflects contributions of administrators, faculty, students, and staff.
> *Main Point 1:* Administrators are in charge of planning and coordinating all aspects of campus life.
> *Main Point 2:* Faculty take the lead in charting the academic character of college life.
> *Main Point 3:* Students are the primary designers of extracurricular life on campus.
> *Main Point 4:* Staff make sure that the initiatives of administrators, faculty, and students are implemented consistently.

EMMA *I'm an orientation counselor, and I think I've been using the star pattern to talk to new students, but I didn't know you called it that. With each new group, I have to tell them about the campus and town and school policies and so forth. With first-year students, I start off by talking about school policies because not knowing them can get the kids in trouble. With junior transfers, I get to that last and just spend a little time on it. With out-of-state students, I spend more time talking about the town and even the region—how the South is, which some of them don't understand. I pretty much cover everything with each group, but how I do it varies a lot, depending on who is in the group.*

The Comparative Pattern As the term suggests, comparative patterns compare two or more objects, people, situations, events, or other phenomena. This structure is also called *comparison/contrast* and *analogical organization*. It encourages listeners to be aware of similarities or differences between two or more things or to understand a new idea, process, or event in terms of one with which they're already familiar.

MAYUMI *I selected comparative organization for my informative speech about American and Japanese marriages because I wanted the class to understand how people from my country think differently about marriage than Americans do. I divided my speech into courtship, division of household work, and meaning of divorce to show the difference between Americans and Japanese in each area.*

Students giving persuasive speeches have used the comparative pattern to argue that computer literacy is as important as oral and written literacy and that undergraduate education is different from career preparation. In each case, the comparative structure invites listeners to perceive how two or more phenomena are alike or different.

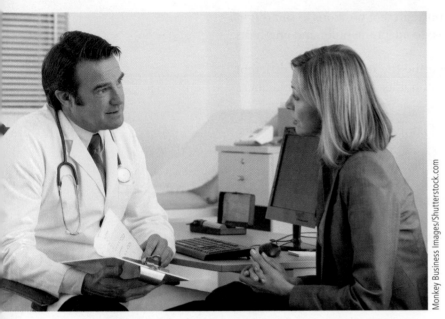

Medical professionals frequently present information to patients.

Thesis: Health maintenance organizations are inferior to private medical practices.

Main Point 1: Health maintenance organizations provide less individualized patient care than private practices do.

Main Point 2: Health maintenance organizations are less likely than private practices to authorize important diagnostic tests.

Main Point 3: Health maintenance organizations place less emphasis on preventive care than private medical practices do.

The Problem–Solution Pattern   This pattern divides a topic into two major areas: a problem and a solution. Usually, a speaker begins by describing a problem and its severity and then proposes a solution. Occasionally, this sequence is inverted when a speaker begins by discussing a solution and then explains the problem it solves.

The problem–solution pattern is effective for persuasive speeches because it lends itself naturally to advocating policies, answers, and actions. Students have used this pattern effectively to persuade others that many people who are severely ill or dying (problem) could be helped if more people were organ donors (solution), and that the overcrowding of jails and the backlog of court cases (problems) could be decreased if all victimless crimes were made misdemeanors (solution).

The power of this pattern derives from the sequential involvement it invites from listeners. If they accept a speaker's description of a problem and believe the problem is important or urgent, they hunger for a solution. The speaker, who presents a solution that addresses the problem they've already acknowledged, has a good chance of convincing listeners to endorse the recommended proposal.

Thesis: Victimless crimes should be reclassified as misdemeanors.

Main Point 1: Currently, courts across the nation are overwhelmed by cases in which there is no victim.

Main Point 2: Reclassifying victimless crimes as misdemeanors would dramatically ease the burden on our courts.

Although most often used for persuasive speeches, the problem–solution structure can be used for informative presentations with thesis statements, such as "The new vendors you've seen in the cafeteria (solution) are in response to student complaints about lack of variety in food options (problem)."

The Cause–Effect and Effect–Cause Patterns   This pattern is used to argue a direct relationship between two things: a cause and an effect. In some instances, speakers want to inform people that a situation, policy, or practice (effect) results from certain previous choices or events (causes). In other cases, speakers argue that a specific action (cause) will lead to an effect. Cause–effect and effect–cause patterns are appropriate for both informative and persuasive speeches.

You should be aware that it is extremely difficult to prove unequivocal causation. Research may show that two things (for example, smoking and lung cancer) are related, but it cannot conclusively prove that smoking directly and unvaryingly causes lung cancer. Thus, speakers using this pattern generally demonstrate relationships, or correlations, between two things, and this is often persuasive to listeners.

> *Thesis:* Raising the minimum wage would be bad for our economy.
> *Main Point 1:* Raising the minimum wage would reduce worker productivity.
> *Main Point 2:* Raising the minimum wage would lead to greater unemployment.
> *Main Point 3:* Raising the minimum wage would increase the costs of what we buy.

The seven patterns we've discussed represent different ways to organize public presentations. To structure your speech effectively, you should consider how each of the eight patterns might shape the content and impact of your presentation.

Designing the Introduction

The introduction to a speech is the first thing listeners hear. A good introduction accomplishes four goals: (a) It captures listeners' attention; (b) it presents a clear thesis statement; (c) it enhances the speaker's credibility; and (d) it previews how the speech will be developed. That's a lot to accomplish in a short time, so careful thought is required to design a strong introduction.

Capture Listeners' Attention   The first objective of an introduction is to gain listeners' attention (Verderber, Sellnow, & Verderber, 2015). There are many ways to gain listeners' attention and interest. You might begin with a dramatic piece of evidence, such as a stirring quotation, a striking visual aid, or a startling statistic or example. Each of these forms of evidence can capture listeners' interest and make them want to hear more.

Review It!

Organizational
Patterns:
- Temporal
- Spatial
- Topical
- Star
- Comparative
- Problem–Solution
- Cause–Effect

Image Source RF/Cadalpe/Getty Images

MindTap®   Does this speaker seem engaging?

You may also open with a question that invites listeners to become involved with the topic. "Do you know the biggest cause of death among college students?" "Would you like to know how to double your chances of getting a job offer?" Questions engage listeners personally at the outset of a speech.

There are other ways to capture listeners' attention. For example, speakers sometimes refer to current events or experiences of listeners that are related to the topic of a speech. A student who spoke on homelessness immediately after fall break opened this way: "If you're like me, you went home over the break and enjoyed good food, a clean bed, and a warm, comfortable house—all the comforts that a home provides. But not everyone has those comforts."

Another effective way to capture listeners' attention is to provide them with direct experience, which is a highly effective foundation for persuasion (Baron & Berne, 1994). For example, in a speech advocating a low-fat diet, a speaker began the presentation by passing out low-fat cookies he had baked. All the listeners then had an immediate experience with delicious and healthful food.

When appropriate to the speaking situation, humor can also be an effective way to open a speech—but only if it succeeds in amusing listeners. Thus, it's a good idea to try jokes out on people who are similar to your listeners.

Present a Clear Thesis Statement   The second function of an introduction is to state the main message of your speech, which is the thesis statement we discussed in Chapter 12. Your thesis should be a short, clear sentence that directly states the overall theme of your presentation.

- "I will describe problems with advising on our campus and ask your help in solving them."

- "I will inform you of your legal rights when interviewing for a job."

- "I will show you that the death penalty is ineffective and discriminatory."

Build Credibility   The third function of an introduction is to establish a speaker's credibility. Listeners regard a speaker as credible if he or she seems qualified to speak on a topic, shows goodwill toward them, and demonstrates dynamism.

To show that they are qualified to speak on a topic, speakers may mention their personal experience: "I am a hemophiliac." Speakers may also explain how they gained expertise on their topics. "For the past 2 years, I have volunteered at the homeless shelter here in town." If you do not have personal experience with a topic, let listeners know that you have gained knowledge in other ways. "I interviewed 10 people who work with abused children."

In addition to letting your listeners know that you are qualified to speak on your topic, you want to demonstrate that you have goodwill and are trustworthy. You might do this by explaining why you think your speech will help them. "What I'm going to tell you might save a life, perhaps your own." "My speech will give you information vital to making an informed choice when you vote next week."

Speakers confront a particular problem in establishing goodwill if they are advocating an unpopular position. They need to demonstrate that they respect listeners' possible objections. One way to do this is to show that you once held their attitudes. "Some of you may think homeless people are just lazy. I thought so, too, before I volunteered at the local shelter and got to know some of them."

Preview the Body   The final purpose of an introduction is to preview your major points so that listeners understand how you will develop ideas and can follow you.

The preview announces the main points of your speech. Typically, a preview enumerates or lists the main points. Here are examples from student speeches:

- "I will show you that there has been a marked decrease in advisers' accessibility and helpfulness to students. Then I will ask you to sign a petition that asks our provost to hire more advisers and provide ongoing training to them."

- "To convince you that the death penalty should be abolished, I will first provide evidence that it is not effective as a deterrent to crime. Second, I will demonstrate that the death penalty discriminates against minorities and people who are poor."

SHARPEN YOUR SKILL

At the end of this chapter, refer to the Sharpen Your Skill feature, Designing Your Introduction, to apply concepts from Chapter 14.

Craft the Conclusion

The next step in organizing a speech is to craft a conclusion. An effective conclusion summarizes content and provides a memorable final thought (Griffin, 2015). As you may realize, these two functions are similar to the attention and preview in introductions. In repeating key ideas and leaving the audience with a compelling final thought, a speaker provides psychological closure on the speech. Like introductions, conclusions are short. Thus, you have to accomplish the two objectives of a conclusion very concisely.

To summarize the content of your speech, it's effective to restate your thesis and each major point. Here are examples from student speeches:

- "Today I've identified two key problems with advising: an insufficient number of advisers and inadequate training of advisers. Both of these problems can be solved if you will join me in urging our president to increase the number of advisers and the training they get."

- "My speech has informed you of your legal rights in interviews and what you can do if an interviewer violates them."

- "I've shown you that the death penalty doesn't prevent crime and that it discriminates against minorities and the poor."

After reviewing main points, a conclusion should offer listeners a final idea, ideally something particularly memorable or strong or an ending that returns to the opening idea to provide satisfying closure. In a speech on environmental activism, the speaker began with "'One earth, one chance' is the Sierra Club motto" and ended with "We have one chance to keep our one earth. Let's not throw it away." This was effective because the ending returned to the opening words but gave them a slightly different twist. A student who argued that the death penalty should be abolished ended the speech with this statement: "We need to kill the death penalty before it kills anyone else." A third example, again from a student speaker, is this memorable closing: "I've given you logical reasons to be a blood donor, but let me close with something more personal: I am alive today because there was blood available for a massive transfusion when I had my automobile accident. Any one of us could need blood tomorrow." Effective conclusions are short and focused. They highlight central ideas one last time and offer listeners a powerful or compelling concluding thought.

Outline Builder accessed through MindTap, includes extensive prompts and a clear framework for organizing and outlining different types of speeches.

Build in Transitions

The final organizational issue is **transitions**—words and sentences that connect ideas and main points in a speech so that listeners can follow a speaker. Transitions signal listeners that you are through talking about one idea and are ready move to the next one. Effective transitions are like signposts for listeners. They tell listeners where you have been and where you are heading (Coopman & Lull, 2015).

Transitions may be words, phrases, or entire sentences. Within the development of a single point, it's effective to use transitional words or phrases such as *therefore, and so, for this reason, as this evidence suggests,* and *consequently.* To make transitions from one point to another in a speech, phrases can be used to signal listeners that you are starting to discuss a new idea:

- "My second point is…"

- "Now that we have seen how many people immigrate to the United States, let's consider what they bring to us."

- "In addition to the point I just discussed, we need to think about…"

To move from one to another of the three major parts of a speech (i.e., introduction, body, and conclusion), you can signal your audience with statements that summarize what you've said in one part and point the way to the next. For example, here is an internal summary and a transition between the body of a speech and the conclusion:

"I've now explained in some detail why we need stronger educational and health programs for new immigrants. Let me close by reminding you of what's at stake."

Transitions also may be nonverbal. For example, you might hold up one, two, and three fingers to reinforce your movement from the first to the second to the third main point in the body of your speech. Changes in vocal intensity, eye contact,

transitions Words and sentences that connect ideas and main points in a speech so that listeners can follow a speaker.

and inflection can effectively mark movement from one idea to the next. For instance, you could conclude the final point of the body of your speech with strong volume and then drop the volume to begin the conclusion. Silence is also effective in marking transitions. A pause after the introduction signals listeners that a speaker is going to a new place. Visual aids also help listeners move with a speaker.

Transitions are vital to effective speaking. If the introduction, body, and conclusion are the bones of a speech, the transitions are the sinews that hold the bones together.

Presenting Public Speeches

We turn now to the final aspect of public speaking: presenting, or delivering, your speech. We'll first discuss building your speaking confidence. We then describe oral style, pointing out how it differs from written style. Then, we'll consider alternative styles of delivery.

Building Speaking Confidence

Speaking confidence enhances effectiveness. Yet there are very few people who don't sometimes feel apprehensive about public speaking (Richmond & McCroskey, 1992). If you are among the 95% of Americans who have some speaking anxiety (Richmond & McCroskey, 1995a), you are in good company. As you prepare to present your speech, it's important for you to understand **communication apprehension**, which is anxiety associated with speaking.

> **communication apprehension** Anxiety associated with real or anticipated communication encounters. Communication apprehension is common and can be constructive.

Communication & Careers

I'd Rather Lose Than Have to Give a Speech

MindTap

Bob Daemmrich/PhotoEdit

Many professions call for occasional public speaking, and that's especially true for celebrities including sports starts such as pro golfer Annika Sorenstam As a high school student, she was so afraid of speaking that she often deliberately played to win second place so that she wouldn't have to give the winner's speech (Morreale, 2003). Her confident speaking style today reminds us that communication apprehension can be managed.

The first thing to understand is that a degree of anxiety is natural and helpful to speakers. It stimulates our bodies to produce adrenaline and extra blood sugar, which increase energy so that we are more dynamic.

Although a degree of anxiety about speaking is natural, too much can interfere with effectiveness. Anxiety strong enough to hinder our ability to interact with others is communication apprehension.

Causes of Communication Apprehension

There are two types of communication apprehension: situational and chronic. For many of us, certain situations spark anxiety. For instance, if you are scheduled to speak to a group that is known to be hostile to you or your ideas, anxiety is to be expected.

Five situational factors may generate apprehension. First, we tend to be more anxious when communicating with people who are unfamiliar to us or whom we perceive as different from us. Apprehension is also likely to be present in new or unfamiliar situations, such as your first job interview. A third situational cause of apprehension is being in the spotlight. When we are the center of attention, we tend to feel self-conscious and anxious that we might embarrass ourselves. Fourth, we may feel apprehensive when we're being evaluated.

A final situational reason for apprehension is a past failure or failures in a particular speaking situation. For example, my doctor called me one day to ask me to coach her for a speech she had to give to a medical society. Eleanor had last given a public speech 8 years earlier in medical school. Just before the speech, her first patient had died, and she was badly shaken. As a result, she was disorganized, flustered, and generally ineffective. That single incident, which followed a history of successful speaking, was so traumatic that Eleanor developed acute speaking anxiety.

Communication apprehension is more difficult to manage when it is chronic. Rather than feeling anxious in specific situations, which is often appropriate, some people are generally apprehensive about communicating. People who have chronic communication anxiety learn to fear communication, just as some of us learn to fear heights or water (Beatty, Plax, & Kearney, 1985; DeFleur & Ball-Rokeach, 1989).

Managing Communication Apprehension

There are ways to manage communication apprehension. First, remember that some anxiety is natural and often helpful in speaking. Second, use positive self-talk, which we discussed in Chapter 3. Tell yourself, "I can do this." "My anxiety is going to keep me on my toes." Also challenge negative, self-defeating thoughts. If you find yourself thinking "I'm going to forget what I want to say and everyone will think I'm incompetent," challenge that by saying, "I will have my notes so I can remind myself of anything I forget. Everyone in the audience has forgotten at times, so they're not going to think anything of it if I refer to my notes." It's a good idea to speak aloud when engaging in self-talk. Hearing yourself reinforces the message.

A third way to reduce communication apprehension is to engage in **positive visualization**, which aims to reduce anxiety by guiding apprehensive speakers through imagined positive speaking experiences (Hamilton, 2015). In professional life, managers are coached to visualize successful negotiations and meetings. In the world of sports, athletes are taught to imagine playing well, and those who engage in positive visualization improve as much as athletes who physically practice

positive visualization A technique of reducing speaking anxiety; a person visualizes herself or himself communicating effectively in progressively challenging speaking situations.

oral style The visual, vocal, and verbal aspects of the delivery of a public speech.

impromptu speaking Public speaking that involves little preparation. Speakers think on their feet as they talk about ideas and positions with which they are familiar.

their sport. Go to the book's online resources for this chapter to read about positive visualization and other ways of reducing speaking anxiety.

If your communication apprehension is not responsive to these suggestions and if it interferes with your ability to express your ideas, ask your instructor to direct you to professionals who can work with you.

Oral Style

Oral style refers to speakers' visual, vocal, and verbal communication with listeners. *Oral style includes everything from* gestures and movement during a presentation to her or his sentence structures, volume, inflection, and speaking rate.

A common mistake of speakers, both new and experienced, is to use written style rather than oral style. But a speech is not a spoken essay. There are three primary qualities of effective oral communication (Wilson & Arnold, 1974). First, it is usually more informal than written communication. Thus, speakers use contractions and sentence fragments that would be inappropriate in a formal written document. The informal character of oral style also means it's appropriate for speakers to use colloquial words in informal speaking contexts. However, speakers shouldn't use slang or jargon that might offend any listener or that might not be understood by some listeners.

Second, effective oral style tends to be more personal than written style. It's generally effective for speakers to include personal stories and personal pronouns, referring to themselves as "I" rather than "the speaker." In addition, speakers should sustain eye contact with listeners and show that they are approachable. Third, effective oral style tends to be more immediate and more active than written style. This is important because listeners must understand ideas immediately as they are spoken, whereas readers can take time to comprehend ideas. In oral presentations, simple sentences ("I have three points") and compound sentences ("I want to describe the current system of selling textbooks, and then I will propose a less costly alternative") are more appropriate than complex sentences ("There are many reasons to preserve the Arctic National Wildlife Refuge, some of which have to do with endangered species and others with the preservation of wilderness environment, yet our current Congress is not protecting this treasure").

Immediacy also involves moving quickly instead of gradually to develop ideas. Rhetorical questions, interjections, and redundancy also enhance the immediacy of a speech.

Styles of Delivery

The style of delivery that's effective at a political rally is different from the style appropriate for an attorney's closing speech in a trial; a toast at a wedding requires a style different from that required for testimony before Congress. There are four presentational styles.

Impromptu Style **Impromptu speaking** involves little preparation. Speakers speak off the cuff, organizing ideas as they talk and working with evidence that is already familiar to them. You use an impromptu style when you make a comment in a class, answer a question you hadn't anticipated in an interview, or respond to a request to share your ideas on a topic. There is no time to prepare or rehearse, so you have to think on your feet.

Impromptu speaking is appropriate when you know a topic well enough to organize and support your ideas without a lot of advance preparation. For instance,

Review It!
....
Managing
Speaking Anxiety:
• Remember It's
Natural and Helpful
• Use Positive Self-Talk
• Engage in Positive
Visualization

Review It!
....
Qualities of
Oral Style:
• Informal
• Personal
• Immediate

Christopher Halloran/Shutterstock.com

President Obama
used different styles of
delivery, depending on
the occasion.

the president of a company could speak off the cuff about the company's philosophy, goals, and recent activities. Impromptu speaking is not an effective style when speakers are not highly familiar with topics and at ease in speaking in public.

Extemporaneous Style   Probably the most common presentational style today, **extemporaneous speaking** relies on preparation and practice, but actual words aren't memorized. Extemporaneous speaking (also called *extemp*) requires speakers to do research, organize ideas, select supporting evidence, prepare visual aids, outline the speech, and practice delivery. Yet the speech itself is not written out in full. Instead, speakers speak from notes or an outline.

Effective extemporaneous speaking requires a fine balance between too little and too much practice. Not rehearsing enough may result in stumbling, forgetting key ideas, and not being at ease with the topic. On the other hand, too much practice tends to result in a speech that sounds canned. Extemporaneous speaking involves a conversational and interactive manner that is generally effective with listeners.

Manuscript Style   As the term suggests, **manuscript speaking** involves speaking from the complete manuscript of a speech. After planning, researching, organizing, and outlining a presentation, a speaker then writes the complete word-for-word text and practices the presentation using that text or text transferred to a teleprompter. One clear advantage of this style is that it provides security to speakers. Even if a speaker gets confused when standing before an audience, he or she can rely on the full text. A second advantage of manuscript speaking is that it ensures precise content, which is important in official ceremonies, diplomatic agreements, and formal press statements and legal proceedings.

There are also disadvantages to manuscript speaking. First, writing a speech in its entirety often results in written, rather than oral, style. A second hazard of manuscript speaking is the tendency to read the speech. It's difficult to be animated and visually engaged with listeners when reading a manuscript.

BRAD   *Most of my professors are pretty good. They talk with us in classes, and they seem to be really involved in interacting with students. But I've had several professors who read their notes — like, I mean, every day. They'd just come in, open a file, and start reading. I had one professor who almost never looked at us. It didn't feel like a person was communicating with us. I'd rather have read his notes on my own.*

extemporaneous speaking A presentational style that includes preparation and practice but not memorization of words and nonverbal behaviors.

manuscript speaking A presentational style that involves speaking from the complete manuscript of a speech.

memorized speaking A presentational style in which a speech is memorized word for word in advance.

Memorized Style   The final presentational style is **memorized speaking**, which carries the manuscript style one step further. After going through all the stages of manuscript speaking (i.e., preparing, researching, organizing, outlining, writing out the full text, and practicing), a speaker commits the entire speech to memory and speaks from a manuscript that is in his or her head. The advantages of this style are the same as those for manuscript speaking: An exact text exists, so everything is prepared in advance and the speaker has security.

There are serious disadvantages to memorizing. Because memorized speaking is based on a full written speech, the presentation may reflect written rather than oral style. In addition, memorized speaking is risky because a speaker has no safety net in case of memory lapses. Speakers who forget a word or phrase

Today, many people rely on tablets or smart phones instead of note cards when speaking.

may become rattled and unable to complete the presentation. Memorized style also can limit effective delivery. It is difficult for a speaker to sound spontaneous when she or he has memorized an entire speech. Because the speaker is preoccupied with remembering the speech, she or he can't interact fully with listeners. These drawbacks of memorized speaking explain why it isn't widely used or recommended.

Knowing the benefits and liabilities of each presentational style provides you with alternatives. For most speaking occasions, extemporaneous style is effective because it combines good preparation and practice with spontaneity. Go to the book's online resources for this chapter for additional tips for effective delivery.

Practice

For all styles except impromptu, practice is important. Practicing allows you to refine your ability to apply the guidelines in Table 14.2. Ideally, you should begin practicing your speech several days before you plan to deliver it. During practice, you should rely on the notes or outline you will use when you actually deliver the speech. This ensures that you will be familiar with your material. You should also practice with visual aids and any other materials you plan to use in your speech so that you are comfortable working with them.

There are many ways to practice a speech. Usually, speakers prefer to practice alone initially so that they gain some confidence and comfort. You may find it helpful to practice in front of a mirror to see how you look and to keep your eyes focused away from the outline. Practicing before a mirror is especially helpful in experimenting with different nonverbal behaviors that can enhance your presentational impact.

You may want to tape yourself during practice so that you can see and hear yourself and make decisions about how to refine your delivery. If the videotape shows you not keeping eye contact, you can work to increase your eye contact when speaking. Take breaks between practices so that you don't wind up memorizing the speech inadvertently.

Review It!

Styles of Delivery:
- Impromptu
- Extemporaneous
- Manuscript
- Memorized

Table 14.2	Guidelines for Effective Delivery

1. Adapt your appearance to your listeners and their expectations.

2. Adapt your appearance to the speaking situation. Formal dress is likely to be appropriate for a speech to executives that is given in an office or board room. However, if that same speech were given at a company retreat by the ocean, casual dress would be more appropriate.

3. Use gestures to enhance impact. Gestures can reinforce ideas and complement verbal messages.

4. Adopt a confident posture. Stand erect, with your shoulders back and your feet slightly apart for optimum balance.

5. Use confident, dynamic body movement to communicate your enthusiasm and confidence. Walk to the speaking podium (or wherever you will speak) with assurance: head up, arms comfortably at your side, at a pace that is neither hurried nor halting. As you speak, move away from the podium to highlight key ideas or to provide verbal transitions from one point to the next.

6. Maintain good eye contact with listeners. Try to vary your visual zone so that you look at some listeners at one moment and then move your gaze to a different segment of listeners.

7. Use volume that is strong but not overpowering. The appropriate volume will vary, depending on the size of your audience. You also need to adapt your volume to the environment. If a noisy air conditioner is running, you'll need to increase your volume to be heard. Be careful not to let your volume drop off at the end of sentences, a common problem for beginning speakers.

8. Use your voice to enhance your message. Pitch, rate, volume, and articulation are vocal qualities that allow you to add emphasis to important ideas. As you practice your speech, decide which words and phrases you want to emphasize.

9. Use pauses for effect. It is often effective to pause for a second or two after stating an important point or presenting a dramatic example or statistic.

10. Do not let accent interfere with clarity. For everyone but professional broadcasters, regional accents are acceptable. However, your speaking must be understandable to listeners.

11. Articulate clearly. Speakers lose credibility when they mispronounce words or when they add or delete syllables. Common instances of added syllables are *cohabitate* for *cohabit*, *orientated* for *oriented*, *preventative* for *preventive*, and *irregardless* for *regardless*.

SHARPEN YOUR SKILL

At the end of this chapter, refer to the Sharpen Your Skill feature, Rehearsing Your Speech, to apply concepts from Chapter 14.

When you've rehearsed enough to feel comfortable with the speech, it's time to practice in front of others. Ask friends to listen, and invite their feedback on ways you can refine your presentation. Practice until you know your material well but haven't memorized it. Then stop! Rehearsing too much is just as inadvisable as not practicing enough. You want to preserve the spontaneity that is important in oral style.

Digital Media and Speech Organization and Delivery

Digital media can assist you in organizing and delivering a speech. One of the most valuable resources is the MindTap platform that accompanies this book. You can use Outline Builder to create an outline for your speech. MindTap also offers

Practice and Present, a tool that allows you to upload a video of you practicing your speech for you to review.

In addition to MindTap, you might use a digital tablet to make a video of a practice presentation that you can then review and critique. Many speakers—students and nonstudents—make multiple videos as they practice their speeches. This allows you to refine your delivery style.

Increasingly, speakers rely on tablets or smart phones rather than paper notes or outlines. Using a digital device for your notes ensures that there will be no rustling of paper as you turn pages or cards; you simply scroll through the material. A digital device also fits in your hand so it is inconspicuous.

Chapter Summary

In this chapter, we focused on ways to organize and present public speeches. We first discussed the importance of speaking confidence and ways to build it. Next, we identified different types of outlines that assist speakers in organizing material. Third, we considered seven patterns for organizing speeches and explored how each pattern affects the residual message of a presentation. Which organizational structure is best depends on a variety of factors, including the topic, your speaking goal, and the listeners with whom you will communicate. The fourth section of the chapter examined the advantages and disadvantages of different styles of delivery. Finally, we considered how speakers may use digital media when organizing and presenting public speeches.

To make sure that you've thought through all important aspects of organizing, outlining, and delivery, review the checklist at the end of this chapter. Then you'll be ready to proceed to Chapter 15, in which we analyze the full text of a student speech to see how organization, evidence, and other facets of public speaking work in an actual presentation.

MindTap

Checklist for Organizing and Presenting a Speech

Complete this checklist to help you organize your next speech.

In addition, you can use Outline Builder to help you organize your speech.

1. How could you structure your speech using each of the organizational patterns we discussed? Write out a thesis statement for each pattern.
    A. temporal: _____
    B. spatial: _____
    C. topical: _____
    D. star: _____
    E. comparative: _____
    F. problem–solution: _____
    G. cause–effect: _____
    H. effect–cause: _____

2. Which pattern have you decided to use?
    A. List the two or three main points into which you've divided your topic: _____, _____, and _____.

3. Describe the three parts of your introduction:
    A. I will gain attention by _____
    _____
    B. My thesis statement is _____
    _____
    C. My preview is _____
    _____

4. Describe the transitions you've developed to move listeners from idea to idea in your speech.
   A. My transition from introduction to the body of the speech is _____
   _____
   _____
   B. My transitions between major points in the body are _____
   _____
   _____
   C. My transition from the body to the conclusion of the speech is _____
   _____
   _____

5. Describe the two parts of your conclusion:
   A. Restatement of thesis and major points: _____
   B. Concluding emphasis: _____

6. The delivery style I will use is _____ because _____

7. I've practiced my speech
   A. on my own
   B. in front of others
   C. in front of a mirror
   D. in the room where I will deliver it
   E. on video

Experiencing Communication in Our Lives

MindTap

CASE STUDY: Analyzing Delivery: Speech of Self-Introduction

Apply what you've learned in this chapter by analyzing the following case study, using the accompanying questions as a guide. These questions and a video of the case study are also available online with your MindTap Speech for *Communication in Our Lives*.

Every year since I've remembered, we've gone back to Iowa and spent a week of that summer just being with my dad's parents, my grandparents. And each year, as I grew, I grew closer and closer to my grandfather. And it got to the point where I no longer just knew him as a relative but I knew him as a human being. Sitting outside on his porch one day, right before he died, he told me about his life. We were talking about what he had done, being in World War II, being a dentist, being a community leader, all the things he had ever achieved in his life—and it all sounded so perfect. I said, "Grandfather, what do you regret most in your life?" He said, "Adam, I regret not seeing more sunsets."

A couple months later, he passed on, and I realized that I didn't enjoy every single minute with him as much as I could've, and I didn't have the time with him that I thought that I had. So I look at my wall now, and I see the quotes on it and see the stories on it and the pictures on it and I realize that everyone I've come into contact with, everyone I've ever met, everything I've done, has all contributed to shaping the person that I am.

QUESTIONS FOR ANALYSIS AND DISCUSSION

1. Was the speaker dynamic—excited about the topic?

2. Was the speaker's language clear, immediate, and vivid?

3. Did the speaker use nonverbal communication to enhance effectiveness?

4. What style of speaking did the speaker use? Was this an appropriate choice for this speech, this occasion, and the particular listeners?

MindTap

Use flashcards to learn key concepts and take a quiz to test your knowledge.

Key Concepts

communication apprehension

extemporaneous speaking

formal outline

impromptu speaking

key word outline

manuscript speaking

memorized speaking

oral style

positive visualization

transitions

working outline

works cited

Sharpen Your Skill

1. Designing Your Introduction

Apply the principles we've discussed to develop an introduction to a speech you plan to give. Using the following outline, fill in full sentences for each element of your introduction.

I. Introduction

A. Attention: _____

B. Thesis: _____

C. Credibility: _____

D. Preview: _____

2. Rehearsing Your Speech

You'll need three 20-minute periods at different times to complete this activity.

a. After you have prepared the outline that you will use when you present your speech, find a quiet place where you will not be disturbed. Present the speech as you intend to deliver it to your class. As you rehearse, practice looking at different parts of the room as you will later engage in eye contact with classmates.

b. Wait at least a few hours after your first practice to do the second one. This time, practice in the same room, but stand in front of a mirror; ideally it should be a full-length mirror so that you can see yourself as listeners will see you. Give your speech as you plan to deliver it to your classmates. As you speak, notice your posture and nonverbal communication. Are you using effective hand gestures, facial expressions, and changes in body posture and position?

c. Wait at least a few hours after your second practice to do the third one. You may want to invite several friends or classmates to join you in this practice session so that you have an audience. For this rehearsal, go to your classroom or another classroom that is set up similarly to yours. Sit down in the room as you would sit in your class. Imagine the teacher announcing that it is your turn to speak. Get up from your seat, go to the podium or front of the classroom, and present your speech as you plan to deliver it to your classmates. Practice looking at different areas of the room or at your friends as you will later engage in eye contact with classmates. If you have access to a video camera, you may tape this third rehearsal and then analyze your presentation as well as feedback from anyone you invited to be your listeners.

For Further Reflection and Discussion

1. Does a speaker have an ethical responsibility to organize a speech well, or is organization strictly a strategic matter—something to help a speaker have impact? Does careful organization reflect ethical issues, such as respect for listeners?

2. Attend a public presentation and keep notes on how the speaker organizes the speech. What is the overall pattern of the presentation? Did the speaker make a wise choice? Identify transitions in the speech, and evaluate their effectiveness. Do the introduction and conclusion serve the appropriate speaking goals?

3. Give a 1- to 2-minute impromptu speech on your favorite activity. Next, spend 2 days preparing an extemporaneous speech on the same topic. How do the two speeches differ in quality and effectiveness?

15

> Information is
> the currency of
> democracy.
>
> **Thomas
> Jefferson**

Image Source/Thinkstock

Informative Speaking

*How common is
informative speaking
in everyday life?*

MindTap®

Review the chapter's
learning objectives and
start with a quick warm-
up activity.

LEARNING OBJECTIVES

After studying the topics in this chapter, you should be able to:

1. Explain four ways in which informative speaking differs from persuasive speaking.

2. List eight guidelines for effective informative speaking.

3. Recall five strategies for informative speaking that will enhance listeners' retention.

4. Provide an example for each of the four ways to involve listeners when presenting an informative speech.

5. Identify five criteria to consider when evaluating information to use as supporting material.

6. Use the online and/or print material in this chapter to prepare an informative speech outline.

Silas savors the steaming coffee as he pulls up the calendar on this laptop and reviews his to-do list for the day. Since he launched his start-up consulting firm, he's been incredibly busy. He's building his team while also trying to attract clients and keep investors satisfied with the firm's progress. At 9 o'clock, he's meeting with his assistant to explain a new procedure for managing client files. At 10 o'clock is the monthly meeting with investors where he will update them on the new clients and the revenue stream. Lunch will be with a woman he's trying to lure away from one of his competitors. He'd love to have her on his team, so Silas has put thought into how he can describe his company, its mission, and its culture.

Like many professionals, Silas does a lot of informational speaking. He has to be able to describe changing practices, explain procedures, and inform people about issues. To live and work effectively in today's world, we need to share information—in the workplace, in social situations, and in community and civic contexts. Skill at informative speaking is critical if you want to be effective personally, professionally, and socially. Go to the book's online resources for this chapter to learn more about the importance of informational speaking in professional life.

Building on what you've learned in Chapters 12, 13, and 14, this chapter will guide you through the process of developing and presenting an informative speech. The process we discuss can also be used to develop short informational presentations, such as some of those Silas has on his calendar. We will first highlight the importance of informative speaking in everyday life and note how it differs from persuasive speaking, which we will cover in Chapter 16. Next, we'll identify ways that digital media assist us when we are preparing for and engaging in informational speaking and then discuss guidelines for effective informative speaking. At the end of the chapter, you'll find a sample informative speech.

The Nature of Informative Speaking

An **informative speech** aims to increase listeners' knowledge, understanding, or abilities. Competence in informative speaking is important if you plan to coach sports, be part of neighborhood and civic groups, succeed in your profession, or teach anything to anyone (Hamilton, 2015; Morreale, Osborn, & Pearson, 2000).

Informative Speaking in Everyday Life

It's likely that you'll give a number of informative speeches in your life. Some will be short; some will be longer. Some will be formal; others will be informal. All of them will have the goal of conveying information to others. Consider these examples of everyday informative speaking:

- Explaining a medical procedure to a patient.
- Informing your neighbors about a community watch program that's decreased burglaries in other neighborhoods.
- Briefing stakeholders on the new strategic plan your firm is implementing.

informative speech A presentation that aims to increase listeners' knowledge, understanding, or abilities.

Informative Speaking on the Job   MindTap

What does skill in informative speaking have to do with career success? A lot. People who can present ideas clearly tend to be noticed and promoted. A 2015 article in *U.S. News & World Report* pointed out that good informative speaking skills are not just for presentations in front of large crowds. They are also critical to presenting ideas in team meetings and informing colleagues and board members of new policies, products, and issues. In other words, speaking skill is part of everyday work situations (Yeager, 2015).

- Describing a new offensive strategy to the Little League team you coach.

- Telling a civic group about traditions in your culture.

- Reporting to your coworkers on what you learned at a conference so that they understand new developments in your field.

SHARPEN YOUR SKILL

At the end of this chapter, refer to the Sharpen Your Skill feature, Informative Speaking in Your Life, to apply concepts from Chapter 15.

Comparing Informative and Persuasive Speaking

Informative speaking and persuasive speaking differ, yet they also have much in common. Both require forethought about listeners and the occasion, research, organization, supporting material, and delivery. There are also overlaps between informative and persuasive goals. For example, in an informative speech, you are trying to persuade listeners to attend to what you say and to care about learning. In persuasive speeches, you often need to inform listeners about certain issues to influence their values, attitudes, or behaviors.

Four differences between informative and persuasive speaking are particularly important.

The Controversial Nature of the Purpose   The purposes of informative speeches tend to be less controversial than the purposes of persuasive speeches. Something is controversial when it can be debated or argued—in other words, when not everyone is likely to agree. Typically, informative presentations aim to give listeners new information: to teach, explain, or describe a person, object, event, process, or relationship. Persuasive speeches, on the other hand, often aim to change listeners' attitudes, beliefs, or behaviors.

Obviously, information can have persuasive impact, so it can be controversial. Yet the degree to which a purpose is controversial is much greater in persuasive speeches. An informative speech might have the specific purpose of describing the historical conditions that led to establishment of affirmative action policies. A persuasive speech on the same topic might have the specific purpose of persuading listeners to support or oppose affirmative action policies. Clearly, the latter purpose is more controversial than the former.

The Response Sought   Related to their differing purposes are the responses informative and persuasive speeches seek from listeners. In the affirmative action example, the speaker giving an informative speech wants listeners to understand certain historical conditions. The speaker giving a persuasive speech wants listeners to believe that affirmative action is right or wrong, justified or not justified, or

Most professionals today engage in informative speaking.

beneficial or harmful. The persuasive speaker might even want to persuade listeners to take specific actions to oppose or support affirmative action at local, regional, or national levels. In seeking to change listeners in some way, persuasive speeches seek a more powerful response: change rather than acceptance of new information.

The Evidence Needed Because persuasive speeches tend to be more controversial and seek to convince listeners to change in some way, they generally need stronger supporting material than informative speeches do. This does not mean that informative speeches don't need proof; they do. However, an effective persuasive speech generally must include more supporting material. Why? Because listeners expect more evidence when they are asked to think, feel, or act differently than when they are asked only to understand something. Listeners will want convincing evidence not only that discrimination exists and is wrong but also that affirmative action policies are an effective response to the problem.

In persuasive speeches, speakers also have a responsibility to anticipate and address listeners' reservations. Doing this effectively requires evidence. Perhaps, in researching public opinions on affirmative action, you learn that the most common objection is based on the assumption that it lowers standards for admission to schools and professions. To persuade listeners to support affirmative action, you should present evidence that shows that standards have not declined in institutions that follow affirmative action policies.

VINCE *Last week, I went to hear a speaker on capital punishment. He was trying to convince us that we should abolish it, but I wasn't convinced. What he mainly did was to inform us that there are cases where innocent people are convicted or even put to death. But he never showed us—or me, anyway—that abolishing capital punishment is the answer. Why can't we just reform it, like, require absolute proof of guilt before someone can be sentenced to die? And what about all the people who really are guilty of horrible things, like school killings or the Oklahoma bombing? Shouldn't they be sentenced to death? He never talked about that.*

Review It!

Differences Between
Informative and
Persuasive Speeches:
- Controversialness
- Response Sought
- Evidence Needed
- Credibility Needed

Credibility Needed   Credibility is important to any speaker's effectiveness. As with evidence, however, the credibility a speaker needs varies with the speaking purpose. In general, a speaker who attempts to change people needs more credibility than a speaker who seeks only to inform them. Because credibility is so important in persuasive speaking, we will discuss it in depth in Chapter 16.

Guidelines for Effective Informative Speaking

Eight guidelines are particularly important for informative speeches.

Provide Listeners with a Clear Thesis Statement

When giving an informative presentation, the speaker should state a simple, clear thesis that tells listeners what the speech will provide or do. The thesis should motivate listeners by alerting them that the information to come will be useful to them. As you'll recall from previous chapters, a good thesis is clear and direct: "At the end of my talk, you will understand the different citizen responsibilities and results of three popular neighborhood watch programs used in our county." Upon hearing this thesis, listeners know exactly what the speaker plans to give them and what they should get out of listening.

Connect with Listeners' Values and Experiences

As with all communication, informative speeches should build connections with listeners. For instance, in a speech with the specific purpose of describing alternative neighborhood watch programs, a speaker might open by saying, "I know we share a concern for safety in our neighborhood. What I want to do is describe the three neighborhood watch programs in our county so that we can make an informed choice about what is right for our community." This opening establishes a common ground between the speaker and listeners by noting that they "share a concern" and by using *we* language: "our neighborhood," "we can make," "our community."

MindTap®   What are your impressions of this speaker?

iStockphoto.com/Cathy Yeulet

Motivate Listeners to Want Information

For an informative speech to be effective, listeners must be motivated to want what the speaker offers. In some cases, listeners are motivated for their own reasons. People who attend cardiopulmonary resuscitation (CPR) class want to learn how to perform CPR. They are already motivated.

In other cases, the speaker may need to motivate people to want information. For example, a supervisor may need to fuel employees' hunger for information on a new procedure the company wants them to follow. In this situation, the supervisor might say, "I know we all get tired of learning new procedures, but the one I'm going to explain today will make your jobs easier and increase your productivity." This statement motivates employees to listen, especially if their pay is based on their productivity.

SARAH   *I went to the placement office the other day for a workshop on interviewing. I wasn't really interested, but I thought I should go, so I was just kind of there but not really paying attention. Then the facilitator got us started. The first thing she said was that students who attend these workshops tended to get more and better job offers than students who don't. That definitely got my attention! From then on, I was listening very carefully and taking lots of notes.*

Build Credibility with Listeners

As we've noted, for a speaker to be effective, listeners must perceive him or her as credible. When giving an informative speech, you should demonstrate that you have some expertise relevant to your topic. You may show you have personal experience ("I took a CPR course"). You may also demonstrate to listeners that you have gained information in other ways ("To prepare to talk to you today, I spoke with emergency department doctors about people whose lives were saved by CPR").

You'll also want to show listeners that you care about them or that the information you are offering will help them in some way. You might say, "This information may enable you to save a life one day."

Adapt to Diverse Listeners

You should speak in ways that include and respect diverse experiences, values, and viewpoints. People whose homes have been burglarized have had a different experience from those whose homes have not been burglarized. Citizens who were raised in highly communal cultures are likely to be more inclined toward communal efforts to protect a neighborhood than are people who were raised in highly individualistic cultures. Families without children may have different security concerns from families with children, especially young ones.

DIMITRI   *I am looking for a new car, so I went to a dealership. I was looking at a model that Consumer Reports said has the highest safety rating. Then the salesman came over and started talking about the car I was looking at. His pitch was that it was cheap and fuel efficient. I asked him a couple of questions about safety issues, which are my primary concerns with cars, and he just brushed them back and kept telling me how economical it was. He lost that sale.*

Organize So Listeners Can Follow Easily

In Chapter 4, we learned that listening is hard work. A speaker should make it easy for listeners to take in information. Applying the principles we discussed in Chapter 14, this means that you should structure your speech clearly. As we learned, your introduction should capture listeners' attention ("Would you like to increase your paycheck by 10%?"), provide a clear thesis ("I'm going to explain a new procedure that will increase your efficiency and income"), and preview what will be covered ("I will demonstrate a new method of sorting and routing stock and show how much faster and more accurate it is than the method we've been using").

Transitions should be woven throughout the speech to assist listeners in following the flow of ideas. The conclusion should summarize key points ("I've shown you how to increase your paycheck") and end with a strong idea or punch ("In this case, what's good for the company is also good for you").

The body of an informative speech should also be organized clearly (see Table 15.1). Temporal and spatial patterns can be effective for speeches that aim to demonstrate, describe, explain, or teach ("In my speech, I will describe how interviews progress from opening stage to substance and closing stage"). Topical patterns are commonly used for reports and briefings that address several areas of a topic ("I will summarize developments in our sales and marketing divisions"). When introducing new or alternative ideas or procedures, the comparative pattern can be effective ("The new method of sorting and routing stock differs from our current method in two key ways").

Although they are less commonly used in informative presentations, problem–solution and cause–effect or effect–cause patterns can be good choices.

Table 15.1	Organizing Informative Speeches	
Specific Purpose	**Thesis**	**Organizational Patterns**
Listeners will learn how to recognize differences between poisonous and nonpoisonous plants.	I will teach you how to tell which plants are safe to eat.	Comparison/contrast
Team members will know management's response to our strategic plan.	I will summarize the feedback from management on our goals and implementation strategies.	Topical
To teach friends how I make crème brûlée.	I am going to take you through the steps involved in making a perfect crème brûlée.	Temporal
Employees will understand the reasons for a new procedure for sorting and routing stock.	I want to explain how the new procedure we're going to start using solves problems that have frustrated us for years.	Problem–solution

For instance, an informative speech might explain how a new procedure for sorting and routing stock solves a problem. The same topic might be organized using a cause–effect pattern to show that the new procedure (cause) will increase productivity (effect).

Outline Builder accessed through MindTap, includes extensive prompts and a clear framework for organizing and developing speeches that incorporate a variety of informative strategies.

Design Your Speech to Enhance Learning and Retention

Much of the information we need to do our jobs and live our lives is not particularly interesting. This poses a challenge for you when you give an informative speech. The informative speaker is responsible for making material interesting to listeners. In addition, information can be complex and difficult to grasp, particularly in oral presentations. This creates a second challenge for informative speakers: You must do all you can to increase the clarity of the information. Five strategies can help you make your information interesting and clear.

Limit the Information You Present   By the time you are ready to give an informative speech, you know a great deal about the topic. It's your job to sort through all your knowledge to choose wisely the two or three points you want to make. You may think five points are important. If you try to present all five, however, you risk having listeners remember none or the less important ones.

If you must cover more than two or three points to inform listeners fully, then you have two choices. You may give multiple informative talks, separated by time to allow listeners to absorb and apply the information you've provided before they get more. A second option is to rely on other principles of increasing clarity and interest that we discuss later in this chapter.

Move from Familiar to Unfamiliar   It's normal to feel uneasy when you are asked to understand new information or learn a new process or skill. Speakers can reduce this anxiety by starting with what is familiar to listeners and moving to what is new. For instance, the supervisor in our example might open an informative speech by saying, "All of you know the sorting and routing procedure we've used for years. The new procedure extends what you already know. What you've done in the past is to sort incoming stock into three piles. From now on, you'll be sorting it into four. It's the same process—just one more pile." Upon hearing this, listeners realize that skills they already have will transfer to the new procedure.

Repeat Important Ideas   Repetition increases retention (Jaffe, 2016; Thompson & Grundgenett, 1999). Have you ever been introduced to someone and not been able to remember the person's name 5 minutes later? That's because you heard it only once. The introduction probably was like this: "Pat, I'd like you to meet Leigh." If the person doing the introduction had wanted to help you remember Leigh's name, it would have been better to say this: "Pat, I'd like you to meet Leigh. Leigh and I go way back; we met in our sophomore year. We got together when Leigh and I were trying out for the chorus, and Leigh got a place when I didn't." In that short introduction, Leigh's name was mentioned four times. You'll probably remember it. You're more likely to remember something you hear four times than something you hear only once.

SHARPEN YOUR SKILL

At the end of this chapter, refer to the Sharpen Your Skill feature, Organizing Your Informative Speech, to apply concepts from Chapter 15.

The same principle applies to informative speaking. As an illustration, let's return to our supervisor. It's important that employees retain the new classifications into which they will be sorting stock, so these bear repeating: "In the past you've sorted stock into new, returns, and used. As most of you know, the stock we've been putting in the return pile has really been of two types: stock that was missing something and stock that was defective. Now we're breaking returns into two separate piles: ones with missing parts and ones that are defective. So we have missings and defects. The missing pile is for stock that is missing a part. We can fix these items by adding the missing part. The defect pile is for stock that has something wrong with it. So missings and defects are the new piles we want to use." The repeated references to *missings* and *defects* increase listeners' ability to retain the new classifications for stock.

Highlight Key Material   Do you become more attentive in class when a teacher says, "This next point is really important" or "You're likely to see this on the test"? Probably you do. That's what the teacher intends. He or she is highlighting key material to get your attention. In this example, the teacher highlighted by framing. "This material is important" is a frame that calls your attention to important material.

"This material is important."

MATERIAL

There are other ways to highlight key material. You might say something direct, such as, "Listen up. This is important." Or you might say, "I hope you'll really tune in to this next point." You could also say, "If you remember only one thing from my talk, it should be this: . . ." All of these statements give verbal clues to listeners that you are presenting especially important material.

You can also provide nonverbal clues to highlight key material. Raising volume or changing inflection tends to capture interest, so listeners are likely to listen more carefully when a speaker alters volume or inflection. Gestures can also emphasize the importance of key ideas. You can change your position—move from behind a podium to in front of it, move from sitting to standing—to draw listeners' attention.

Rely on Multiple Communication Channels   If a speaker says, "Red berries often are poisonous," you might get the point. You'd be more likely to retain it if the speaker made that statement and also showed you pictures of red berries or gave you red berries. When we use multiple channels to communicate, we increase the likelihood that listeners will retain new information.

When you're presenting a lot of information or complex information, handouts can greatly increase listeners' retention and ability to use new information. Listeners both hear the talk and see the notes summarizing key points. Visual aids can also highlight information. The supervisor in our example might develop a visual aid to show the two new classifications that grow out of the one former one (Figure 15.1). Showing this while also talking about the two new classifications lets listeners learn and retain through two senses: seeing and hearing. The visual aid would be especially effective if the two new classifications stood out visually. They might be larger or a different color font.

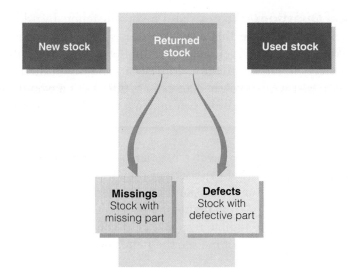

FIGURE 15.1
A Visual Aid to Illustrate
a New Procedure

Involve Listeners

Have you ever been a passenger when someone else was driving and later been unsure how to get back to where the two of you went? If you drive yourself, there's a greater likelihood that you'll learn how to get to the place. This common experience reminds us that we learn best when we do something ourselves rather than just hear or see someone else do it. There are many ways to involve listeners in informative speeches. We'll highlight four of the most effective (see Table 15.2).

Call for Participation You might give sticks to Boy Scouts and so they can rub them together as you demonstrate how to do this to start a fire (but only if fire codes allow this and if you can control possible danger). You might let people try a new procedure at a demonstration stand you set up. You might bring plants that are poisonous and nonpoisonous so that listeners can see, smell, and touch them as you describe how they differ.

Table 15.2	Generating a Sense of Listener Participation
Specific Informative Purpose: To Teach Listeners How to Recognize Poisonous Plants	
Method	**Example**
Direct participation	I want each of you to smell the berries I'm handing out.
Rhetorical question	If you were stranded on a camping trip, would you know how to survive?
Poll listeners	How many of you have ever pulled a ripe berry off a bush and wondered if it was safe to eat?
Refer to specific listeners	Jane, remember when you watched Tom Hanks in *Castaway* and wondered how he knew what was safe to eat on the island?

Ask Rhetorical Questions   You can also involve listeners by asking rhetorical questions. These are questions that a speaker doesn't actually expect listeners to answer. By asking them, however, a speaker invites listeners' mental participation: They are likely to answer rhetorical questions silently in their heads. "How many of you have ever wished you had an extra $100?" "What would you do if you made 20% more each week? Would you take a vacation, buy a new car, or pay some bills?"

Poll Listeners   Another way to involve listeners is to poll them to find out what they think, feel, or want or what experiences they have had. "How many of you have ever left your home for a vacation and worried about whether someone was going to break into it?" "How many of you would like to earn $100 more a week?" Speakers can ask for audible responses ("If you have had this experience, say yes") or a show of hands ("Let me see the hands of everyone who has had this experience").

Refer to Specific Listeners   You may also speak directly to or about particular members of your audience. Ethically, you must be careful not to speak to or about others in ways that could embarrass them or reveal information they consider private. Speaking to or about specific listeners generates a sense of participation and community. "Bill and Sally, we've all heard about the break-in at your house." "Just the other day, I overheard Ed talking about what he'd do if he won the lottery. Well, Ed, I've got good news for you: You may not win the lottery, but you can get more money."

Use Effective and Ethical Supporting Materials

To be effective in informing listeners, speeches must include supporting material that is both effective and ethical. Effective supporting materials add interest, force, and clarity to a speech. Ethical supporting materials present accurate information fairly and without distortion (Lehman & DuFrene, 1999).

Returning to our previous example, the supervisor might take the average employee's salary and show how much it should go up using the new procedure. The speaker might develop a visual aid to show how that increase would multiply over a period of time (Figure 15.2).

To be ethical, supporting material should meet the criteria we discussed in Chapter 13 (see Table 13.4 on page 261). To review, supporting material should be:

• Sufficient to achieve the speaking purpose, such as teaching or describing (sufficiency).

• Accurate, correct and complete, with sources cited, presented in its original context (accuracy).

• Relevant to the topic and claims made (relevance).

• Timely, usually current or in some cases historically situated (timeliness).

• Free of biases, such as vested interests (impartiality).

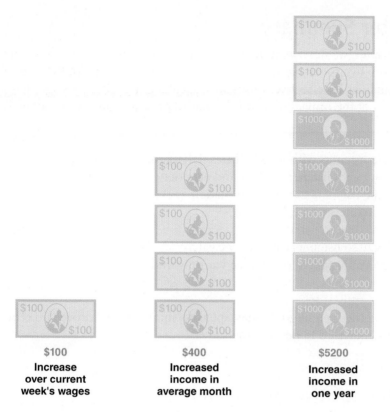

FIGURE 15.2

A Visual Aid to Motivate Employees

Using these criteria, it would be ethical for the speaker to tell employees that their wages should increase an average of 20% only if the speaker had adequate data to support that claim (the criterion of accuracy). If only 25% of employees who have used the new procedure increase their productivity, it would not be ethical to state that they could expect to increase their wages because only one in four could reasonably expect that. If most employees do increase their productivity by 20% but only after 4–6 months of adjusting to the new procedure, the speaker would be ethically obligated to inform them of the time lag (the criterion of timeliness). If employees who use the new procedure at other plants have different working conditions and tools, the change in their productivity might not generalize to the listeners in this case (the criterion of relevance).

Digital Media and Informative Speaking

In prior chapters, we have noted many ways that digital media assist people who are preparing for and presenting public speeches. Informative speakers, like other speakers, may rely on digital media to conduct research, find experts and verify their qualifications, and conduct interviews and surveys.

MindTap includes tools that can help you prepare an effective informative speech. You will find a tool, Outline Builder, for organizing your speech and another tool, Practice and Present, for uploading practice deliveries that you can review and critique.

Chapter Summary

In this chapter, we described the many types of informative speeches and noted how informative speaking differs from persuasive speaking. We then highlighted eight guidelines for effective informative speaking. Because these guidelines are at the heart of the impact of your informative presentations, we summarize them here:

1. Provide listeners with a clear thesis statement.
2. Connect with listeners' values and experiences.
3. Motivate listeners to want information.
4. Build credibility with listeners.
5. Adapt to diverse listeners.
6. Organize so listeners can follow easily.
7. Design your speech to enhance learning and retention.
8. Involve listeners.

In following these eight guidelines, speakers should use effective and ethical supporting materials to develop their ideas.

Informative Speech Outline

General Purpose: _____

Specific Purpose: _____

Introduction

I.   Attention device _____

II. Motivation for listening _____

III. Thesis statement _____

IV. Preview of speech _____

Body

I.   First main point _____
   A. Supporting material _____
   B. Supporting material (You may have only two main points) _____
   C. Transition _____

II. Second main point (You may have more than two kinds of supporting materials for main points)

   _____
   A. Supporting material _____
   B. Supporting material _____
   C. Transition _____

Transition to conclusion _____

Conclusion

I.   Summary of main points _____

II. Strong closing statement _____

References _____

Evaluation Form for Informative Speeches

Speaker's Name: _____ Date: _____

Speech Topic: _____

_____

1. Did the speaker capture listeners' initial attention? _____

2. Did the speaker motivate listeners to want information? _____

3. Did the speaker state a clear thesis? _____

4. Did the speaker preview the body of the speech? _____

5. Was the speech structured clearly and appropriately? _____

6. Were strong transitions provided between parts of the speech and main points in the body of the speech? _____

7. Did the speaker provide effective supporting material? _____

8. Did the speaker use ethical supporting material? _____

9. Did the speaker involve listeners directly by polling them, asking rhetorical questions, or speaking to or about particular listeners? _____

10. Did the speaker use strategies to enhance listeners' learning and retention?
_____

11. Did the speaker connect the topic to listeners' experiences and values? _____

12. Did the conclusion summarize main points of the speech? _____

13. Did the speech end on a strong note? _____

_____

Experiencing Communication in Our Lives   MindTap

CASE STUDY: Informative Speech: Anytown USA

Apply what you've learned in this chapter by analyzing the following case study, using the accompanying questions as a guide. These questions and a video of the case study are also available online with your MindTap Speech for *Communication in Our Lives*.

I would not be the person I am today if it was not for Anytown. I would not be in this room if it was not for this organization. You're probably wondering what I'm talking about. What can so dramatically change someone's life?

Anytown is a summer leadership camp. Now there are thousands of summer leadership camps all around the world. You have science camps, young life camps, all kinds of camps—camps that change our lives in positive ways.

The summer before my junior year, I attended Anytown. Before camp, I was a deviant young man. After camp I was never the same. So what exactly is Anytown? What is its history and what goes on at camp that's so powerful? Today I'll discuss these three things with you.

According to the website, Anytown Arizona is a youth development program that focuses on diversity awareness, social justice, and personal empowerment. Its mission is to be a catalyst and facilitator for social change. This camp brings together people from different backgrounds and different cultures.

The Anytown USA organization has several types of programs: Anytown Junior is for junior highers; Unitowns are for weekend programs; Beyond Anytown is for people who have attended Anytown; and Powertown focuses on parents and community members.

The weeklong camp is filled with activities geared toward understanding diversity through a great deal of educational activities that have emotional impact. Typically, the counselors act out different levels of violence that are seen everywhere. They start with verbal violence—someone saying an inappropriate comment to somebody just because they are a different color. They continue to physical violence, ganging up and pummeling another counselor because they are a different color. They finish with genocide. Genocide consists of four or six counselors acting out being Jewish, killed by two counselors acting out being Nazis. This is only one of the activities and there are many others.

So where did Anytown come from? What's its history? According to the Anytown website, Anytown began in 1957 known as the National Conference for Christians and Jews, now better known as the National Conference for Community and Justice. The goal then and now was to bring together a group of diverse young youth from a variety of different backgrounds, empower them to understand each other, and learn from each other.

In one cabin you will have a young man who has been very wealthy growing up and a young man who has had a very dysfunctional past. Together, throughout the week, they come together and they learn about each other and where they're from and what they've lived. Toward the end of the week they become kind of like brothers.

The staff, in a way, tests the students. They segregate them. Each day has a different theme, such as "know yourself," "know your friends," and "know your family." During the week in the end, when they become segregated they either continue to stay segregated or they desegregate themselves. These students never fail the test of desegregating themselves.

Each camp reacts differently to the segregation. Some break it and integrate to the camp. Some stay segregated until one specific student speaks up.

I hope you have learned a thing or two about this great organization that has been around for years. I'm sure that Anytown will be around for the future, helping our youth understand diversity, and understand each other. Jared Cohan, an Anytown alumni, quotes, "One person can achieve wonders by helping one person—an individual. Then that individual passes those things to another and so on and so on." This is the power Anytown has, changing the world one person at a time.

QUESTIONS FOR ANALYSIS AND DISCUSSION

1. Did Enriques Ruiz effectively capture your attention at the beginning of his speech?

2. Did the preview forecast coverage adequately?

3. Did he provide effective and ethical evidence to support his ideas?

4. Were there good transitions between main points?

5. Did the conclusion summarize main points in the speech?

Key Concepts

informative speech

Sharpen Your Skill

1. Informative Speaking in Your Life

How common is informative speaking in your everyday life? For the next week, keep a record of the informative speeches you hear (those given by others), grouped into the four categories listed here. Remember that an informative speech need not be long—it may be just a couple of minutes in which someone teaches you how to do something or explains a new procedure, describes a rule or policy, or tells you the background of an issue.

a. Informative speaking in classes

b. Informative speaking on the job

c. Informative speaking with friends

d. Other informative speaking

2. Organizing Your Informative Speech

Apply the principles of effective organization as you develop your informative speech. Provide the following information for your speech:

Introduction

To capture listeners' attention and motivate them to listen, I will _____

My thesis statement is _____

To establish my initial credibility, I will _____

To preview my speech, I will say _____

My transition from the introduction to the body is _____

Body

    My organizational pattern is _____

    To provide transitions from one main point to the next, I will say

    A. Points one to two: _____

    B. Points two to three: _____

    C. Point three to conclusion: _____

    My transition from body to conclusion is

Conclusion

    I will summarize the key points in my speech by saying _____

    I will close with this strong statement: _____

For Further Reflection and Discussion

1. Attend an informative speech. Identify the thesis and the organizational pattern. Evaluate the ethical and strategic quality of the speaker's evidence.

2. Go to the book's online resources for this chapter to find quotations that are relevant to your speech.

3. Ted Talks offer many examples of informative speeches that employ different delivery styles. Go to www.Ted.com to find speeches on topics that interest you or go to the book's online resources for this chapter to view three examples of informative speeches.

Blend Images/Getty Images

16

Whatever words
we utter should
be chosen with
care for people
will hear them
and be influenced
by them for good
or ill.

Buddha

Persuasive Speaking

LEARNING OBJECTIVES

After studying the topics in this chapter, you should be able to:

1. Explain why persuasion is transactional, artistic, and gradual.

2. Summarize the nature of each of the three pillars of persuasion.

3. Define and provide an example for each of the three types of credibility.

4. Recall three criteria to consider when deciding whether a persuasive speech should be one-sided or two-sided.

5. Name the five steps in the motivated sequence.

6. Apply chapter guidelines to prepare an effective persuasive speech.

What leads you to perceive a speaker as credible?

MindTap®

Review the chapter's learning objectives and **start** with a quick warm-up activity.

- You want to persuade a patient to eat less and exercise more.
- You are a finalist for a key position and have 3 minutes to explain why you should be selected.
- You want to convince the town council not to build a commercial center on the edge of your neighborhood.

Although most of us won't give persuasive speeches regularly, nearly all of us will find ourselves speaking persuasively at times. For instance, your manager might want you to persuade a potential client that your firm can provide the best service. In other cases, your values and commitments will compel you to speak in an effort to persuade others to ideas or actions that you think are right or desirable.

Building on the knowledge you've gained from the previous chapters, this chapter begins by defining persuasive speaking. Second, we discuss three pillars of persuasion and ways to build your credibility as a speaker. Next, we'll identify organizational patterns that are particularly effective for persuasive speeches. Fourth, note how digital technologies that can assist in preparing and presenting persuasive speeches. We close the chapter with guidelines for effective persuasive speaking.

Understanding Persuasive Speaking

Persuasive speeches aim to change others by prompting them to think, feel, believe, or act differently. You may want to alter the strength of others' attitudes for or against particular issues. You may want to convince others to use seat belts, vote for a candidate, or volunteer for community service. In each case, your goal is persuasive: You aim to change the people with whom you speak.

In thinking about persuasive speaking, it's important to keep three points in mind. First, like all other communication, persuasive speaking involves multiple communicators. The transactional model of communication we discussed in Chapter 1 is as relevant to persuasive speaking as it is to other kinds of communication. Effective persuasion is not something speakers do to listeners. Instead, it is engagement between a speaker and listeners. Although the speaker may be in the spotlight, the listeners are part of effective persuasive speaking, from planning to delivery. Speakers should consider listeners' experiences, expectations, values, and attitudes as they plan, research, and present speeches. Speakers should also attend to listeners' feedback during speeches.

Second, remember that persuasion is not coercion or force. The great rhetorical scholar Aristotle distinguished between what he called inartistic proofs and artistic proofs. An inartistic proof requires no art or skill on our part. For instance, if you hold a gun to someone's head and say, "Give me your money or I'll shoot you," you may get the money. In that sense, you've been effective in getting the money (although you might wind up in jail). However, you haven't been artistic, and you haven't engaged in persuasion. To do that, you would need to use reasons and words to motivate, not force, the other person to do what you want. Persuasion relies on artistic, not inartistic, proofs.

Third, persuasive impact usually is gradual and incremental. Although people's positions occasionally change abruptly, usually we move gradually toward

persuasive speech
A presentation that aims to change listeners by prompting them to think, feel, or act differently.

Communication Highlight

The Persuasive Campaign for Designated Drivers

MindTap®

Have you ever been a designated driver? Have you ever been driven home by a designated driver? Today, most of us are familiar with the idea of a designated driver, but that wasn't always the case. In 1988, the Harvard School of Public Health launched the Harvard Alcohol Project, an intensive persuasive campaign to diffuse the concept of designated driver through American society. A pioneering venture, the Harvard Alcohol Project was the first time that a health organization partnered with mass media communication specialists (Harvard Alcohol, 2012).

The campaign began when Harvard convinced writers for top-rated television programs to weave references to "designated driver" into characters' dialogue, making them part of story lines. This was designed to influence viewers' perceptions of appropriate behavior and to model the specific behaviors of asking for and serving as a designated driver.

Simultaneous with the introduction of the term into prime-time television shows, Harvard asked ABC, CBS, and NBC to air public service announcements encouraging the use of designated drivers. This was another first: the first time the three major networks simultaneously aired a public service campaign's messages.

By 1991, the term *designated driver* was added to *Merriam-Webster's Collegiate Dictionary*, signaling its widespread usage. Also in 1991, a Roper poll showed that 9 of 10 respondents in the United States knew about the designated driver program and rated it favorably.

When Harvard launched the campaign in 1988, annual fatalities attributed to drivers under the influence of alcohol were 23,626. By 1994, annual fatalities were 16,580, a decline of 30% in 6 years.

new ideas, attitudes, and actions. When we hear a persuasive speech, we compare its message with our experience and knowledge. If the speaker offers strong arguments, good evidence, and coherent organization, we may shift our attitudes or behaviors to some degree. If we later encounter additional persuasion, we may shift our attitudes further.

Because persuasion tends to happen gradually and incrementally, speakers should understand the attitudes and behaviors of listeners and adapt their persuasive goals accordingly. For example, assume you believe that the Electoral College should be abandoned and you want to persuade others to your point of view.

Communication & Careers

Sell Your Products, Sell Yourself

MindTap®

Forbes magazine published the results of a poll on the requirements for professional success. Seventy percent of business leaders who were polled said the ability to present ideas was critical to career advancement. The ability to speak effectively allows professionals to inspire others, sell products and services, attract funding, and—in general—sell oneself as a leader (Gallo, 2014).

Presenting ideas persuasively is a critical skill for professional advancement.

How would an effective persuasive speech differ if you knew in advance that listeners strongly favor the current Electoral College system or if you knew that they already have reservations about it?

In the first case, it would be unrealistic and ineffective to try to persuade listeners to support abolition of the Electoral College. A more realistic speaking purpose would be to persuade listeners that there are some disadvantages to the current electoral system. In this instance, you would be effective if you could reduce the strength of their position favoring the Electoral College. Because the second group of listeners already has reservations, you can build on those and lead them closer to supporting abolition of the Electoral College.

The Three Pillars of Persuasion

Teachers in ancient Greece and Rome recognized three pillars of persuasion, which are also called three forms of proof, or reasons people are persuaded: These are *ethos, pathos,* and *logos* (Kennedy, 1991). Although these three forms of proof are also important in other kinds of speaking, they assume special prominence when we engage in persuasion (Figure 16.1).

Ethos

Ethos refers to the perceived personal character of the speaker. We are more likely to believe the words of people whom we perceive as having strong, good character. We tend to attribute high ethos to people if we perceive that

- they have integrity
- they can be trusted
- they have goodwill toward us
- they know what they are talking about
- they are committed to the topic (show enthusiasm, dynamism)

ethos The perceived personal character of the speaker.

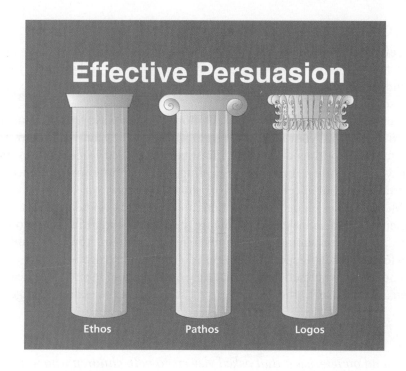

FIGURE 16.1
The Three Pillars of Persuasion

CARL *Last year, I had a teacher who didn't know anything about the subject. She made a lot of really vague statements, and when we tried to pin her down on specifics, she would blow off hot air—saying nothing at all. Nobody in the class thought she had any credibility.*

Because ethos is critical to persuasive impact, you should do what you can to demonstrate to your listeners that you are of good character. Table 16.1 identifies specific ways that you can influence listeners' perceptions of your ethos.

Table 16.1	Demonstrating Ethos
DIMENSIONS OF ETHOS	**WAYS TO DEMONSTRATE**
Goodwill	Identify common ground between you and listeners.
	Show respect for listeners' attitudes and experiences.
	Show that what you're saying will benefit them.
Expertise	Provide strong support for your claims.
	Document sources of support.
	Address concerns about or objections to your position.
	Demonstrate personal knowledge of the topic.
Trustworthiness	Use supporting materials ethically.
	Address other points of view fairly.
	Demonstrate that you care about your listeners.
Dynamism	Use appropriate volume and vocal emphasis.
	Assume a confident posture.
	Use gestures and kinesics to enhance forcefulness.
	Be energetic in presentation.

Pathos

Pathos refers to emotional reasons for attitudes, beliefs, or actions. We are influenced by appeals to our passions, fears, love, compassion, and so forth. Emotional proofs address the more subjective reasons for our beliefs in people, ideas, causes, and courses of action.

In preparing your persuasive presentation, develop ways to help your listeners not just to understand your ideas but also to feel a certain way about them. You may want them to feel outraged about an injustice, compelled to help others, or afraid of a policy or possibility. Appealing to feelings such as these may enhance the persuasive impact of your speech. Table 16.2 shows particular ways to enhance pathos.

As Melanie notes, appeals to emotions are powerful—and dangerous. They can easily alienate listeners instead of involving them. Fear and guilt are uncomfortable emotions, so speakers should be cautious in arousing them. You may want your listeners to fear what will happen if they don't do what you advocate, but you don't want them to be so overwhelmed by fear that they quit listening to you. Also, fear appeals can decrease a speaker's ethos if listeners are skeptical of the claimed dangers.

pathos Emotional proofs for claims.

MELANIE   *Last night, I saw an ad on television that asked viewers to help children who were starving in other countries. At first, I paid attention, but it just went over the top. The pictures were so heartbreaking that I just couldn't watch. I felt disgusted and guilty and mainly, what I really felt was turned off.*

Table 16.2	Enhancing Pathos
WAYS TO ENHANCE PATHOS IN PERSUASIVE SPEAKING	**EXAMPLE**
Personalize the issue, problem, or topic.	Include detailed examples.
	Tell stories that give listeners a sense of being in situations, experiencing problems.
	Translate statistics to make them interesting and personal.
Appeal to listeners' needs and values.	Show how your position satisfies listeners' needs, is consistent with their values.
	Use examples familiar to listeners to tie your ideas to their values and experiences.
	Show listeners how doing or believing what you advocate helps them live up to their values.
	Include quotations from people whom listeners respect.
Bring material alive.	Use visual aids to give listeners a vivid, graphic understanding of your topic.
	Use striking quotes from people involved with your topic.
	Use active, concrete language to paint verbal pictures.

Generally, it's more effective to encourage listeners to do something they will feel good about (e.g., send money to help starving children overseas) than to berate them for what they are or aren't doing (e.g., living well themselves while others starve).

Logos

The third reason for belief is **logos**, which is rational or logical proof. In persuasive speeches, logical proofs are arguments, reasoning, and evidence to support claims.

Forms of Reasoning   Most reasoning can be classified as one or the other of two basic forms. **Inductive reasoning** begins with specific examples and uses them to draw a general conclusion (Faigley & Selzer, 2000). Suppose you want to present a speech arguing that climate change is damaging our environment. To reason inductively, you would start by citing specific places where global climate change has demonstrable impact and document the harm in each case. Then you would advance the general conclusion that global climate change threatens life on our planet.

Deductive reasoning begins with a broad claim that listeners accept. Following this, the speaker then offers a specific claim. The conclusion follows from the general claim combined with the specific claim. Reasoning deductively, you would start by stating a commonly accepted claim (i.e., "Climate change is having a negative impact on the world") and then advance a specific claim (i.e., "Our region is part of the world"). From these two claims, it naturally follows that "Climate change is having negative impact on our region" (your conclusion).

The Toulmin Model   Another way to think about reasoning was originated by philosopher Stephen Toulmin (1958; Toulmin, Rieke, & Janik, 1984). Toulmin said that logical reasoning consists of three primary components: claims, grounds for the claims, and warrants that connect the claims to the grounds for them. In addition to these three basic parts of logical reasoning, Toulmin's model includes qualifiers and rebuttals. Figure 16.2 shows the **Toulmin model of reasoning**.

logos Rational or logical proofs.

inductive reasoning
A form of reasoning that begins with specific instances and forms general conclusions based on them.

deductive reasoning
A form of reasoning in which a general premise followed by a specific claim establishes a conclusion.

Toulmin model of reasoning A representation of effective reasoning that includes five components: claim, grounds (evidence), warrant (link between grounds and claim), qualifier, and rebuttal.

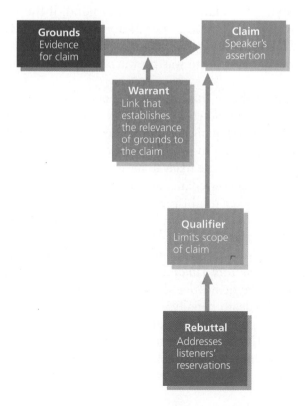

FIGURE 16.2
The Toulmin Model of Reasoning

The first component of Toulmin's model is the **claim,** which is an assertion. For instance, you might advance this claim: "The death penalty does not deter crime."

To give persuasive impact to a claim, you need to provide some *grounds* for believing it. **Grounds** are evidence or data that support the claim. For example, you might cite statistics showing that crime did not diminish when some states enacted the death penalty or that crime did not rise when other states repealed the death penalty.

Consider a second example. You assert, or claim, that global climate change is harming the planet. Grounds, or evidence, to support that claim might include statistics to document the occurrence of global climate change, detailed examples of people whose lives have been negatively affected by changes in the earth's temperature, the testimony of credible scientists, and photos that show changes over time. All these kinds of evidence support your claim that global climate change harms the planet.

Grounds are necessary to support claims. However, they aren't sufficient; the grounds must be justified. That justification is a **warrant**—an explanation of the relevance of the grounds to the claim. You've probably heard the word *warrant* in connection with law enforcement. If a police officer wants to search the home of Pat Brown, the officer must obtain a search warrant from a judge. The officer shows the judge evidence suggesting that Brown has engaged in criminal activity. If the judge agrees that the evidence links Brown to criminal activity, a search warrant is issued. However, if the judge thinks the evidence is insufficient to link Brown to criminal activity, a warrant is not issued. Warrants operate the same way in persuasive speaking. If listeners perceive your evidence as relevant to and supportive of the claim, they're likely to believe your claim.

Let's return to the example of a speech against the death penalty. To support your claim that the death penalty does not deter crime, you provide statistics showing that crime rates did not increase when certain states repealed the death penalty. If the statistics were compiled by the Department of Justice, your listeners may perceive them as justifying the claim. On the other hand, if the statistics were compiled by an organization that opposes the death penalty, your listeners might perceive the source of the evidence as biased and therefore untrustworthy. In that case, listeners might decide that there was no warrant to justify linking the evidence to the claim.

A **qualifier** is a word or phrase that limits the scope of your claim. "Everyone can be rehabilitated" is a very broad claim—so broad that it is difficult to support. A more qualified claim would be qualified: "Some people who commit crimes can be rehabilitated." Finally, Toulmin's model includes **rebuttal,** which anticipates and addresses reservations that listeners are likely to have about claims. Speakers demonstrate respect for listeners by acknowledging and addressing their reservations.

In our example, the speaker might realize that listeners could say to themselves, "The death penalty may not deter all crimes, but it deters serious crimes like homicide." If the speaker has reason to think listeners may resist the claim on this basis, the speaker would offer a rebuttal to the reservation. It would be effective for the speaker to cite the *New York Times* 2012 investigative report that shows that since 1976, states without the death penalty have had homicide rates no higher than those of states with the death penalty.

Careful reasoning and good evidence allow you to offer logical appeals that are sound, effective, and ethical. Later in this chapter, we'll discuss some of the most common kinds of logical fallacies so that you can avoid them when you make persuasive presentations.

Review It!

Elements of Toulmin Model:
- Claim
- Grounds
- Warrant
- Qualifier
- Rebuttal

Review It!

Forms of Proof:
- Ethos
- Pathos
- Logos

---

claim An assertion. A claim advanced in speaking requires grounds (evidence) and warrants (links between evidence and claims).

grounds Evidence that supports claims in a speech.

warrant A justification for grounds (evidence) and claims in persuasive speaking.

qualifier A word or phrase that limits the scope of a claim. Common qualifiers are *most, usually,* and *in general.*

rebuttal A response to listeners' reservations about a claim made by a speaker.

Building Credibility

We've noted that the three forms of proof—ethos, pathos, and logos—are the bases of effective persuasive speaking. Now, we want to consider more closely the key issue of speaker credibility.

Understanding Credibility

A speaker earns **credibility** by convincing listeners that he or she has integrity and goodwill toward them and can be trusted. Notice that credibility is tied to listeners' perceptions of a speaker. This means that credibility doesn't reside in the speaker. Instead, listeners confer or withhold it.

> **SOYANA** *The greatest teacher I ever had taught a class in government policies and practices. Before coming to campus, he had been an adviser to three presidents. He had held a lot of different offices in government, so what he was teaching us was backed up by personal experience. Everything he said had so much more weight than what I hear from professors who've never had any practical experience.*

Credibility arises from the three pillars of persuasion: ethos, pathos, and logos. Listeners are likely to find speakers credible if they demonstrate their personal integrity, establish emotional meaning for their topics, and present ideas logically and with good evidence.

Types of Credibility

Credibility is not static; it can change in the course of communication (Figure 16.3). Have you ever attended a public speech by someone you respected greatly and found the presentation disappointing? Did you think less of the speaker after the speech

credibility The perception that a person is informed and trustworthy. Listeners confer it, or refuse to confer it, on speakers.

Communication Highlight — Goodwill and Credibility

More than 2,000 years ago, the Greek rhetorician Aristotle wrote that a speaker's credibility depended on listeners' perceptions of the speaker's intelligence, character, and goodwill. Since Aristotle's time, research has established empirical support for strong links between credibility and perceived intelligence and character. But what about goodwill?

In a 1999 investigation, Jim McCroskey and Jason Teven found that perceived goodwill is positively linked to perceptions of likableness and believability. In other words, when listeners think a speaker cares about them and has ethical intentions toward them, they are likely to trust and like the speaker. The practical implication of this study is that speakers who want to be judged credible should establish goodwill toward listeners.

According to McCroskey and Teven (1999), goodwill tends to be established in three ways: showing understanding of listeners' ideas, feelings, and needs; demonstrating empathy, or identification, with listeners' feelings; and being responsive to listeners while speaking.

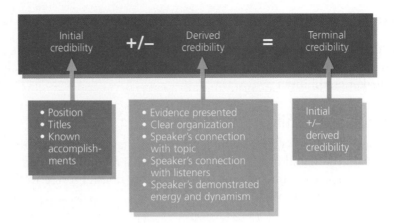

FIGURE 16.3
Developing Credibility

initial credibility The expertise and trustworthiness that listeners attribute to a speaker before a presentation begins. Initial credibility is based on the speaker's titles, positions, experiences, or achievements known to listeners before they hear the speech.

derived credibility The expertise and trustworthiness that listeners attribute to a speaker as a result of how the speaker communicates during a presentation.

than before it? Have you ever gone to a presentation without knowing much about the speaker and found it so impressive that you changed an attitude or behavior? If so, then you know that credibility can increase or decrease as a result of a speech.

Developing Credibility

Initial Credibility   Some speakers have high **initial credibility,** which is the expertise and trustworthiness recognized by listeners before a presentation begins. Initial credibility is based on titles, positions, experiences, or achievements that are known to listeners before they hear a speech. For example, most listeners would grant the Secretary of State high credibility on foreign affairs.

Derived Credibility   In addition to initial credibility, speakers may also gain **derived credibility,** which is the expertise and trustworthiness that listeners confer on speakers as a result of how speakers communicate during presentations. Speakers earn derived credibility by demonstrating care for listeners, by organizing ideas clearly

Effective speakers increase credibility in the course of presenting a speech.

and logically, by including convincing and emotionally compelling evidence, and by speaking dynamically. Speakers who are not well known tend not to have high initial credibility, so they must derive credibility from the quality of their presentations.

Terminal Credibility   The credibility of speaker at the end of a presentation is terminal credibility. It is the cumulative expertise, goodwill, and trustworthiness listeners attribute to a speaker—a combination of initial and derived credibility. Terminal credibility may be greater or less than initial credibility, depending on how effectively a speaker has communicated.

Enhancing Credibility

As you plan, develop, and present a persuasive speech, you should aim to earn credibility. Below are ways to establish initial credibility and build derived and terminal credibility:

- State your qualifications for speaking on this topic: experiences you have had, research you have conducted.

- Show listeners that you care about them; make the speech relevant to their welfare.

- Appeal to listeners' emotions, but don't alienate or overwhelm listeners with excessively dramatic appeals.

- Use effective, ethical supporting materials.

- Communicate both verbally and nonverbally that you care about the topic and are involved with it.

Organizing Speeches for Persuasive Impact

In Chapter 14, we discussed ways to organize speeches. The principles you learned in that chapter apply to persuasive speaking:

- Your introduction should capture listeners' attention, provide a clear thesis statement, establish your credibility, and preview your speech.

- Your conclusion should summarize main points and end with a strong closing statement.

- You should provide internal summaries of main points.

- You should provide smooth transitions between the parts of your speech.

- The body of your speech should be organized to reinforce your thesis and show listeners how your ideas cohere.

To build on these general principles for organizing speeches, we want to focus on special organizational concerns relevant to persuasive speaking. We will discuss two topics: the motivated sequence pattern, which is particularly well adapted to persuasive goals, and the relative merits of one-sided and two-sided presentations.

The Motivated Sequence Pattern

Any of the organizational patterns that we discussed in Chapter 14 can be used to structure persuasive speeches. Table 16.3 shows how each of the seven patterns we discussed could support a persuasive thesis.

Review It!

Types of Credibility:
- Initial
- Derived
- Terminal

terminal credibility
The cumulative expertise and trustworthiness listeners attribute to a speaker as a result of the speaker's initial and derived credibility; may be greater or less than initial credibility, depending on how effectively a speaker communicates.

Table 16.3	Organizing for Persuasion

Lloyd Bennett works for a public relations firm that wants to convince Casual Cruise Lines to become a client. Lloyd could use any of the eight basic organizational patterns to structure his speech to persuade the cruise line to hire his firm.

PATTERN	THESIS AND MAIN POINTS
Time	Our firm can move Casual Cruise Lines into the future. I. Originally, Casual Cruise Lines attracted customers whose average age was 58 years. II. In recent years, that customer base has shrunk. III. To thrive in the years ahead, Casual Cruise Lines needs to appeal to younger customers.
Spatial	Our proposal focuses on redesigning the space on cruise ships to appeal to the 30- to 45-year-old market. I. In the staterooms, we propose replacing the conventional seafaring motif with abstract, modernistic art. II. In the public area of the lower deck, we propose replacing the current coffee shops with sushi and espresso bars and adding fitness rooms. III. On the upper deck, we propose building hot tubs beside the pool.
Topical	Our firm has the most experience advertising cruise lines and the most innovative staff. I. Our firm has increased revenues for three other cruise lines. II. Our firm has won more awards for innovation and creativity than the other firms Casual Cruise Lines is considering for this account.
Star	Let's consider how younger customers might be attracted if we revamped ship décor, activities, and cuisine. I. Younger customers like modern décor. II. Younger customers want youthful activities. III. Younger customers want trendy food.
Comparative	Casual Cruise Lines needs to adapt to younger customers whose needs and interests differ from those of older customers. I. We recommend 3-, 5-, and 7-day cruises because, although older people have the time for extended cruises, 30- to 45-year-olds can usually spare only a week or less at a time. II. Casual Cruise Lines should get rid of bingo and shuffleboard and add dancing and nightclubs, which are favorite leisure activities of 30- to 45-year-olds. III. We recommend adding 24-hour espresso bars and onboard fitness rooms to meet the preferences of 30- to 45-year-olds.
Problem–solution	We have a solution to Casual Cruise Lines' inability to attract younger customers. I. Casual Cruise Lines hasn't been able to get a substantial share of the lucrative 30- to 45-year-old market. II. Our advertising campaign specifically targets this market.

Table 16.3	Organizing for Persuasion (*Continued*)
Cause–effect	The advertising campaign we propose will attract young, affluent customers by appealing to their interests and lifestyles. I. Our proposal's emphasis on luxury features of the cruise caters to this market's appreciation of extravagance. II. Our proposal to feature adults-only cruises caters to this market's demonstrated preferences. III. Our proposal to offer 2-day to 4-day cruises meets this market's interest in long weekend getaways.

In addition to the patterns we have already discussed, there is an eighth structure that can be highly effective in persuasive speaking: the **motivated sequence pattern** (Monroe, 1935). It has proven quite effective in diverse communication situations (Gronbeck, McKerrow, Ehninger, & Monroe, 1994; Jaffe, 2007). The primary reason for the effectiveness of the motivated sequence pattern is that it follows a natural pattern of human thought by gaining listeners' attention, demonstrating a need, offering a solution, and then helping them visualize and act on the solution. This pattern progressively increases listeners' motivation and personal involvement with a problem and its solution. The motivated sequence pattern includes five sequential steps.

In the first step, listeners' attention is drawn to the subject. Here, a speaker makes a dramatic opening statement (e.g., "Imagine this campus with no trees whatsoever"), shows the personal relevance of the topic (e.g., "The air you are breathing right now exists only because we have trees"), or otherwise captures listeners' attention.

The second step establishes need with evidence and reasoning that a real and serious problem exists (e.g., "Acid rain is slowly but surely destroying the trees on our planet"). Next is the satisfaction step, in which a speaker recommends a solution (e.g., "Stronger environmental regulations and individual efforts to use environmentally safe products can protect trees and thus the oxygen we breathe"). The fourth step, visualization, increases listeners' commitment to the solution identified in the satisfaction step by helping them imagine the results that would follow from adopting the recommended solution (e.g., "You will have ample air to breathe, and so will your children and grandchildren. Moreover, we'll all have the beauty of trees to enrich our lives").

Outline Builder, accessed through MindTap, includes extensive prompts and a clear framework for organizing and developing speeches that incorporate a variety of persuasive strategies.

Finally, speakers move to the action step, which involves a direct appeal for concrete action on the part of listeners (e.g., "Refuse to buy or use any aerosol products," "Sign this petition that I am sending to our senators in Washington, D.C."). The action step calls on listeners to take action to bring about the solution the speaker helped them visualize.

motivated sequence pattern A pattern for organizing persuasive speeches that consists of five steps: attention, need, satisfaction, visualization, and action.

> **VELMA** *I've heard a lot of speeches on discrimination, but the most effective I ever heard was Cindy's in class last week. Other speeches I've heard focused on the idea that discrimination is wrong, but that's something I already believe, so they weren't helpful. Cindy, on the other hand, told me how to do something about discrimination. She showed me how I could act on what I believe.*

SHARPEN YOUR SKILL

At the end of this chapter, refer to the Sharpen Your Skill feature, Using the Motivated Sequence Pattern, to apply concepts from Chapter 16.

Review It!

Steps in Motivated Sequence:
- Attention
- Need
- Satisfaction
- Visualization
- Action

Velma's commentary explains why the motivated sequence pattern is especially suited to persuasive speaking: It goes beyond identifying a problem and recommending a solution. In addition, it intensifies listeners' desire for a solution by helping them visualize what it would mean and gains their active commitment to being part of the solution. When listeners become personally involved with an idea and with taking action, they are more enduringly committed. Go to the book's online resources for this chapter to read tips and see a sample speech using the motivated sequence patterns.

One-Sided and Two-Sided Presentations

Perhaps you are wondering whether it's more effective to present only your own point of view or both sides of an issue in a persuasive speech. Research tells us that it depends on the particular audience a speaker addresses, which reminds us again that audience analysis and adaptation are critical to effective public speaking. Specifically, deciding whether to present one or both sides of an issue depend on the particular listeners' expectations, attitudes, and knowledge.

Listeners' Expectations   As we've noted before, effective speakers always try to learn what listeners expect so they don't fail to meet expectations. In educational settings, listeners are likely to expect speakers to discuss more than one side of an issue (Lasch, 1990). On the other hand, at campaign rallies, candidates are generally expected to present only their own views. Expectations may also be shaped by prespeech publicity. Imagine that you decide to attend a speech after seeing a flyer for a presentation on the pros and cons of requiring students to purchase meal plans. You might be irritated if the speaker presented only the pros or only the cons of the proposed requirement.

Listeners' Attitudes   It makes a difference whether listeners are likely to be favorably disposed toward your ideas (Griffin, 2015). If they already favor your position, you may not need to discuss alternative positions in depth. However, if listeners favor a position different from yours, then it's essential to acknowledge and deal with their views. If your listeners oppose what you propose, it's unlikely that you will persuade them to abandon their position and adopt yours. With an audience hostile to your views, it's more reasonable to try to lessen their hostility to your ideas or to diminish the strength of their commitment to their present position (Trenholm, 1991).

Failure to consider listeners' opposing ideas diminishes a speaker's credibility because listeners may assume that the speaker either is uninformed about another side or is informed but trying to manipulate them by not discussing it. Either assumption lessens credibility. Speakers have an ethical responsibility to give respectful consideration to listeners' ideas and positions. Doing so encourages reciprocal respect from listeners for the ideas you present. R. J.'s commentary illustrates this.

R. J.   *In my ROTC unit, there's a lot of bad will toward the idea of gays in the military. Some of the guys have really strong feelings against it, so I was interested in what would happen at a required seminar last week with a guest speaker who was arguing that gays should be allowed in the services. He was really good! He spent the first 10 minutes talking about all of the concerns, fears, and reasons why officers and enlisted personnel disapprove of having gays in the military, and he showed a lot of respect for those reasons. Then he presented his own ideas and showed how they answered most of the concerns people had. I won't say everyone was persuaded 100% that gays should be allowed in, but I will say he managed to get a full hearing with a group that I thought would just turn him off from the word go. Since he talked to us, I've heard some of the guys saying that maybe gays wouldn't be a problem.*

Listeners' Knowledge   What an audience already knows or believes about a topic should influence decisions on whether to present one or more sides of an issue. Listeners who are well informed about a topic are likely to be aware of more than one side, so your credibility will be enhanced if you include all sides in your presentation (Jackson & Allen, 1990). Also, highly educated listeners tend to realize that most issues have more than one side, so they may be suspicious of speakers who present only one point of view.

In some instances, speakers know that later on listeners will be exposed to *counterarguments*—arguments that oppose those of a speaker. In such cases, it's advisable to inoculate listeners. **Inoculation** in persuasion is similar to inoculation in medicine. Vaccines give us limited exposure to diseases so that we won't contract them later. Similarly, persuasive inoculation "immunizes" listeners in advance against opposing ideas and arguments they may encounter in the future. If listeners later hear the other side, they have some resistance to arguments that oppose your position (Kiesler & Kiesler, 1971). For example, in political campaigns, candidates often make statements such as this: "Now, my opponent will tell you that we don't need to raise taxes, but I want to show you why that's wrong." By identifying and rebutting the opposing candidate's ideas in advance, the speaker inoculates listeners against an opponent's ideas (Allen et al., 1990).

There is no quick and easy formula for deciding whether to present one-sided or two-sided discussions of a topic. Like most aspects of public speaking, this decision involves judgment on the speaker's part. That judgment should be informed by ethical considerations of what listeners have a right to know and what content is necessary to represent the issues fairly. In addition, judgments of whether to present more than one side should take into account listeners' expectations, attitudes, and knowledge and the likelihood that listeners have been or will be exposed to opposing arguments.

SHARPEN YOUR SKILL

At the end of this chapter, refer to the Sharpen Your Skill feature, Deciding Whether to Present One or Two Sides, to apply concepts from Chapter 16.

Digital Media and Persuasive Speaking

In prior chapters, we have noted many ways that digital media assist people who are preparing for and presenting public speeches. Persuasive speakers, like other speakers, may rely on digital media to conduct research, find experts and verify their qualifications, and conduct interviews and surveys.

MindTap includes tools that can help you prepare an effective persuasive speech. You will find a tool, Outline Builder for organizing your speech and another tool, Practice and Present, for uploading practice deliveries that you can review and critique.

Guidelines for Effective Persuasive Speeches

In this chapter, we've already discussed some guidelines for effective persuasive speaking. For instance, we discussed the importance of developing a speech that includes the three pillars of persuasion: ethos, pathos, and logos. We also emphasized the importance of speaker credibility, and we identified specific ways to build yours when you speak. We extended our previous discussion of organizing speeches to discuss the motivated sequence pattern and the merits of presenting one or two sides of arguments. In addition to these guidelines, three other principles are important for effective persuasive speaking.

Create Common Ground with Listeners

In any communication context, common ground is important. That general principle has heightened importance in persuasive speaking. A persuasive speaker tries

inoculation "Immunization" of listeners to opposing ideas and arguments that they may later encounter.

to move listeners to a point of view or action. It makes sense that they will be more likely to move with the speaker if they perceive some common ground with him or her. In other words, speakers seek to create with listeners a sense of **identification**, which is a recognition of commonalities (Burke, 1950). Listeners may think, "If we share all of these values and concerns, then maybe I should rethink my position on this one issue we disagree on."

Effective persuasive speakers seek out similarities between themselves and their listeners and bring those similarities into listeners' awareness. A few years ago, a student of mine wanted to persuade his listeners that fraternities are positive influences on members' lives. From polling students on campus, Steve knew that many held negative stereotypes of "frat men." He reasoned that most of his listeners, who did not belong to Greek groups, would be likely to view him both negatively and as different from them. This is how he established common ground in opening his speech:

> You've probably heard a lot of stories about wild fraternity parties and "frat men" who spend most of their time drinking, partying, and harassing pledges. I confess, I've done all of that as a brother in Delta Sigma Phi. I've also spent every Sunday for the last semester volunteering in the Big Brother Program that helps underprivileged kids in the city. And I've built friendships with brothers that will last my entire life. Like many of you, I felt a little lost when I first came to this campus. I wanted to find a place where I belonged at college. Like you, I want to know people and be involved with projects that help me grow as a person. For me, being in a fraternity has done that.

This is an effective opening. Steve began by showing listeners that he realized they might hold some negative views of fraternity men. He went further and acknowledged that he personally fit some of those stereotypes. But then Steve challenged the adequacy of the stereotypes by offering some information that didn't fit with them. Having recognized and challenged stereotypes his listeners were likely to hold, Steve then began to create common ground. Most of his listeners could remember feeling lost when they first came to college. Most of them could identify with wanting to belong and to grow as people. Steve's opening successfully identified similarities between himself and his listeners, so they were open to considering his argument that fraternities are valuable.

Adapt to Listeners

A good persuasive speech is not designed for just anyone. Instead, it is adapted to specific listeners' knowledge, attitudes, motives, experiences, values, and expectations. As a speaker, your job is to apply what you learn about your listeners as you develop and present your speech.

In 1998, Raymond W. Smith, chairperson of Bell Atlantic, spoke about hate speech on the Internet. Smith spoke at the Simon Wiesenthal Center, which is dedicated to human rights (Smith, 1998). Although Smith spoke against censoring hate speech on the Internet, he realized that his largely Jewish listeners had acute knowledge of the dangers of hate speech. In his opening remarks Smith said,

> Neo-Nazis and extremists of every political stripe who once terrorized people in the dead of night with burning crosses and painted swastikas are now sneaking up on the public—especially our kids—through the World Wide Web.

identification The recognition and enlargement of common ground between communicators.

Although Smith went on to argue against censorship, he let his listeners know that he was well aware of hate speech and the harms it can cause. Within his speech, Smith further adapted to his listeners by quoting Jewish leaders, who had high credibility with listeners.

Knowing that many of his listeners favored censorship, Smith presented a two-sided speech. He began by considering the arguments of those who favor censorship, treating them thoroughly and respectfully. He then turned to the other side (the one he favored): not censoring hate speech on the Internet. Smith argued that censorship will not get to the source of the problem, which is hate. Instead, he said the solution is to teach tolerance and respect. In making this argument, Smith adapted to his listeners at the Wiesenthal Center by saying,

> *While cyberhate cannot be mandated or censored out of existence, it can be countered by creating hundreds of chat lines, home pages, bulletin boards, and websites dedicated to social justice, tolerance, and equality for all people. . . . Moral leadership can have a tremendous impact. Quite simply, we need more Simon Wiesenthal Centers.*

To adapt to his listeners, Smith acknowledged their cultural history, quoted authorities they respected, and thoughtfully considered the argument for censorship. Therefore, his listeners were then willing to give an equally thoughtful hearing to Smith's argument against censorship.

Avoid Fallacious Reasoning

A **fallacy** is an error in reasoning. Fallacies present false, or flawed, logic, which renders them ineffective with educated or thoughtful audiences. To be effective and ethical, you should avoid using fallacies in your speeches. To be a critical listener, you should be able to recognize fallacies used by others. We'll discuss eight of the most common fallacies in reasoning.

fallacy An error in reasoning.

Ethical speakers do not engage in fallacious reasoning.

Cultura Creative/Alamy Stock Photo

***Ad Hominem* Arguments**   In Latin, the word *ad* means "to," and *hominem* means "human being." Thus, *ad hominem* arguments are ones that go to the person instead of the idea. It is not ethical to argue for your point of view by attacking the integrity of someone who has taken a stand opposing yours.

"You can't trust what George Boxwood says about the importance of a strong military. After all, he never served a day in the military." Although it may be true that Boxwood didn't serve in the military, that doesn't necessarily discredit his argument about the importance of a strong military. Boxwood may have researched the topic vigorously, interviewed military personnel, and studied historical effects of strong and weak military forces. Boxwood's own service—or lack thereof—is not directly relevant to the quality of his argument for a strong military. Unethical speakers sometimes try to undercut people whose positions oppose their own by attacking the people, not the arguments. Critical listeners recognize this fallacy and distrust speakers who engage in it.

Post Hoc, Ergo Propter Hoc   *Post hoc, ergo propter hoc* is a Latin phrase meaning "after this, therefore because of this." Sometimes when one thing follows another, we mistakenly think the first thing caused the second. Unethical speakers sometimes try to persuade us to think that a coincidental sequence is causal. For instance, the U.S. economy faltered and verged on recession after George W. Bush became president. Does that mean Bush and his administration caused the economic slowdown? Not necessarily. To support the claim that Bush caused the economic slowdown, a speaker would need to demonstrate that policies implemented by Bush hurt the economy.

The Bandwagon Appeal   When I was a child, I often tried to persuade my parents that I should be allowed to do something because all of my friends were doing it. Invariably, my parents rejected that reason and replied, "If all of your friends jumped off the roof, would you?" At the time, that answer exasperated me. But my parents were right. They rejected the bandwagon appeal, which argues that because most people believe or act a particular way, you should too. Widely held attitudes are not necessarily correct, as Galileo proved.

Slippery Slope   The slippery slope fallacy claims that once we take the first step, more and more steps inevitably will follow until some unacceptable consequence results. For example, an unethical speaker who wanted to argue against a proposal to restrict logging in a protected environmental area might state, "Restricting logging is only the first step. Next, the environmentalists are likely to want to prohibit any timber cutting. Pretty soon, we won't be able to build homes or furniture." The idea that we won't have lumber to build homes and furniture is extreme. It has little to do with the question of whether we should restrict logging in one particular area.

Hasty Generalization   A hasty generalization is a broad claim based on insufficient evidence. It is unethical to assert a broad claim when you have only anecdotal or isolated evidence or instances. Consider two examples of hasty generalizations based on inadequate data:

- Three congressional representatives have had affairs. Therefore, members of Congress are adulterers.

- An environmental group illegally blocked loggers and workers at a nuclear plant. Therefore, environmentalists are radicals who take the law into their own hands.

In each case, the conclusion is based on limited evidence. In each case, the conclusion is hasty and fallacious.

***ad hominem* arguments**
Arguments that attack the integrity of the person instead of the person's ideas.

post hoc, ergo propter hoc
Latin phrase meaning "After this, therefore because of this." The fallacy of suggesting or assuming that because event B follows event A, event A has therefore caused event B.

bandwagon appeal The fallacious argument that because many people believe or act in a certain way, everyone should.

slippery slope The fallacy of suggesting or assuming that once a certain step is taken, other steps will inevitably follow that will lead to some unacceptable consequence.

hasty generalization
A broad claim based on too few examples or insufficient evidence.

Red Herring Argument   Years ago, fox hunters sometimes dragged a dead herring across the trail of a fox to see whether the dogs would be diverted (Gass, 1999). They were trying to train the dogs not to let the smell of the herring deflect them from hunting the fox. Speakers who try to deflect listeners from relevant issues engage in **red herring arguments.** They say something that is irrelevant to their topic or that doesn't really respond to a listener's question. The point is to divert the listener from something the speaker can't or doesn't want to address.

Either–Or Logic   What is wrong with the following statement: "Either abolish fraternities on our campus or accept the fact that this is a party school where drinking is more important than learning." The fallacy in this statement is that it implies there are only two options: either get rid of fraternities altogether or allow partying to eclipse academics. Are there no other alternatives? In most instances, **either–or logic** is simplistic and fallacious.

Reliance on the Halo Effect   The **halo effect** occurs when we generalize a person's authority or expertise in a particular area to other areas that are irrelevant to the person's experience and knowledge. It is fallacious to think that because a person is knowledgeable on particular topics, he or she is knowledgeable on all topics. William Shatner, who starred in *Star Trek*, encourages us to use priceline.com. Well-known people appear in the mustache advertisements promoting milk. Are any of these people experts on the products they are urging us to buy and use?

To be effective and ethical, persuasive speakers should avoid fallacies in reasoning (Table 16.4). Likewise, effective critical listeners should be able to detect fallacies in reasoning and to resist being persuaded by them.

red herring argument An argument that is irrelevant to the topic; an attempt to divert attention from something the arguer can't or doesn't want to address.

either–or logic The fallacy of suggesting or assuming that only two options or courses of action exist when in fact there may be more.

halo effect The tendency to assume that an expert in one area is also an expert in other unrelated areas.

Table 16.4	Fallacies in Reasoning
Ad hominem attack	You can't believe what Jane Smith says about voting because she doesn't vote.
Post hoc, ergo propter hoc	The new flextime policy is ineffective because more people have been late getting to work since it went into effect.
Bandwagon appeal	You should be in favor of the new campus meal plan because most students are.
Slippery slope	If we allow students to play a role in decisions about hiring and tenure of faculty, pretty soon students will be running the whole school.
Hasty generalization	People should not be allowed to own Rottweilers because there have been three instances of Rottweilers attacking children.
Either–or	Tenure should be either abolished or kept exactly as it is.
Red herring argument	People who own Rottweilers should own cats instead. Let me tell you why cats are ideal pets.
Reliance on the halo effect	World-famous actor Richard Connery says that we should not restrict people's right to own firearms.

Chapter Summary

This chapter focused on persuasive speaking. After noting the many situations in which persuasive speaking occurs, we identified ethos, pathos, and logos and the cornerstones of effective persuasion, and we highlighted ways in which speakers can incorporate each into presentations. Extending this, we discussed credibility, which is especially important in persuasive speaking. We identified three types of credibility—initial, derived, and terminal—and discussed ways in which speakers can build their credibility during the process of planning, developing, and presenting persuasive speeches. The next section of the chapter reviewed general organizational principles and highlighted organizational concerns that are particularly relevant to persuasive speaking.

We introduced the motivated sequence pattern, which can be powerful in moving listeners to accept and act on persuasive appeals. We also discussed the merits of one-sided and two-sided presentations, and we identified criteria for choosing the one that will be most effective in particular situations and with particular listeners.

The last section of the chapter provided guidelines for persuasive speaking. The first is to build common ground between a speaker and a listener. The second is to adapt to particular listeners by tailoring a persuasive speech to their expectations, knowledge, experiences, motives, values, and attitudes. The third is to avoid fallacies in reasoning, which are usually ineffective and always unethical.

MindTap°

Experiencing Communication in Our Lives

CASE STUDY: Persuasive Speech: No Child Left Behind: Addressing the School Dropout Rate Among Latinos

Apply what you've learned in this chapter by analyzing the following case study, using the accompanying questions as a guide. These questions and a video of the case study are also available online with your MindTap Speech for *Communication in Our Lives*.

Dana gave this speech in an introductory public speaking class. The assignment was to give a 4- to 6-minute speech, with a minimum of four sources cited. Students were also asked to create a preparation outline that included a Works Cited section.

I'll begin with a story from the *Santa Fe New Mexican* newspaper about a young woman named Mabel Arellanes. After becoming pregnant and dropping out of school at the age of 16 years, Mabel has reenrolled in high school and is now the junior class president. Although her dynamic change in attitude toward education has led her to the hope of becoming a lawyer, Mabel's story is not representative of the current trends among other Latinos. I have been conducting extensive research on trends in the socioeconomic status, graduation rates, and the population of Latinos in the United States. Today, I will discuss the problem of the Latino dropout rate from high school and college, as well as provide a solution for addressing this intensifying issue. Let me begin by discussing the problem.

The dropout rate among Latinos in secondary schools and colleges must be addressed. Why? Because the dropout rate is simply excessive. Statistics and first-hand accounts attest to this fact. According to the *News and Observer*, 1 in 12 Latino students dropped out of high school in North Carolina during the 2003–2004 school year, but this statistic does not account for the 47.5% of Latino students who have not graduated in the four years since the beginning of the 1999–2000 academic year. Gamaliel Fuentes, who dropped out of school at the age of 15 years, said, "We have no money; that's why I dropped out of school. [My father] asked me [to stay in school], but I decided. Now, if I could go back in time, I would stay still in school." The tendency for Latinos to drop out is triggered by their generally low socioeconomic status and a lack of family support. The *Hispanic Outlook in Higher Education* explains that students coming from families of lower socioeconomic status are less likely to succeed in college because high schools do not prepare them well. In addition, Latino families expect their teens and young adults to contribute to the family's economic needs, and work schedules often conflict with studies.

Next, I will discuss the importance of addressing the Latino dropout rate. Addressing the dropout rate will keep Latinos from remaining at a generally low economic status. It is no secret that income is heavily dependent on education level. According to the *Daily Evergreen* newspaper, a person with a bachelor's degree is likely to earn almost one million dollars more over their course of their lifetime than someone with no college education. While a census report in the *San Antonio Express-News* found that Latinos earned merely 6.2% of bachelor's degrees awarded in 2001, the U.S. Census Bureau found that Latinos made up 12% of the national population in 2000 and 13.3% in 2002. In her essay, "Canto, Locura, y Poesia," Olivia Castellano, Latina professor at California State University, writes, "[Latinos] carry a deeply ingrained sense of inferiority, a firm conviction that they are not worthy of success." Ultimately, all who hold the belief that our country is the "land of opportunity" are affected by the Latino dropout rate. Again, referencing the 2001 findings of the U.S. Census Bureau, 2 out of every 10 Hispanics live below the poverty line, while only one out of every four earned a yearly salary of $35,000 or more. Comparatively, around 50% of non-Hispanic whites earned $35,000 or more that year. These figures are far from exemplifying opportunity for Latinos.

What will happen if the problem is not solved? Since the percentage of Latinos in our population is still climbing, ignoring this issue will lead to a greater gap between the life of the typical American and the life of the Latino American. As I proceed to discuss the solutions for this problem, are you beginning to sense the urgency of this situation?

To solve the problem of a high dropout rate, we must fund teacher sensitivity training programs that help Latinos succeed in education, and Latinos must change their perspective on the importance of education and their ability to succeed. Let me first address teacher sensitivity training. Programs that educate teachers about Latino culture and beliefs and that help Latino students succeed in education will have the most impact on the dropout rate. Properly educated teachers will become aware of how they are able to meet the needs of Latino students. For example, the *Santa Fe New Mexican* reported on the success of a program called AVID, which boasts a 95% college entrance rate among its Latino students. This solution, which can be implemented at the national, state, and local levels, is dependent on increased funding and the efforts of educators with experience in Latino culture. Increased funding will help reform educational budgets for Latino communities and fund college success programs like AVID. This solution also requires the collective efforts of highly knowledgeable professionals with experience in education and in Latino culture who can train other educators.

Given proper attention and execution, the plan to address the Latino dropout rate will help the dropout rate begin to fall and will instill pride in the Latino community. Although it will take at least a decade before results are fully apparent, perhaps even a generation, ideally the plan will result in an increase in Latinos earning bachelor's, master's, and doctoral degrees. The sense of accomplishment gained by furthering education will change the typical Latino mindset regarding education and instill an overall sense of pride in the U.S. Latino community.

In summary, today I have discussed the problem of high dropout rate among Latinos, and I have discussed a possible solution for addressing the issue. Hopefully, you can clearly see that the high Latino dropout rate is an issue of great concern, one that requires prompt and thorough attention.

QUESTIONS FOR ANALYSIS AND DISCUSSION

1. Did Dana provide a strong introduction with an attention device, a clear thesis, and a clear preview?

2. Are the sources of evidence credible? Why or why not? Is there any reason to suspect that the sources are biased?

3. What other kinds of evidence might Dana have used to strengthen the persuasive impact of her message?

4. Did Dana's speech reflect awareness of ethos, pathos, and logos?

5. How did Dana adapt the message to listeners who were 19- to 24-year-old college students? Can you think of additional ways she might have adapted this message to these particular listeners?

MindTap

Use flashcards to learn key concepts and take a quiz to test your knowledge.

Key Concepts

ad hominem arguments
bandwagon appeal
claim
credibility
deductive reasoning
derived credibility
either–or logic
ethos
fallacy
grounds
halo effect

hasty generalization
identification
inductive reasoning
initial credibility
inoculation
logos
motivated sequence
    pattern
pathos
persuasive speech

post hoc, ergo propter hoc
qualifier
rebuttal
red herring argument
slippery slope
terminal credibility
Toulmin model of
    reasoning
warrant

Sharpen Your Skill

1. Using the Motivated Sequence Pattern

Think about how you might organize a speech using the motivated sequence pattern. Write a thesis and five main points for a motivated sequence appeal.

Thesis _____

1. Attention: _____

2. Need: _____

3. Satisfaction: _____

4. Visualization: _____

5. Action: _____

2. Deciding Whether to Present One or Two Sides

Apply what you have learned to decide whether you should present one or two sides in your persuasive speech.

1. Are your listeners likely to expect to hear more than one side of the issue?

   A. How much education do they have? _____

   B. Has there been any prespeech publicity? _____

   C. Is there any reason to think that listeners do or do not care about hearing both sides? _____

2. What are your listeners' attitudes toward your topic? _____

   A. Do they have a position on the topic? If so, is it the same as yours?

   _____

   B. How strongly do listeners hold their opinions on the topic?

   _____

3. What level of knowledge about the topic do your listeners have?

   _____

   A. Do they know about more than one side of the issues?

   _____

   B. How much information about the topic have they already gained?

   _____

4. Are your listeners likely to hear counterarguments after your speech?

   _____

For Further Reflection and Discussion

1. Reread this chapter's discussion of one-sided and two-sided persuasive speeches. When is it ethical to present only one side of a topic? When is it unethical? In answering this question, remember that ethical considerations are not necessarily the same as strategic ones. A speaker who uses unethical arguments or evidence might be effective in convincing listeners to think or do something.

2. Go to the book's online resources for this chapter to see and hear famous speeches.

3. Go to the book's online resources for this chapter to read an article on the importance of skill in persuasive speaking for top-level positions in business.

4. Apply the principles of persuasive speaking to prepare a 1-minute "elevator speech," which we mentioned in Chapter 12.

5. Ted Talks offer many examples of persuasive speeches that employ different delivery styles. Go to www.Ted.com to find speeches on topics that interest you or go to the book's online resources for this chapter to view two examples of persuasive speeches.

Anton Gvozdikov/Shutterstock.com

Closing: Pulling Ideas Together

C ommunication is an intricate tapestry woven from the threads of self, others, perceptions, relationships, contexts, culture, climate, listening, and verbal and nonverbal messages. Each thread has its own distinct character, and yet each thread is also woven into the complex, ever-changing tapestry of human communication. We've taken time to discuss each thread in its own right and then explored how it blends with other threads in particular communication situations.

Sometimes a particular thread stands out boldly, as individual threads sometimes do in woven fabric. For instance, the thread of delivery is quite prominent in public speaking, and the thread of listening is less visible. Yet to be effective, speakers must understand and adapt to their listeners because listeners decide how credible a speaker is and how effective public communication can be. Similarly, in personal relationships the thread of climate stands out as particularly important. Yet, the climate we create through our communication is also important in organizational communication and small group work. Thus, even when threads of communication are muted in particular contexts of interaction, they are present and important.

At other times, an individual thread blends so completely with other threads that we don't perceive it as separate from the overall pattern of the tapestry. Organization, for example, is present in interaction between friends as they decide what to talk about and how to sequence the topics. Yet in friends' conversation, the thread of organization is subdued, and other threads, such as sensitive listening, stand out. Similarly, the thread of delivery is subtle in casual conversations, yet our communication with friends is affected by how we articulate our ideas—by vocal force, volume, pace, and other aspects of delivery. The many threads that make up the tapestry of communication vary in intensity and prominence from one point in the tapestry to another, yet all are part of the whole.

To conclude our study of the communication tapestry, let's review what we've discussed and what it means for us. The overall goal of this book is to increase your insight into the ways in which communication is an integral part of our everyday lives.

We launched our journey in Chapter 1, which described the range of human communication and the modern academic field that bears its name. Chapter 2 allowed us to delve into the complicated process of perception so that we could understand how perception, thought, and communication interact. We learned that we seldom, if ever, perceive the full, raw reality around us. Instead, we perceive selectively, noticing only some things and overlooking others. The labels we use to name, classify, and evaluate our perceptions reverberate in our consciousness to shape what we perceive and what it means to us. In fact, most of the time, how we think, feel, and act are based less on objective realities in the external world than on how we label our selective perceptions of it. This is normal, yet it can cause us trouble if we forget that we are responding to our labels, not to the world itself. In Chapter 3, we explored the profound ways in which communication shapes personal identity and, in turn, the ways in which our identities shape how we communicate.

Chapters 4–6 focused on primary forms of communication: listening, verbal communication, and nonverbal behavior. As we considered each topic, we examined ways to improve our personal effectiveness as communicators. Particularly important to our understanding of these topics is the realization that people differ in their styles of listening and their verbal and nonverbal communication. Awareness of these differences helps us understand others on their terms. The principles and skills we discussed in these chapters should serve you well throughout your life as you seek to interact effectively and sensitively with others in personal, social, and professional contexts.

The second part of the book extended the first six chapters by weaving basic communication concepts and skills into contexts of interaction. In Chapter 7, we explored interpersonal communication in general and as it occurs in friendships and romantic relationships. The intimate bonds that grace our lives are communicative achievements because we create and sustain them largely through interaction and the meanings we assign to it. Communication is the lifeblood of intimacy. In dramatic forms, such as declarations of love and disclosure of secrets, and in everyday small talk, it is communication that continually breathes life and meaning into our relationships with others.

We moved to quite a different context in Chapter 8, which examined communication in small groups. There, we learned what types of communication facilitate and hinder effective group discussion and what communication responsibilities accompany effective membership and leadership. We also studied the standard agenda for problem solving, which gives participants an effective method of organizing group discussion.

Chapter 9 focused on organizational communication, with particular emphasis on how interaction among members of an organization creates an overall culture for the organization. The elaborate and fascinating relationships between culture and communication were the focus of Chapter 10. There, we unmasked the subtle

Communication skills are a foundation for effectiveness in personal, professional, and social life.

ways in which communication creates and sustains the beliefs, values, and practices that define cultures and social communities. Equally important, we saw that cultures shape the forms and content of communication by telling us what is and is not important and what are appropriate and inappropriate ways of interacting with others. Understanding differences between cultures and social communities allows us to appreciate the distinct character of each one and to enlarge our own repertoire of communication skills. In Chapter 11, we explored mass communication and social media, which permeate our lives. Here, we focused on ways to develop critical skills that enhance your media literacy.

Part III of this book concentrated on public speaking. From the early stages of planning presentations, to researching and developing evidence, and finally to organizing, outlining, and practicing, public speaking involves skills that most of us already have and use in other communication situations. As is true for all interactions, good public speaking centers on others; the values, interests, knowledge, and beliefs of listeners guide what speakers can and cannot wisely say and how they develop and present their ideas. Effective public speaking, like effective everyday conversation, is a genuine interaction between people in which the views and values of all participants should be taken into account.

Throughout *Communication in Our Lives*, we've seen that people differ in their communication and in the meanings they attach to words and actions. The cornucopia of cultures and social communities in our world gives rise to a fascinating range of communication styles. No single way of communicating is inherently superior to any other; the differences result from diverse cultural heritages and practices.

Learning not to impose our own communication patterns and our culture's judgments on others allows us to enlarge and enrich who we are individually and collectively. Curiosity, appreciation, and openness to unfamiliar ways of communicating are vital to a healthy pluralistic society in which each of us preserves our own distinct identity while remaining part of and engaged with a larger whole.

If you have learned these principles and skills of human communication, then you have the foundation to be effective in personal, professional, and social settings. If you are committed to practicing and continually enlarging the principles and skills introduced in this book, then you can look forward to a life of personal growth, meaningful relationships, professional success, and social impact. What is more, you are on the threshold of a life filled with joy.

Julia T Wood

Annotated Sample Speeches

MindTap® Are you ready to give a special occasion speech? Use the following speech as a model. Brandon gave this speech in an introductory public speaking class. The assignment was to give a 3- to 5-minute speech commemorating a special person, place, or thing in the speaker's life. In addition, go to MindTap to access video clips of other commemorative speeches, such as Tara Flanagan's "My Grandfather, John Flanagan Sr."

Water

Brandon Perry

Specific Purpose: To commemorate the strength, flexibility, and beauty of water

Thesis Statement: I'm thankful for all that water's enduring strength, everlasting flexibility, and exciting beauty have done for us and given us.

It is in the sky. It is on the ground. It is in us. Do you know what IT is? Father Time has no control over it, weapons weep at its power, and like an architect, it chisels and creates. Do you know what IT is? Water is what I speak of, and nowadays we view water passively—nothing more than a convenience—but it is more than that. Every day I see the strength of water in how it shapes the landscape of this earth. I see its flexibility in giving me the ability to shape snow to throw. And I see a beauty that competes with the most beautiful sunset.

Discovering the amazing strength of water doesn't require going halfway across the Earth. Think about the strange and mysterious creatures of the deep blue sea. Turn your head toward the purple majestic skyscrapers of the West. Listen to the sounds of a roaring old-man-winter blizzard in Colorado. Take a walk down the hallway, then a right, arrive at the fountain, and take a nice long relaxing cool drink. Water, like a lifelong friend, is the regenerator, the reviver, the reliever of your life that you can't live without.

Water is uniquely flexible to many contexts. Little kids throwing water balloons and running through sprinklers would be unheard of without water. College students, enjoying a day off from classes, throwing snowballs at each other and building snowmen, would be unimaginable without water. The clouds that crowd and bustle through our bright blue sky, giving inspiration to artists and kids alike, would be unthinkable without water. The water we use every day once quieted the

Commentary

By asking a series of questions, Brandon piques his audience's curiosity and draws them in. He then reveals the topic of his speech.

In his introduction, Brandon indicates how he appreciates his topic by describing some of water's virtues. In addition, by talking about water's "strength," "flexibility," and "beauty," he previews his main points.

He connects to his audience by inking his topic to human senses—he asks his audience to think about, move toward, and listen to the sounds of water.

The use of alliteration ("the regenerator, the reviver, the reliever") helps make the speech appealing to listeners.

Brandon includes an anecdote about playing in the snow to relate to his audience of college-aged students.

In using personification ("the clouds that crowd and bustle . . . . giving inspiration"), he helps bring life to his topic.

Notice the vivid imagery and rhythm Brandon uses in this paragraph to describe water's beauty.

In his conclusion, Brandon provides a short summary of the three virtues he admires most about water.

cries of an early Earth, quenched the thirst of a dinosaur, and gave blood to the mighty trees of the past and present of our world.

Beauty, they say, is in the eye of the beholder. But for those who claim they cannot see water's beauty, they need to look again. The glistening songs of blooming flowers in a midday spring afternoon are water's beauty transformed. Stand by a remote mountain lake, and a perfect, clear reflection of the mighty trees and peaks in the crystal clear water might just say hello. What makes water's beauty more unique and special, though, than any other is its ability to pass it on. The mighty Amazon rainforest or slopes covered in twenty feet of snow are just a couple examples. This beauty also allows all of us to view ourselves in a different light, like a mirror—it tells no lies. So, when you stop and stare into a reflection that water gives you, do you see just yourself, or can you see deeper things, deeper ideas, deeper emotions?

Water was here long before and will be here long past our deaths on this planet or the next. Life without water's enduring strength, everlasting flexibility, and exciting beauty would be all but impossible for most living things on this Earth. Be thankful for all that water has done for us; it has given us all that we see before us, in one form or another.

Martin Luther King Jr. Remembrance Speech: Transcript of 2010 Speech

Barack Obama

Abstract: President Obama honors Martin Luther King Jr.'s life and activism while also encouraging Americans that his work is not finished and that individual people must work hard and persevere to end discrimination of all kinds and make our country and world more stable and safe.

Full Text: Address by Barack Obama, 44th president of the United States, during his presidency at the Vermont Avenue Baptist Church in Washington, DC, delivered on January 17, 2010.

Barack Obama, Martin Luther King Jr. Remembrance Speech, delivered on January 17, 2010, at Vermont Avenue Baptist Church, Washington, DC.

Good morning. Praise be to God. Let me begin by thanking the entire Vermont Avenue Baptist Church family for welcoming our family here today. It feels like a family. Thank you for making us feel that way. To Pastor Wheeler, first lady Wheeler, thank you so much for welcoming us here today. Congratulations on Jordan Denice—aka Cornelia.

> He acknowledges and thanks audience and those who invited him.

Michelle and I have been blessed with a new nephew this year as well—Austin Lucas Robinson. So maybe at the appropriate time we can make introductions. Now, if Jordan's father is like me, then that will be in about 30 years. That is a great blessing.

> He uses humor to make a connection.

Michelle and Malia and Sasha and I are thrilled to be here today. And I know that sometimes you have to go through a little fuss to have me as a guest speaker. So let me apologize in advance for all the fuss.

We gather here, on a Sabbath, during a time of profound difficulty for our nation and for our world. In such a time, it soothes the soul to seek out the Divine in a spirit of prayer; to seek solace among a community of believers. But we are not here just to ask the Lord for His blessing. We aren't here just to interpret His Scripture. We're also here to call on the memory of one of His noble servants, the Reverend Dr. Martin Luther King, Jr.

> He identifies the purpose of the speech: to honor Dr. Martin Luther King Jr.

Now, it's fitting that we do so here, within the four walls of Vermont Avenue Baptist Church—here, in a church that rose like the phoenix from the ashes of the civil war; here in a church formed by freed slaves, whose founding pastor had worn the union blue; here in a church from whose pews congregants set out for marches and from whom choir anthems of freedom were heard; from whose sanctuary King himself would sermonize from time to time.

> He shows respect by honoring the history of the church at which he is speaking.

One of those times was Thursday, December 6, 1956. Pastor, you said you were a little older than me, so were you around at that point? You were 3 years old—okay. I wasn't born yet.

On Thursday, December 6, 1956. And before Dr. King had pointed us to the mountaintop, before he told us about his dream in front of the Lincoln Memorial,

> He provides background information to inform the audience and build credibility.

King came here, as a 27-year-old preacher, to speak on what he called "The Challenge of a New Age." "The Challenge of a New Age." It was a period of triumph, but also uncertainty, for Dr. King and his followers—because just weeks earlier, the Supreme Court had ordered the desegregation of Montgomery's buses, a hard-wrought, hard-fought victory that would put an end to the 381-day historic boycott down in Montgomery, Alabama.

He uses detailed imagery to help the audience imagine being at the church at a particular time.

And yet, as Dr. King rose to take that pulpit, the future still seemed daunting. It wasn't clear what would come next for the movement that Dr. King led. It wasn't clear how we were going to reach the Promised Land. Because segregation was still rife; lynchings still a fact. Yes, the Supreme Court had ruled not only on the Montgomery buses, but also on *Brown v. Board of Education*. And yet that ruling was defied throughout the South—by schools and by states; they ignored it with impunity. And here in the nation's capital, the federal government had yet to fully align itself with the laws on its books and the ideals of its founding.

He continues the use of imagery.

So it's not hard for us, then, to imagine that moment. We can imagine folks coming to this church, happy about the boycott being over. We can also imagine them, though, coming here concerned about their future, sometimes second-guessing strategy, maybe fighting off some creeping doubts, perhaps despairing about whether the movement in which they had placed so many of their hopes—a movement in which they believed so deeply—could actually deliver on its promise.

He uses a transition to make a connection between the past and present.

So here we are, more than half a century later, once again facing the challenges of a new age. Here we are, once more marching toward an unknown future, what I call the Joshua generation to their Moses generation—the great inheritors of progress paid for with sweat and blood, and sometimes life itself.

We've inherited the progress of unjust laws that are now overturned. We take for granted the progress of a ballot being available to anybody who wants to take the time to actually vote. We enjoy the fruits of prejudice and bigotry being lifted—slowly, sometimes in fits and starts, but irrevocably—from human hearts. It's that progress that made it possible for me to be here today; for the good people of this country to elect an African American the 44th President of the United States of America.

He addresses a popular counter-argument.

Reverend Wheeler mentioned the inauguration, last year's election. You know, on the heels of that victory over a year ago, there were some who suggested that somehow we had entered into a post-racial America, all those problems would be solved. There were those who argued that because I spoke of a need for unity in this country that our nation was somehow entering into a period of post-partisanship. That didn't work out so well. There was a hope shared by many that life would be better from the moment that I swore that oath.

Thesis: the work Dr. King began is not finished.

Of course, as we meet here today, 1 year later, we know the promise of that moment has not yet been fully fulfilled. Because of an era of greed and irresponsibility that sowed the seeds of its own demise, because of persistent economic troubles unaddressed through the generations, because of a banking crisis that brought the financial system to the brink of catastrophe, we are being tested—in our own lives and as a nation—as few have been tested before.

He uses general statistical information to support the thesis.

Unemployment is at its highest level in more than a quarter of a century. Nowhere is it higher than in the African American community. Poverty is on the rise. Home ownership is slipping. Beyond our shores, our sons and daughters are fighting two wars. Closer to home, our Haitian brothers and sisters are in desperate need. Bruised, battered, many people are legitimately feeling doubt, even despair, about the future. Like those who came to this church on that Thursday in 1956, folks are wondering, where do we go from here?

I understand those feelings. I understand the frustration and sometimes anger that so many folks feel as they struggle to stay afloat. I get letters from folks around the country every day; I read 10 a night out of the 40,000 that we receive. And there are stories of hardship and desperation, in some cases, pleading for help: I need a job. I'm about to lose my home. I don't have health care—it's about to cause my family to be bankrupt. Sometimes you get letters from children: My mama or my daddy have lost their jobs, is there something you can do to help? Ten letters like that a day we read.

He identifies with audience to create a connection.

He uses and emotional appeal.

So, yes, we're passing through a hard winter. It's the hardest in some time. But let's always remember that, as a people, the American people, we've weathered some hard winters before. This country was founded during some harsh winters. The fishermen, the laborers, the craftsmen who made camp at Valley Forge—they weathered a hard winter. The slaves and the freedmen who rode an underground railroad, seeking the light of justice under the cover of night—they weathered a hard winter. The seamstress whose feet were tired, the pastor whose voice echoes through the ages—they weathered some hard winters. It was for them, as it is for us, difficult, in the dead of winter, to sometimes see spring coming. They, too, sometimes felt their hopes deflate. And yet, each season, the frost melts, the cold recedes, the sun reappears. So it was for earlier generations and so it will be for us.

He uses a metaphor to advance his point.

(metaphor continues)

What we need to do is to just ask what lessons we can learn from those earlier generations about how they sustained themselves during those hard winters, how they persevered and prevailed. Let us in this Joshua generation learn how that Moses generation overcame.

He uses more concrete language to suggest a solution to the problem addressed in the thesis.

Let me offer a few thoughts on this. First and foremost, they did so by remaining firm in their resolve. Despite being threatened by sniper fire or planted bombs, by shoving and punching and spitting and angry stares, they adhered to that sweet spirit of resistance, the principles of nonviolence that had accounted for their success.

He continues to suggest specific actions for the identified problem.

Second, they understood that as much as our government and our political parties had betrayed them in the past—as much as our nation itself had betrayed its own ideals—government, if aligned with the interests of its people, can be—and must be—a force for good. So they stayed on the Justice Department. They went into the courts. They pressured Congress, they pressured their President. They didn't give up on this country. They didn't give up on government. They didn't somehow say government was the problem; they said, we're going to change government, we're going to make it better. Imperfect as it was, they continued to believe in the promise of democracy; in America's constant ability to remake itself, to perfect this union.

He continues to suggest specific actions for the identified problem.

He urges people to take action.

Third, our predecessors were never so consumed with theoretical debates that they couldn't see progress when it came. Sometimes I get a little frustrated when folks just don't want to see that even if we don't get everything, we're getting something. King understood that the desegregation of the Armed Forces didn't end the civil rights movement, because black and white soldiers still couldn't sit together at the same lunch counter when they came home. But he still insisted on the rightness

He uses specific historical examples to encourage the audience toward action in the present.

of desegregating the Armed Forces. That was a good first step—even as he called for more. He didn't suggest that somehow by the signing of the Civil Rights that somehow all discrimination would end. But he also didn't think that we shouldn't sign the Civil Rights Act because it hasn't solved every problem. Let's take a victory, he said, and then keep on marching. Forward steps, large and small, were recognized for what they were—which was progress.

He continues to suggest specific actions for the identified problem.

Fourth, at the core of King's success was an appeal to conscience that touched hearts and opened minds, a commitment to universal ideals—of freedom, of justice, of equality—that spoke to all people, not just some people. For King understood that without broad support, any movement for civil rights could not be sustained. That's why he marched with the white auto worker in Detroit. That's why he linked arm with the Mexican farm worker in California, and united people of all colors in the noble quest for freedom.

He effectively makes use of a quotation.

Of course, King overcame in other ways as well. He remained strategically focused on gaining ground—his eyes on the prize constantly—understanding that change would not be easy, understanding that change wouldn't come overnight, understanding that there would be setbacks and false starts along the way, but understanding, as he said in 1956, that "we can walk and never get weary, because we know there is a great camp meeting in the promised land of freedom and justice."

He summarizes the previous main points: To accomplish the task, people must persevere.

And it's because the Moses generation overcame that the trials we face today are very different from the ones that tested us in previous generations. Even after the worst recession in generations, life in America is not even close to being as brutal as it was back then for so many. That's the legacy of Dr. King and his movement. That's our inheritance. Having said that, let there be no doubt the challenges of our new age are serious in their own right, and we must face them as squarely as they faced the challenges they saw.

He uses general examples to encourage and bring a more positive tone.

I know it's been a hard road we've traveled this year to rescue the economy, but the economy is growing again. The job losses have finally slowed, and around the country, there's signs that businesses and families are beginning to rebound. We are making progress.

He uses repetition of a phrase (i.e., "I know it's been a hard road we've traveled . . .") to emphasize and engage.

He uses repetition again (e.g., "This will be a victory . . .").

I know it's been a hard road that we've traveled to reach this point on health reform. I promise you I know. But under the legislation I will sign into law, insurance companies won't be able to drop you when you get sick, and more than 30 million people—our fellow Americans—will finally have insurance. More than 30 million men and women and children, mothers and fathers, won't be worried about what might happen to them if they get sick. This will be a victory not for Democrats; this will be a victory for dignity and decency, for our common humanity. This will be a victory for the United States of America.

He uses repetition again ("Don't give up on . . .")

He uses an effective quotation that supports his point.

Let's work to change the political system, as imperfect as it is. I know people can feel down about the way things are going sometimes here in Washington. I know it's tempting to give up on the political process. But we've put in place tougher rules on lobbying and ethics and transparency—tougher rules than any administration in history. It's not enough, but it's progress. Progress is possible. Don't give up on voting. Don't give up on advocacy. Don't give up on activism. There are too many needs to be met, too much work to be done. Like Dr. King said, "We must accept finite disappointment but never lose infinite hope."

Let us broaden our coalition, building a confederation not of liberals or conservatives, not of red states or blue states, but of all Americans who are hurting today, and searching for a better tomorrow. The urgency of the hour demands that we make common cause with all of America's workers—white, black, brown—all of whom are being hammered by this recession, all of whom are yearning for that spring to come. It demands that we reach out to those who've been left out in the cold even when the economy is good, even when we're not in recession—the youth in the inner cities, the youth here in Washington, D.C., people in rural communities who haven't seen prosperity reach them for a very long time. It demands that we fight discrimination, whatever form it may come. That means we fight discrimination against gays and lesbians, and we make common cause to reform our immigration system.

> He briefly returns to the metaphor (of winter and spring) used before.

And finally, we have to recognize, as Dr. King did, that progress can't just come from without—it also has to come from within. And over the past year, for example, we've made meaningful improvements in the field of education. I've got a terrific Secretary of Education, Arne Duncan. He's been working hard with states and working hard with the D.C. school district, and we've insisted on reform, and we've insisted on accountability. We're putting in more money and we've provided more Pell Grants and more tuition tax credits and simpler financial aid forms. We've done all that, but parents still need to parent. Kids still need to own up to their responsibilities. We still have to set high expectations for our young people. Folks can't simply look to government for all the answers without also looking inside themselves, inside their own homes, for some of the answers.

> He builds credibility by citing his own work toward the goals that he encourages his audience to work toward.

Progress will only come if we're willing to promote that ethic of hard work, a sense of responsibility, in our own lives. I'm not talking, by the way, just to the African American community. Sometimes when I say these things people assume, well, he's just talking to black people about working hard. No, no, no, no. I'm talking to the American community. Because somewhere along the way, we, as a nation, began to lose touch with some of our core values. You know what I'm talking about. We became enraptured with the false prophets who prophesized an easy path to success, paved with credit cards and home equity loans and get-rich-quick schemes, and the most important thing was to be a celebrity; it doesn't matter what you do, as long as you get on TV. That's everybody.

> He uses vivid, emotional language (i.e., "false prophets," Biblical language for those who pretend to be messengers of God) that will appeal to his audience (i.e., church members).

We forgot what made the bus boycott a success; what made the civil rights movement a success; what made the United States of America a success—that, in this country, there's no substitute for hard work, no substitute for a job well done, no substitute for being responsible stewards of God's blessings.

What we're called to do, then, is rebuild America from its foundation on up. To reinvest in the essentials that we've neglected for too long—like health care, like education, like a better energy policy, like basic infrastructure, like scientific research. Our generation is called to buckle down and get back to basics.

> He personalizes his message by referring to specific individuals (i.e., his nephew and the pastor's daughter, who were mentioned at the start of the speech).

We must do so not only for ourselves, but also for our children, and their children. For Jordan and for Austin. That's a sacrifice that falls on us to make. It's a much smaller sacrifice than the Moses generation had to make, but it's still a sacrifice.

Yes, it's hard to transition to a clean energy economy. Sometimes it may be inconvenient, but it's a sacrifice that we have to make. It's hard to be fiscally responsible when we have all these human needs, and we're inheriting enormous

> He connects with audience by acknowledging their circumstances.

He continues to connect with the audience by acknowledging their challenges.

deficits and debt, but that's a sacrifice that we're going to have to make. You know, it's easy, after a hard day's work, to just put your kid in front of the TV set—you're tired, don't want to fuss with them—instead of reading to them, but that's a sacrifice we must joyfully accept.

Sometimes it's hard to be a good father and good mother. Sometimes it's hard to be a good neighbor, or a good citizen, to give up time in service of others, to give something of ourselves to a cause that's greater than ourselves—as Michelle and I are urging folks to do tomorrow to honor and celebrate Dr. King. But these are sacrifices that we are called to make. These are sacrifices that our faith calls us to make. Our faith in the future. Our faith in America. Our faith in God.

He suggests a way (i.e., faith) to meet the difficult challenge he has asked of them.

And on his sermon all those years ago, Dr. King quoted a poet's verse:
Truth forever on the scaffold
Wrong forever on the throne . . .
And behind the dim unknown stands God
Within the shadows keeping watch above his own.

He uses a quotation.

Even as Dr. King stood in this church, a victory in the past and uncertainty in the future, he trusted God. He trusted that God would make a way. A way for prayers to be answered. A way for our union to be perfected. A way for the arc of the moral universe, no matter how long, to slowly bend towards truth and bend towards freedom, to bend towards justice. He had faith that God would make a way out of no way.

You know, folks ask me sometimes why I look so calm. They say, all this stuff coming at you, how come you just seem calm? And I have a confession to make here. There are times where I'm not so calm. Reggie Love knows. My wife knows. There are times when progress seems too slow. There are times when the words that are spoken about me hurt. There are times when the barbs sting. There are times when it feels like all these efforts are for naught, and change is so painfully slow in coming, and I have to confront my own doubts.

He shares personal information and makes himself vulnerable to relate to the audience.

But let me tell you—during those times it's faith that keeps me calm. It's faith that gives me peace. The same faith that leads a single mother to work two jobs to put a roof over her head when she has doubts. The same faith that keeps an unemployed father to keep on submitting job applications even after he's been rejected a hundred times. The same faith that says to a teacher even if the first nine children she's teaching she can't reach, that that 10th one she's going to be able to reach. The same faith that breaks the silence of an earthquake's wake with the sound of prayers and hymns sung by a Haitian community. A faith in things not seen, in better days ahead, in Him who holds the future in the hollow of His hand. A faith that lets us mount up on wings like eagles; lets us run and not be weary; lets us walk and not faint.

He makes a Biblical reference to further emphasize the point (i.e., faith).

So let us hold fast to that faith, as Joshua held fast to the faith of his fathers, and together, we shall overcome the challenges of a new age. Together, we shall seize the promise of this moment. Together, we shall make a way through winter, and we're going to welcome the spring. Through God all things are possible.

He thanks his audience.

May the memory of Dr. Martin Luther King continue to inspire us and ennoble our world and all who inhabit it. And may God bless the United States of America.

Josh, a drummer, takes his topic from his interest in music. He catches his audience's attention by asking them to imagine using a musical instrument to communicate language, something people in the United States don't typically do.

Thank you very much, everybody. God bless you.

"The Dun Dun Drum"

Joshua Valentine

Josh gave this speech in an introductory public speaking class. The assignment was to give a 4- to 6-minute speech with visual aids. Students were also asked to create a preparation outline that indicated where in the speech the visual aids were to be displayed [these indications appear in brackets in the speech below], that cited the sources of the visual aids, and that included a Works Cited section. As you watch Josh's speech, consider the effectiveness of his use of photographs and audio to illustrate and clarify points.

Imagine that your friend comes up to you and asks you what you did this weekend, and instead of using words, your friend simply beats a drum. You've probably never had this type of encounter. However, there are many cultures in the world where music is used for customs that we're really not accustomed to.

Webster's Dictionary defines language as "any system of symbols, sounds, or gestures used for the purpose of communication." Here in America we don't really have instrumental sounds that represent English words, but there are many cultures around the world where sounds do have meaning.

I've been playing percussion since junior high. I first learned about the *dun dun* drum while attending a percussion workshop 2 years ago. So, today I'll explain the origins of the *dun dun* drum, its uses as a linguistic tool, and its uses as a musical instrument.

The *dun dun* drum, also known as the Nigerian talking drum, actually does talk in the Yoruba language. [*Display photograph of* dun dun *drum downloaded and used with permission from http://media.dickinson.edu/gallery/Sect5 .html.*] The *dun dun* originated in the Oyo Empire of Yoruba-land during the fifteenth century A.D. for the purposes of communication, mainly for spiritual communication. As such, the Yoruba language is easily adaptable to the *dun dun* drum.

Now, the Yoruba language is a tonal language, which basically means it uses three basic tones, or pitches, with glides between them—this is an essential part of how words are pronounced. Listen to this sound clip and see if you can examine the three different glides. [*Play a sound clip downloaded for one-time use from the Internet.*] I'll play that again for you. If you have a sharp ear, you may also be able to pick out three glides that are essential to the pronunciation of the Yoruba language. Melody is the basis for the Yoruba language, since the same word pronounced with a different melody might mean something completely different.

The Yoruba drum, the *dun dun*, functions mainly by using and changing the tension between two different skin heads. [*Point out the straps on the PowerPoint slide.*] By doing such, they can actually have a lot of control about how the *dun dun* operates and its use in communication. And, the *dun dun* was originally created for the purpose of communication.

The Yoruba are people of southwestern Nigeria who have used the *dun dun* drum for communication throughout their history. [*Show photo of carved drum downloaded from* www.hamillgallery.com . . .*YorubaDrum01.html.*] It was

---

MindTap

In the second main point of his introduction, he introduces his topic. He adapts his topic to his audience by using a familiar source, *Webster's Dictionary*, to define what language is and then explain that although Americans don't use music as language, other cultures do.

He establishes his credibility by indicating that he is a musician and that he learned about his topic in a percussion workshop.

In the last point of his introduction, Josh previews the two main points of his speech.

Because his audience is unfamiliar with his topic, Josh uses his first main point to explain what the *dun dun* drum is, where it originated, and what it is used for.

By allowing his audience to see and hear a *dun dun* drum, Josh helps his audience better understand his topic. In particular, the audio clips let the audience hear what is complicated to explain in words alone.

He kept a careful record of from where he obtained his visual and audio aids so he could cite his sources accurately in his speech. Note that he downloaded copyrighted material according to the terms of use posted by the

websites he accessed—
he requested permission
or agreed to use the ma-
terial only for his speech
in class.

The visual aid Josh used
for subpoint D of his first
main point clarifies how
the drum works.

In his second main point,
Josh explains how the
drum is used to communi-
cate. He continues to use
his visual and audio aids
to enhance and clarify the
information in his speech.

In subpoint B, he provides
details that his audience
can relate to: "saying hi,"
"cracking jokes," "telling
stories." Notice that he
cites his sources simply
but effectively.

Here Josh uses a specific
example to explain how
the Yoruba "talk" with
the *dun dun* drum.

Here he adapts to his
audience by explaining
how the *dun dun* drum
is used in a way that is
familiar to people in the
United States, as a musi-
cal instrument.

Josh ends the body of his
speech with an audio clip
that reinforces his final
sub-subpoint, that the
dun dun drum is now an
international instrument.

Josh begins his conclu-
sion by reinforcing that
the drum is used for
both language and mu-
sic. He then summarizes
his main points.

He ends his speech with
an intriguing statement
that encourages his audi-
ence to remember what
he's told them about a
particular African drum.

originally, of course, created first for spiritual communication. Since its inception, the drum has mainly been used to create religious songs and hymns of praise, and these songs are still recited today among the modern Yoruba people.

Here's an example of a very intense spiritual worship song done on talking drums. *[Play example downloaded for one-time use from http://www.world-beats.com/instruments/dundun.htm.]*

The Yoruba talking drum is also used heavily for day-to-day social communication. According to worldbeats.com, a master drummer can maintain a regular monologue while cracking jokes, saying hi to different people, even telling stories on the *dun dun* drum. Additionally, many *dun dun* drummers are known to say the names of friends and family on the *dun dun* drums as a sign of greeting and as a form of respect. So it's used very heavily in those senses, and it's very important—it's a huge part of the Yoruba culture.

And, additionally, the most obvious use of the *dun dun* drum, and its secondary use, really, is as a musical instrument. Now, we've already gone over the fact that the *dun dun* drum originally was used for spiritual communication. But since corporate worship in Yoruba is so prolific, people come together, and making music on the *dun dun* was born. That's essentially an example of how it's evolved. In fact, today, modern Yoruba people still use the *dun dun* for religious songs, although mainly for their musical purposes.

Everyday speech on the Yoruba drum becomes rhythmic when it's used. For example, the word *kabo*, which means "welcome" in the Yoruba language, is only a two-syllable word, so it's really not that exotic—it's not that interesting; it's not that musical. According to Drum Talk Limited, a more common phrase that someone might speak on the Yoruba talking drum is, "Welcome, we are happy that you arrived safely," because it's more musical. It has more of that flair to it. And even when a word spoken, or a phrase spoken, with regular words wouldn't be rhythmic, it is when the Yoruba people use the talking drum, because melody, as I said, is the basis of the talking drum.

The use of the Nigerian talking drum has spread far beyond Nigeria. In fact, next to the *djembe* drum, the *dun dun* is the most well-known and recognizable African drum used in America today. It's also very versatile. According to Francis Awe, a renowned African American musician, the *dun dun* drum fares well in jazz, blues, R&B, rock and roll, reggae, classical, even choral music. Here's one particular clip from renowned African American musician Francis Awe. *[Play sample clip downloaded from http://www.nitade.com/html/cd1.html.]*

So, in conclusion, whether the *dun dun* drum is used in language or in song, it always has a very unusual and beautiful sound. Today I've talked about the origins of the *dun dun* drum. I've also talked about its linguistic uses, and its uses as a musical instrument. So next time you hear music as simple as someone beating a drum, you might think to yourself that maybe that drummer, maybe that musician, is communicating much more than you first think.

Interviewing

You've probably participated in a number of interviews during your life. Perhaps you were interviewed by committees that appoint students to leadership positions at your school or award scholarships to students. You may have had interviews with members of groups you sought to join. Probably you have interviewed for part-time or full-time jobs.

You've probably been on the other side of the interviewing process, too; you may have interviewed people who were applying to join organizations to which you belong. You may have interviewed experts to gain information about a topic on which you were writing a paper or preparing a speech. Because interviews are common, learning to communicate effectively in interviews is important to your personal and professional success.

An interview is a communication transaction that emphasizes questions and answers. In this appendix, we will discuss interviewing and identify ways you can enhance your effectiveness as both interviewer and interviewee. First, we will identify a range of purposes or types of interviews. Second, we will discuss the typical structure and style of interviews. Third, we will describe different kinds of questions interviewers use. Then, we will identify challenges that are part of interviewing. We will focus on hiring interviews because those are particularly important to many college students. Our discussion will provide tips for preparing to interview and for dealing with inappropriate or illegal questions.

Understanding Communication in Interviews

Types and Purposes of Interviews

Communication scholars have identified distinct types of interviews. Each interview is defined by its primary purpose, although many interviews have multiple, and sometimes conflicting, purposes. For example, an interviewer may want to gain objective information for a speech, yet may be biased about the topic that he or she wants to support. We'll discuss 11 types of interviews.

Information-Giving Interviews   In the first type of interview, the interviewer provides information to the interviewee. Doctors engage in information-giving interviews when they explain to patients how to prepare for procedures, take medicines, follow exercise programs, and observe symptoms. Academic advisers give students information about curricular requirements and administrative processes. Team leaders often inform new members of a work unit about expectations and operating procedures.

interview A communication transaction that emphasizes questions and answers.

information-giving interviews Interviews in which the interviewer provides information to the interviewee.

Information-Getting Interviews   In this type of interview, the interviewer asks questions to learn about the interviewee's opinions, knowledge, attitudes, experience, and so forth. Public opinion polls, census taking, and research surveys are common examples of **information-getting interviews**. Physicians also use these to gain insight into patients' medical histories and current conditions (Farnill, Hayes, & Todisco, 1997). Journalists devote a great deal of time to information-getting interviews to obtain background material for stories they are writing and to learn about experts' opinions on newsworthy topics.

Persuasive Interviews   Interviews designed to influence attitudes or actions are **persuasive interviews**. We're all familiar with the sales interview, in which a salesperson attempts to persuade a customer to buy a product or service. Persuasive interviews can sell more than products. They may also promote people (political candidates) and ideas (persuading an administrator to act on your team's report, convincing a company to implement environmental regulations).

Problem-Solving Interviews   When people need to address a dilemma, they may engage in **problem-solving interviews**. Perhaps you have met with a professor to discuss difficulties in a course. The two of you may have collaborated to identify ways to improve your note taking, study habits, and writing. Supervisors sometimes hold problem-solving interviews with employees to discover and resolve impediments to maximally effective work.

Counseling Interviews   Like problem-solving interviews, **counseling interviews** focus on a problem. In counseling interviews, however, the problem is not mutual. A client has a problem, such as stress, depression, or compulsiveness, which she or he wants to overcome. The counselor attempts to help the client understand the problem more fully and collaborates with the client to develop strategies for coping with or overcoming the difficulty (Evans, Coman, & Goss, 1996). Counseling interviews also occur outside the therapeutic setting: We may seek counseling from attorneys to address (or avoid) legal problems, from accountants to get help with financial matters, and from religious leaders to deal with spiritual issues.

Employment Interviews   The purpose of **employment interviews** is to allow employers and job candidates to assess each other and decide whether there is a good fit between them. Typically, employment interviews include periods of information giving and information getting as well as persuasive efforts on the part of both participants. The prospective employer wants to convince the job candidate of the quality of the company, and the candidate wants to convince the prospective employer of the quality of his or her qualifications. Ideally, both participants gain enough information to make a sound judgment of the fit between the candidate and the job.

Complaint Interviews   **Complaint interviews** allow people to register complaints about a product, service, or person. Many firms have departments whose sole purpose is to accept and respond to complaints. Of primary importance is showing the people who complain that they are heard and that they matter. The interviewer (company representative) attempts to gain information about the customer's dissatisfaction: What was defective or disappointing about the product? Was service inadequate? What would it take to satisfy the customer now? The person

information-getting interviews Interviews in which the interviewer asks questions to learn about the interviewee's qualifications, background, experience, opinions, knowledge, attitudes, or behaviors.

persuasive interviews Interviews designed to influence attitudes, beliefs, values, or actions.

problem-solving interviews Interviews in which people collaborate to identify sources of a mutual problem and to develop ways to address or resolve it.

counseling interviews Interviews in which one person with expertise helps another to understand a problem and develop strategies to overcome the difficulty or cope more effectively with it.

employment interviews Interviews in which employer and job candidate assess each other and decide whether there is a good fit between them.

complaint interviews Interviews conducted for the purpose of allowing someone to register a complaint about a product, service, person, or company.

conducting complaint interviews should call recurring complaints to the attention of those who can diagnose and solve underlying problems.

Performance Reviews   Most organizations require **performance reviews,** or performance appraisals, at regular intervals. By building performance appraisals into work life, organizations continually monitor employees' performance and foster their professional growth. The performance review is an occasion on which a supervisor comments on a subordinate's achievements and professional development, identifies any weaknesses or problems, and collaborates to develop goals for future performance. During the interview, subordinates should offer their perceptions of their strengths and weaknesses and participate actively in developing goals for professional development (Kikoski, 1998).

Reprimand Interviews   When a person's work is unsatisfactory, a supervisor may conduct a **reprimand interview.** The goals are to identify lapses in professional conduct, determine sources of problems, and establish a plan for improving future performance. Because reprimands tend to evoke defensiveness, developing a constructive, supportive climate for these interviews is especially important. Supervisors may foster a good climate by opening the interview with assurances that the goal is to solve a problem together, not to punish the subordinate. Supervisors should also invite subordinates to express their perceptions and feelings fully.

Stress Interviews   **Stress interviews** are designed to create anxiety in respondents or interviewees. Stress interviews are unique in their deliberate intent to apply pressure. Frequently used communication techniques for inducing stress are rapid-fire questions, intentional misinterpretations and distortions of the interviewee's responses, and hostile or skeptical nonverbal expressions.

Why, you might ask, would anyone deliberately create a high-stress interview situation? Actually, stress interviews may be useful in several contexts. Attorneys may intentionally intimidate reluctant or hostile witnesses or people whose honesty is suspect. Similarly, prison administrators and police officers may communicate aggressively with people they think are withholding important information. This kind of interview also may be used in hiring people for high-stress jobs. By deliberately trying to rattle job candidates, interviewers can assess how well they manage and respond to stress.

Exit Interviews   In academic and professional life, **exit interviews** have become increasingly popular. The goal of this type of interview is to gain information, insights, and perceptions about a place of work or education from a person who is leaving. While people are in a job or learning environment, they may be reluctant to mention dissatisfactions or to speak against those who have power over them. When people are leaving an organization or school, however, they can offer honest insights and perceptions with little fear of reprisal. Thus, exit interviews can be especially valuable in providing information about policies, personnel, and organizational culture.

The Structure of Interviews

To be effective, interviews should follow a structure that builds a good communication climate and allows the interviewer and the interviewee to deal with substantive matters. Experienced interviewers, even those without professional training, tend

Review It!

Types of Interviews:
- Information-Giving
- Information-Getting
- Persuasive
- Problem-Solving
- Counseling
- Employment
- Complaint
- Performance Review
- Reprimand
- Stress
- Exit

performance reviews Interviews in which a supervisor comments on a subordinate's achievements and professional development, identifies any weaknesses or problems, and collaborates with the subordinate to develop goals for future performance. Subordinates should offer perceptions of their strengths and weaknesses and participate actively in developing goals for professional development. Also known as a *performance appraisal.*

reprimand interview An interview conducted by a supervisor with a subordinate to identify lapses in the subordinate's professional conduct, determine sources of problems, and establish a plan for improving future performance.

stress interviews A style of interviewing in which an interviewer deliberately attempts to create anxiety in the interviewee.

exit interviews Interviews designed to gain information, insights, and perceptions about a place of work or education from a person who is leaving.

to organize interview communication into a three-stage sequence. Interviewees who understand the purpose of each stage in the sequence increase their ability to participate effectively.

The Opening Stage   The initial stage of an interview tends to be brief and aims to create an effective climate for interaction, clarify the purpose, and preview issues to be discussed (Wilson & Goodall, 1991). Typically, opening small talk encourages a friendly climate:

- "I see you're from Buffalo. Are the winters there still as harsh as they used to be?"

- "It's been 6 months since our last performance review. What do you think has changed in that time?"

- "I noticed you got your B.A. from State University. I graduated from there, too. Did you ever take any courses with Doctor Barnette in anthropology?"

After opening small talk, effective interviewers state the purpose of the interview and how they plan to accomplish that purpose:

- "As you know, I'm on campus today to talk with liberal arts majors who are interested in joining Hodgeson Marketing. I'd like to ask you some questions about yourself and your background, and then I want to give you an opportunity to ask me anything you want about Hodgeson."

- "Pat, the reason I asked you to meet with me today is that there have been some complaints about your attitude from others on your work team. I know you are good at your job and have a fine history with the firm, so I want us to put our heads together to resolve this matter. Let's begin with me telling you what I've heard, and then I'd like to hear your perceptions of what's happening."

The Substantive Stage   The second stage of an interview, which generally consumes the bulk of time, deals with substance or content relevant to the purpose of the interview. For example, in reprimand interviews, the substantive stage would zero in on identifying problem behaviors and devising solutions. In a hiring interview, the substantive stage might concentrate on the job candidate's background, experience, and qualifications.

Because the goal of the substantive stage is to exchange information, it takes careful planning and thought. Most interviewers prepare lists of topics or specific questions and use their notes to make sure they cover all the important topics. During the interview, they may also take notes of responses. Communication during this phase tends to progress from broad topic areas to increasingly specific questions within each topic. After introducing a topic, the interviewer may ask some initial general questions and then follow up with more detailed probes. Because the pattern of communication moves from broad to narrow, it has been called the **funnel sequence** (Cannell & Kahn, 1968; Moffatt, 1979). The interviewer may repeat the funnel sequence for each new topic area in an interview.

During the substantive stage, an interviewer may invite the interviewee to take the lead in communication, either by posing questions or by volunteering perceptions and ideas in response to what has been covered thus far. To be an effective

funnel sequence A pattern of communication in interviews that moves from broad, general questions to progressively narrower, more probing questions.

interviewee, you should be prepared with questions and topics that you want to introduce. This portrays you as someone who prepares and takes initiative. It is also important to monitor your nonverbal communication. Interviewers tend to be most impressed with interviewees whose paralanguage and kinesics convey enthusiasm, confidence, and an outgoing personality (Mino, 1996).

The Closing Stage   Like the opening stage, the closing stage tends to be brief. Its purposes are to summarize what has been discussed, state what follow-up will occur, if any, and create good will in parting. Summarizing the content of the interview increases the likelihood that an accurate and complete record of the interview will survive. If the interviewer overlooks any topics, the interviewee may appropriately offer a reminder. Interviewees also may ask about follow-up if interviewers fail to mention this.

Most interviews follow the three-step sequence we've discussed, but not all do. Some interviewers are ineffective because they are disorganized, unprepared, and inadequately trained in effective interviewing. They may ramble for 15 minutes or more and fail to provide any closing other than "Gee, our time is up." In other instances, interviewers may deliberately violate the standard pattern to achieve their goals. For example, in stress interviews designed to test how well a person responds to pressure, the interviewer may skip opening comments and jump immediately into tough substantive questions. This allows the interviewer to assess how well the respondent copes with unexpected pressure.

> **Review It!**
> ....
> Interview Stages:
> - Opening
> - Substantive
> - Closing

Styles of Interviewing

Interviews may be more or less formal. In highly formal interviews, participants tend to stay within social and professional roles. The content of highly formal interviews tends to follow a standard format, often one that the interviewer has written to structure the interaction. Nonverbal communication provides further clues to formality: clothes, a formal meeting room, stilted postures, and a stiff handshake are all signs of formality.

In contrast, informal interviews are more relaxed, personal, and flexible. The interviewer attempts to engage the interviewee as an individual, not just a person in a general role. Typically, informal interviews aren't as rigidly structured as formal interviews. The interviewer may have a list of standard topics (either memorized or written down), but these provide only guidelines, not a straitjacket for communication. Informal interviews often include nonverbal cues such as smiling, relaxed postures, casual surroundings, and informal dress.

Most interviews fall between the extremes of formality and informality. Also, interviews may become more or less formal as a result of communication between participants. A person who communicates in a stilted manner is likely to encourage formality in the other person. Conversely, a person who communicates casually promotes a relaxed style of response.

Another influence on the communication climate in interviews is the balance of power between interviewer and interviewee. Power may be evenly balanced between participants or skewed toward the interviewer or the interviewee.

Mirror Interviews   Interviewees have the greatest power to direct communication in **mirror interviews,** in which the interviewer consistently reflects the interviewee's comments to the interviewee. This may be done by restating verbatim

> **mirror interviews** A style of interviewing in which an interviewer's questions reflect previous responses and comments of the interviewee. Mirror interviews allow interviewees substantial power.

what an interviewee says, paraphrasing an interviewee's comments, or making limited inferences about an interviewee's thoughts and feelings based on the communication. Skillful listening is essential for effectively using the mirror style (Banville, 1978). Consider this sample excerpt from a mirror interview:

> INTERVIEWER: Tell me about your studies.
> INTERVIEWEE: I'm a communication major.
> INTERVIEWER: So you've studied communication?
> INTERVIEWEE: Yes, especially organizational communication and leadership.
> INTERVIEWER: Then you're particularly interested in leadership in organizations?
> INTERVIEWEE: Yes. I think communication is the heart of effective leadership, so majoring in communication prepares me to lead.
> INTERVIEWER: So you see communication as the heart of effective leadership?
> INTERVIEWEE: Well, I see leadership as motivating others and empowering them to achieve their goals. A person who knows how to communicate clearly, listen well, and establish rapport with others is most able to motivate them.

In this exchange, the interviewer lets the interviewee to lead. What the interviewee says is the basis for the interviewer's subsequent questions and probes. Astute interviewees realize that mirror interviews give them significant opportunity to highlight their strengths and introduce topics they wish to discuss.

Distributive Interviews   In **distributive interviews**, power is equally divided (or distributed) between participants. Both ask and answer questions, listen and speak, and contribute to shaping the direction and content of communication. The distributive style of interviewing is generally used when participants are equal in professional or social standing. Distributive interviews may also be used between people with unequal power if the interviewer wants to create a relaxed exchange. Recruiters often use distributive styles to put job candidates at ease.

Authoritarian Interviews   In **authoritarian interviews**, the interviewer exercises primary control over interaction. The interviewer may avoid or quickly cut off discussion of any topics not on the list and may give the interviewee little or no opportunity to ask questions or initiate topics. Efficiency is the primary strength of the authoritarian style of interviewing: Many topics can be covered quickly. But the authoritarian style of interviewing can be frustrating to interviewees, and the interviewer may miss relevant information by failing to specifically seek it and by not giving the interviewee an opportunity to initiate topics.

In stress interviews, which we discussed previously in this appendix, the interviewer has primary control, as in authoritarian interviews. Unlike authoritarian interviews, however, stress interviews are a deliberate attempt to create anxiety in the interviewee. Thus, the interviewer controls not only the pace and content of interaction but also the psychological agenda.

Interviewees have even less control than in authoritarian interviews because stress interviews often rely on trick questions, surprise turns in topic, and unsettling

distributive interviews
A style of interviewing in which roughly equal power is held by interviewer and interviewee.

authoritarian interviews
An interviewing style in which the interviewer has and exerts greater power than the interviewee.

responses to interviewees. If you find yourself in a stress interview, recognize that it is probably a deliberate attempt to test your ability to cope with pressure. Stay alert and flexible to deal with unpredictable communication from the interviewer.

Forms of Questions in Interviews

Most interviews follow a question–answer pattern in which each person speaks only briefly before the other person speaks. Consequently, skill in asking and responding to questions is central to effectiveness. Skillful interviewers understand that different kinds of questions shape responses, and effective interviewees recognize the opportunities and constraints of distinct forms of questions. We'll consider eight of the most common types of questions and discuss the responses invited by each.

Review It!

Interview Styles:
- Mirror
- Distributive
- Authoritarian

Open Questions   Open questions are general queries that invite expansive responses: "What can you tell me about yourself?" "What is your work experience?" Because open questions are broad, they give interviewees opportunities to steer communication toward topics that interest or reflect well on them.

Closed Questions   Unlike open questions, closed questions do not invite broad answers. Instead, they ask for a concrete, narrow reply, often in the form of "yes" or "no." Closed questions are often used to follow up on general replies to open questions. "How many business courses have you taken?" "What was your position at the summer camp?" "Do you prefer working individually or on teams?" Closed questions call for short, direct answers, and an interviewer may interpret more broad responses negatively.

Mirror Questions   Mirror questions paraphrase or reflect the previous communication. If an interviewee says, "I have worked in a lot of stressful jobs," the interviewer might respond reflectively by saying, "So you can handle pressure, right?" At the content level of meaning, a mirror question seems pointless because it merely repeats what preceded it. At the relationship level of meaning, however, mirror questions say, "Elaborate; tell me more." Thus, they represent opportunities to expand on ideas.

Hypothetical Questions   Hypothetical questions ask a person to speculate. Recruiters often pose hypothetical questions to see how well candidates can think on their feet. A student of mine provided the following example of a hypothetical question she was asked in a job interview: "Assume you are supervising an employee who is consistently late to work and sometimes leaves early. What would you do?" My student responded that her first course of action would be to talk with the employee to determine the reason for his or her tardiness and early departures. Next, she said, she would work with the employee to eliminate the source or, if company policies allowed it, to rearrange the schedule to accommodate the employee's circumstances.

This response showed that the job candidate was collaborative and supportive—precisely the qualities the recruiter wanted to assess. Hypothetical questions are designed to find out how you grasp and approach complex situations (Gladwell, 2000).

Probing Questions   When we probe something, we go beneath its surface to find out more about it. During interviews, probing questions go beneath the surface of a response to gather additional information and insight. Consider this example of several probing questions that follow an open question and a broad response:

> INTERVIEWER: Tell me about your work history.
> INTERVIEWEE: I've held 10 jobs while I've been attending college.
> INTERVIEWER: Why have you held so many different jobs instead of sticking with one of them?
> INTERVIEWEE: I kept switching in the hope of finding one that would be really interesting.
> INTERVIEWER: What makes a job interesting to you?
> INTERVIEWEE: It would have to be challenging and have enough variety not to bore me.
> INTERVIEWER: Are you easily bored?

Note how the interviewer probes to learn more about the interviewee's responses. Each probe seeks more details about the interviewee's attitudes toward work.

Leading Questions   Leading questions predispose a certain response. For example, "You believe in teamwork, don't you?" encourages "Yes" as a response, whereas "You don't drink on a regular basis, do you?" encourages "No" as a response. Leading questions generally are not a good way to get candid responses because they suggest how you want a person to respond (Stewart & Cash, 1991). Leading questions can be useful, however, if an interviewer wants to test an interviewee's commitment to an idea. An acquaintance of mine who recruits employees for sales positions that require a lot of travel often poses this leading question: "After a year or two of travel, the novelty wears off. I assume you expect a permanent location after a year or so with us, right?" Applicants who answer "yes" do not get job offers because travel is an ongoing part of the sales positions.

Loaded Questions   Loaded questions are worded to reflect the emotions or judgments of the person asking the question. The language in the question is laden with emotion and may cause an interviewee to respond emotionally. "How do you feel about slackers who expect to leave work at 5 p.m. every day?" In this question, the word *slackers* suggests the interviewer's negative judgment of employees who expect to quit at 5 p.m. each day. An interviewee is likely to pick up on the bias in the question and reply, "I think an employee should work until the job is done, not until the clock strikes 5 p.m." But this may not reflect the interviewee's actual views, so the question isn't effective in probing the interviewee's attitudes.

Another version of the loaded question involves baiting an interviewee. The classic example of a loaded question is, "When did you stop beating your dog?" The question presumes something (in this case, that the interviewee at some point did beat his or her dog) that hasn't been established. This kind of loaded question is likely to foster defensiveness in an interviewee and to limit what an interviewer learns about the interviewee.

Summary Questions   A final kind of question is the summary question, which covers what has been discussed. Although summary questions often are phrased as statements, they function as questions. For example, "I believe we've covered everything" should be perceived as, "Do we need to discuss anything else?" "It seems we've agreed on expectations for your performance during the next quarter" should be perceived as, "Do you feel we have a common understanding of what's expected of you?" Communication that summarizes topics in an interview provides an opportunity for participants to check whether they agree about what they've discussed and what will follow.

What we've discussed gives us a foundation for discussing two important challenges for communicating in interviews.

Guidelines for Communicating Effectively in Interviews

Like all other kinds of interaction, interviewing presents challenges that require communication skills. We will discuss two specific challenges: preparing to be interviewed and dealing with illegal questions. We will use the hiring interview to illustrate these challenges, but the ideas we'll discuss pertain to other kinds of interviews as well.

Prepare

My students sometimes tell me that they can't prepare for interviews because they don't know what the interviewer will ask. Even without knowing exactly what questions will arise, you can do a great deal to prepare yourself for a successful interview. First, prepare a résumé that is concise, accurate in content and style (proofread carefully!), and professional in appearance. Your résumé is your first chance to "advertise yourself" to potential employers (Krannich & Banis, 1990).

Conduct Research   Every type of interview benefits from advance research, although the appropriate research varies according to the interview's purpose. Before performance appraisals, both the supervisor and the subordinate should review any previous performance appraisals. In addition, both participants should think about what has happened since the last appraisal: Have goals that were set been met? Have there been notable achievements, such as development of new skills or receipt of awards? It's also appropriate to talk with others to learn what is expected of employees at various stages in their careers.

Research is critical for effective employment interviewing. To learn about an organization, you'll want information about its products and services, self-image, history, benefits, organizational culture, and so on. If you know someone who works for the company, ask that person to share perceptions and information with you. If you aren't personally acquainted with employees at the company, check for materials in your library or placement office or an online service. Standard references such as *Moody's Manuals* and *Standard & Poor's Index* provide information about the size, locations, salary levels, structure, employee benefits, and financial condition of many organizations.

The Internet is an additional source of information. Many companies have Web pages that allow you to learn such things as how the company thinks of itself, the image it wants to project, and its size and geographic scope. Because websites are updated regularly, visiting a company's website is a good way to get the current information about a company that interests you.

Research enhances your effectiveness in two ways. First, the information you gather provides a basis for questions that show you have done your homework and understand the company. Second, when you know something about a company's

Review It!

Forms of Questions:
- Open
- Closed
- Mirror
- Hypotehtical
- Probing
- Leading
- Loaded
- Summary

or program's priorities, image, and goals, you can adapt your communication to acknowledge the expectations and norms of the company.

Engage in Person-Centered Communication   In Chapter 2, we discussed person-centered communication, in which one person recognizes and respects the perspective of another person. To prepare for an interview, ask yourself, "What would I want to know if I were interviewing me for this position?" Don't ask what you want to tell the interviewer about yourself or what you think is most important about your record. Instead, take the perspective of the interviewer as you anticipate the interaction.

You are not likely to know the interviewer personally, so you can't realistically expect to understand him or her as a unique individual. What matters is to recognize that in the interview situation, the recruiter is a representative of a particular company with distinct goals, history, expectations, and culture. If you have researched the company, you will be able to adapt your communication to the interviewer's frame of reference.

Person-centered communication also requires sensitivity to cultural differences. For instance, people who were raised in some Asian cultures tend to be modest about personal achievements and abilities. Viewed from a Western perspective, such modesty might be misinterpreted as lack of confidence (Kikoski, 1998; U.S. Department of Labor, 1992).

Practice Responding   One of the most common complaints of employment recruiters is that candidates are unprepared for interviews (DeVito, 1994). Examples of appearing unprepared include not bringing a résumé to the interview, not knowing about the company, and not recalling specific information, such as names of former supervisors and dates of employment. Ability to recall specific information shows you are prepared and knowledgeable. Yet many people fumble when asked about specifics. Why? Because they assume they know about themselves—after all, it's their life—so they don't bother to review details and practice responses.

You can avoid appearing unprepared by taking time before an interview to review your experiences and accomplishments and to remind yourself of key names, places, and dates. It's also a good idea to practice responding aloud to questions. You want your communication to reflect what employers look for— attentiveness, positive attitude, preparation, clarity, and motivation (Anderson & Killenberg, 1998; Farnill et al., 1997; Peterson, 1997; Ramsay, Gallois, & Callan, 1997). Figure B.1 lists questions commonly asked during employment interviews.

Conducting research, engaging in person-centered communication, and practicing responses will not prepare you for everything that can happen in an interview. However, they will make you better prepared and more impressive than candidates who don't follow the guidelines we've discussed.

Manage Illegal Questions in Interviews

Just a couple of years ago, a student who was completing a professional degree was asked this question by a job recruiter: "What methods of birth control do you use?" Fortunately, this student knew the question was discriminatory, so she refused to answer and reported the interviewer to the campus placement service.

Know the Law   The Equal Employment Opportunity Commission (EEOC) is a federally created entity that monitors various kinds of discrimination in hiring

1. Why did you decide to attend this school?
2. Why did you choose _____ as your major?
3. Tell me about yourself.
4. Why are you interested in our company (firm)?
5. How does your academic background pertain to this job?
6. What do you consider your most serious weakness?
7. What are your long-term professional goals?
8. Which of the jobs you've held has been most satisfying to you? Why?
9. What is the most difficult situation you have ever been in? How did you handle it?
10. Who has been the biggest influence in your life?
11. What are your hobbies? How do you spend spare time?
12. How do you define success in sales (marketing, management, training, etc.)?
13. Why should we hire you instead of another person?
14. What kind of people do you prefer to work with? Why?
15. Are you willing to travel?
16. What do you expect your employer to do for you?
17. What do you think of the president's budget proposal (or another current national issue)?
18. Describe your closest friend.
19. How long would you expect to remain with our company?
20. Define *teamwork*. Give me an example of a team on which you worked.

FIGURE B.1
Common Questions Asked in Employment Interviews

decisions. In 1970, the EEOC issued initial guidelines pertinent to employment interviews, and these have been updated periodically. EEOC guidelines also apply to tests, application forms, and other devices used to screen job applicants.

EEOC regulations prohibit discrimination on the basis of criteria that are legally irrelevant to job qualifications. Because the EEOC is an arm of the federal government, it protects interviewees in all states from intrusive questions about race, ethnicity, marital status, age, sex, disability, and arrests. Individual states and institutions may impose additional limits on information about candidates that may be used in hiring decisions. For instance, my school has a policy against discrimination based on military service or sexual orientation.

An illegal question reflects either an interviewer's ignorance of the law or his or her willful disregard of it. People who conduct interviews should review restrictions on questions in a good source such as Arthur Bell's 1989 book *The Complete Manager's Guide to Interviewing*. Whether interviewers intend to ask illegal questions or not, it's important for interviewees to know what questions are not legally permissible in employment interviews. If you don't understand the legal boundaries on questions, you cannot protect your rights.

Respond Deliberately to Illegal Questions   Knowing which questions are out of bounds doesn't tell us what to do if we are asked an inappropriate question. You may choose to respond if it doesn't bother you. You also have the right to object and to point out to an interviewer that a question is inappropriate. If you don't care about the job, this is a reasonable way to respond. But realize that even if you exercise your rights diplomatically, doing so may lessen an interviewer's interest in hiring you.

One effective way to respond to unlawful questions is to provide only information that may be sought legally. This strategy preserves a supportive climate in the interview by not directly reprimanding the interviewer. For instance, if an employer asks whether you are a native Chinese speaker, you might respond, "I am fluent in both English and Chinese." If you are asked whether you belong to any political organizations, be wary because this is often an effort to determine your religion or political affiliation. You might answer, "The only organizations to which I belong that are relevant to this job are the Training and Development Association and the National Communication Association." If a diplomatic response, such as a partial answer, doesn't satisfy the interviewer, it is appropriate for you to be more assertive. You might ask, "How does your question pertain to qualifications for this job?" This more direct response can be effective in protecting your rights without harming the climate. It is possible to be both assertive and cordial, and this is generally advisable. Figure B.2 lists some questions that can and cannot legally be asked by employment interviewers.

FIGURE B.2
Legal and Illegal
Questions

It's legal to ask:
1. Are you a law-abiding person?
2. Do you have the physical strength to do this job?
3. Are you fluent in any languages other than English?
4. Could you provide proof that you are old enough to meet the age requirements for this job?
5. Your transcript shows you took a course in socialism. Did you find it valuable?

But illegal to ask:
1. Are you physically disabled?
2. Are you a native speaker of English?
3. How old are you?
4. Are you a socialist?
5a. Would you be willing to live in a town without a temple/church/synagogue?
5b. Does your religion allow to work on Saturdays?
6. May I have a picture to put with your file?
7. Do you have (plan to have) children?
8. Are you married?
9. Do you have reliable child care?
10. Do you own a car or a house?
11. What is your political affiliation?

Summary

In this appendix, we have gained insight into the structure and processes involved in interviewing. We have learned that most interviews follow a three-part sequence and that different styles and forms of questions are used to achieve different objectives in interview situations.

In the second section of this appendix, we focused on three guidelines for effective communication when interviewing, especially in the context of job seeking. The first guideline is to prepare by researching the company and the interviewer, by reviewing your qualifications and experience, and by practicing dealing with questions, including difficult ones. A second guideline for effectiveness in interviews is to be person-centered in your communication. Adapting the content and style of your communication to the person with whom you are interacting is important. A final suggestion is to become familiar with legal issues relevant to interviewing. Whether you are an interviewer or an interviewee, you should know and abide by laws governing what can and cannot be asked in interviews.

Experiencing Communication in Our Lives

MindTap

CASE STUDY: Tough Questions

Apply what you've learned in this chapter by analyzing the following case study and using the accompanying questions as a guide. These questions and a video of the case study are also available online in MindTap Speech.

Elliott Miller is a second-semester senior who has double-majored in business and communication. Today, he is interviewing with Community Savings and Loan, which is recruiting managerial trainees. Elliott has dressed carefully. He is wearing his good suit, a light blue shirt, a conservative necktie, and wingtips. At 10 a.m. sharp, he knocks on the office door of Karen Bourne, the person with whom he will interview. She is in her mid-thirties and is dressed in a conservative navy blue suit. She opens the door and offers her hand to Elliott.

BOURNE: Mr. Miller, I see you're right on time. That's a good start. (*They shake hands.*)

MILLER: Thank you for inviting me to interview today.

BOURNE: Sit down. (*He sits in the chair in front of her desk; she sits behind the desk.*) So, you're about to finish college, are you? I remember that time in my own life—exciting and scary!

MILLER: It's definitely both for me. I'm particularly excited about the job here at Community Savings and Loan.

BOURNE: (*smiles*) Then there's a mutual interest. We had a lot of applications, but we're interviewing only eight of them. What I'd like to do is get a sense of your interests and tell you about our managerial trainee program here, so that we can see if the fit between us is as good as it looks on paper. Sound good to you?

MILLER: Great.

BOURNE: Let me start by telling you about a rather common problem we've had with our past managerial trainees. Many of them run into a problem—something they have trouble learning or doing right. That's normal enough—we expect that. But a lot of the trainees seem to get derailed when that happens. Instead of finding another way to approach the problem, they get discouraged and give up. So I'm very interested in hearing what you've done when you've encountered problems or roadblocks in your life.

MILLER: Well, I can remember one time when I hit a real roadblock. I was taking an advanced chemistry course, and I just couldn't seem to understand the material. I failed the first exam, even though I'd studied hard.

BOURNE: Good example of a problem. What did you do?

MILLER: I started going to all the tutorial sessions that grad assistants offer. That helped a little, but I still wasn't getting the material the way I should. So, I organized a study team and offered to pay for pizzas so that the students who were on top of the class would have a reason to come.

BOURNE: (*nodding with admiration*) That shows a lot of initiative and creativity. Did the study team work?

MILLER: (*smiling*) It sure did. I wound up getting a B in the course, and so did several other members of the study team who had been in the same boat I was in early in the semester.

BOURNE: So you don't mind asking for help if you need it?

MILLER: I'd rather do that than flounder, but I'm usually pretty able to operate independently.

BOURNE: So you prefer working on your own to working with others?

MILLER: That depends on the situation or project. If I have all that I need to do something on my own, I'm comfortable working solo. But there are other cases in which I don't have everything I need to do something well—maybe I don't have experience in some aspect of the job or I don't have a particular skill or I don't understand some perspectives on the issues. In cases like that, I think teams are more effective than individuals.

BOURNE: Good. Banking management requires the ability to be self-initiating and also the ability to work with others. Let me ask another question. As I was looking over your transcript and résumé, I noticed that you changed your major several times. Does that indicate you have difficulty making a commitment and sticking with it?

MILLER: I guess you could think that, but it really shows that I was willing to explore a lot of alternatives before making a firm commitment.

BOURNE: But don't you think that you wasted a lot of time and courses getting to that commitment?

MILLER: I don't think so. I learned something in all of the courses I took. For instance, when I was a philosophy major, I learned about logical thinking and careful reasoning. That's going to be useful to me in management. When I was majoring in English, I learned how to write well and how to read others' writing critically. That's going to serve me well in management too.

BOURNE: So what led you to your final decision to double-major in business and communication? That's kind of an unusual combination.

MILLER: It seems a very natural one to me. I wanted to learn about business because I want to be a manager in an organization. I need to know how organizations work, and I need to understand different management philosophies and styles. At the same time, managers work with people, and that means I have to have strong communication skills.

Key Concepts

authoritarian interviews
complaint interviews
counseling interviews
distributive interviews
employment interviews
exit interviews
funnel sequence

information-getting
  interviews
information-giving
  interviews
interview
mirror interviews
performance reviews

persuasive interviews
problem-solving
  interviews
reprimand interview
stress interviews

For Further Reflection and Discussion

1. Arrange an information-seeking interview with a person in the field you
   hope to enter. Ask the person to tell you about the job—its advantages and
   disadvantages and the skills it requires.

2. Schedule an interview with a peer on a topic of mutual interest. During the
   interview, experiment with different forms of questions (e.g., open, closed,
   mirror, probing, hypothetical). How do the different types of questions affect
   the interviewee's comfort and responses?

3. Think about the ethical issues in choosing how to respond to illegal questions
   if the questions are not personally offensive or bothersome. For instance,
   Christians might think they have nothing to lose by responding honestly to
   the question, "Can you work on Saturdays?" If only members of minority
   religions refuse to answer questions about religion, how effective are the legal
   protections provided by EEOC guidelines? If all Protestants answer questions
   about religion honestly, are members of other religions jeopardized?

Ethics

4. Identify a company that is of interest to you for future employment. Visit the
   company's website and record what is presented there. How does information
   on the website help you prepare for an effective job interview? Compare what
   you find on the website with what is available in printed materials (brochures,
   annual reports, etc.) about the company.

5. Go to the book's online resources for this chapter if you would like tips for
   how to be effective in a virtual interview.

Glossary

abstract Removed from concrete reality. Symbols are abstract because they are inferences and generalizations derived from a total reality.

***ad hominem* argument** Argument that attacks the integrity of the person instead of the person's ideas.

agenda setting Mass media's ability to select and call to the public's attention ideas, events, and people.

ambiguous Subject to more than one interpretation. Symbols are ambiguous because their meanings vary from person to person and context to context.

ambushing Listening carefully in order to attack a speaker.

arbitrary Random; not determined by necessity. Symbols are arbitrary because there is no particular reason for any one symbol to stand for a certain referent.

artifacts Personal objects we use to announce our identities and personalize our environments.

assimilation The giving up of one's own culture's ways for those of another culture.

attachment style Any of several patterns of attachment that result from particular parenting styles that teach children who they are, who others are, and how to approach relationships.

attribution A causal account that explains why a thing happened or why someone acted a certain way.

authoritarian interview An interviewing style in which the interviewer has and exerts greater power than the interviewee.

bandwagon appeal The fallacious argument that because many people believe or act in a certain way, everyone should.

chronemics A type of nonverbal communication concerned with how we perceive and use time to define identities and interaction.

claim An assertion. A claim advanced in speaking requires grounds (evidence) and warrants (links between evidence and claims).

climate communication One of three constructive forms of participation in group decision making. Climate communication focuses on creating and sustaining an open, engaged atmosphere for discussion.

cognitive complexity The number of constructs used, how abstract they are, and how elaborately they interact to create perceptions.

cognitive restructuring A method of reducing communication apprehension that involves teaching people to revise how they think about speaking situations.

cohesion Closeness among members of a group; *esprit de corps*.

commitment A decision to remain with a relationship. One of three dimensions of enduring romantic relationships, commitment has more impact on relational continuity than does love alone. It is also an advanced stage in the process of escalation in romantic relationships.

communication A systemic process in which people interact with and through symbols to create and interpret meanings.

communication apprehension Anxiety associated with real or anticipated communication encounters. Communication apprehension is common and can be constructive.

communication network A set of formal and informal links between members of organizations.

communication rules Shared understandings of what communication means and what behaviors are appropriate in various situations.

comparison A form of evidence that uses associations between two things that are similar in some important way.

complaint interview An interview conducted for the purpose of allowing someone to register a complaint about a product, service, person, or company.

constitutive rules Communication rules that define what communication means by specifying how certain communicative acts are to be counted.

constructivism The theory that we organize and interpret experience by applying cognitive structures, called *schemata*.

content level of meaning One of the two levels of meaning in communication. The content level of meaning is the literal, or denotative, information in a message.

convergence The integration of mass media, computers, and telecommunications.

counseling interview An interview in which one person with expertise helps another to understand a problem and develop strategies to overcome the difficulty or cope more effectively with it.

credibility The perception that a person is informed and trustworthy. Listeners confer it, or refuse to confer it, on speakers.

critical listening Attending to communication to analyze and evaluate the content of communication or the person speaking.

critical thinking Examining ideas reflectively and carefully to decide what you should believe, think, or do.

cultivation The cumulative process by which television fosters beliefs about social reality.

cultivation theory The theory that television promotes an inaccurate worldview that viewers nonetheless assume reflects real life.

cultural intelligence Motivational, cognitive, and behavioral abilities to understand and adapt to a range of contexts, people, and patterns of interaction.

cultural relativism The idea that cultures vary in how they think, act, and behave as well as in what they believe and value; not the same as moral relativism.

culture Beliefs, understandings, practices, and ways of interpreting experience that are shared by a number of people.

deductive reasoning A form of reasoning in which a general premise followed by a specific claim establishes a conclusion.

defensive listening Perceiving personal attacks, criticisms, or hostility in communication when no offense is intended.

demographic audience analysis A form of audience analysis that seeks information about the general features of a group of listeners.

derived credibility The expertise and trustworthiness that listeners attribute to a speaker as a result of how the speaker communicates during a presentation.

digital divide The gap between people and communities with access to media, especially social media, and people and communities with less or no access.

direct definition Communication that explicitly tells us who we are by specifically labeling us and reacting to our behaviors. Direct definition usually occurs first in families and then in interaction with peers and others.

distributive interview A style of interviewing in which roughly equal power is held by interviewer and interviewee.

dual perspective The ability to understand another person's perspective, beliefs, thoughts, or feelings.

dynamic Evolving and changing over time.

ego boundaries A person's internal sense of where he or she stops and the rest of the world begins.

egocentric communication An unconstructive form of group contribution that blocks others or calls attention to oneself.

either–or logic The fallacy of suggesting or assuming that only two options or courses of action exist when in fact there may be more.

emotional intelligence The ability to recognize which feelings are appropriate in which situations and the ability to communicate those feelings effectively.

empathy The ability to feel with another person or to feel what that person feels in a given situation.

employment interview An interview in which employer and job candidate assess each other and decide whether there is a good fit between them.

environmental factors Elements of settings that affect how we feel and act. Environmental factors are a type of nonverbal communication.

ethnocentrism The tendency to regard ourselves and our way of life as superior to other people and other ways of life.

ethos The perceived personal character of the speaker.

evidence Material used to support claims. Types of evidence are statistics, examples, comparisons, and quotations. Visual aids may be used to represent evidence graphically.

example A form of evidence; a single instance that makes a point, dramatizes an idea, or personalizes information. The four types of examples are undetailed, detailed, hypothetical, and anecdotal.

exit interview An interview designed to gain information, insights, and perceptions about a place of work or education from a person who is leaving.

extemporaneous speaking A presentational style that includes preparation and practice but not memorization of words and nonverbal behaviors.

fallacy An error in reasoning.

feedback Response to a message; may be verbal, nonverbal, or both. In communication theory, the concept of feedback appeared first in interactive models of communication.

formal outline A complete outline of a speech, including the parts of a speech, main points, supporting material, transitions, and citations for sources.

funnel sequence A pattern of communication in interviews that moves from broad, general questions to progressively narrower, more probing questions.

gatekeeper A person or group that decides which messages pass through the gates of media that control information flow to consumers.

grounds Evidence that supports claims in a speech.

group Three or more people who interact over time, are interdependent, and follow shared rules of conduct to reach a common goal. The team is one type of group.

groupthink The cessation of critical, independent thought on the part of a group's members about ideas generated by the group.

halo effect The tendency to assume that an expert in one area is also an expert in other unrelated areas.

haptics Nonverbal communication that involves physical touch.

hasty generalization A broad claim based on too few examples or insufficient evidence.

hearing The physiological activity that occurs when sound waves hit our eardrums. Unlike listening, hearing is a passive process.

high-context communication style The indirect and undetailed communication favored in collectivist cultures.

hypothetical thought Cognitive awareness of experiences and ideas that are not part of the concrete, present situation.

identification The recognition and enlargement of common ground between communicators.

identity script A guide to action based on rules for living and identity. Initially communicated in families, identity scripts define our roles, how we are to play them, and basic elements in the plot of our lives.

impromptu speaking Public speaking that involves little preparation. Speakers think on their feet as they talk about ideas and positions with which they are familiar.

indexing A technique of noting that statements reflect specific times and circumstances and may not apply to other times or circumstances.

individualism/collectivism One of five dimensions of variation among cultures, this refers to the extent to which members of a culture understand themselves as part of, and connected to, their families, groups, and cultures.

inductive reasoning A form of reasoning that begins with specific instances and forms general conclusions based on them.

informational listening Listening to gain and understand information; tends to focus on the content level of meaning.

information-getting interview An interview in which the interviewer asks questions to learn about the interviewee's qualifications, background, experience, opinions, knowledge, attitudes, or behaviors.

information-giving interview An interview in which the interviewer provides information to the interviewee.

informative speech A presentation that aims to increase listeners' knowledge, understanding, or abilities.

initial credibility The expertise and trustworthiness that listeners attribute to a speaker before a presentation begins. Initial credibility is based on the speaker's titles, positions, experiences, or achievements known to listeners before they hear the speech.

inoculation "Immunization" of listeners to opposing ideas and arguments that they may later encounter.

interpersonal communication Communication between people, usually in close relationships such as friendship and romance.

interpretation The subjective process of evaluating and explaining perceptions.

interview A communication transaction that emphasizes questions and answers.

intrapersonal communication Communication with ourselves; self-talk.

investment Something put into a relationship that cannot be recovered should the relationship end. Investments, more than rewards and love, increase commitment.

key word outline An abbreviated speaking outline that includes only key words for each point in a speech. The key words trigger the speaker's memory of the full point.

kinesics Body position and body motions, including those of the face.

leadership A set of functions that assists groups in accomplishing tasks efficiently and well while maintaining a good climate.

listening A complex process that consists of being mindful, physically receiving messages, selecting and organizing information, interpreting, responding, and remembering.

literal listening Listening only to the content level of meaning and ignoring the relational level of meaning.

loaded language An extreme form of evaluative language that relies on words that strongly slant perceptions and hence meanings.

logos Rational or logical proofs.

long-term/short-term orientation One of five dimensions of variation among cultures, this refers to the extent to which members of a culture think about long term (history and future) versus short term (present).

low-context communication style The direct, precise, and detailed communication favored in individualistic cultures.

mainstreaming The process by which mass communication stabilizes and homogenizes social perspectives; a concept in cultivation theory.

manuscript speaking A presentational style that involves speaking from the complete manuscript of a speech.

masculinity/femininity One of five dimensions of variation among cultures, this refers to the extent to which a culture values aggressiveness, competitiveness, looking out for yourself, and dominating others and nature (considered masculine orientations) versus gentleness, cooperation, and taking care of others and living in harmony with the natural world (considered feminine orientations).

mass media Channels of mass communication, such as television and radio.

meaning The significance we attach to phenomena, such as words, actions, people, objects, and events.

media literacy The ability to understand the influence of mass media and to access, analyze, evaluate, and respond to mass media in informed, critical ways.

memorized speaking A presentational style in which a speech is memorized word for word in advance.

metaphor An implicit comparison of two different things that have something in common.

mindfulness Being fully present in the moment; the first step of listening and the foundation of all other steps.

mind map A holistic record of information on a topic. Mind mapping is a method that can be used to narrow speech topics or to keep track of information gathered during research.

mind reading Assuming that we understand what another person thinks or how another person perceives something.

minimal encouragers Communication that, by expressing interest in hearing more, gently invites another person to elaborate.

mirror interview A style of interviewing in which an interviewer's questions reflect previous responses and comments of the interviewee. Mirror interviews allow interviewees substantial power.

monopolizing Continually focusing communication on oneself instead of on the person who is talking.

motivated sequence pattern A pattern for organizing persuasive speeches that consists of five steps: attention, need, satisfaction, visualization, and action.

multilingual Able to speak and think in more than one language.

neutralization One of the four responses to relational dialectics; involves balancing or finding a compromise between two dialectical poles.

noise Anything that has potential to interfere with intended communication.

nonverbal communication All forms of communication other than words themselves; includes inflection and other vocal qualities as well as several other behaviors.

norm An informal rule that guides how members of a group or culture think, feel, act, and interact. Norms define what is normal or appropriate in various situations.

oral style The visual, vocal, and verbal aspects of the delivery of a public speech.

organizational culture Ways of thinking, acting, and understanding work that are shared by members of an organization and that reflect an organization's distinct identity.

paralanguage Vocal communication that does not include actual words; for example, sounds, vocal qualities, accents, and inflection.

paraphrasing A method of clarifying others' meaning by restating their communication.

participation A response to cultural diversity in which people incorporate some practices, customs, and traditions of other groups into their own lives.

particular others One source of social perspectives that people use to define themselves and guide how they think, act, and feel. The perspectives of

particular others are the viewpoints of people who are significant to the self.

passion Intensely positive feelings and desires for another person. Passion is based on the rewards of involvement and is not equivalent to commitment.

pathos Emotional proofs for claims.

perception The process of actively selecting, organizing, and interpreting people, objects, events, situations, and activities.

performance review An interview in which a supervisor comments on a subordinate's achievements and professional development, identifies any weaknesses or problems, and collaborates with the subordinate to develop goals for future performance. Subordinates should offer perceptions of their strengths and weaknesses and participate actively in developing goals for professional development. Also known as a *performance appraisal.*

personal construct A bipolar mental yardstick that allows us to measure people and situations along specific dimensions of judgment.

personal relationship A relationship defined by uniqueness, rules, relational dialectics, and commitment and affected by contexts. Personal relationships, unlike social ones, are irreplaceable.

person-centered perception The ability to perceive another as a unique and distinct individual apart from social roles and generalizations.

perspective of the generalized other Viewpoint based on the rules, roles, and attitudes endorsed by the whole social community in which we live.

persuasive interview An interview designed to influence attitudes, beliefs, values, or actions.

persuasive speech A presentation that aims to change listeners by prompting them to think, feel, or act differently.

physical appearance Physical features of people and the values attached to those features; a type of nonverbal communication.

policy A formal statement of an organizational practice. An organization's policies reflect and uphold the overall culture of the organization.

positive visualization A technique of reducing speaking anxiety; a person visualizes herself or himself communicating effectively in progressively challenging speaking situations.

post hoc, ergo propter hoc Latin phrase meaning "After this, therefore because of this." The fallacy of suggesting or assuming that because event B follows event A, event A has therefore caused event B.

power The ability to influence others; a feature of small groups that affects participation.

power distance One of the five dimensions of variation among cultures, this refers to the size of the gap between people with high and low power and the extent to which that gap is regarded as normal.

power over The ability to help or harm others. Power over others usually is communicated in ways that highlight the status and influence of the person using the power.

power to The ability to empower others to reach their goals. People who use power to help others generally do not highlight their own status and influence.

problem-solving interview An interview in which people collaborate to identify sources of a mutual problem and to develop ways to address or resolve it.

procedural communication One of three constructive ways of participating in group decision making. Procedural communication orders ideas and coordinates the contributions of members.

process Something that is ongoing and continuously in motion, the beginnings and endings of which are difficult to identify. Communication is a process.

prototype A knowledge structure that defines the clearest or most representative example of some category.

proxemics A type of nonverbal communication that includes space and how we use it.

pseudo-listening Pretending to listen.

psychological responsibility The responsibility for remembering, planning, and coordinating domestic work and child care. In general, women assume the psychological responsibility for child care and housework even if both partners share in the actual tasks.

puffery In advertising, superlative claims for a product that seem factual but are actually meaningless.

punctuation Defining the beginning and ending of interaction or interaction episodes.

qualifier A word or phrase that limits the scope of a claim. Common qualifiers are most, usually, and in general.

quotation A form of evidence that uses exact citations of statements made by others. Also called *testimony*.

rebuttal A response to listeners' reservations about a claim made by a speaker.

red herring argument An argument that is irrelevant to the topic; an attempt to divert attention from something the arguer can't or doesn't want to address.

reflected appraisal Our perceptions of others' views of us.

reframing One of four responses to relational dialectics. The reframing response transcends the apparent contradiction between two dialectical poles and reinterprets them as not in tension.

regulative rules Communication rules that regulate interaction by specifying when, how, where, and with whom to talk about certain things.

relational culture A private world of rules, understandings, and patterns of acting and interpreting that partners create to give meaning to their relationship; the nucleus of intimacy.

relational dialectics Opposing forces or tensions that are normal parts of all relationships. The three relational dialectics are autonomy/connectedness, novelty/predictability, and openness/closedness.

relational listening Listening to support another person or to understand another person's feelings and perceptions; focuses on the relational level of meaning as much as on the content level of meaning.

relationship level of meaning One of the two levels of meaning in communication; expresses the relationship between communicators.

reprimand interview An interview conducted by a supervisor with a subordinate to identify lapses in the subordinate's professional conduct, determine sources of problems, and establish a plan for improving future performance.

resistance A response to cultural diversity in which the cultural practices of others are attacked or the superiority of one's own cultural traditions is proclaimed.

resonance The extent to which media representations are congruent with personal experience.

respect A response to cultural diversity in which one values others' customs, traditions, and values, even if one does not actively incorporate them into one's own life.

rite A dramatic, planned set of activities that brings together aspects of an organization's culture in a single event.

ritual A form of communication that occurs regularly and that members of an organization perceive as a familiar and routine part of organizational life.

rules Patterned ways of behaving and interpreting behavior; all relationships develop rules.

role The collection of responsibilities and behaviors associated with and expected of a specific position in an organization.

schemata (singular: *schema*) Cognitive structures we use to organize and interpret experiences. Four types of schemata are prototypes, personal constructs, stereotypes, and scripts.

script One of four cognitive schemata. A script defines an expected or appropriate sequence of action in a particular setting.

segmentation One of four responses to relational dialectics. Segmentation responses meet one dialectical need while ignoring or not satisfying the contradictory dialectical need.

selective listening Focusing on only selected parts of communication. We listen selectively when we screen out parts of a message that don't interest us or with which we disagree and also when we rivet attention on parts of communication that do interest us or with which we agree.

self A multidimensional process in which the individual forms and acts from social perspectives that arise and evolve in communication.

self-disclosure Revelation of information about ourselves that others are unlikely to discover on their own.

self-fulfilling prophecy An expectation or judgment of ourselves brought about by our own actions.

self-sabotage Self-talk that communicates that we're no good, we can't do something, we can't change, and so on. Undermines belief in ourselves and motivation to change and grow.

self-serving bias The tendency to attribute our positive actions and successes to stable, global, internal influences that we control and to attribute negative actions and failures to unstable, specific, external influences beyond our control.

separation One of four responses to relational dialectics, in which friends or romantic partners assign one pole of a dialectic to certain spheres of activities or topics and the contradictory dialectical pole to distinct spheres of activities or topics.

silence The lack of verbal communication or paralanguage. Silence is a type of nonverbal communication that can express powerful messages.

simile A direct comparison that typically uses the words *like* or *as* to link two things.

situational audience analysis A method of audience analysis that seeks information about specific listeners that relates directly to a topic, speaker, and occasion.

skills training A method of reducing communication apprehension that assumes that anxiety is a result of lack of speaking skills and therefore can be reduced by learning skills.

slippery slope The fallacy of suggesting or assuming that once a certain step is taken, other steps will inevitably follow that will lead to some unacceptable consequence.

social climbing The attempt to increase personal status in a group by winning the approval of high-status members.

social community A group of people who live within a dominant culture yet who also have common distinctive experiences and patterns of communicating.

social comparison Comparing ourselves with others to form judgments of our own talents, abilities, qualities, and so on.

social loafing Exists when members of a group exert less effort than they would if they worked alone.

social media Electronic tools that allow people to connect and to interact actively.

specific purpose A behavioral objective or observable response that a speaker specifies as a gauge of effectiveness; reinforces a speaker's more general speaking goals.

speech to entertain A speech the primary goal of which is to amuse, interest, or engage listeners.

speech to inform A speech the primary goal of which is to increase listeners' understanding, awareness, or knowledge of some topic.

speech to persuade A speech the primary goal of which is to change listeners' attitudes, beliefs, or behaviors or to motivate listeners to action.

standpoint theory The theory that a culture includes social groups that differently shape the knowledge, identities, and opportunities of members of those groups, which can lead to political consciousness.

static evaluation Assessments that suggest something is unchanging or static. "Bob is impatient" is a static evaluation.

statistics A form of evidence that uses numbers to summarize a great many individual cases or to demonstrate relationships between phenomena.

stonewalling Refusal to discuss issues that are creating tension in a relationship. Stonewalling is especially corrosive in relationships because it blocks the possibility of resolving conflicts.

stereotype A predictive generalization about people and situations.

stress interview A style of interviewing in which an interviewer deliberately attempts to create anxiety in the interviewee.

structure In an organization, the set of procedures, relationships, and practices that provides predictability for members so that they understand roles, procedures, and expectations and so that work gets done.

survey research Research that involves asking a number of people about their opinions, preferences, actions, or beliefs relevant to a speaking topic.

symbol An arbitrary, ambiguous, and abstract representation of a phenomenon. Symbols are the basis of language, much nonverbal behavior, and human thought.

synergy Collaborative vitality that enhances the efforts, talents, and strengths of individual members.

system A group of interrelated elements that affect one another. Communication is systemic.

systematic desensitization A method of reducing communication apprehension that teaches people how to relax physiologically and then helps them practice feeling relaxed as they imagine themselves in progressively difficult communication situations.

task communication One of the three constructive forms of participation in group decision making; focuses on giving and analyzing information and ideas.

team A special kind of group characterized by different and complementary resources of members and a strong sense of collective identity. All teams are groups, but not all groups are teams.

terminal credibility The cumulative expertise and trustworthiness listeners attribute to a speaker as a result of the speaker's initial and derived credibility; may be greater or less than initial credibility, depending on how effectively a speaker communicates.

thesis statement The main idea of an entire speech. It should capture the key message in a concise sentence that listeners can remember easily.

tolerance A response to diversity in which one accepts differences even though one may not approve of or even understand them.

totalizing Responding to people as if one aspect of them were the sum total of who they are.

Toulmin model of reasoning A representation of effective reasoning that includes five components: claim, grounds (evidence), warrant (link between grounds and claim), qualifier, and rebuttal.

transitions Words and sentences that connect ideas and main points in a speech so that listeners can follow a speaker.

uncertainty avoidance One of five dimensions of variation among cultures, this refers to the extent to which people try to avoid ambiguity and vagueness.

understanding A response to cultural diversity in which it is assumed that differences are rooted in cultural teachings and that no traditions, customs, and behaviors are intrinsically more valuable than others.

uses and gratification theory The theory that people choose to attend to mass communication in order to fulfill personal needs and preferences.

visual aids Presentation of evidence by visual means such as charts, graphs, photographs, and physical objects to reinforce ideas presented verbally or to provide information.

warrant A justification for grounds (evidence) and claims in persuasive speaking.

working outline A sketch of main ideas and their relationships; used by and intended only for the speaker.

works cited A list of sources used in preparing a speech.

References

Acker, J. (2013). Is capitalism gendered and racialized? In M. Andersen & Ph.H. Collins (Eds.), *Race, class, and gender: An anthology* (8th ed., pp. 125–133). Boston, MA: Cengage.

Adams, K., & Galanes, G. (2011). *Communicating in groups*. New York: McGraw-Hill.

Adams, S. (2014, April 21). How women breadwinners can save their relationships. *Forbes*. Retrieved from http://www.forbes.com /sites/susanadams/2014/04/21/how-women-breadwinners-can-save-their-relationships/

Adler, J. (2007, March 12). The great sorority purge. *Newsweek*, p. 47.

Adler, R., Hirsch, S., & Mordaunt, M. (Eds.). (2012). *Voice and communication therapy for the transgender/transsexual client: A comprehensive clinical guide* (2nd ed.). San Diego, CA: Plural Publications.

Adler, R., & Proctor, R., II. (2013). *Looking out /looking in* (14th ed.). Boston, MA: Cengage.

Alberts, J., Tracy, S., & Trethewey, A. (2011). An integrative theory of the division of domestic labor: Threshold level, social organizing and sense-making. *Journal of Family Communication*, 11, 21–28.

Allen, B. J. (2006). Communicating race at WeighCo. In J. T. Wood & S. W. Duck (Eds.), *Composing relationships: Communication in everyday life* (pp. 146–155). Belmont, CA: Thomson Wadsworth.

Allen, M., Hale, J., Mongeau, P., Berkowitz-Stafford, S., Stafford, S., Shanahan, W., & Ray, C. (1990). Testing a model of message sidedness: Three replications. *Communication Monographs*, 37, 275–291.

American Society for Plastic Surgeons. (2014). *Celebrating 15 years of trustworthy plastic surgery statistics*. Retrieved from http://www.surgery .org/media/news-releases/celebrating-15-years-of-trustworthy-plastic-surgery-statistics

Amodio, D., & Showers, C. (2006). "Similarity breeds liking" revisited: The moderating role of commitment. *Journal of Social and Personal Relationships*, 22, 817–836.

Andersen, M. L., & Collins, P. H. (Eds.). (2013). *Race, class, and gender: An anthology* (8th ed.). Belmont, CA: Wadsworth.

Angier, N. (2013, November 26). Families. *New York Times*, pp. D1, D2–D3.

Ansari, A. (2015, June 15). Love in an age of like. *Time*, pp. 40–46.

Ansari, A., & Klinenberg, E. (2015). *Modern romance*. New York: Penguin

Aratani, L. (2007, February 27). Teens aren't studying at 100%. *Raleigh News & Observer*, p. 4A.

Argyle, M., & Henderson, M. (1984). The rules of friendship. *Journal of Social and Personal Relationships*, 1, 211–237.

Argyris, C. (2012). *Organizational traps*. New York: Oxford University Press.

Arroyo, A., & Harwood, J. (2012). Exploring the causes and consequences of engaging in fat talk. *Journal of Applied Communication Research*, 40, 167–187.

Ashcraft, K. L., & Mumby, D. K. (2004). *Reworking gender: A feminist communicology of organization*. Thousand Oaks, CA: Sage.

Badiou, A. (2012). *In praise of love*. London: Serpent's Tail.

Bailey, A. (1998, February 29). Daily bread. *Durham Herald-Sun*, p. C5.

Baird, J. (2014, April 7). Neither female nor male. *New York Times*, p. A21.

Bakalar, N. (2012, July 24). Fitness products come mostly filled with fiction. *New York Times*, p. D5.

Balaji, M., & Worawongs, T. (2010). The new Suzie Wong: Normative assumptions of white male and Asian female relationships. *Communication, Culture & Critique*, 3, 224–241.

Balcetis, E., & Dunning, D. (2010). Wishful seeing: Desirable objects are seen as closer. *Psychological Science*, 21, 147–152.

Banse, R. (2004). Adult attachment and marital satisfaction: Evidence for dyadic configuration effects. *Journal of Social and Personal Relationships*, 21, 273–282.

Barash, S. (2006). *Tripping the prom queen.* New York: St. Martin's Griffin.

Barge, K. (2009). Social groups, workgroups, and teams. In W. F. Eadie (Ed.), *21st century communication: A reference handbook* (pp. 340–348). Thousand Oaks, CA: Sage.

Bargh, J. (1997). *The automaticity of everyday life.* Mahwah, NJ: Erlbaum.

Bargh, J. (1999, January 29). The most powerful manipulative messages are hiding in plain sight. *Chronicle of Higher Education,* p. B6.

Baron, N. (2010). *Always on: Language in an online and mobile world.* New York: Oxford University Press.

Baron, R. A., & Berne, D. (1994). *Social psychology* (7th ed.). Boston, MA: Allyn & Bacon.

Barstead, M. G., Bouchard, L. C., & Shih, J. H. (2013). Understanding gender differences in co-rumination and confidant choice in young adults. *Journal of Social and Clinical Psychology, 32,* 791–808.

Bartlett, T. (2003, March 7). Take my chair (please). *Chronicle of Higher Education,* pp. A36–A38.

Baxter, L. A. (1990). Dialectical contradictions in relational development. *Journal of Social and Personal Relationships, 7,* 69–88.

Baxter, L. A. (1993). The social side of personal relationships: A dialectical perspective. In S. Duck (Ed.), *Understanding relationship processes, Vol. 3: Social context and relationships* (pp. 139–165). Newbury Park, CA: Sage.

Baxter, L. A., & Montgomery, B. (1996). *Relating: Dialogues and dialectics.* New York: Guilford Press.

Beatty, M. J., Plax, T., & Kearney, P. (1985). Reinforcement vs. modeling theory in the development of communication apprehension: A retrospective analysis. *Communication Research Reports, 12,* 80–95.

Beebe, S., & Masterson, J. (2011). *Communication in small groups: Principles and practices.* New York: Allyn & Bacon.

Begley, S. (2009, February 16). Will the BlackBerry sink the presidency? *Newsweek,* pp. 36–39.

Beil, L. (2011, November 29). The certainty of memory has its day in court. *New York Times,* pp. D1, D6.

Bellamy, L. (1996, December 18). Kwanzaa cultivates cultural and culinary connections. *Raleigh News & Observer,* pp. 1F, 9F.

Bendavid, N. (2013, October 31). Countries expand recognition for alternative 'intersex' gender. *The Wall Street Journal,* p. A9.

Benenson, J., Gordon, A., & Roy, R. (2000). Children's evaluative appraisals in competition in tetrads versus dyads. *Small Group Research, 31,* 635–652.

Bergen, K., & Braithwaite, D. O. (2009). Identity as constituted in communication. In W. F. Eadie (Ed.), *21st century communication: A reference handbook* (pp. 166–173). Thousand Oaks, CA: Sage.

Bergner, R. M., & Bergner, L. L. (1990). Sexual misunderstanding: A descriptive and pragmatic formulation. *Psychotherapy, 27,* 464–467.

Berne, E. (1964). *Games people play.* New York: Grove Press.

Berrett, D. (2011, November 18). What spurs students to stay in college and learn? Good teaching and diversity. *Chronicle of Higher Education,* p. A27.

Berrett, D. (2012, February 3). "Adrift" in adulthood: Students who struggled in college find life harsher after graduation. *Chronicle of Higher Education,* p. A20.

Berry, L. (2014, May 21). "Ideal" body image differs by race. *Medscape Medical News.* Retrieved from http://www.medscape.com/viewarticle/825489

Birdwhistell, R. (1970). *Kinesics and context.* Philadelphia, PA: University of Pennsylvania Press.

Blow, C. M. (2009, February 21). A nation of cowards? *New York Times,* p. A17.

Bodey, K., & Wood, J. T. (2009). Grrrlpower: What counts as voice and who does the counting? *Southern Journal of Communication, 74,* 325–337.

Bohill, C., Owen, C., Jeong, E., Alicea, B., & Bocca, F. (2009). Virtual reality. In W. F. Eadie (Ed.), *21st century communication: A reference handbook* (pp. 534–542). Thousand Oaks, CA: Sage.

Borchers, T. (2006). *Rhetorical theory: An introduction.* Belmont, CA: Thomson Wadsworth.

Bornstein, M., & Bradley, R. (Eds.). (2003). *Socioeconomic status, parenting, and child development.* Mahwah, NJ: Earlbaum.

Bornstein, R., & Languirand, M. (2003). *Healthy dependency.* New York: Newmarket Press.

Bowlby, J. (1973). *Separation: Attachment and loss* (Vol. 2). New York: Basic Books.

Bowlby, J. (1988). *A secure base: Parent-child attachment and healthy human development.* New York: Basic Books.

Brady, J. (2013, May 22). Some companies foster creativity, others fake it. *The Wall Street Journal,* p. A15.

Brady, M. (2015). *Understanding auditory learning: Integrating-listening K-12 classroom.* Retrieved from http://ltd.edc.org/understanding-auditory-learning-integrating-listening-k-12-classroom

Brody, J. (2015, July 14). Limit children's screen time, and your own. *New York Times*, p. D7.

Braithwaite, D., & Kellas, J. K. (2006). Shopping for and with friends: Everyday communication at the shopping mall. In J. T. Wood & S. W. Duck (Eds.), *Composing relationships: Communication in everyday life* (pp. 86–95). Belmont, CA: Thomson Wadsworth.

Braithwaite, S. R., Delevi, R., & Fincham, F. D. (2010). Romantic relationships and the physical and mental health of college students. *Personal Relationships, 17,* 1–12.

Brenning, K., Soenens, B., Braet, C., & Bosmans, G. (2011). An adaptation of the experiences in close relationships scale-revised for use with children and adolescents. *Journal of Personal and Social Relationships, 28,* 1048–1072.

Bruess, C. (2015). Yard sales and yellow roses: rituals in enduring relationships. In D. O. Braithwaite & J. T. Wood (Eds.), *Casing interpersonal communication* (2nd ed., pp. 111–116). Dubuque, IA: Kendall Hunt.

Bruess, C., & Hoefs, A. (2006). The cat puzzle recovered: Composing relationships through family ritual. In J. T. Wood & S. W. Duck (Eds.), *Composing relationships: Communication in everyday life* (pp. 65–75). Belmont, CA: Thomson Wadsworth.

Bryant, J., & Oliver, M. B. (Eds.). (2008). *Media effects* (3rd ed.). New York: Routledge.

Buber, M. (1970). *I and thou* (Walter Kaufmann, Trans.). New York: Scribner.

Burchell, J. L., & Ward, J. (2011). Sex drive, attachment style, relationship status and previous infidelity as predictors of sex differences in romantic jealousy. *Personality and Individual Differences, 51,* 657–661.

Burke, K. (1950). *A rhetoric of motives.* Englewood Cliffs, NJ: Prentice Hall.

Burleson, B. R., & Rack, J. (2008). Constructivism theory. In L. A. Baxter & D. O. Braithwaite (Eds.), *Engaging theories in interpersonal communication: Multiple perspectives* (pp. 51–63). Thousand Oaks, CA: Sage.

Burney, M. (2012, March 15). Standing up to bullies. *Chronicle of Higher Education*, pp. 50–53.

Buzzanell, P., & Kirby, E. (2013). Communicating work-life issues. In L. Putnam & D. Mumby (Eds.), *The SAGE handbook of organizational communication: Advances in theory, research and methods* (pp. 351–374). Thousand Oaks, CA: Sage.

Calero, H. (2005). *The power of nonverbal communication: What you do is more important than what you say.* Los Angeles, CA: Silver Lake.

Cancian, F. (1987). *Love in America.* Cambridge, UK: Cambridge University Press.

Carnegie, D. (1936). *How to win friends and influence people.* New York: Simon & Schuster.

Carr, N. (2011). *The shallows: What the Internet is doing to our brains.* New York: Norton.

Cassirer, E. (1944). *An essay on man.* New Haven, CT: Yale University Press.

Caughlin, J., & Vangelisti, A. (2000). An individual difference explanation of why married couples engage in the demand/withdraw pattern of conflict. *Journal of Social and Personal Relationships, 17,* 523–551.

Center for Health Communication. (2012). *Harvard alcohol project.* Retrieved from http://www.hsph.harvard.edu/research/chc/harvard-alcohol-project/index.html

Centers for Disease Control and Prevention. (2009). *STD surveillance 2009.* Retrieved from http://www.cdc.gov/std/stats09/ chlamydia.htm

Centers for Disease Control and Prevention. (2011). *HIV/AIDS.* Retrieved from http://www.cdc.gov/hiv/default.htm

Chan, Y. (1999). Density, crowding, and factors intervening in their relationship: Evidence from a hyper-dense metropolis. *Social Indicators Research, 48,* 103–124.

Chang, K. (2015, March 3). New stage of progress in science. *New York Times*, pp. D1, D5.

Chen, H., Luo, S., Yue, G., Xu, D., & Zhaoyang, R. (2009). Do birds of a feather flock together in china? *Personal Relationships, 16,* 167–186.

Chen, P. (2012, June 5). The trouble with "doctor knows best." *Raleigh News & Observer*, p. D5.

Choi, C. (2015, June 11). Taco Bell executives bone up on youth lingo. *Raleigh News & Observer*, p. 6A.

Choose Your Parents Wisely. (2014, July 26). *The Economist*, pp. 21–25.

Ciarrochi, J., & Mayer, J. (2007). *Applying emotional intelligence.* Florence, KY: Psychology Press.

Clancy, C. M. (2011, May 3). *Safety culture creates better care for patients.* U.S. Department of Health and Human Services: Agency for Healthcare Research. Retrieved from http://www.ahrq.gov/consumer/cc/cc050311.htm

Clydesdale, T. (2009, January 23). Wake up and smell the new epistemology. *Chronicle of Higher Education*, pp. B7–B9.

Cockburn-Wootten, C., & Zorn, T. (2006). Cabbages and headache cures: Work stories within the family. In J. T. Wood & S. W. Duck (Eds.), *Composing relationships: Communication in everyday life* (pp. 137–145). Belmont, CA: Thomson Wadsworth.

Cole, T., & Leets, L. (1999). Attachment styles and intimate television viewing: Insecurely forming relationships in a parasocial way. *Journal of Social and Personal Relationships, 16,* 495–511.

Collins, F. S., & Fauci, A. S. (2010, May 23). AIDS in 2010: How we're living with HIV. *Parade,* pp. 10–12.

Conrad, C., & Poole, M. (2012). *Strategic organizational communication in a global economy* (7th ed.). New York: Harcourt.

Cooley, C. H. (1912). *Human nature and the social order.* New York: Scribner.

Coombs, W. T., Falkheimer, J., Heide, M., & Young, P. (2016). *Strategic communication, social media, land democracy.* New York: Routledge.

Coontz, S. (2014, July 27). The new instability. *New York Times,* pp. SR1, 7.

Cooper, L. (1997). Listening competency in the workplace: A model for training. *Business Communication Quarterly, 60,* 75–84.

Coopman, S., & Lull, J. (2013). *Public speaking: The evolving art.* Belmont, CA: Wadsworth.

Covey, S. (2012). *The 7 habits for managers.* Grand Haven, MI: Franklin Covey Brilliance Audio.

Coontz, S. (2013). Gender equality. *The New York Times,* pp. 1, 6, 7.

Cox, J. R. (2016). Personal communication.

Cronen, V., Pearce, W. B., & Snavely, L. (1979). A theory of rule-structure and types of episodes and a study of perceived enmeshment in undesired repetitive patterns ("URPs"). In D. Nimmo (Ed.), *Communication yearbook* (Vol. 3, pp. 225–240). New Brunswick, NJ: Transaction Books.

Cross, G. (2008). *Men to boys: The making of modern immaturity.* New York: Columbia University Press.

Crossen, C. (1997, July 10). Blah, blah, blah. *The Wall Street Journal,* pp. 1A, 6A.

Cummings, M. (1993). Teaching the African American rhetoric course. In J. Ward (Ed.), *African American communication: An anthology in traditional and contemporary studies* (pp. 239–248). Dubuque, IA: Kendall/Hunt.

Davies-Popelka, W. (2015). Mirror, mirror on the wall: Weight, identity, and self-talk. In D. O. Braithwaite & J. T. Wood (Eds.), *Casing interpersonal communication* (2nd ed., pp. 25–32). Dubuque, IA: Kendall Hunt.

DeFleur, M. L., & Ball-Rokeach, S. (1989). *Theories of mass communication* (5th ed.). White Plains, NY: Longman.

Delia, J., Clark, R. A., & Switzer, D. (1974). Cognitive complexity and impression formation in informal social interaction. *Speech Monographs, 41,* 299–308.

DeMaris, A. (2007). The role of relationship inequity in marital disruption. *Journal of Social and Personal Relationships, 24,* 177–195.

Demographics. (2009, January 26). *Newsweek,* p. 70.

Dennis, A., & Wood, J. T. (2012). "We're not going to have this conversation, but you get it": Black mother-daughter communication about sexual relations. *Women's Studies in Communication, 35,* 204–223. doi: 10.1080/07491409.2012.724525

DeVito, J. (1994). *Human communication: The basic course* (6th ed.). New York: HarperCollins.

Dewey, C. (2014, January 17). How many of this year's Oscar nominees pass the Bechdel test? Not many. *Washington Post Blog.* Retrieved from http://www.washingtonpost.com/blogs/style-blog/wp/2014/01/17/howmany-of-this-years-oscar-nominees-pass-thebechdel-test-not-many/

Dickson, F. (1995). The best is yet to be: Research on long-lasting marriages. In J. T. Wood & S. W. Duck (Eds.), *Understanding relationship processes, 6: Understudied relationships: Off the beaten track* (pp. 22–50). Thousand Oaks, CA: Sage.

Dijck, J. (2013). *The culture of connectivity: A critical history of social media.* New York: Oxford University Press.

Domrose, C. (2010, August 23). *The time is now: "culture of safety" key to preventing errors.* Retrieved from Nurse.com: http://news.nurse.com/article/20100823/NATIONAL01/108230030/-1/frontpage

Douglas, W. (2012, May 17). House Oks anti-domestic violence bill. *Raleigh News & Observer,* p. 3A.

Doyle, G. (2008). *Understanding media economics* (2nd ed.). Thousand Oaks, CA: Sage.

Duck, S. W. (2006). The play, playfulness, and the players: Everyday interaction as improvised rehearsal of relationships. In J. T. Wood & S. W. Duck (Eds.), *Composing relationships:*

Communication in everyday life (pp. 15–23). Belmont, CA: Thomson Wadsworth.

Duck, S. W., & McMahan, D. (2012). *Basics of communication* (2nd ed.). Thousand Oaks, CA: Sage.

Duck, S. W., & Wood, J. T. (2006). What goes up may come down: Gendered patterns in relational dissolution. In M. Fine & J. Harvey (Eds.), *The handbook of divorce and dissolution of romantic relationships* (pp. 169–187). Mahwah, NJ: Erlbaum.

Dunbar, R. (2012). *The science of love and betrayal.* London, UK: Faber & Faber.

Edelman, B., & Larkin, I. (2014). Social comparisons and deception across workplace hierarchies: Field and experimental evidence. *Organizational Science, 26,* 78–98.

Edwards, H. (2015, August 3). The next social security crisis. *Time,* pp. 48–52.

Einhorn, L. (2000). *The Native American oral tradition: Voices of the spirit and soul.* Westport, CT: Praeger.

Eisenberg, E., Goodall, H., & Trethewey, A. (2013). *Organizational communication: Balancing creativity and constraint.* Boston, MA: Bedford /St. Martin's.

Ellis, A. (1988). *How to stubbornly refuse to make yourself miserable about anything—yes, anything.* New York: Lyle Stuart.

Engeln, R. (2015, March 15). The problem with 'fat talk.' *New York Times,* p. SR 12.

Emmons, S. (1998, February 3). The look on his face: Yes, it was culture shock. *Raleigh News & Observer,* p. 5E.

Epley, N. (2014). *Mindwise: How we understand what others think, believe, feel and want.* New York: Borzoi/Knopf.

Erbert, L. (2000). Conflict and dialectics: Perceptions of dialectical contradictions in marital conflict. *Journal of Social and Personal Relationships, 17,* 638–659.

Eytan, T., Benabio, J., Golla, V., Parikh, V., & Stein, S. (2011, Winter). Social media and the health system. *Permanente Journal, 15,* 71–74.

Fackelmann, K. (2006, March 6). Arguing hurts the heart in more ways than one. *USA Today,* p. 10D.

Faigley, L., & Selzer, J. (2000). *Good reasons.* Needham Heights, MA: Allyn & Bacon.

Fehr, B. (1993). How do I love thee: Let me consult my prototype. In S. W. Duck (Ed.), *Understanding relationship processes,*
1: Individuals in relationships (pp. 87–122). Newbury Park, CA: Sage.

Fehr, B., & Russell, J. A. (1991). Concept of love viewed from a prototype perspective. *Journal of Personality and Social Psychology, 60,* 425–438.

Ferguson, S. D. (2008). *Public speaking: Building competency in stages.* New York: Oxford University Press.

Ferrante, J. (2009). *Sociology: A global perspective* (7th ed.). Belmont, CA: Thomson Wadsworth.

Fitch, N. (Ed.). (2000). *How sweet the sound: The spirit of African American history.* New York: Harcourt College.

Fogg, P. (2008, July 25). Thinking in black and white. *Chronicle of Higher Education,* p. B19.

Foley, M. (2006). Locating "difficulty": A multi-site model of intimate terrorism. In C. D. Kirpatrick, S. W. Duck, & M. K. Foley (Eds.), *Relating difficulty: The processes of constructing and managing difficult interaction* (pp. 43–59). Mahwah, NJ: Erlbaum.

Ford Foundation. (1998, October 6). *Americans see many benefits to diversity in higher education, finds first ever national poll on topic.* Press release via Business Wire.

Forsyth, D. (2009). *Group dynamics* (5th ed.). Belmont, CA: Wadsworth Cengage.

Freeman, J. (2009). *The tyranny of e-mail.* New York: Simon & Schuster/Scribner.

Fryberg, S. A., & Markus, H. R. (2003). On being American Indian: Current and possible selves. *Self and Identity, 2,* 325–344.

Fujishin, R. (2014). *Creating effective groups.* Summit, PA: Rowman & Littlefield.

Furnham, A., & Xenikou, A. (2013). *Group dynamics and organizational culture.* New York: Palgrave Macmillan.

Gallo, C. (2014, September 25). New survey: 70% say presentational skills are critical for career success. *Forbes.* http://www.forbes.com/sites /carminegallo/2014/09/25/new-survey-70-percent-say-presentation-skills-critical-for-career-success/

Galvin, K., Braithwaite, D., & Bylund, C. (2015). *Family communication: Cohesion and change.* Upper Saddle Ridge, NJ: Pearson.

Galvin, K., Dickson, F., & Marrow, S. (2006). Systems theory: Patterns and (w)holes in family communication. In D. O. Braithwaite & L. A. Baxter (Eds.), *Engaging theories in family communication: Multiple perspectives* (pp. 308–324). Thousand Oaks, CA: Sage.

Gass, R. (1999). *Fallacy list: SpCom 335. Advanced argumentation.* Fullerton, CA: California State University. Retrieved from http://commfaculty.fullerton.edu/rgass/fallacy31.htm

Gentner, D., & Boroditsky, L. (2009). Early acquisition of nouns and verbs: Evidence from the Navajo. In V. Gathercole (Ed.), *Routes to language* (pp. 5–86). New York: Taylor & Francis.

George, L. (1995, December 26). Holiday's traditions are being formed. *Raleigh News & Observer,* pp. C1, C3.

Gerbner, G. (1990). Epilogue: Advancing on the path of righteousness (maybe). In N. Signorielli & M. Morgan (Eds.), *Cultivation analysis: New directions in media effects research* (pp. 250–261). Thousand Oaks, CA: Sage.

Global Analytics. (n.d.). Retrieved from http://globalworkplaceanalytics.com/telecommuting-statistics

Goldstein, J. (2013, June 11). A not-for-tourists guide to navigating a multicultural city (It's for the police). *The Wall Street Journal,* pp. A18, A19.

Goleman, D. (1995). *Emotional intelligence.* New York: Bantam.

Goleman, D. (1998). *Working with emotional intelligence.* New York: Bantam.

Goleman, D. (2007). *Social intelligence: The new science of human relationships.* New York: Bantam.

Goleman, D. (2011). *The brain and emotional intelligence.* Florence, MA: More than Sound.

Goleman, D., McKee, A., & Boyatzis, R. (2002). *Primal leadership: Realizing the power of emotional intelligence.* Cambridge, MA: Harvard Business School Press.

González, A., Houston, M., & Chen, V. (Eds.). (2012). *Our voices: Essays in culture, ethnicity, and communication.* New York: Oxford University Press.

GooLeave, S. (2015, February 19). The skills Americans say kids need to succeed in life. *Pew Research Centre.* Retrieved from http://www.pewresearch.org/fact-tank/2015/02/19/skills-for-success/

Gottman, J. (1993). The roles of conflict engagement, escalation, or avoidance in marital interaction: A longitudinal view of five types of couples. *Journal of Consulting and Clinical Psychology, 61,* 6–15.

Gottman, J. (1994a). *What predicts divorce? The relationship between marital processes and marital outcomes.* Hilllsdale, NJ: Erlbaum.

Gottman, J. (1994b). Why marriages fail. *Family Therapy Newsletter,* pp. 41–48.

Gottman, J. (1999). *Seven principles for making marriages work.* New York: Crown.

Gottman, J., & Carrère, S. (1994). Why can't men and women get along? Developmental roots and marital inequities. In D. Canary & L. Stafford (Eds.), *Communication and relational maintenance* (pp. 203–229). New York: Academic Press.

Grayling, A. (2013). *Friendship.* New Haven, CT: Yale University Press.

Gregory, G., Healy, R., & Mazierska, E. (2007). *The essential guide to careers in media and film.* Thousand Oaks, CA: Sage.

Gregory, T. (2012, March 5). Young adults in an age of "hyper-connectivity." *Raleigh News & Observer,* p. D1.

Griffin, C. (2015). *An invitation to public speaking* (5th ed.). Belmont, CA: Wadsworth.

Gronbeck, B. E., McKerrow, R., Ehninger, D., & Monroe, A. H. (1994). *Principles and types of speech communication* (12th ed.). Glenview, IL: Scott, Foresman.

Groopman, J. (2007). *How doctors think.* Boston, MA: Houghton Mifflin.

Gueguen, N., & De Gail, M. (2003). The effect of smiling on helping behavior: Smiling and good Samaritan behavior. *Communication Reports, 16,* 133–140.

Guerrero, L. (1996). Attachment style differences in intimacy and involvement: A test of the four-category model. *Communication Monographs, 63,* 269–292.

Guerrero, L., Andersen, P., & Afifi, W. (2008). *Close encounters: Communication in relationships* (2nd ed.). Thousand Oaks, CA: Sage.

Guerrero, L., & Floyd, K. (2006). *Nonverbal communication in close relationships.* Mahwah, NJ: Erlbaum.

Guerrero, L., La Valley, A., & Farinelli, L. (2008). The experience and expression of anger, guilt, and sadness in marriage: An equity theory explanation. *Journal of Social and Personal Relationships, 25,* 699–724.

Gupta, S. (2012, August 1). More treatment, more mistakes. *New York Times,* p. A21.

Hacker, K., Goss, B., & Townley, C. (1998). Employee attitudes regarding electronic mail policies: A case study. *Management Communication Quarterly, 11,* 422–432.

Hall, E. T. (1966). *The hidden dimension*. New York: Anchor.

Hall, E. T. (1977). *Beyond culture*. New York: Doubleday.

Hall, J. A., Coats, E., & Smith-LeBeau, L. (2004). Nonverbal behavior and the vertical dimension of social relations: A meta-analysis. *Psychological Bulletin, 131*, 898–924. [Cited in M. L. Knapp & J. A. Hall (2006), *Nonverbal communication in human interaction*. Belmont, CA: Thomson Wadsworth.]

Hall, J., Park, N., Song, H., & Cody, J. (2010). Strategic misrepresentation in online dating: The effects of gender, self-monitoring, and personality traits. *Journal of Social and Personal Relationships, 27*, 117–135.

Hamachek, D. (1992). *Encounters with the self* (3rd ed.). Fort Worth, TX: Harcourt Brace Jovanovich.

Hamilton, C. (2015). *Essentials of public speaking* (7th ed.). Belmont, CA: Wadsworth.

Hamilton, N. (2011–2012). Effectiveness requires listening: How to assess and improve listening skills. *Florida Coastal Law Review, 13*, 145–180.

Hamermesh, D. (2011). *Beauty pays: Why attractive people are more successful*. Princeton, NJ: Princeton University Press.

Haraway, D. (1988). Situated knowledges: The science question in feminism and the privilege of partial perspective. *Signs, 14*, 575–599.

Harding, S. (1991). *Whose science? Whose knowledge? Thinking from women's lives*. Ithaca, NY: Cornell University Press.

Hargie, O. (Ed.). (2006). *The handbook of communication skills*. Florence, KY: Psychology Press.

Harmon, A. (2002). Talk, type, read e-mail: The trials of multitasking. In E. Bucy (Ed.), *Living in the information age* (pp. 79–81). Belmont, CA: Thomson Wadsworth.

Harris, G. (2011, July 11). For aspiring doctors, the people skills test. *New York Times*, pp. A1, A12.

Harris, T., & Sherblom, J. (2010). *Small group and team communication*. Boston, MA: Allyn & Bacon.

Harris, T. J. (1969). *I'm OK, you're OK*. New York: Harper & Row.

Hart Research Associates. (2013). It takes more than a major. *Employer priorities for college learning and student success*. Washington, D.C.: Author.

Harvard Business Press. (2010). *Leading virtual teams*. Boston, MA: Author.

Heider, F. (1958). *The psychology of interpersonal relations*. New York: Wiley.

Heine, S. J., & Hamamura, T. (2007). In search of East Asian self-enhancement. *Personality and Social Psychology Review, 11*, 1–24.

Heine, S. J., & Raineri, A. (2009). Self-improving motivations and culture: The case of Chileans. *Journal of Cross-Cultural Psychology, 40*, 158–163.

Helmrich, B. (August 10, 2015) Email Etiquette 101: The Do's and Don'ts of Professional Emails. *Business News Daily*. Retrieved from and http://www.businessnewsdaily.com/8262-email-etiquette-tips.html

Hendrick, C., & Hendrick, S. (1996). Gender and the experience of heterosexual love. In J. T. Wood (Ed.), *Gendered relationships* (pp. 131–148). Mountain View, CA: Mayfield.

Hendrick, C., Hendrick, S., Foote, F. H., & Slapion-Foote, M. J. (1984). Do men and women love differently? *Journal of Social and Personal Relationships, 2*, 177–196.

Hendrick, S., & Hendrick, C. (2006). Measuring respect in close relationships. *Journal of Social and Personal Relationships, 23*, 881–899.

Henrich, J., & Norenzayan, A. (2010). The weirdest people in the world? *Behavioral and Brain Sciences, 33*, 61–135.

Hesmondhaigh, D. (2007). *The cultural industries* (2nd ed.). Thousand Oaks, CA: Sage.

Hewes, D. (Ed.). (1995). *The cognitive bases of interpersonal perception*. Mahwah, NJ: Erlbaum.

Hickey, W. (2014, April 1). The dollar-and-cents case against Hollywood's exclusion of women. *Five Thirty Eight*. Retrieved from http://fivethirtyeight.com/features/the-dollar-andcents-case-against-hollywoods-exclusion-ofwomen/

Hillis, K., Petit, M., & Jarrett, K. (2012). *Google and the culture of search*. New York: Routledge.

Hochschild, A., & Machung, A. (2003). *The second shift* (Rev. ed.). New York: Viking.

Hoffman, J. (2010, June 28). Online bullies pull schools into the fray. *New York Times*, pp. A13, A14, A15.

Hoffman, J. (2012, June 4). A warning to teenagers before they start dating. *New York Times*, pp. A12, A13.

Hofstede, G. (1991). *Culture and organizations: Software of the mind*. New York: McGraw-Hill.

Hofstede, G. (2001). *Cultures' consequences: Comparing values, behaviors, institutions, and organizations across nations*. Thousand Oaks, CA: Sage.

Hofstede, G., Hofstede, G. J., & Minkov, M. (2010). *Cultures and organizations: Software of the mind* (3rd ed.). New York: McGraw-Hill.

Holt-Lunstad, J., Smith, T. B., & Layton, J. B. (2010). Social relationships and mortality risk: A meta-analytic review. *PLoS Medicine, 7,* 1–20.

Honoré, C. (2005). *In praise of slowness.* San Francisco, CA: Harper.

Hoon, H., & Tan, M. (2008). Organizational citizenship behavior and social loafing: The role of personality, motives, and contextual factors. *Journal of Psychology, 142,* 89–108.

Hoover, E. (2010, January 29). An immigrant learns 2 new languages. *Chronicle of Higher Education,* p. A22.

Houston, M., & Wood, J. T. (1996). Difficult dialogues, expanded horizons: Communicating across race and class. In J. T. Wood (Ed.), *Gendered relationships* (pp. 39–56). Mountain View, CA: Mayfield.

Hrabi, D. (2013, June 22–23). Nestle while you work. *The Wall Street Journal,* pp. D1, D8.

Huesmann, L. R., Moise-Titus, J., Podolski, C., & Eron, L. D. (2003). Longitudinal relations between children's exposure to TV violence and their aggressive and violent behavior in young adulthood: 1977–1992. *Developmental Psychology, 39,* 201–221.

Hunter, S. (2012). *Lesbian and gay couples: Lives, issues, and practice.* Chicago, IL: Lyceum Books, Inc.

Inman, C. C. (1996). Friendships among men: Closeness in the doing. In J. T. Wood (Ed.), *Gendered relationships* (pp. 95–110). Mountain View, CA: Mayfield.

ILA (2011). Retrieved from http://www.listen.org/

Irvine, M. (2012, June 4). Does texting ruin the art of conversation? *Raleigh News & Observer,* p. 3A.

Italie, L. (2014, July 31). Fashion industry, retailers face gender divide. *Raleigh News & Observer,* p. 8D.

Jackson, S., & Allen, J. (1990). *Meta-analysis of the effectiveness of one-sided and two-sided argumentation.* Paper presented at the International Communication Association, Montreal, Canada.

Jacobson, L. (2015, August 27). More Americans killed by guns since 1968 than in all U.S. wars, columnist Nicholas Kristof writes. *Tampa Bay Times.* Retrieved from http://www.politifact.com/punditfact/statements/2015/aug/27/nicholas-kristof/more-americans-killed-guns-1968-all-wars-says-colu/

Jaffe, C. (2016). *Public speaking: Concepts and skills for a diverse society* (8th ed.). Belmont, CA: Wadsworth.

Jaffe, E. (2004). Peace in the Middle East may be impossible: Lee D. Ross on naïve realism and conflict resolution. *American Psychological Society Observer, 17,* 9–11.

Jandt, F. (2012). *An introduction to intercultural communication: Identities in a global community.* Thousand Oaks, CA: Sage.

Janis, I. L. (1989). *Crucial decisions: Leadership in policymaking and crisis management.* New York: Free Press.

Jensen, B. (2014, June–July). The new American family. *AARP Magazine,* pp. 34–38.

Jhally, S., & Katz, J. (2001, Winter). Big trouble, little pond. *UMass,* pp. 26–31. Retrieved from https://www.umass.edu/umassmag/archives/2001/winter2001/athens.html.

Johnson, F. L. (1996). Friendships among women: Closeness in dialogue. In J. T. Wood (Ed.), *Gendered relationships* (pp. 79–94). Mountain View, CA: Mayfield.

Jones, D. (2007, March 30). Do foreign executives balk at sports jargon? *USA Today,* pp. 1B–2B.

Jordan, M. (2012, February 17). More marriages cross race, ethnicity lines. *The Wall Street Journal,* p. A2.

Joshi, N. (2015, January 5). Doctor, shut up and listen. *New York Times,* p. A15.

June, A. (2012, March 23). Work-life balance is out of reach for many scientists, and not just women. *Chronicle of Higher Education,* p. A29.

Katzman, M. (2015, July 5). Baffled by buzzwords. *New York Times,* p. BU7.

Kaufman, M., & Kimmel, M. (2011). *The guy's guide to feminism.* Berkeley, CA: Seal Press.

Keizer, G. (2010). *The unwanted sound of everything we want: A book about noise.* New York: Perseus-Public Affairs.

Kellerman, K. (2011, November). From communication professor to trial consultant. *Spectra,* pp. 11–15.

Kelley, H. H. (1967). Attribution theory in social psychology. In D. Levine (Ed.), *Nebraska symposium on motivation* (Vol. 15, pp. 192–238). Lincoln, NE: University of Nebraska Press.

Kendall, D. (2011). *Framing class.* Lanham, MD: Rowman.

Kennedy, G. (Ed. & Trans.). (1991). *Aristotle on rhetoric*. London, UK: Oxford University Press.

Kiesler, C. A., & Kiesler, S. B. (1971). Role of forewarning in persuasive communications. *Journal of Abnormal and Social Psychology, 18,* 210–221.

Kimbrough, A. M., Guadagno, R. E., Muscanell, N. L., & Dill, J. (2013). Gender differences in mediated communication: Women connect more than do men. *Computers in Human Behavior, 29,* 896–900.

Kim, J. & Meyers, R. (2012). Cultural differences in conflict management styles in east and west organizations. *Journal of Intercultural Communication, 29.* Retrieved from http://www.immi.se/intercultural

Kimmel, M. (2008). *Guyland: The perilous world where boys become men.* New York: Macmillan.

Kimmel, M. (2013). *Angry white men.* New York: Nation.

Kimmel, M. & Messner, M. (2012). *Men's lives* (9th ed.). Upper Saddle Ridge, NJ: Pearson.

Kimmelman, M. (2014, August 22). In redesigned room, hospital patients may feel better already. *New York Times*, pp. A1, A13.

Knapp, M., & Hall, J. A. (2006). *Nonverbal communication in human interaction.* Belmont, CA: Thomson Wadsworth.

Knapp, M. L., Hall, J. A., & Hogan, T. (2013). *Nonverbal communication in human interaction.* Stamford, CT: Cengage.

Kohlberg, L. (1958). *The development of modes of thinking and moral choice in the years 10 to 16.* Unpublished doctoral dissertation, University of Chicago.

Korkki, P. (2013, June 16). Business schools know how you think, but how do you feel? *The Wall Street Journal*, p. B1.

Korzybski, A. (1948). *Science and sanity* (4th ed.). Lakeville, CT: International Non-Aristotelian Library.

Krasnova, H., Wenninger, H., Widjaja, T., & Buxmann, P. (2013). Envy on Facebook: A hidden threat to users' life satisfaction. 11th International Conference on Wirtschaftsinformatik, Leipzig, Germany. Retrieved from http://warhol.wiwi.hu-berlin.de/~hkrasnova/Ongoing_Research_files/WI%202013%20Final%20Submission%20Krasnova.pdf

Kreps, G. L. (2010). *Health communication.* Thousand Oaks, CA: Sage.

Kristof, N. (2014, March 9). To end the abuse, she grabbed a knife. *New York Times*, pp. SR1, 11.

Kurtzberg, T. (2014). *Virtual teams: Mastering communication and collaboration in the digital age.* Santa Barbara, CA: Praeger.

Landrum, R., & Harrold, R. (2003). What employers want from psychology graduates. *Teaching of Psychology, 30,* 131–133.

Langer, S. (1953). *Feeling and form: A theory of art.* New York: Scribner.

Langer, S. (1979). *Philosophy in a new key: A study in the symbolism of reason, rite, and art* (3rd ed.). Cambridge, MA: Harvard University Press.

Lasch, C. (1990, Spring). Journalism, publicity and the lost art of argument. *Gannett Center Journal*, pp. 1–11.

Laswell, H. D. (1948). The structure and function of communication in society. In L. Bryson (Ed.), *The communication of ideas* (pp. 37–51). New York: Harper & Row.

Lawless, B. (2012). More than white: Locating an invisible class identity. In A. González, M. Houston, & V. Chen (Eds.), *Our voices: Essays in culture, ethnicity, and communication* (pp. 247–253). New York: Oxford University Press.

Le, B., & Agnew, C. (2003). Commitment and its theorized determinants: A meta-analysis of the investment model. *Personal Relationships, 10,* 37–57.

Leaper, N. (1999). How communicators lead at the best global companies. *Communication World, 16,* 33–36.

Lee, J. A. (1973). *The colours of love: An exploration of the ways of loving.* Don Mills, Ontario, Canada: New Press.

Lee, J. A. (1988). Love-styles. In R. J. Sternberg & M. L. Barnes (Eds.), *The psychology of love* (pp. 38–67). New Haven, CT: Yale University Press.

Lee, W. (1994). On not missing the boat: A processual method for intercultural understandings of idioms and lifeworld. *Journal of Applied Communication Research, 22,* 141–161.

Lee, W. (2000). That's Greek to me: Between a rock and a hard place in intercultural encounters. In L. Samovar & R. Porter (Eds.), *Intercultural communication: A reader* (9th ed., pp. 217–224). Belmont, CA: Wadsworth.

Lehman, C., & DuFrene, D. (1999). *Business communication* (12th ed.). Cincinnati, OH: South-Western.

Lerner, B. (2015, February 24). Please stop making that noise. *New York Times*, p. D4.

Levine, M. (2004, June 1). Tell the doc all your problems, but keep it to less than a minute. *New York Times*, p. D6.

Levy, D., Nardick, D., Turner, J., & McWatters, L. (2011, May 13). No cellphone? No internet? So much less stress. *Chronicle of Higher Education*, pp. B27–B28.

Levy, S. (2006, March 27). (Some) attention must be paid! *Newsweek*, p. 16.

Livermore, D. A. (2015) *Leading with cultural intelligence: The real secret to success* (2nd ed.). New York: AMACOM.

Lowry, J. (2013, June 13). Hands-free devises not risk-free, study says. *Raleigh News & Observer*, p. 5A.

Lublin, J.S. (2010, July 6). The keys to unlocking your most successful career: Five simple but crucial lessons culled from many years of offering advice to workers, bosses and job seekers. *The Wall Street Journal*. Retrieved from http://www.wsj.com/articles/SB1000142405274870429360457 5343322516508414

Lumsden, G., & Lumsden, D. (2009). *Communicating in groups and teams* (6th ed.). Belmont, CA: Wadsworth.

Lund, M. (1985). The development of investment and commitment scales for predicting continuity of personal relationships. *Journal of Social and Personal Relationships, 2*, 3–23.

Luhrmann, T. M. (2014, December 4). Wheat people vs. rice people. *New York Times*, p. A29.

Luttrell, R. (2014). *Social media: How to engage, share, and connect*. Landham, MD: Rowman & Littlefield.

Lutz-Zois, C., Bradley, A., Mihalik, J., & Moorman-Eavers, E. (2006). Perceived similarity and relationship success among dating couples: An idiographic approach. *Journal of Social and Personal Relationships, 23*, 865–880.

Major, B., Schmidlin, A. M., & Williams, L. (1990). Gender patterns in social touch: The impact of setting and age. In C. Mayo & N. M. Henley (Eds.), *Gender and nonverbal behavior* (pp. 3–37). New York: Springer-Verlag.

Manusov, V., & Harvey, J. (2001). *Attribution, communication behavior, and close relationships*. Port Chester, NY: Cambridge University Press.

Manusov, V., & Patterson, M. L. (2006). *The Sage handbook of nonverbal communication*. Thousand Oaks, CA: Sage.

Manusov, V., & Spitzberg, B. (2008). Attribution theory. In L. A. Baxter & D. O. Braithwaite (Eds.),

Engaging theories in interpersonal communication: Multiple perspectives (pp. 37–49). Thousand Oaks, CA: Sage.

Matsumoto, D., Franklin, B., Choi, J., Rogers, D., & Tatani, H. (2002). Cultural influences on the expression and perception of emotion. In W. Gudykunst & B. Mody (Eds.), *The handbook of international and intercultural communication* (2nd ed., pp. 107–126). Thousand Oaks, CA: Sage.

McCombs, M., Ghanem, S., & Chernov, G. (2009). Agenda setting and framing. In W. F. Eadie (Ed.), *21st century communication: A reference handbook* (pp. 516–524). Thousand Oaks, CA: Sage.

McCroskey, J., & Teven, J. (1999). Goodwill: A reexamination of the construct and its measurement. *Communication Monographs, 66*, 90–103.

McGuire, W. J. (1989). Theoretical foundations of campaigns. In R. E. Rice & C. K. Atkin (Eds.), *Public communication campaigns* (2nd ed., pp. 43–65). Newbury Park, CA: Sage.

McMurtrie, B. (2011, November 18). International enrollments at U.S. colleges grow but still rely on China. *Chronicle of Higher Education*, pp. A16–A20.

Mead, G. H. (1934). *Mind, self, and society*. Chicago, IL: University of Chicago Press.

Mehrabian, A. (1981). *Silent messages: Implicit communication of emotion and attitudes* (2nd ed.). Belmont, CA: Wadsworth.

Metts, S. (2006a). Hanging out and doing lunch: Enacting friendship closeness. In J. T. Wood & S. W. Duck (Eds.), *Composing relationships: Communication in everyday life* (pp. 76–85). Belmont, CA: Thomson Wadsworth.

Metts, S. (2006b). Gendered communication in dating relationships. In B. Dow & J. T. Wood (Eds.), *Handbook of gender and communication research* (pp. 25–40). Thousand Oaks, CA: Sage.

Meyers, D. G. (1993). *Social psychology* (4th ed.). New York: McGraw-Hill.

Milbank, D. (2014, August 7). A welcome end to American whiteness. *Raleigh News & Observer*, p. 7A.

Milia, T. (2003). *Doctor, you're not listening*. Philadelphia, PA: Xlibris.

Miller, C. (2015a). Can an algorithm hire better than a human? *New York Times*, p. SR 4.

Miller, C. (2015b, August 1). Millennial men aren't the dads of their hopes. *New York Times*, pp. A1, A3.

Miller, C. (2014). *Organizing communication: Approaches and processes* (8th ed.). Belmont, CA: Wadsworth/Cengage.

Modaff, D., Butler, J., & DeWine, S. (2011). *Organizational communication: Foundations, challenges, and misunderstandings* (3rd ed.). Boston, MA: Allyn & Bacon.

Mokros, H. (2006). Composing relationships at work. In J. T. Wood & S. W. Duck (Eds.), *Composing relationships: Communication in everyday life* (pp. 175–185). Belmont, CA: Thomson Wadsworth.

Monastersky, R. (2002, March 29). Speak before you think. *Chronicle of Higher Education,* pp. A17–A18.

Monroe, A. H. (1935). *Principles and types of speech.* Glenview, IL: Scott, Foresman.

Morreale, S. (2003, September). Importance of communication. *Spectra,* p. 14.

Morreale, S., Osborn, M., & Pearson, J. (2000). Why communication is important: A rationale for the centrality of the study of communication. *Journal of the Association for Communication Administration, 29,* 1–25.

Muehlhoff, T. (2006). "He started it": Everyday communication in parenting. In J. T. Wood & S. W. Duck (Eds.), *Composing relationships: Communication in everyday life* (pp. 46–54). Belmont, CA: Thomson Wadsworth.

Mumby, D. K. (2006a). Constructing working-class masculinity in the workplace. In J. T. Wood & S. W. Duck (Eds.), *Composing relationships: Communication in everyday life* (pp. 166–174). Belmont, CA: Thomson Wadsworth.

Mumby, D. K. (2006b). Introduction to Part II. In B. J. Dow & J. T. Wood (Eds.), *The handbook of gender and communication* (pp. 89–95). Thousand Oaks, CA: Sage.

Muwanguzi, S., & Musambira, G. (2013). Communication experiences of Ugandan immigrants during acculturation to the United States: A preliminary study. *Journal of Intercultural Communication, 31.* Retrieved from http://www.immi.se/intercultural/

Nagourney, E. (2006, May 9). Surgical teams found lacking, in teamwork. *New York Times,* p. D6.

Nass, C. (2012, May/June). The keyboard and the damage done. *Pacific Standard,* pp. 22–25.

Neuliep, J. (2014). *Intercultural communication: A contextual approach.* Thousand Oaks, CA: Sage.

Newman, J. (2015, August 28). The perils of email auto-fill. The New York Times. Retrieved from http://mobile.nytimes.com/2015/08/30/fashion/the-perils-of-email-auto-fill.html?referrer=

Newsbeast. (2012, January 30). *Newsweek,* p. 12.

Nichols, M. (2009). *The lost art of listening: How learning to listen can improve relationships.* New York: Guilford Press.

Nicotera, A., Clinkscales, M., & Walker, F. (2002). *Understanding organization through culture and structure.* Thousand Oaks, CA: Sage.

Niedenthal, P. M., Krauth-Gruber, S., & Ric, F. (2006). *Psychology of emotion.* Thousand Oaks, CA: Sage.

O'Hair, D., & Eadie, W. F. (2009). In W. F. Eadie (Ed.), *21st century communication: A reference handbook* (pp. 3–11). Thousand Oaks, CA: Sage.

Ohanian, H. (2009). *Einstein's mistakes.* New York: W.W. Norton.

Olson, J. M., & Cal, A. V. (1984). Source credibility, attitudes, and the recall of past behaviors. *European Journal of Social Psychology, 14,* 203–210.

Opfer, C. (2011, November/December). Disappearing ink: The burgeoning business of tattoo removal. *Miller-McCune,* pp. 20–21.

Orbe, M., & Harris, T. (2015). *Interracial communication: Theory into practice* (3rd ed.). Belmont, CA: Wadsworth.

Pacanowsky, M., & O'Donnell-Trujillo, N. (1983). Organizational communication as cultural performance. *Communication Monographs, 30,* 126–147.

Palmieri, P., Peterson, L., Pesta, B., Flit, M., & Saettone, D. (2010). Safety culture as a contemporary healthcare construct: Theoretical review, research assessment, and translation to human resource management. *Advances in Health Care Management, 9,* 97–133.

Parker-Pope, T. (2009a, January 13). A problem of the brain, not the hands: Group urges phone ban for drivers. *New York Times,* p. D5.

Parker-Pope, T. (2009b, January 20). Your nest is empty? Enjoy each other. *New York Times,* p. D5.

Parker-Pope, T. (2014, August 26). Marital bliss, one decision after another. *New York Times,* pp. D1, D4.

Pearce, W. B., Cronen, V. E., & Conklin, F. (1979). On what to look at when analyzing communication: A hierarchical model of actors' meanings. *Communication, 4,* 195–220.

Pedulla, D., & Thébaud, S. (2015). Can we finish the revolution? Gender, work-family ideals, and institutional constraint. *American Sociological Review, 80,* 116–139.

Perlow, L. (2013). *Sleeping with your smartphone.* Boston, MA: Harvard Business Review Press.

Petronio, S., & Caughlin, J. (2006). Communication privacy management theory: Understanding families. In D. O. Braithwaite & L. A. Baxter (Eds.), *Engaging theories in family communication: Multiple perspectives* (pp. 35–49). Thousand Oaks, CA: Sage.

Piaget, J. (1932/1965). *The moral judgment of the child.* New York: Free Press.

Porath, C. (2015, June 21). No time to be nice. *New York Times,* pp. SR 1, 6, 7.

Potter, J. (2009). *Media literacy* (4th ed.). Thousand Oaks, CA: Sage.

Prevalence of Domestic Violence. (2013, August). *The advocates for human rights.* Retrieved from http://www.stopvaw.org /prevalence_of_domestic_violence

Qin, X. (2014). Exploring the impact of culture in five communicative elements: A case of intercultural misunderstandings between Chinese and American. *Journal of Intercultural Communication, 34.* Retrieved from http://www .immi.se/intercultural/

Quenqua, D. (2014, August 3). Tell me, even if it hurts me. *New York Times,* pp. SR 1, 8–9.

Quesenberry, K. (2015). *Social media strategy.* Landham, MD: Rowman & Littlefield.

Rae-Dupree, J. (2008, December 7). Teamwork, the true mother of invention. *New York Times,* p. B3.

Rawlins, W. K. (1981). *Friendship as a communicative achievement: A theory and an interpretive analysis of verbal reports.* Unpublished doctoral dissertation, Temple University, Philadelphia, PA.

Rawlins, W. K. (1994). Being there and growing apart: Sustaining friendships during adulthood. In D. Canary & L. Stafford (Eds.), *Communication and relational maintenance* (pp. 275–294). New York: Academic Press.

Ream, Diane Show. (2012, June 25). Aired on NPR 10–11 a.m. EDS.

Reinhard, C. D., & Dervin, B. J. (2009). Media uses and gratifications. In W. F. Eadie (Ed.), *21st century communication: A reference handbook* (pp. 506–515). Thousand Oaks, CA: Sage.

Rhodewalt, F. (Ed.). (2007). *Personality and social behavior.* Florence, KY: Psychology Press.

Rice, A. (2011, November 25). Bleary-eyed students can't stop texting, even to sleep, a researcher finds. *Chronicle of Higher Education,* p. A13.

Rice, R., & Leonardi, P. (2013). Information and communication technologies in organizations. In L. Putnam & D. Mumby (Eds.), *The SAGE handbook of organizational communication: Advances in theory, research and methods* (pp. 425–448). Thousand Oaks, CA: Sage.

Richmond, V. P., & McCroskey, J. C. (1992). *Communication: Apprehension, avoidance, and effectiveness* (3rd ed.). Scottsdale, AZ: Gorsuch Scarisbrick.

Richmond, V. P., & McCroskey, J. C. (1995a). *Communication: Apprehension, avoidance, and effectiveness.* Scottsdale, AZ: Gorsuch Scarisbrick.

Richmond, V. P., & McCroskey, J. C. (1995b). *Nonverbal communication in interpersonal relations* (3rd ed.). Boston, MA: Allyn & Bacon.

Richtel, M. (2011, December 15). As doctors use more devices, potential for distraction grows. *New York Times,* pp. A1, A4.

Ritchel, M. (2015). *A deadly wandering.* New York: William Morrow/HarperCollins.

Robinson, G. (2001, March 4). Sometimes a thank you is enough. *New York Times,* pp. 16, 18.

Robinson, J. D. (2009). Media portrayals and representations. In W. F. Eadie (Ed.), *21st century communication: A reference handbook* (pp. 497–505). Thousand Oaks, CA: Sage.

Rosenbaum, L. (2011, November 22). The doctor feels your pain. *Raleigh News & Observer,* pp. 1D–2D.

Ross, K. (2013). *Gendered media: Women, men, and identity politics.* Landham, MD: Rowman & Littlefield.

Rothenberg, P. (2006). *Race, class, and gender in the United States* (7th ed.). New York: Worth.

Rothwell, J. D. (2015). *In mixed company: Small group communication* (9th ed.). Belmont, CA: Wadsworth.

Rowe, A. C., & Carnelley, K. B. (2005). Preliminary support for the use of a hierarchical mapping technique to examine attachment networks. *Personal Relationships, 12,* 499–519.

Rowe Finkbeiner, K. (2014, April 30). The motherhood penalty. *Politico Magazine.* http:// www.politico.com/magazine/story/2014/04/the-motherhood-penalty-106173.html#.U6aurdJOXq4

Rudman, L. A., & Glick, P. (2010). *The social psychology of gender.* New York: Guilford Press.

Rusli, E. (2013, June 12). When words just aren't enough some turn to flatulent bunnies. *The Wall Street Journal*, pp. A1, A14.

Salas, E., & Frush, K. (2012). *Improving patient safety through teamwork and team training*. New York: Oxford University Press.

Salerno, S. (2005). *Sham: How the self-help movement made America helpless*. New York: Three Rivers Press.

Samovar, L., Porter, R., McDaniel, E., & Roy, C. (2017). *Communication between cultures* (9th ed.). Boston, MA: Cengage.

Samovar, L., Porter, R., McDaniel, E. R., & Roy, C. (Eds.). (2015). *Intercultural communication: A reader* (14th ed.). Belmont, CA: Wadsworth.

Samp, J. A., & Palevitz, C. E. (2009). Dating and romantic partners. In W. F. Eadie (Ed.), *21st century communication: A reference handbook* (pp. 322–330). Thousand Oaks, CA: Sage.

Sawyer, K. (2008). *Group genius: The power of creative collaboration*. New York: Basic.

Schiavo, R. (2007). *Health communication: From theory to practice*. San Francisco, CA: Jossey-Bass.

Schmidt, J., & Uecker, D. (2007). Increasing understanding of routine/everyday interaction in relationships. *Communication Teacher, 21,* 111–116.

Scholz, M. (2005, June). A "simple" way to improve adherence. *RN, 68,* 82.

Schram, P., & Schwartz, H. (2000). *Stories within stories: From the Jewish oral tradition*. Leonia, NJ: Jason Aronson.

Schramm, W. (1955). *The process and effects of mass communication*. Urbana, IL: University of Illinois Press.

Schumpeter. (2011, December 31). *Economist*, p. 50.

Schwab, H. (2014, October 9). 'Nude' improved. *Raleigh News & Observer*, pp. D1, 2.

Scott, J., & Leonhardt, D. (2013). Shadowy lines that still divide. In M. Andersen & P. H. Collins (Eds.), *Race, class, and gender: An anthology* (8th ed., pp. 117–124). Boston, MA: Cengage.

Segrin, C., Hanzal, A., & Domschke, T. (2009). Accuracy and bias in newlywed couples' perceptions of conflict styles and the association with marital satisfaction. *Communication Monographs, 76,* 207–233.

Seligman, M. E. P. (2002). *Authentic happiness*. New York: Free Press.

Selingo, J. (2012, September 28). Colleges and employers point fingers over skills gap. *Chronicle of Higher Education*, p. A20.

Servaty-Seib, H., & Burleson, B. (2007). Bereaved adolescents' evaluations of the helpfulness of support-intended statements: Associations with person centeredness and demographic, personality, and contextual factors. *Journal of Social and Personal Relationships, 24,* 207–223.

Shanahan, J., & Jones, V. (1999). Cultivation and social control. In D. Demers & K. Viswanath (Eds.), *Mass media, social control, and social change* (pp. 89–116). Ames, IA: Iowa State University Press.

Shannon, C., & Weaver, W. (1949). *The mathematical theory of communication*. Urbana, IL: University of Illinois Press.

Shattuck, T. R. (1980). *The forbidden experiment: The story of the wild boy of Aveyron*. New York: Farrar, Straus & Giroux.

Shellenbarger, S. (2013, September 11). The biggest distraction in the office is sitting next to you. *The Wall Street Journal*, pp. D1, D3.

Shifman, P., & Tillet, S. (2015, February 3). To stop violence, start at home. New York Times, A21.

Shimanoff, S. B. (1980). *Communication rules: Theory and research*. Beverly Hills, CA: Sage.

Sias, P., Heath, R., Perry, T., Silva, D., & Fix, B. (2004). Narratives of workplace friendship deterioration. *Journal of Social and Personal Relationships, 21,* 321–340.

Siebold, D., Hollingshead, A., & Yoon, K. (2013). Embedded teams and embedding organizations. In L. Putnam & D. Mumby (Eds.), *The SAGE handbook of organizational communication: Advances in theory, research and methods* (pp. 327–350). Thousand Oaks, CA: Sage.

Smith, R. (1998, December 1). *Civility without censorship: The ethics of the Internet cyberhate*. Speech delivered at the Simon Wiesenthal Center/Museum of Tolerance, Los Angeles, CA.

Smith, S., Choueiti, M., & Pieper, K. (2013). Race/ethnicity in 500 popular films: Is the key to diversifying cinematic content held in the hand of the black director? Retrieved from http://annenberg.usc.edu/sitecore/shell/Applications/~/media/PDFs/RaceEthnicity.ashx

Spaeth, M. (1996, July 1). "Prop" up your speaking skills. *The Wall Street Journal*, p. A15.

Spar, D. (2013). *Wonder women: Sex, power and the quest for perfection*. New York: Sarah Crichton Books.

Spitzberg, B., & Cupach, W. (2014). *The dark side of relational pursuit* (2nd ed.). New York: Routledge.

Stafford, L. (2009). Spouses and other intimate partnerships. In W. F. Eadie (Ed.), *21st century communication: A reference handbook* (pp. 296–302). Thousand Oaks, CA: Sage.

Stapel, D. A., & Blanton, H. (Eds.). (2006). *Social comparison theories: Key readings*. Florence, KY: Psychology Press.

Staples, W. (2014). *Everyday surveillance: Vigilance and visibility in postmodern life*. Landham, MD: Rowman & Littlefield.

Stobbe, M. (2012, March 22). Move-in before marriage no longer predicts divorce. *Raleigh News & Observer*, p. 4A.

Stolberg, S. (2009, January 29). From the top, the White House unbuttons formal dress code. *New York Times*, pp. A1, A14.

Streitfeld, D. (2015, August 19). The 24-hour timecard. *New York Times*, pp. B1, 2.

Swain, S. (1989). Covert intimacy: Closeness in men's friendships. In B. Risman & P. Schwartz (Eds.), *Gender and intimate relationships* (pp. 71–86). Belmont, CA: Wadsworth.

Swidler, A. (2001). *Talk of love: How culture matters*. Chicago, IL: University of Chicago Press.

Tabuchi, H. (2012, May 30). Educated, but not fitting in. *New York Times*, pp. B1, B2.

Tashiro, T., & Frazier, P. (2003). "I'll never be in a relationship like that again": Personal growth following romantic relationship breakups. *Personal Relationships, 10*, 113–128.

Tavris, C., & Aronson, E. (2007). *Mistakes were made (but not by me): Why we justify foolish beliefs, bad decisions, and hurtful acts*. New York: Harcourt.

Terlecki, M., Brown, J., Harner-Steciw, L., Irvin-Hannum, J., Marchetto-Ryan, N., Ruhl, L., & Wiggins, J. (2011). Sex differences and similarities in video game experience, preferences, and self-efficacy: Implications for the gaming industry. *Current Psychology, 30*, 22–33.

Thompson, F., & Grundgenett, D. (1999). Helping disadvantaged learners build effective learning skills. *Education, 120*, 130–135.

Thrun, S. (2011, December 6). Leave the driving to the car, and reap benefits in safety and mobility. *New York Times*, p. D4.

Tierney, J. (2013, March 19). Good news beats bad on social networks. *New York Times*, p. D3.

Tierney, J. (2015, June 30). Love at gradually evolving sight. New York Times, p. D6.

Tilsley, A. (2010, July 2). New policies accommodate transgender students. *Chronicle of Higher Education*, pp. A19–A20.

Ting-Toomey, S. (2005). The matrix of face: An updated face-negotiation theory. In W. B. Gudykunst (Ed.), *Theorizing about intercultural communication* (pp. 71–92). Thousand Oaks, CA: Sage.

Toulmin, S. (1958). *The uses of argument*. Cambridge, MA: Cambridge University Press.

Toulmin, S., Rieke, R., & Janik, A. (1984). *An introduction to reasoning* (2nd ed.). New York: Macmillan.

Trenholm, S. (1991). *Human communication theory* (2nd ed.). Englewood Cliffs, NJ: Prentice Hall.

Trice, H., & Beyer, J. (1984). Studying organizational cultures through rites and ceremonials. *Academy of Management Review, 9*, 653–669.

Tropp, L. R., & Wright, S. C. (2003). Evaualions and perceptions of self, in-group, and out-group: Comparisons between Mexican-American and European-American children. *Self and Identity, 2*, 203–221.

Tsai, F., & Reis, H. (2009). Perceptions by and of lonely people in social networks. *Personal Relationships, 16*, 221–238.

Tugend, A. (2011, July 2). Comparing yourself to others: It's not all bad. *New York Times*, p. B6.

Turkle, S. (2011). *Alone together: Why we expect more of technology and less of each other*. New York: Basic.

Turow, J. (2008). *Media today* (3rd ed.). New York: Routledge.

Tusing, K., & Dillard, J. (2000). The sounds of dominance: Vocal precursors of perceived dominance during interpersonal influence. *Human Communication Research, 26*, 148–171.

A Victory for Tolerance. (2014, June 21). *Raleigh News & Observer*, p. 9A.

Virtual Team Challenges. (n.d.). Retrieved from http://onlinemba.unc.edu/research-and-insights/developing-real-skills-for-virtual-teams/virtual-team-challenges/

Walker, S. (2007). *Style and status: Selling beauty to African American women*. Lexington, KY: University of Kentucky Press.

Watters, E. (2013, March/April). We aren't the world. *Pacific Standard*, pp. 46–53.

Watzlawick, P., Beavin, J., & Jackson, D. D. (1967). *Pragmatics of human communication*. New York: W. W. Norton.

Weber, L. (2013, June 13). Why dads don't take paternity leave. *The Wall Street Journal*, pp. B1, B7.

Weger, H., Bell, G. C., Minei, E., & Robinson, M. (2014). The relative effectiveness of active

Listening in initial interactions. *International Journal of Listening, 28*, 13–31.

Wegner, H., Jr. (2005). Disconfirming communication and self-verification in marriage: Associations among the demand/withdraw interaction pattern, feeling understood, and marital satisfaction. *Journal of Social and Personal Relationships, 22*, 19–31.

Weimann, G. (2000). *Communicating unreality: Modern media and the reconstruction of reality.* Newbury Park, CA: Sage.

Wen, L., & Kosowsky, J. (2013). *When doctors don't listen.* New York: St. Martin's/Thomas Dunne.

West, C., & Zimmerman, D. H. (1987). Doing gender. *Gender and Society, 1*, 125–151.

Whitman, T., White, R., O'Mara, K., & Goeke-Morey, M. (1999). Environmental aspects of infant health and illness. In T. Whitman & T. Merluzzi (Eds.), *Life-span perspectives on health and illness* (pp. 105–124). Mahwah, NJ: Erlbaum.

Whorf, B. (1956). *Language, thought, and reality.* New York: MIT Press/Wiley.

Williams, G. (1995). *Life on the color line: The true story of a white boy who discovered he was black.* New York: Plume.

Williams, J. (2013, June 6). Paygap deniers. *Huffington Post.* Retrieved from http://www .huffingtonpost.com/joan-williams/pay-gap-deniers_b_3391524.html

Williams, R. (1994). *The non-designer's design book: Design and typographic principles for the visual novice.* Berkeley, CA: Peachpit Press.

Wilson, J. F., & Arnold, C. C. (1974). *Public speaking as a liberal art* (4th ed.). Boston, MA: Allyn & Bacon.

Winans, J. A. (1938). *Speechmaking.* New York: Appleton-Century-Crofts.

Wines, M. (2011, November 12). Picking the pitch-perfect brand name in China. *New York Times*, p. A4.

Wolvin, A. (2009). Listening, understanding and misunderstanding. In W. F. Eadie (Ed.), *21st century communication: A reference handbook* (pp. 137–146). Thousand Oaks, CA: Sage.

Wood, J. T. (1982). Communication and relational culture: Bases for the study of human relationships. *Communication Quarterly, 30*, 75–84.

Wood, J. T. (1992). Telling our stories: Narratives as a basis for theorizing sexual harassment. *Journal of Applied Communication Research, 4*, 349–363.

Wood, J. T. (1994a). Engendered identities: Shaping voice and mind through gender. In D. Vocate (Ed.), *Intrapersonal communication: Different voices, different minds* (pp. 145–167). Hillsdale, NJ: Erlbaum.

Wood, J. T. (1994c). *Who cares? Women, care, and culture.* Carbondale, IL: Southern Illinois University Press.

Wood, J. T. (2005). Feminist standpoint theory and muted group theory: Commonalities and divergences. *Women & Language, 28*, 61–64.

Wood, J. T. (2006a). Chopping the carrots: Creating intimacy moment by moment. In J. T. Wood & S. W. Duck (Eds.), *Composing relationships: Communication in everyday life* (pp. 15–23). Belmont, CA: Thomson Wadsworth.

Wood, J. T. (2007a). *Gendered lives* (7th ed.). Belmont, CA: Wadsworth.

Wood, J. T. (2010). The can-do discourse and young women's anticipations of future. *Women & Language, 33*, 103–107.

Wood, J. T. (2011). Which ruler do we use? Theorizing the division of domestic labor. *Family Communication Journal, 11*, 39–49.

Wood, J. T., Dendy, L., Dordek, E., Germany, M., & Varallo, S. (1994). Dialectic of difference: A thematic analysis of intimates' meanings for differences. In K. Carter & M. Presnell (Eds.), *Interpretive approaches to interpersonal communication* (pp. 115–136). New York: State University of New York Press.

Wood, J. T., & Dow, B. (2010). The invisible politics of "choice" in the workplace. In S. Hayden & L. Hallstein (Eds.), *Contemplating maternity in an era of choice* (pp. 203–225). New York: Lexington.

Wood, J. T., & Duck, S. (2006). Introduction. In J. T. Wood & S. Ducks (Eds.), *Composing relationships: Communication in everyday life* (pp. 1–13). Belmont, CA: Thomson Wadsworth.

Wood, J. T., & Fixmer-Oraiz, N. (2017). *Gendered Lives* (12th ed.). Boston, MA: Cengage.

Wood, J. T., & Inman, C. C. (1993). In a different mode: Masculine styles of communicating closeness. *Journal of Applied Communication Research, 21*, 279–295.

Woolfolk, A. E. (1987). *Educational psychology.* Englewood Cliffs, NJ: Prentice Hall.

Workers of the World, Log In. (2014, August 16). *The Economist*, pp. 51–53.

Workplace Privacy (2011). Fact Sheet 7. Retrieved from http://management.about.com/gi/o .htm?zi=1/XJ&zTi=1&sdn=management&cdn =money&tm=53&gps=464_1035_1001_

592&f=00&su=p560.11.336.ip_&tt=2&bt=
0&bts=0&zu=http%3A//www.privacyrights
.org/fs/fs7-work.htm

Wu, C., & Shaffer, D. R. (1988). Susceptibility to persuasive appeals as a function of source credibility and prior experience with attitude object. *Journal of Personal and Social Psychology, 52,* 677–688.

Yeager, M. (June, 2015). How to use public speaking skills at work. *U.S. News & World Report.* Retrieved from http://money.usnews.com /money/blogs/outside-voices-careers/2015/06/25 /how-to-use-public-speaking-skills-at-work

Ye, Z. & Palomares, N. A. (2013). Effects of conversation partners' gender-language consistency on references to emotion, tentative language, and gender salience. *Journal of Language and Social Psychology, 32,* 433–451.

Yen, H. (2012, May 17). Minority birthrate now surpasses whites in US, Census shows. *Huffington Post.* Retrieved from http://www .huffingtonpost.com/2012/05/17/minorities-birth-rate-now-surpass-whites-in-us-census_n_1523230 .html

Young, S., Wood, J., Phillips, G., & Pedersen, D. (2001). *Group discussion* (3rd ed.). Prospect Heights, IL: Waveland.

Zarocostas, J. (2014, May 14). U.S. alone in not paying maternity leave. *Raleigh News & Observer,* p. 3A.

Zhang, Q. (2010). Asian Americans beyond the model minority stereotype: The nerdy and the left out. *Journal of International and Intercultural Communication, 3,* 20–37.

Zuckerberg, R. (2013). *Dot complicated.* New York: HarperCollins.

Index

Note: Page numbers followed by *f* indicate figures or photos and those followed by *t* indicate tables.